PRESIDENTIAL
POWER

The Politics of Leadership
from FDR to Carter

PRESIDENTIAL POWER

The Politics of Leadership
from FDR to Carter

Richard E. Neustadt
HARVARD UNIVERSITY

MACMILLAN PUBLISHING COMPANY
New York

COLLIER MACMILLAN PUBLISHERS
London

To Bert and Roger

Macmillan Publishing Company
866 Third Avenue, New York, New York 10022

Collier Macmillan Canada, Inc.

Library of Congress Cataloging in Publication Data:

Neustadt, Richard E.
   Presidential power.

   Includes bibliographical references and index.
   I. Title.
JK516.N4   1980   353.03′2   79-19474
ISBN 0-02-386670-5

Printed in the United States of America

Printing   16   Year   9 0

ISBN 0-02-386670-5

Preface to the
Original Edition

When we inaugurate a President of the United States we give a man the powers of our highest public office. From the moment he is sworn the man confronts a personal problem: how to make those powers work for *him*. That problem is the subject of this book. My theme is personal power and its politics: what it is, how to get it, how to keep it, how to lose it. My interest is in what a President can do to make his own will felt within his own Administration; what he can do, as one man among many, to carry his own choices through that maze of personalities and institutions called the government of the United States.

This is not a book about the Presidency as an organization, or as legal powers, or as precedents, or as procedures. It is not about the politics of getting to the White House; nor is it a history of what has happened there. Least of all is it a list of what occurs there hour by hour. Fortunately, we have many books on all these other aspects of the Presidency: historical treatments, administrative surveys, nomination and election studies, contemporary commentaries, biographies galore. The reader who seeks background is referred to these; their contributions are not duplicated here.

The purpose here is to explore the power problem of the man inside the White House. This is the classic problem of the man on top in any political system: how to be on top in fact as well as name. It is a problem common to Prime Ministers and Premiers, and to dictators, however styled, and to those kings who rule as well as reign. It is a problem also for the heads of private "governments," for corporation presidents, trade union leaders, churchmen. But this book is not comparative,

vi   PREFACE TO THE ORIGINAL EDITION

though possibly it may facilitate comparisons. This is an effort to look closely at the problem of one officeholder in one political system: the office is the Presidency, the system is American. The objects of this examination are our most recent Presidents. The problem for the man inside that office has not been the same at every time. We deal here only with the "present" time. This book does not compare historical periods any more than it compares political systems. Comparisons are not my present purpose.

The search for personal influence is at the center of the job of being President. To analyze the problem of obtaining personal power one must try to view the Presidency from over the President's shoulder, looking out and down with the perspective of *his* place. This is not the way that we conventionally view the office; ordinarily we stand outside it, looking in. From outside, or from below, a President is "many men," or one man wearing many "hats," or playing many "roles." Conventionally we divide the job of being President according to the categories such a view suggests, "Chief Legislator," "Chief Administrator," "Chief of Party," and the like, and analyze the job by treating chieftainships in turn. For many purposes this framework of analysis is valuable. For present purposes, however, it becomes a block to insight. The President himself plays every "role," wears every "hat" at once. Whatever he may do in one role is by definition done in all, and has effects in all. When he attempts to make his wishes manifest, his own will felt, he is one man, not many. To analyze this aspect of his job we need a frame of reference as unlike the usual categories as the view from inside out is unlike that from outside in.

Nothing has been harder in the writing of this book than the effort to escape from chiefs-of-this-and-that. Nothing may be harder in the reading. But the effort must be made if we are to explore the power problem of the man on top in our political system.

Because my purpose is analytical and my framework unconventional, I have illustrated every major step in the analysis with cases from the record of recent Administrations, mainly Truman's and Eisenhower's. To lighten the load of sheer description and to save the reader from dependence on my word alone, I have tried to meet two standards in selecting these cases: first, that they should have been widely publicized and much discussed when they occurred; second, that they should have been described elsewhere in studies to which readers can refer for more detail and for a judgment independent of my own. In the few instances when it has not been possible to meet the latter standard—lacking independent studies from another source—I have sought to compensate by relatively detailed treatment here. For the most part, however, at the start of my examples readers will find notes on other writings. These are noted with the hope they will be read.

My illustrations are designed to shed light on a problem, not to give a balanced view of recent Administrations. With one exception every major illustration in this book is in some sense the story of a failure; without exception every case turns on dramatic incidents. This does not mean that recent Presidents knew no successes, or that presidential business is invariably dramatic. It merely means that negative examples tend to be the most illuminating, and dramatic ones tend to be best remembered and recorded. These cases serve my purpose, but my aim is not historical. My treatment of events and men has no other objective than to clarify the nature of the search for personal power.

In several instances my illustrations have involved men and events still on the stage as I was writing. School integration at Little Rock is an example. Another example is the ''new'' Eisenhower of 1959. In instances like these I have not tried to bring the record up to date beyond July of 1959. My observations and conclusions rest on what occurred in that month and before. When one deals with contemporary matters one must stop somewhere; this is where I stopped. To help the reader place that point in time: the American economy had virtually recovered from the 1958 recession; a steel strike had just begun; the Little Rock high schools were soon to reopen; Congress was approaching adjournment; so was a Foreign ministers' conference on Berlin; the Vice-President was in the Soviet Union; the President was about to visit Western Europe; the Soviet Premier had accepted an invitation to visit the United States. This book takes no account of what has happened since.

While writing, I have been aware that there will soon be rich additions to the literature concerning modern Presidents at work in modern government. The Inter-University Case Program, which pioneered depth case studies of policy decisions, is now preparing several studies focused in large part upon decisions at the White House. The Twentieth Century Fund, through its project on civil-military relations, is about to publish a notable series of case studies in foreign and military policy-making; these cases also reach into the White House. A comparable, complementary series has been undertaken by the Columbia University Institute of War and Peace Studies. In 1960 and in 1961, publications from these sources will provide detailed accounts of governmental action at the highest levels on a rather wide variety of foreign, military, budgetary, scientific, and economic policy decisions made in Roosevelt's time, and Truman's, and in Eisenhower's. I have been mindful of that prospect in preparing this book. Three of my major illustrations, most of my incidental illustrations, and the general organization of my argument were planned to provide links between the presentation here and that prospective case material. Students, I hope, will find it easy to move from the particular perspective of this book, focused on the President himself, to the wider focus of these forthcoming case studies.

It is a matter of regret to me that I have had personal contact with only one of the Presidents involved in my illustrations. In President Truman's instance I saw aspects of the man at work while I served on his staff and have had later opportunities to exchange views with him. His readiness in those exchanges to respect my scholarly purpose, regardless of our former association, was as kind as it was useful; I note it gratefully. In President Roosevelt's case I had a partial substitute: the recollections of my father's friends and of my own acquaintances who served in his Administration, and opportunities to talk with certain members of his family. In President Eisenhower's instance, on the other hand, although his aides were helpful and informative they felt themselves unable to extend to me the privilege of direct contact with him or with their work. This is not noted in complaint but in acknowledgment of limits on my resources for personal observation. Recognizing these limits I have sought compensation in the usual way, by interviewing men who had the contacts I did not.

This book is my responsibility, of course, but many others have contributed to its development. I began it when I first returned to teaching at the close of the Truman Administration, after a decade of staff work in the Office of Price Administration, the Navy, the Budget Bureau, and the White House. During the seven years since then I have imposed on numbers of my former colleagues for access to their memories and their personal files. I have buttonholed assorted friends and strangers in the Washington press corps and at the Capitol. And I have interviewed officials in the Eisenhower Administration with the student's usual unconcern for other people's time. Everywhere I have been met with courtesy and candor, as well as information. I am profoundly grateful for all three. Many of my Washington informants were assured that there would be no attribution of their information. Since I cannot thank them all by name, I shall name none. But I can state the debt I owe them all: without their help this study could not have been done.

My work was aided, also, by financial grants in 1955 and 1957 from the Columbia University Council for Research in the Social Sciences. Research and writing were completed while I held an appointment from Columbia as Ford Research Professor in American Government. The University's help in these respects is noted with a great deal of appreciation.

While this book was in draft form, four friends and colleagues gave me detailed comments on the entire manuscript: Roger Jones, Wallace Sayre, Harold Stein, and David Truman. I am enormously obliged to them for criticisms and suggestions which have certainly made this a better book. I am equally obliged to several others who commented on portions of the draft: Daniel Bell, Douglass Cater, Violet Coffin, Herbert Deane, Henry Graff, Samuel Huntington, Frances Low, Warner Schilling, and Kenneth Young. My thanks are due also to Everard Meade and Rose Marie O'Reilly of the Columbia Broadcasting System, and to George Gallup and John Fenton of the American Institute of Public Opinion, for their time and good counsel as well as for the data they so generously provided.

Finally, I owe more than I can readily express to Elinor Truman, who masqueraded as a typist but performed as an editor, to Bertha Neustadt, who joined in this enterprise not only as my wife but also as my research assistant, and to Rick and

Betsy Neustadt who spent a whole year heeding the injunction, "Shhh—he's *writing*."

Columbia University   Richard E. Neustadt
New York City
December, 1959

Preface to the 1980 Edition

In writing this book twenty years ago, I sought to characterize the power of a modern American President. I addressed not the office but rather the person as one among many in an institution. "Power" I defined as personal influence on governmental action. This I distinguished sharply—a novel distinction then—from formal powers vested in the Presidency. In considering Dwight D. Eisenhower and Harry S. Truman, with Franklin D. Roosevelt in their immediate background, I found that sort of influence to be a risky thing, hard to consolidate, easy to dissipate, rarely assured. Presidential weakness was the underlying theme of *Presidential Power*.

This remains my theme. It runs through the eight original chapters, here reprinted, and through the three new ones that are meant to supplement, bring up to date, revise and reconsider, as befits a new edition. The doing has not brought a change of themes. Weakness is still what I see. Expectations rise again and clerkly tasks increase, priorities are needed more than ever but are harder to maintain, and prospects for sustained support from any quarter worsen as political parties wane.

Stated so flatly this may cause surprise. Since 1960 we have had five Presidents. Broadly speaking, the experience of three supports that view, although they served for such short spans as to reduce their usefulness in evidential terms, less than eight years among them so far: John F. Kennedy, Gerald R. Ford, and Jimmy Carter up to now. But the other two, with nearly eleven years of office between them, successively displayed what most Americans regard, at least in retrospect, as altogether too much influence on far too many acts of government: Lyndon B. Johnson and

Richard M. Nixon. Their power is symbolized by the Americanization of the Vietnam War and our continued involvement, and in Nixon's case as well by all the
things we lump together under "Watergate." Their strength was in a sense illusory,
however, for these also are the symbols of their self-destruction.

In 1960 my concern with personal power turned upon the problem of conserving
and applying it, taken in strategic terms, "looking toward tomorrow from today."
Presidents, I argued, ought to think about their personal stakes in every choice,
deriving either guidance for the present or warnings for the future. The better this
was done the likelier to buttress future influence and also chosen policies. But
Johnson and Nixon, by all accounts assiduous in thinking about power—both,
indeed, preoccupied with it to the point of obsession—set themselves on disastrous
courses, leading one to premature retirement, and the other to forced resignation. In
the process they either damaged or demolished (history will tell) their dearest policy
objectives: Johnson's Great Society at home, Nixon's balance-of-power in the
world.

Two questions arise. Can what they did be squared with what I wrote twenty
years ago? If not, how should I change my words in light of their years at the White
House? Having thought about these questions, I address them in the tenth chapter of
this edition. That essay is intended as a commentary on the whole of the original
book. It adjusts details but not essentials. Despite appearances, Johnson and Nixon
found their power as contingent and variable as that of others. Judging by their
experience, my proffered line of thought appears less useful than I had hoped; this
does not render power less contingent. So I think it was for them as for the others, at
least strategically, looking ahead.

Some critics of the original edition cannot fathom how such strength as, for
example, Nixon showed in 1973 when he impounded funds appropriated by Congress, can be viewed by me as consonant with weakness. But that is to confuse the
first bite of invoked authority with longer-run effects on power prospects. Nixon
complicated his relations with the Democratic Congress just before his cover-up of
Watergate collapsed. He provoked a batch of lawsuits brought by congressmen,
which overturned his more adventurous impoundments. He invited a restrictive
statute that eventually deprived the Presidency of its right to impound in his fashion
ever: all this for a short-run show of success. Power? Not in prospective terms!

Chapter 10 is preceded by another commentary with a different purpose. Chapter
9 adapts this book's analysis of power, viewed in prospect, so as to provide the
terms for judgment of a President's performance on the job in retrospect. These
terms, I hope, are applicable to anyone, but only retrospectively; they make it plain,
for instance, how premature are early judgments about Carter's "passion." Here
the terms have been applied to JFK, the man history squeezed between Eisenhower
and Johnson. Kennedy was also the first President to deal directly with a nuclear
confrontation and the second to involve us directly in Vietnam. On these scores,
among others, his incumbency projects beyond its two years and ten months. Thus

Chapter 9 does double duty, not only offering terms for general use but also helping to bring readers from the Fifties toward the Eighties.

Chapter 11, the third essay this edition adds to the original text, continues with that latter task, comparing, among others, Kennedy and Carter as they went about learning by doing. This is an inescapable aspect of the office and one that Carter's difficulties cast in sharp relief; it seems to be both harder and more critical than formerly. "Transition," taken as inclusive of the learning-time, was hazardous for Kennedy but still more so for Carter. Personal style aside, this reflects changes in our system. These, while cumulative since the Fifties, have accelerated in the Seventies so that they render Carter's institutional surroundings very different even from Johnson's. Chapter 11 suggests how and why. It also spells out, with two new case studies, what transition hazards are. The Bay of Pigs of 1961 and the Lance affair of 1977 serve as cases in this chapter. Thereby it adds fresh illustrative material to Chapters 1 through 4, and adds to Chapter 5 a dimension of television.

This final essay thus does four-way duty, summarizing changes, setting forth exacerbated problems, bringing the analysis into the TV age, and coming to grips, as best I can in his unfinished term, with Carter's troubles.

Carter is the latest President to find the Presidency weak in prospects for effective influence. Granting all the changes of detail in institutions and in public moods, I think his power problems now somewhat resemble Truman's. But beyond these details lie substantial differences of substance. The United States no longer is the overwhelming military power in the world, no longer sure of never losing wars, no longer confident of having learned how to maintain employment and to check inflation, no longer revelling in resource independence, technological supremacy, favorable exchange rates, and the privileged life abroad. If there was an "American Century," as Henry Luce proclaimed after the Second World War, it lasted only twice as long as Adolph Hitler's Thousand Year Reich. Tantalizingly, unlike the Reich, conditions favoring this country's sense of independence and security—if not quite the old substance—could return with a few well-placed technological breakthroughs. No wonder there is still a general disbelief (current polls put it at 70 percent) in the genuineness of prospective fuel crises. Substantively Carter's problems may be worse than Truman's; psychologically they surely are, especially since Carter, up to now, has had no Stalins to stage educational dramas overseas. Yet this is very relative. Fearfulness not confidence marked public moods in many of the Truman years, and also anger at the President. Carter evokes shrugs or head-shaking; Truman evoked cries of "treason."

The power problems I addressed in 1960 were defined as time-bound, bearing on the Presidency in a given setting. I chose the then contemporary setting, labelled it "mid-century," and defined it in political and institutional terms drawn from the years since the Second World War. Hence, the stress on Truman and Eisenhower. I did not think it likely that two decades later all the changes in the setting would have taken such a shape as to leave all the problems roughly what they were for Truman, if not more so. Change was bound to come; I did not foresee this result. Sometime during the Seventies I thought we might see strengthened partisan alignments, linking President and Congress through their nominating processes. "Sometime" could be any time, if not the Seventies perhaps the Eighties or the Nineties (or is the prospect but pie in the sky?); however, for the present we have seen the opposite occur. Those links are so frayed now that policy results hark back in some respects to Franklin Roosevelt, *circa* 1939, when Congress was as feisty with the President on foreign policy as on domestic programs. Of course it was a very different Congress, in a very different world of parties, staffs, departments, interests, issues, populations, economics, armaments, and governments. Yet the terms and conditions of employment for a President who seeks to husband his resources and extend his grasp appear alike from then to now in significant ways. Why difference leads toward sameness—and where sameness stops—are questions variously addressed by all the added chapters, especially the last one, in this edition.

The new chapters lengthen the book, something I deplore. It once had something I admire, brevity. But I ruled out the alternative. Revising the original text struck me as inappropriate, a bit Orwellian. Books should stand where they first saw the light of day, expressive of their setting and confined by it. Therefore, the only thing that I have done to Chapters 1 through 8 in this edition is to find and strike a misused "hopefully." Otherwise these chapters remain as they were twenty years ago, warts and all; just as they have been cited, quoted, criticized. Chapters 9 through 11 build on them, comment on them, differ with them now and then, but do not obfuscate (I hope) their analytic argument. That remains the heart of the book.

Two of the three chapters added in this edition have been seen before. They too remain unchanged, except for striking another "hopefully" and adding a couple of clarifying phrases. Chapter 9 is virtually identical with the Afterword initially prepared in 1968 for a French edition and then carried at the back of subsequent American printings. Chapter 10 is, in condensed form, the text of the three William W. Cook Lectures delivered in the spring of 1976 at the Law School of the University of Michigan, under the title "Presidential Power Revisited: Reflections on Johnson and Nixon." I am grateful to the Law School for suggesting the subject and also for agreeing that my text should be published where it belongs, in this book rather than in a separate volume. Initially published as an Introduction to the 1976 printing, it is now placed, much more logically, *after* the analysis that it revisits.

This edition's Chapter 11 is in expanded form the Phi Beta Kappa Lecture I gave in the early months of 1979 as a Visiting Scholar at several universities and colleges. I am grateful to the National Phi Beta Kappa Society for those interesting visits, and to the Center for Advanced Study in the Behavioral Sciences for an immensely satisfying place to write and edit this chapter, among other things, while on sabbatic leave. The chapter was completed there in May, 1979, a time when the inflation rate was 12 percent, with recession a prospect, when gasoline was short in California, when Salt II was completed but not yet before the Senate, when Egypt and Israel were starting their West Bank negotiation, and when Carter's Gallup Poll approval stood at 32 percent, seven points below his previous low the year before. I take no account of what has happened since.

Numbers of friends read drafts and gave advice on these three chapters at one stage or another. For their help I am very grateful. I owe thanks as well to Pennie Gonzoule and to Barbara Witt for typing. I am grateful for research help to Thomas Balliett and to Bruce Harley. Needless to say, their assistance was all to the good; anything bad remains mine.

The first edition of *Presidential Power* and now this one have been dedicated to two people. One is my wife Bert, who helped this book (and me) along at every stage, some of them hard to bear. The other is a one-time boss in the then Budget Bureau, Roger W. Jones, who helped to launch me on an academic career and subsequently disciplined my interest in the Presidency, by first insisting that I go on leave and do a doctoral dissertation from our files, and then, years later, by thoughtfully reviewing every draft of this book's original text. Twenty years ago he did not wish to be identified. Now I am unwilling to let him remain anonymous.

Since 1960 we have had not only five more Presidents but also, and in greater number, new works on the Presidency, some of them major contributions. I have been tempted to dwell on these as well as on the Presidents. I have resisted the temptation lest I alter this book's character. *Presidential Power* never was, and is not now, a comprehensive commentary on the literature. The new material for this edition is not even comprehensive in its dealings with the critics of the earlier edition. The criticism I have heeded is my own, which sometimes coincides with that of others, sometimes not. The book remains then what it was originally, one man's argument, illustrated from the public record of the Presidency, drawing on my own experience and observation, an argument thus limited in its ambitions and its uses. My experience has been considerably enlarged since 1960, also the opportunities for observation, as a consultant to the Kennedy and Johnson White House and occasionally to Carter's Reorganization Project. I have always tried to turn participant-observership to the account of scholarship which might assist participants. I leave to others, or at least until another time, the wider task.

Harvard University   Richard E. Neustadt
Cambridge, Massachusetts
June, 1979

Contents

PART One

THE ORIGINAL STUDY

CHAPTER 1

Leader or Clerk?

In the United States we like to ''rate'' a President. We measure him as ''weak'' or ''strong'' and call what we are measuring his ''leadership.'' We do not wait until a man is dead; we rate him from the moment he takes office. We are quite right to do so. His office has become the focal point of politics and policy in our political system. Our commentators and our politicians make a specialty of taking the man's measurements. The rest of us join in when we feel ''government'' impinging on our private lives. In the third quarter of the twentieth century millions of us have that feeling often.

This book is an endeavor to illuminate what we are measuring. Although we all make judgments about presidential leadership, we often base our judgments upon images of office that are far removed from the reality. We also use those images when we tell one another whom to choose as President. But it is risky to appraise a man in office or to choose a man for office on false premises about the nature of his job. When the job is the Presidency of the United States the risk becomes excessive. I hope this book can help reduce the risk.

We deal here with the President himself and with his influence on governmental action. In institutional terms the Presidency now includes 2000 men and women. The President is only one of them. But *his* performance scarcely can be measured without focusing on *him*. In terms of party, or of country, or the West, so-called, his leadership involves far more than governmental action. But the sharpening of spirit and of values and of purposes is not done in a vacuum. Although governmental action may not be the whole of leadership, all else is nurtured by it and gains meaning from it. Yet if we treat the Presidency as the President, we cannot measure him as though he were the government. Not action as an outcome but his impact on the outcome is the measure of the man. His strength or weakness, then, turns on his personal capacity to influence the conduct of the men who make up government. His influence becomes the mark of leadership. To rate a President according to these rules, one looks into the man's own capabilities as seeker and as wielder of effective influence upon the other men involved in governing the country. That is what this book will do.

"Presidential" on the title page means nothing but the President. "Power" means *his* influence. It helps to have these meanings settled at the start.

There are two ways to study "presidential power." One way is to focus on the tactics, so to speak, of influencing certain men in given situations: how to get a bill through Congress, how to settle strikes, how to quiet Cabinet feuds, or how to stop a Suez. The other way is to step back from tactics on those "givens" and to deal with influence in more strategic terms: what is its nature and what are its sources? What can *this* man accomplish to improve the prospect that he will have influence when he wants it? Strategically, the question is not how he masters Congress in a peculiar instance, but what he does to boost his chance for mastery in any instance, looking toward tomorrow from today. The second of these two ways has been chosen for this book.

II

To look into the strategy of presidential influence one must decide at whom to look. Power problems vary with the scope and scale of government, the state of politics, the progress of technology, the pace of world relationships. Power in the Nineteen-sixties cannot be acquired or employed on the same terms as those befitting Calvin Coolidge, or Theodore Roosevelt, or Grover Cleveland, or James K. Polk. But there is a real likelihood that in the next decade a President will have to reach for influence and use it under much the same conditions we have known since the Second World War. If so, the men whose problems shed most light on the White House prospects are Dwight David Eisenhower and Harry S. Truman. It is at them, primarily, that we shall look. To do so is to see the shadow of another, Franklin D. Roosevelt. They worked amidst the remnants of his voter coalition, and they filled an office that his practice had enlarged.

Our two most recent Presidents have had in common something that is likely to endure into our future: the setting for a great deal of their work. They worked in an environment of policy and politics marked by a high degree of continuity. To sense the continuity from Truman's time through Eisenhower's one need only place the newspapers of 1959 alongside those of 1949. Save for the issue of domestic communists, the subject matter of our policy and politics remains almost unchanged.

We deal as we have done in terms of cold war, of an arms race, of a competition overseas, of danger from inflation, and of damage from recession. We skirmish on the frontiers of the Welfare State and in the borderlands of race relations. Aspects change, but labels stay the same. So do dilemmas. Everything remains unfinished business. Not in this century has there been comparable continuity from a decade's beginning to its end; count back from 1949 and this grows plain. There even has been continuity in the behavior of our national electorate; what Samuel Lubell nine years ago called "stalemate" in our partisan alignments has not broken yet.

The similarities in Truman's setting and in Eisenhower's give their years a unity distinct from the War Years, or the Depression Era, or the Twenties, or before. In governmental terms, at least, the fifteen years since V-J Day deserve a designation all their own. "Mid-century" will serve for present purposes. And what distinguishes mid-century can be put very briefly: emergencies in policy with politics as usual.

"Emergency" describes mid-century conditions only by the standards of the past. By present standards what would once have been emergency is commonplace. Policy dilemmas through the postwar period resemble past emergencies in one respect, their difficulty and complexity for government. Technological innovation, social and political change abroad, population growth at home impose enormous strains not only on the managerial equipment of our policy-makers but also on their intellectual resources. The gropings of mature men at mid-century remind one of the intellectual confusions stemming from depression, thirty years ago, when men were also pushed past comprehension by the novelty of their condition. In our time innovation keeps us *constantly* confused; no sooner do we start to comprehend than something new is added, and we grope again. But unlike the Great Difficulties of the past, our policy dilemmas rarely produce what the country feels as "crisis." Not even the Korean War brought anything approaching sustained national "consensus." Since 1945 innumerable situations have been felt as crises inside government; there rarely has been comparable feeling outside government. In the era of the Cold War we have practiced "peacetime" politics. What else could we have done? Cold War is not a "crisis"; it becomes a way of life.

Our politics has been "as usual," but only by the standard of past *crises*. In comparison with what was once normality, our politics has been *un*usual. The weakening of party ties, the emphasis on personality, the close approach of world events, the changeability of public moods, and above all the ticket-splitting, none of this was "usual" before the Second World War. The symbol of mid-century political conditions is the White House in one party's hands with Congress in the other's—a symbol plainly visible in eight of the past fifteen years and all but visible in four of the remaining seven. Nothing really comparable has been seen in this country since the Eighteen-eighties. And the Eighties were not troubled by emergencies in policy.

As for politics and policy combined, we have seen some precursors of our setting at mid-century. Franklin Roosevelt had a reasonably comparable setting in his middle years as President, though not in his first years and not after Pearl Harbor. Indeed, if one excepts the war, mid-century could properly be said to start with Roosevelt's second term. Our recent situation is to be compared, as well, with aspects of the Civil War. Abraham Lincoln is much closer to us in condition than in time, the Lincoln plagued by Radicals and shunned by Democrats amidst the managerial and intellectual confusions of twentieth-century warfare in the nineteenth century. And in 1919 Woodrow Wilson faced and was defeated by conditions something like our own. But save for these men one can say of Truman and of Eisenhower that they were the first who had to fashion presidential influence out of mid-century materials. Presumably they will not be the last.

III

We tend to measure Truman's predecessors as though "leadership" consisted of initiatives in economics, or diplomacy, or legislation, or in mass communication. If we measured him and his successors so, they would be leaders automatically. A striking feature of our recent past has been the transformation into routine practice of the actions we once treated as exceptional. A President may retain liberty, in Woodrow Wilson's phrase, "to be as big a man as he can." But nowadays he cannot be as small as he might like.

Our two most recent Presidents have gone through all the motions we traditionally associate with strength in office. So will the man who takes the oath on January 20, 1961. In instance after instance the exceptional behavior of our earlier "strong" Presidents has now been set by statute as a regular requirement. Theodore Roosevelt once assumed the "steward's" role in the emergency created by the great coal strike of 1902; the Railway Labor Act and the Taft-Hartley Act now make such interventions mandatory upon Presidents. The other Roosevelt once asserted personal responsibility for gauging and for guiding the American economy; the Employment Act binds his successors to that task. Wilson and F.D.R. became chief spokesmen, leading actors, on a world stage at the height of war; now UN membership, far-flung alliances, prescribe that role continuously in times termed "peace." Through both world wars our Presidents grappled experimentally with an emergency-created need to "integrate" foreign and military policies; the National Security Act now takes that need for granted as a constant of our times. F.D.R. and Truman made themselves responsible for the development and first use of atomic weapons; the Atomic Energy Act now puts a comparable burden on the back of every President. And what has escaped statutory recognition has mostly been accreted into presidential common law, confirmed by custom, no less binding: the "fireside chat" and the press conference, for example, or the personally presented legislative program, or personal campaigning in congressional elections.

In form all Presidents are leaders, nowadays. In fact this guarantees no more than that they will be clerks. Everybody now expects the man inside the White House to do something about everything. Laws and customs now reflect acceptance of him as the Great Initiator, an acceptance quite as widespread at the Capitol as at his end of Pennsylvania Avenue. But such acceptance does not signify that all the rest of government is at his feet. It merely signifies that other men have found it practially impossible to do *their* jobs without assurance of initiatives from him. Service for themselves, not power for the President, has brought them to accept his leadership in form. They find his actions useful in their business. The transformation of his routine obligations testifies to their dependence on an active White House. A President, these days, is an invaluable clerk. His services are in demand all over Washington. His influence, however, is a very different matter. Laws and customs tell us little about leadership in fact.

IV

Why have our Presidents been honored with this clerkship? The answer is that no one else's services suffice. Our Constitution, our traditions, and our politics provide no better source for the initiatives a President can take. Executive officials need decisions, and political protection, and a referee for fights. Where are these to come from but the White House? Congressmen need an agenda from outside, something with high status to respond to or react against. What provides it better than the program of the President? Party politicians need a record to defend in the next national campaign. How can it be made except by "their" Administration? Private persons with a public axe to grind may need a helping hand or they may need a grinding stone. In either case who gives more satisfaction than a President? And outside the United States, in every country where our policies and postures influence home politics, there will be people needing just the "right" thing said and done or just the "wrong" thing stopped *in Washington*. What symbolizes Washington more nearly than the White House?

A modern President is bound to face demands for aid and service from five more or less distinguishable sources: from Executive officialdom, from Congress, from his partisans, from citizens at large, and from abroad. The Presidency's clerkship is expressive of these pressures. In effect they are constituency pressures and each President has five sets of constituents. The five are not distinguished by their membership; membership is obviously an overlapping matter. And taken one by one they do not match the man's electorate; one of them, indeed, is outside his electorate. They are distinguished, rather, by their different claims upon him. Initiatives are what they want, for five distinctive reasons. Since government and politics have offered no alternative, our laws and customs turn those wants into his obligations.

Why, then, is the President not guaranteed an influence commensurate with services performed? Constituent relations are relations of dependence. Everyone with any share in governing this country will belong to one (or two, or three) of his "constituencies." Since everyone depends on him why is he not assured of everyone's support? The answer is that no one else sits where he sits, or sees quite as he sees; no one else feels the full weight of his obligations. Those obligations are a tribute to his unique place in our political system. But just because it is unique they fall on him alone. *The same conditions that promote his leadership in form preclude a guarantee of leadership in fact.* No man or group at either end of Pennsylvania Avenue shares his peculiar status in our government and politics. That is why his services are in demand. By the same token, though, the obligations of all other men are different from his own. His Cabinet officers have departmental duties and constituents. His legislative leaders head *congressional* parties, one in either House. His national party organization stands apart from his official family. His political allies in the States need not face Washington, or one another. The private groups that seek him out are not compelled to govern. And friends abroad are not compelled to run in our elections. Lacking his position and prerogatives, these men cannot regard his obligations as their own. They have their jobs to do; none is the same as his. As they perceive their duty they may find it right to follow him, in fact, or they may not. Whether they will feel obliged *on their responsibility* to do what he wants done remains an open question. That question serves to introduce this book.

2

Three Cases of Command

In the early summer of 1952, before the heat of the campaign, President Truman used to contemplate the problems of the General-become-President should Eisenhower win the forthcoming election. "He'll sit here," Truman would remark (tapping his desk for emphasis), "and he'll say, 'Do this! Do that!' *And nothing will happen*. Poor Ike—it won't be a bit like the Army. He'll find it very frustrating."

Eisenhower evidently found it so. "In the face of the continuing dissidence and disunity, the President sometimes simply exploded with exasperation," wrote Robert Donovan in comment on the early months of Eisenhower's first term. "What was the use, he demanded to know, of his trying to lead the Republican Party. . . ."[1] And this reaction was not limited to early months alone, or to his party only. "The President still feels," an Eisenhower aide remarked to me in 1958, "that when he's decided something, that *ought* to be the end of it . . . and when it bounces back undone or done wrong, he tends to react with shocked surprise."

Truman knew whereof he spoke. With "resignation" in the place of "shocked surprise" the aide's description would have fitted Truman. The former senator may have been less shocked than the former general, but he was no less subjected to that painful and repetitive experience: "Do this, do that, and nothing will happen." Long before he came to talk of Eisenhower he had put his own experience in other words: "I sit here all day trying to persuade people to do the things they ought to have sense enough to do without my persuading them. . . . That's all the powers of the President amount to."

In these words of a President, spoken on the job, one finds the essence of the problem now before us: "powers" are no guarantee of power; clerkship is no guarantee of leadership. The President of the United States has an extraordinary range of formal powers, of authority in statute law and in the Constitution. Here is testimony that despite his "powers" he does not obtain results by giving orders—or not, at any rate, merely by giving orders. He also has extraordinary status, *ex officio,* according to the customs of our government and politics. Here is testimony that despite his status he does not get action without argument. Presidential *power* is the power to persuade.

This testimony seems, at first glance, to be contradicted flatly by events in the public record of Truman's own administration and of Eisenhower's. Three cases, out of many, illustrate the seeming contradiction. In 1951 Douglas MacArthur was ordered to relinquish his commands; he did as he was told. In 1952 Truman seized the nation's steel mills; they remained in government possession for some seven weeks until he ordered them released when the Supreme Court held that he exceeded his authority. And in 1957 Eisenhower ordered Federal troops to Little Rock; the mob was dispersed, and the Negro children went to school. Evidently some commands are effective; some results can be gained simply by giving orders; some actions do not get taken without argument. Truman's comments seem to be belied by his own acts and those of his successor in these instances, among others.

The contradiction is superficial. It exists if Truman's words are stretched to mean that formal powers have no bearing upon influence. It disappears the moment one takes Truman to imply that mere assertion of a formal power rarely is enough. Taken in that second sense his words are actually *substantiated* by these cases of command. For the recall of MacArthur, the seizure of the steel mills, and the Federal troops at Little Rock go far to show how special are the circumstances favoring command. They also show how narrow may be its effective reach, how costly its employment. An analysis of presidential power must begin by marking out the limits upon presidential "powers." These examples tell us much about the limits.

II

Before I turn to what these cases show, let me review the facts in each of them. Chronologically, the MacArthur case comes first, the steel seizure second, and the Little Rock case third. For purposes of factual review it is convenient to discuss them in that order. Once the facts are stated, chronology can be ignored.

When the Korean War broke out in late June 1950 with a drive on South Korea from the North, MacArthur was in Tokyo, 600 miles away, as supreme commander for the allied occupation of Japan and as commander of American forces in the Far East, posts he had assumed five years before when he accepted Japanese surrender. To him and his forces, necessarily, Truman first entrusted military aid for South

Korea.[2] No other forces were at hand. When the United Nations made the war its own and gave command to the United States, Truman added to MacArthur's other titles a designation as the UN field commander.

By August the General had demonstrated both that he could keep a foothold in Korea and that he, personally, might have more in mind than throwing back the North Korean Communists. In the first days of the war Washington had "neutralized" Formosa, ordering the Seventh Fleet to interpose itself between the Communist regime in mainland China and the Nationalist regime which held the island. MacArthur soon met Chiang Kai-shek, and public statements by the two of them implied some sort of underwriting for Chiang's cause and some sort of involvement by the Nationalists in Korea. These statements were at variance with policy in Washington, to say nothing of its UN associates, and Truman, ultimately, had to tell MacArthur to withdraw a further statement he had sent the Veterans of Foreign Wars.

Within three weeks of this episode Washington was ready to forgive it and forget it in delight at the successes on the battlefield. On September 15 MacArthur's forces landed at Inchon; thereafter, virtual victory came in a rush. A month later Truman met the General at Wake Island. They then agreed that they had no dispute about the Chinese Nationalists, and they looked forward confidently to an early end of fighting with the occupation of all North Korea.

Their confidence was not to last. In the first week of November it was shaken as the UN troops encountered Chinese Communists. In the last week of November it was shattered by a Chinese Communist attack that caught MacArthur unprepared and woefully deployed. To extricate his forces he was compelled to retreat two thirds of the way down the peninsula. Not until mid-January 1951 did Washington begin to feel assured that new lines could form, hold, and support real recovery. Meanwhile, MacArthur had announced the coming of a "new war." He had despaired of holding any part of the peninsula, and he had publicly blamed his defeat on Washington's insistence that the fighting should be confined to Korea. Immediately after Chinese intervention he began campaigning for war measures against the Chinese Communists on their home grounds.

Truman, and his advisers, and most allied governments had quite the opposite reaction to Peking's attack. Their eyes were fixed on Europe as the cold war's greatest stake. They hoped to minimize the risk of long involvement elsewhere, and especially the risk of World War III. If the original objective of the fighting, South Korea, could be salvaged without deepening those risks, they would be well content. By February General Ridgway, who commanded the ground forces in Korea, was assuring them it could be done. By March his troops were doing it. Before that month was out substantially the whole of South Korea was again in UN hands, and Ridgway's troops were reaching north toward natural defense lines past the border.

It now seemed likely that hostilities might end with restoration, roughly, of the situation as it had been at the start. To Washington and to its European allies this seemed the best of a bad bargain; to MacArthur, and to many fellow citizens at home, it seemed the worst. Rather than accept it he began a new barrage of public statements aimed, apparently, at pushing Washington to "win" the war. On March 7 in a statement to the press, he called for action to "provide on the highest international levels the answer to the obscurities [of] Red China's undeclared war. . . ."[3] On March 25 he published a demand for enemy surrender, undermining a planned presidential statement that would have expressed interest in negotiated settlement. On April 5 Joseph Martin, the Minority Leader of the House of Representatives, read into the record a letter from the General which deplored the policies of his superiors, and ended with the words, "There is no substitute for victory."

By April 5 Truman's decision already had been taken; five days later Mac-Arthur was relieved. An extraordinary burst of popular emotion heralded his homecoming. Emotion faded, and so did he, during the course of Senate hearings which poked into every corner of official policy. Meanwhile the war remained limited. In July truce talks began; two years later these produced an armistice along a line the troops had reached by June of 1951.

So much for the facts of the MacArthur case. Next is the steel seizure case. On December 31, 1951, five months after the start of truce talks in Korea, contracts between the United Steelworkers and major steel concerns expired with a stalemate in collective bargaining.[4] At Truman's personal request the men continued work without a contract, while he referred their dispute to the Wage Stabilization Board, a body composed equally of labor, industry, and public members, which had charge of wage control and allied functions during the Korean War. Because this Wage Board still was hearing the case, the union twice postponed a strike, again at Truman's insistence. Then, with the strike set for April 9, 1952, labor and public members of the Board agreed, March 20, on terms of settlement to recommend to the disputing parties. Industry members dissented. At first sight of these majority proposals the union embraced them, the companies denounced them, and in echelons above the Board officials thought them "high."

The Wage Stabilization Board was part of a complex administrative hierarchy established in the first six months of the Korean War. At the top was the Office of Defense Mobilization (ODM), headed by Charles E. (General Electric) Wilson whom Truman had entrusted with "direction," "supervision," and "control" of the entire home-front economic effort. ODM had been superimposed on everything else in the immediate aftermath of Chinese intervention. Next in line was an Economic Stabilization Agency (ESA), which had been created before Wilson's appointment. On paper, this Agency administered discretionary powers over prices and wages conferred upon the President by the Defense Production Act. In fact, those powers were administered by two subordinate units: the Office of Price Stabilization, headed by Ellis Arnall, former governor of Georgia, and the Wage Board itself. The Office was organized like a regular line agency. The Board was run like a regulatory commission with one of its public members in the chair. The Board had statutory authority by delegation through the ESA, to *set* maximum limits on wages. It also had a direct authorization from the White House to *recommend* solutions for nonwage issues in labor disputes. Both functions were involved in the steel case. Wage rulings by the Board were legally enforceable; its nonwage proposals were not. Theoretically, its wage ceilings were subject to revision by the Economic Stabilizer, or the Defense Mobilizer, or the President. But practically speaking, case by case, the Board's tripartite composition and quasi-judicial procedures made majority decisions irreversible on wages and not even reviewable on other issues. In comparison, the Office of Price Stabilization was an administrative unit with no more independence of its nominal superiors than it could win by bureaucratic in-fighting, and with no nonprice duties to distract it from concern for price control. One thing, however, wage and price controllers had in common: they mistrusted those above them and were cool to one another.

The Wage Board proposals of March 20 precipitated a crisis in the steel case. The industry pronounced them unacceptable. The union termed them the least it would accept. The Administration could not disavow them without wrecking the machinery for wage stabilization. A strike was just three weeks away. According to the Pentagon the possibility of enemy offensives in Korea precluded any loss of steel production. In these circumstances Wilson, as Director of Defense Mobilization, took personal charge. His answer for the crisis was a *price* concession to the companies sufficient to induce a settlement of wage and other issues before the strike deadline. After hurried consultation with the President, who was ending a vacation at Key West, Wilson sounded out the industry on price relief. Unfortunately, in an impromptu press conference he had exposed a private distaste for the Wage Board's terms of settlement. This ended union confidence in him and cast doubt on his claims to act for the Administration. Immediately after, Wilson was rebuffed by industry officials who wanted higher prices than he had in mind and made no promises to settle with the union. Immediately after that, Wilson's nominal subordinate Ellis Arnall, the Price Director, won support from Truman for a firmer stand on price controls. Concessions were to be allowed for cost increases in the normal course, but only *after* costs had been incurred. A labor-management agreement must come first. So Arnall argued. Truman sympathized. Wilson resigned on March 29.

In the remaining days before the strike the White House, now involved directly, tried to press the companies and union to a settlement without a price concession in advance. Collective bargaining was resumed and mediation was attempted. Much jockeying and many misadventures then ensued but not a settlement. Finally, to escape a shutdown of production Truman seized the industry two hours before the strike deadline. He ordered the Secretary of Commerce to administer the mills and called upon the men to work as government employees.

The union honored Truman's call; the companies accepted government control—and went to court. In ordering his seizure the President had acted without statutory sanction. Indeed, he had ignored a statute on the books, the Taft-Hartley Act, which gave him the alternative of seeking an injunction against union strike-calls for another eighty days. In these circumstances the steel companies asserted that his seizure was illegal. So they argued in the press and in a Federal District Court on April 9 and after. Government attorneys answered with appeals to the necessities of national defense. They also laid claims to unlimited, "inherent" presidential powers. The President, himself, repudiated these claims. The Court, however, was infuriated by them. The fury was shared by Congressmen and editors.

On April 29 the District Judge denied Truman's authority to seize the industry. A strike began at once. Three days later the order of that Judge was stayed by an Appeals Court decision which allowed the government to put its case before the Supreme Court. The men then straggled back to work. At Truman's request, company and union leaders went into the White House to bargain with each other then and there. On May 3 while bargaining was under way, the Supreme Court took jurisdiction of the case and pending its decision ordered that there be no change in wages. White House bargaining broke down at once; all parties turned, instead, to the Court.

On June 2 a Supreme Court majority upheld the District Judge with a set of opinions so diverse as to establish nothing but the outcome. The President at once returned the mills to private hands. Again there was a strike. This time the mills remained shut down for seven weeks until collective bargaining and White House promises of price relief produced a settlement on July 24. The men gained terms a shade less favorable than the Wage Board members had proposed; the companies gained considerably more price relief than Wilson once had offered.

Such was the outcome of steel seizure. Between it and the third case there are five years and Eisenhower's two elections. The Little Rock affair began in the first months of his second term.[5] In April 1957 a Federal Court of Appeals approved the integration plan prepared by school authorities in Little Rock, following the Supreme Court decision of 1954 that school segregation was unconstitutional. The Little Rock School Board announced that integrated schooling would begin at Central High School in September. It intensified its efforts to accustom the community to that prospect. So matters stood in August 1957, when a local citizen brought suit, successfully, in local court to halt the integration. The local court's injunction was declared void by a Federal Judge, and legally the way was cleared for integrated classes when the school reopened on September 3.

But on September 2, Orval Faubus, Governor of Arkansas, sent National Guardsmen to surround the school. These troops, at his instruction, kept all Negroes out in order to preclude the violent citizen reaction he announced might follow from their entry. Unable to carry out its integration plan, the School Board sought instruction from the Federal Judge. He ordered the Board to proceed as planned. Faubus's troops, however, barred compliance with his order. A petition to enjoin the Governor was put before the Judge September 10 with the United States Attorney General, among others, a petitioner. The next day Faubus asked Eisenhower for a conference; the President assented. He was then on vacation in Newport, Rhode Island, and a meeting was arranged there for September 14. But the meeting produced no action on either side.

On September 20, the Federal Judge enjoined the Governor from further interference with the School Board's plan. The Governor withdrew the National Guard and on the next school day, September 23, a noisy crowd broke through police lines and molested various bystanders. The Negro children who had come to school were taken home. That afternoon the President issued a proclamation to the citizens of Little Rock ordering "all persons" to cease the obstruction of justice. That night the White House and the Mayor of Little Rock held consultations. The next morning Eisenhower called the Arkansas National Guard into Federal service, thus removing it from Faubus's hands, and ordered regular Army troops to Little Rock. Order was restored and the Negro children returned to school. They remained in school, and federal troops remained on hand, through the school year until June 1958.

Thereafter, Little Rock's attempted integration entered a new phase. By school reopening in 1958, Faubus had proposed, received, and then invoked State legislation authorizing him to close the school if it were integrated. In 1959 the Federal courts struck down that legislation, and arrangements were made to open the school on roughly the same terms as in 1957. At the time of writing, the Governor had indicated an intention to set those terms aside if he could find a way to do it. This summary concludes without an ending.

III

The dismissal of MacArthur, the seizure of the steel mills, the dispatch of troops to Little Rock share a common characteristic: in terms of immediate intent the President's own order brought results as though his words were tantamount to action. He said, "Do this, do that," and *it was done*. From a presidential standpoint these three orders were self-executing. To give them was to have them carried out. Literally, no orders carry themselves out; self-executed actually means executed-by-others. But self-executing does describe the practical effect as it appeared to those who gave the orders. In the order-giver's eyes command amounted to compliance.

What lay behind "self-execution" of these orders? When troops were sent to Little Rock, Eisenhower's action took the form of an executive order which "authorized and directed" the Secretary of Defense to enforce the orders of the District Court in Arkansas, utilizing "such of the armed forces of the United States . . . as necessary." To implement this order there were successive delegations of authority from the Secretary of Defense through the Secretary of the Army down to units of the 101st Airborne Division and the Arkansas National Guard, the physical executors of Eisenhower's order. In form each delegation was discretionary. In fact, according to a White House participant, "The President decided which troops to use and how fast they should get there and what they should do when they arrived. That was worked out right here and all those fellows at the Pentagon had to do was turn the crank. They knew exactly what they were to do the minute the order was signed." They knew, also, that the President intended to address the nation justifying action *taken*. Under such circumstances, command and compliance are easy to equate.

In the MacArthur case the equation is even easier, for the circumstances were the simplest possible: Truman, as Commander-in-Chief, signed the order that relieved the General and the latter, himself, was its executor, transferring his commands to his designated successor. Misunderstanding was impossible; argument was precluded by publication of the order and by a presidential radio address explaining it.

As for seizure of the steel industry, Truman announced his action in a nationally televised address and at the same time, by executive order, he directed the Secretary of Commerce, Charles S. Sawyer, to take possession of the mills as government administrator. To carry out this order all that was initially required of Sawyer was a telegraphed notification to the managements and a delegation of authority to company executives, with a request that they stay on the job and fly the flag over the mills. Following the nationwide announcement the Secretary scarcely could do less and the government, thereby, was in possession without his having to do more.

This brief recital is enough to show what lay behind the ready execution of these orders. At least five common factors were at work. On each occasion the President's involvement was unambiguous. So were his words. His order was widely publicized. The men who received it had control of everything needed to carry it out. And they had no apparent doubt of his authority to issue it to them. It is no accident that these five factors can be found in all three instances. These are the factors that produce self-executing orders. Lacking any one of them the chances are that mere command will not produce compliance.

To see what happens in the absence of these favorable factors let me turn to incidents in the same factual setting as the three orders just described. These three were promptly executed. Preceding them, or following them, however, were many other orders that did not get carried out. Those others serve to illustrate what happens when a favorable factor is missing.

The first factor favoring compliance with a presidential order is assurance that the President has spoken. The three self-executing orders were given by the man himself, and not only in form but very much in fact. They were *his* orders in the double sense that they both came from him and expressed a definite decision by him personally. Recipients were left no room for doubt on either score; wording, timing, and publicity took care of that. To see what can occur when this factor is absent, one need but contrast the incident precipitating the dismissal of MacArthur: his publicized demand for enemy surrender on March 24, 1951.

The General's call for enemy surrender came at a moment when the President, in consultation with allied governments, was planning a statement that would virtually invite negotiated compromise to end the war. MacArthur got on record first with threats to spread the war. The White House statement then was set aside. To Truman, this action on MacArthur's part signified two things: deliberate sabotage of presidential policy and a deliberate violation of explicit orders. On the record there is no doubt that the President was right in both respects. For the General had been told through channels, in advance, of the impending White House initiative. And he had been under orders since the previous December to make no public statements on foreign or military policy without prior clearance from the Departments of State and Defense. "By this act," Truman writes, "MacArthur left me no choice—I could no longer tolerate his insubordination."[6]

Truman's comment implies what the record makes plain: he virtually invited this result by tolerating a long string of prior acts nearly as insubordinate. Since the Korean outbreak, as for years past, MacArthur had regularly used press statements to counter or to influence the views of his superiors. He had not previously used this means to stop their *acts*. But no penalties of consequence had been invoked for anything he had done short of that. To Truman this extension of the General's tactic was the final straw. MacArthur may have had no notion that the White House would react so strongly.

It is true that MacArthur violated an explicit order. But on its face the order seemed another form for form's sake. Dated December 6, 1950, it was addressed to all government departments and reached Tokyo routinely from the Pentagon. The order was expressed in terms more easily construed as the concoction of press attachés to hush Assistant Secretaries than as Truman's word to his Supreme Commander. In fact MacArthur *was* the target of this order; his press statements immediately after Chinese intervention were the cause of it. His conduct was of great concern to Truman personally. But how was the General to know? The order's widespread application and routine appearance were meant to spare him personal embarrassment (a fact which speaks volumes in itself). Their effect was to minimize its impact and to blur its source. Even had he recognized himself as addressee and Truman personally as sender, MacArthur may have noted that his press offensive at the start of the "new war" had drawn from Washington no more by way of a rebuke than this pale order. When stakes of policy and pride are high, convictions sharp (and political allies powerful), why should not a Supreme Commander try in March a somewhat bolder move than he had gotten away with in December?

A second factor making for compliance with a President's request is clarity about his meaning. If it helps to have respondents know that *he* wants what he asks, it also helps to have them know precisely what he wants. To shift the illustration, when the Governor of Arkansas met Eisenhower at Newport, a week before the troops were sent to Little Rock, there is no doubt that Faubus knew it was the President who wanted something done. But whether he was clear on what that something was remains uncertain; they met alone and the terms of their conversation left room for misunderstanding, apparent or real. According to an Eisenhower aide, "Faubus knew perfectly well what the President wanted: the order of the court complied with and the kids in school, peaceably . . . and he promised to produce. We were double-crossed, that's all." But Ashmore of the *Arkansas Gazette* records the impression that the Governor, believing he could "put off the dread day" until after his next gubernatorial campaign, "carried this illusion with him to Newport . . . and brought it home intact. . . ."[7]

A somewhat comparable piece of business marked the steel crisis of 1952 and led to resignation of the Mobilization Director, Wilson. At the outset of the crisis Wilson had conferred with Truman in Key West, talking at length and alone. But scarcely a week later, in exchanging letters upon Wilson's resignation, they recorded widely different notions of their Key West conversation. Wilson charged Truman with a change of tune; Truman charged Wilson with misconstruing orders. And both may have been right. For Wilson had returned from Key West with a mandate, as he saw it, to settle the dispute by price concessions if and as he could. This was a task demanding wide discretion for effective execution, and hence some open-endedness in its assignment. When a degree of ambiguity is inescapable, as in this case, it may take but a pinch of verbal imprecision or a dash of vacation atmosphere to produce misunderstanding. Both were in the recipe at Key West— and at Newport, five years later.

A third factor favoring compliance with a President's directive is publicity. Even when there is no need for ambiguity, no possibility of imprecision, no real discretionary leeway and nothing to misunderstand, compliance may depend not only on the respondent's awareness of what he is to do, but also on the awareness of others that he has been told to do it. In sending troops to Little Rock, in seizing the steel industry, in firing MacArthur, the whole country was taken into camp, informed of the President's commitment, invited to watch the response. But the circle of observers is rarely so broad. Often it may be entirely too narrow for presidential comfort. A case in point is Secretary Sawyer's interesting behavior in his first weeks as administrator of the seized steel industry.

Having seized the mills in desperation to avert production losses, the White House wanted to be rid of them as fast as possible—which meant as fast as it could gain assurance that production would continue once they were returned to private hands. This called for some settlement of the labor dispute whose lack of settlement had led to seizure in the first place. The circle could be broken only if continued government control were made so unattractive in the eyes of both disputants that they would prefer agreement with each other. To that end a tactic was devised: the Secretary of Commerce, as administrator of the mills, was to put into effect a *portion* of the union's wage demands to which the men were automatically entitled under the existing rules of wage control (a so-called cost-of-living adjustment). At the same time, he was to ask the price controllers for the amount of price relief to which the companies were automatically entitled under "pass through" provisions of existing legislation (the so-called Capehart Amendment). Secretary Sawyer then was to announce that he would do no more. Management and labor would be faced by a *fait accompli* that satisfied neither the union's wage demands nor the company's price demands but put some things beyond dispute and foreclosed better terms for the duration. With this prospect before them both sides might conclude that more was to be gained from settlement than from continued government direction. So, at least, the White House hoped.

Within a week of seizure Truman had decided to proceed along these lines. He asked that Sawyer act at once and planned to call for bargaining by companies and union with his Secretary's action in the background. The President's intent was clear. There were no ambiguities. But Sawyer did not act. The Secretary of Commerce spoke for business in the Cabinet. Officially and personally Sawyer had no liking for the seizure. He had not wanted to administer the mills, and he had taken the assignment with distaste. He was evidently unhappy at the prospect of his signature on wage orders and price requests committing the steel industry. Although he did not refuse to act, he managed to immerse himself in preparations. Presently the District Court relieved him of embarrassment (and the government of opportunity) by denying his authority to run the mills.[8] When the Appeals Court restored his powers, Sawyer reached the point of action only after he had won agreement from the President that in the public record his department should be seen to act on the advice of others. It was nearly four weeks after seizure when Truman brought the union and the companies together to bargain in his office. The Secretary's action was set for two days hence. By then it was too late. On the opening day of the bargaining session the Supreme Court barred changes in wages.

Had the President initially publicized his plan, Sawyer would have had to execute it promptly or resign. That was his choice upon the night of seizure. But Truman did not publicize this scheme of wage adjustments. Toward the end of the four weeks his pressure on the Secretary came to be an open secret. At the start, however, it was little known and Sawyer did not face so sharp a choice. When officials are reluctant to do as they are told, publicity spurs execution. But publicity performs this service at the risk of turning private reluctance into public defiance. Sometimes that may not matter very much, or may even promise some advantage, or the President may have no option. Here it mattered greatly. Truman had just lost his Director of Defense Mobilization (and he had just fired his Attorney General for reasons unrelated to steel). He could ill afford to lose his Secretary of Commerce, particularly on an issue involving the administration of the mills which he had just placed in the Secretary's hands. Truman had an option and he took it. He gave instructions privately and tolerated slow response.

A fourth factor favoring compliance with a President's request is actual ability to carry it out. It helps to have the order-taker in possession of the necessary means. In one respect Sawyer's situation after seizure paralleled his situation on the night of seizure: he had authority enough and resources enough to carry out the President's immediate intention. All that Sawyer needed was a staff to prepare papers, a pen with which to sign them, and access to the telegraph. Those resources were at his disposal. In this respect, on both occasions, Sawyer was in very much the same position as MacArthur when his last orders arrived, or the Secretary of the Army when the word came through on Little Rock. Each had the necessary means at *his* disposal. Without the wherewithal in his own hands a presidential agent may be unable to do as he is told no matter how good his understanding or honest his intention.

An example of a man without the means is Wilson, the Mobilization Director, in the preseizure phase of the steel crisis. Whatever Truman may or may not have said to him at Key West, it is reasonably clear that the President wanted the labor dispute settled without a strike, even at some cost to price control. But the moment Wilson tried to satisfy this want, two things became clear. The companies were in a mood to demand guarantees of price relief, but not to promise settlement. And the Price Director, Ellis Arnall, was in a mood to refuse *any* price increase save what the law would automatically require *after* settlement. In effect, Arnall's stand became "play my way or fire me," and though Wilson ranked him bureaucratically, Arnall was a *presidential* appointee. Wilson actually controlled neither the companies nor the Price Director. He could not even bring much influence to bear upon them since his claims to speak for Truman had been clouded by a clumsy press remark about the Wage Board. Wilson had no recourse but to return to the President empty-handed. When Truman leaned toward Arnall, Wilson resigned. But even had the President renewed Wilson's mandate, it is not clear what he could have done.

Another illustration of the same point can be drawn from the act of seizure itself. I have described Truman's order in this instance as "self-executing" in effect, with Sawyer the executor in fact. But Sawyer had a silent partner, the United Steelworkers. The purpose of the seizure was production. Truman's order was effective upon issuance because the men honored their union's pledge that they would work if their employer were the government. Yet until just two hours before seizure was announced, the President had planned, simultaneously, to invoke the fact-finding procedure of the Taft-Hartley Act.[9] This plan was dropped upon the urgent plea that wildcat strikes in protest, and thus losses of production, might result. In order to assure that Sawyer's silent partner could achieve the purpose of the presidential order, Truman had to modify it in advance.

A fifth factor making for compliance with a President's request is the sense that what he wants is his by right. The steelworkers assumed, as Truman did, that he had ample constitutional authority to seize and operate the mills. An interjection of the term "Taft-Hartley" might have altered their response, but in its absence they conformed to the convention that they would not strike against their government, accepting as *legitimate* the President's claim upon them. The sense of legitimate obligation, legitimately imposed, was present in MacArthur's transfer of his own commands and in the Army's response to its Little Rock directive, no less than in the union's action after seizure. Without a sense of that sort on the part of order-takers, those orders would not have been carried out so promptly. But judging by the illustrations offered up to now the obverse does not follow. There is no assur-ance that orders will be executed just because they seem legitimate to their recipi-ents. In none of the instances cited—not even in the case of Faubus at Newport—was a President's request considered *illegitimate* by those who *failed* to carry it out.

Perhaps legitimacy exerts a stronger influence the more distinct is its relation-ship to some specific grant of constitutional authority. Truman's final order to MacArthur, for example, had a clearer constitutional foundation than Eisenhower's *tête-à-tête* with Faubus, where authority was shared and therefore blurred. But Truman's earlier order to MacArthur on the clearance of public statements had precisely the same constitutional foundation as dismissal did. That earlier order had no more effect upon the General than Eisenhower had upon the Governor. Whatever its source or its relative strength, a sense of legitimacy taken alone does not assure compliance with a President's request.

When MacArthur was dismissed, when the steel mills were seized, when troops were sent to Little Rock, five factors made command appear the equal of compliance. In each of these three instances an unambiguous directive from a determined and committed President was carried out by persons who were capable of prompt response and who accepted his authority. The appearance of self-execution was produced by all these things combined. And when in other instances there was no such combination, there was also no effect of automatic execution.

How often is that combination likely to occur? How much, then, can a Presi-dent rely on sheer command to get him what he wants? It takes but a glance at the examples in this chapter to suggest the answers: not very often and not very much. "Do this, do that, and nothing will happen" was the rule in incidents surrounding the dismissal of the General, and the seizure of the steel mills, and the use of Federal troops at Central High School. Viewed in their surroundings these become excep-tions to the rule. So it is with presidential business generally. Under mid-century conditions self-executing orders are anything but everyday affairs. Indeed, in the whole sweep of Truman's record and of Eisenhower's, those three stand out pre-cisely for that reason: what they represent is relatively rare.

IV

The recall of MacArthur, the steel seizure, and the dispatch of troops to Little Rock share still another notable characteristic: in each case, the decisive order was a painful last resort, a forced response to the exhaustion of all other remedies, sugges-tive less of mastery than failure—the failure of attempts to gain an end by softer means.

Truman records in his memoirs that in April 1951, after reading the Pentagon file, General Marshall "concluded that MacArthur should have been fired two years ago."[10] Not everything that Marshall read is on the public record, but quite enough is there to lend substance to the view that MacArthur's dismissal was remarkably long delayed. Even if one sets aside all pre-Korean matters, ignores all questions of *professional* performance after Inchon, and scans the record only for the insubordination that provoked the firing, one finds at least two earlier cases somewhat comparable in all respects *except* the President's response. These two are MacArthur's outcry after Chinese intervention (leading to the clearance order of December 1950), and, months earlier, his public dissent from Formosa policy.[11] The White House announcement of his recall in April 1951, could have been issued in August or December 1950, without changing a word. Yet Truman stayed his hand on those earlier occasions (though apparently dismissal crossed his mind) and tried to patch the damage, bridge the differences, without offense to anybody's dignity except his own. The record indicates that he definitely did not want to let MacArthur go. At every challenge, save the final one, before and during the Korean War, the President sought means to keep the General both contained and on the job. Whatever his reasons Truman's pursuit of this objective—at considerable risk to policy, real sacrifice of pride—seems as persistent as anything in his career. In that sense the dismissal, when it finally came, marked failure.

And so it was with Eisenhower in the Little Rock affair. There were few things he wanted *less* than federal troops enforcing the desegregation of a Southern school. Indeed he may have helped to set the stage for Faubus by observing in July of 1957:

> I can't imagine any set of circumstances that would ever induce me to send Federal troops . . . into any area to enforce the orders of a Federal Court, because I believe that common sense of America will never require it.
>
> Now there may be that kind of authority resting somewhere, but certainly I am not seeking any additional authority of that kind, and I would never believe that it would be a wise thing to do in this country.[12]

And when, as schools reopened in September, the Governor had National Guardsmen interfere with execution of court orders, the President made a determined effort to avoid the use of force, an effort culminating in the inconclusive Newport conversation. Eisenhower agreed to meet Faubus at Newport without exacting advance guarantees. This is testimony to the President's desire for a way out other than the one he finally chose. So is the sense of "double-cross" that long persisted in the White House *after* Newport, a natural result of wanting to believe there was another way.

As for the steel seizure, the element of failure is self-evident. Truman had sought to settle the labor dispute in order to insure against a shutdown of production. When the union contract expired in December 1951, he tried to obtain settlement without a shutdown by referring the dispute to the Wage Stabilization Board. When the Board's report brought on a crisis instead, Wilson and the President took up the search for settlement. Their disagreement had to do with tactics, not the goal. After Wilson's resignation, the search continued under White House auspices right up to the day before the seizure. That drastic act was not even considered as a serious alternative until the week before, nor chosen with finality until the very day. The White House was so anxious for a settlement that Truman cancelled plans to state his case on television some days in advance of the strike deadline, lest there be an adverse effect on last-minute collective bargaining. In consequence, when seizure came, he had to combine a grave announcement with a contentious argument— hardly the choice of a President bent on seizure in the first place. But he had no such bent. Truman did not try to prepare the country for that course, because, until the last, he was intent on an alternative.

In this instance, as in the others, command became a last resort; but save in very short-run terms, it was not "last" at all. Truman did not want the steel mills; he wanted steel production and reasonably strong price controls. Those aims could only be achieved by terms of settlement between the union and the companies not inconsistent with existing control policies. The President had no power—and seizure gave him none—to gain his ends by fiat. Seizure merely staved off their abandonment and changed the *context* of his efforts to *induce* a satisfactory settlement. Initially, the new context put new inducements at the President's disposal. But seizure produced complications also, and these ultimately cost him both of his objectives. Two months' production vanished with the strike that followed judicial invalidation of his seizure. And price controls were breached beyond repair in White House efforts to conclude the strike. Yet it does not require hindsight to perceive that seizure's nature, from the start, was that of an emergency expedient, powerfully affecting possible solutions but solving nothing of itself. This would have been the case had the outcome been happier from Truman's point of view. At best, not seizure *per se*, but the added leverage it gave to his persuasion might have brought the settlement he wanted.

The same point can be made regarding Little Rock, where Eisenhower's use of troops bought time and changed the context of his appeals to the "hearts and minds" of Southerners but solved no desegregation problems, not even the local one at Central High School. As for the MacArthur case, his removal certainly resolved command relationships in the Korean War, but these were scarcely the sole concern. What was at stake was nothing less than our strategic purpose in the conduct of the war. And Truman's order did not end MacArthur's challenge to Administration policy, however much it may have changed the context of their quarrel. The General's threat to policy was ended by the Senate inquiry that followed his removal—and by the start of truce talks in Korea. Truman dug a grave, but that alone did not suffice to push MacArthur in. Without the push administered by Senate hearings it is not entirely clear whose grave it might have been.

Not only are these "last" resorts less than conclusive, but they are also costly. Even though the order is assured of execution, drastic action rarely comes at bargain rates. It can be costly to the aims in whose defense it is employed. It can be costly, also, to objectives far afield.

When he dismissed MacArthur, for example, Truman had to pay at least one price in the coin of Korean policy. The price was public exposition, at the Senate hearings, of his regime's innermost thoughts about the further conduct of hostilities. Whatever its effect on subsequent events, Peking and Moscow thus were put on notice of American intentions through the rest of Truman's term, and at home the reading public was informed that Washington saw little point in a renewed attempt to conquer North Korea. Against this background there began the long ordeal of truce negotiations. The Chinese may not have been influenced by those disclosures; Americans certainly were. Henry Kissinger, among many others, has argued with considerable justice that ". . . by stopping [offensive] military operations . . . at the very beginning of armistice negotiations . . . we removed the only Chinese incentive for a settlement; we produced the frustration of two years of inconclusive negotiations."[13] But no one has suggested how we were to stay on the offensive after Washington officialdom had formulated for itself and then expressed in public an intense desire to have done as soon as Peking tired of hostilities. Belabored in the hearings to define a "way out" other than MacArthur's, the Administration crystallized its own responsiveness toward offers to negotiate before they were ever made. When offers came they were seized on as "vindication." Even without the whole MacArthur uproar, it would not have been easy to press the offensive as truce talks began. After Senate hearings it seems psychologically if not politically impossible.

Besides such costs as this, directly chargeable against the purpose he was trying to protect, Truman's dismissal of MacArthur involved other costs as well, charged against other policy objectives. These "indirect" costs are hard to isolate because causation is no single-track affair, but certainly they were not inconsiderable. Among others, it is possible that Truman's inability to make his case with Congress, Court, and public in the steel crisis of 1952 resulted from exhaustion of his credit, so to speak, in the MacArthur battle a year earlier. That there is something in this will be clear from later chapters.

Drastic action may be costly, but it can be less expensive than continuing inaction. Truman could no longer have retained MacArthur without yielding to him the conduct of the war. Eisenhower could no longer stay his hand in Little Rock without yielding to every Southern Governor the right—even the duty—to do what Faubus did. These consequences threatened for the obvious reason that the instant challenge openly discounted the position of the Presidency and bluntly posed the question, "Who is President?" In either case, a soft response would have been tantamount to abdication, so public was the challenge in these terms. When Truman seized the steel mills, the Pentagon was warning that a new Chinese offensive, even Soviet intervention, might be coming in Korea "as soon as the mud dries." The seizure proved a very costly venture. But on the information then available, an April shutdown of the mills could have been far more costly. By hindsight it appears that a strike instead of seizure was the cheapest course available. The Chinese did not move as forcefully as had been feared. If they had done so, seizure might have proved a notable success. Truman acted without benefit of hindsight.

Self-executing orders have their uses, however inconclusive or expensive they may be. In each of these three cases, even steel, the presidential order brought assurance that a policy objective would remain in reach just as its loss seemed irretrievable. This is a real accomplishment. But necessarily it is a *transitory* accomplishment. Even the last resorts turn out to share the character of all the softer measures they replace. They turn out to be incidents in a persuasive process whereby someone lacking absolute control seeks to get something done through others who have power to resist.

Truman was quite right when he declared that presidential power is the power to persuade. Command is but a method of persuasion, not a substitute, and not a method suitable for everyday employment.

CHAPTER 3

The Power to Persuade

The limits on command suggest the structure of our government. The constitutional convention of 1787 is supposed to have created a government of "separated powers." It did nothing of the sort. Rather, it created a government of separated institutions *sharing* powers.[1] "I am part of the legislative process," Eisenhower often said in 1959 as a reminder of his veto.[2] Congress, the dispenser of authority and funds, is no less part of the administrative process. Federalism adds another set of separated institutions. The Bill of Rights adds others. Many public purposes can only be achieved by voluntary acts of private institutions; the press, for one, in Douglass Cater's phrase, is a "fourth branch of government."[3] And with the coming of alliances abroad, the separate institutions of a London, or a Bonn, share in the making of American public policy.

What the Constitution separates our political parties do not combine. The parties are themselves composed of separated organizations sharing public authority. The authority consists of nominating powers. Our national parties are confederations of state and local party institutions, with a headquarters that represents the White House, more or less, if the party has a President in office. These confederacies manage presidential nominations. All other public offices depend upon electorates confined within the states.[4] All other nominations are controlled within the states. The President and congressmen who bear one party's label are divided by dependence upon different sets of voters. The differences are sharpest at the stage of nomination. The White House has too small a share in nominating congressmen,

and Congress has too little weight in nominating Presidents for party to erase their
constitutional separation. Party links are stronger than is frequently supposed, but
nominating processes assure the separation.[5]

The separateness of institutions and the sharing of authority prescribe the terms
on which a President persuades. When one man shares authority with another, but
does not gain or lose his job upon the other's whim, his willingness to act upon the
urging of the other turns on whether he conceives the action right for him. The
essence of a President's persuasive task is to convince such men that what the White
House wants of them is what they ought to do for their sake and on their authority.

Persuasive power, thus defined, amounts to more than charm or reasoned
argument. These have their uses for a President, but these are not the whole of his
resources. For the men he would induce to do what he wants done on their own
responsibility will need or fear some acts by him on his responsibility. If they share
his authority, he has some share in theirs. Presidential "powers" may be inconclusive when a President commands, but always remain relevant as he persuades. The
status and authority inherent in his office reinforce his logic and his charm.

Status adds something to persuasiveness; authority adds still more. When
Truman urged wage changes on his Secretary of Commerce while the latter was
administering the steel mills, he and Secretary Sawyer were not just two men
reasoning with one another. Had they been so, Sawyer probably would never have
agreed to act. Truman's status gave him special claims to Sawyer's loyalty, or at
least attention. In Walter Bagehot's charming phrase "no man can *argue* on his
knees." Although there is no kneeling in this country, few men—and exceedingly
few Cabinet officers—are immune to the impulse to say "yes" to the President of
the United States. It grows harder to say "no" when they are seated in his oval
office at the White House, or in his study on the second floor, where almost tangibly
he partakes of the aura of his physical surroundings. In Sawyer's case, moreover,
the President possessed formal authority to intervene in many matters of concern to
the Secretary of Commerce. These matters ranged from jurisdictional disputes
among the defense agencies to legislation pending before Congress and, ultimately,
to the tenure of the Secretary, himself. There is nothing in the record to suggest that
Truman voiced specific threats when they negotiated over wage increases. But
given his *formal* powers and their relevance to Sawyer's other interests, it is safe to
assume that Truman's very advocacy of wage action conveyed an implicit threat.

A President's authority and status give him great advantages in dealing with the
men he would persuade. Each "power" is a vantage point for him in the degree that
other men have use for his authority. From the veto to appointments, from publicity
to budgeting, and so down a long list, the White House now controls the most
encompassing array of vantage points in the American political system. With hardly
an exception, the men who share in governing this country are aware that at some
time, in some degree, the doing of *their* jobs, the furthering of *their* ambitions, may
depend upon the President of the United States. Their need for presidential action,

or their fear of it, is bound to be recurrent if not actually continuous. Their need or fear is his advantage.

A President's advantages are greater than mere listing of his "powers" might suggest. The men with whom he deals must deal with him until the last day of his term. Because they have continuing relationships with him, his future, while it lasts, supports his present influence. Even though there is no need or fear of him today, what he could do tomorrow may supply today's advantage. Continuing relationships may convert any "power," any aspect of his status, into vantage points in almost any case. When he induces other men to do what he wants done, a President can trade on their dependence now *and* later.

The President's advantages are checked by the advantages of others. Continuing relationships will pull in both directions. These are relationships of mutual dependence. A President depends upon the men he would persuade; he has to reckon with his need or fear of them. They too will possess status, or authority, or both, else they would be of little use to him. Their vantage points confront his own; their power tempers his.

Persuasion is a two-way street. Sawyer, it will be recalled, did not respond at once to Truman's plan for wage increases at the steel mills. On the contrary, the Secretary hesitated and delayed and only acquiesced when he was satisfied that publicly he would not bear the onus of decision. Sawyer had some points of vantage all his own from which to resist presidential pressure. If he had to reckon with coercive implications in the President's "situations of strength," so had Truman to be mindful of the implications underlying Sawyer's place as a department head, as steel administrator, and as a Cabinet spokesman for business. Loyalty is reciprocal. Having taken on a dirty job in the steel crisis, Sawyer had strong claims to loyal support. Besides, he had authority to do some things that the White House could ill afford. Emulating Wilson, he might have resigned in a huff (the removal power also works two ways). Or emulating Ellis Arnall, he might have declined to sign necessary orders. Or, he might have let it be known publicly that he deplored what he was told to do and protested its doing. By following any of these courses Sawyer almost surely would have strengthened the position of management, weakened the position of the White House, and embittered the union. But the whole purpose of a wage increase was to enhance White House persuasiveness in urging settlement upon union and companies alike. Although Sawyer's status and authority did not give him the power to prevent an increase outright, they gave him capability to undermine its purpose. If his authority over wage rates had been vested by a statute, not by revocable presidential order, his power of prevention might have been complete. So Harold Ickes demonstrated in the famous case of helium sales to Germany before the Second World War.[6]

The power to persuade is the power to bargain. Status and authority yield bargaining advantages. But in a government of "separated institutions sharing powers," they yield them to all sides. With the array of vantage points at his disposal, a President may be far more persuasive than his logic or his charm could make him. But outcomes are not guaranteed by his advantages. There remain the counter pressures those whom he would influence can bring to bear on him from vantage points at their disposal. Command has limited utility; persuasion becomes give-and-take. It is well that the White House holds the vantage points it does. In such a business any President may need them all—and more.

II

This view of power as akin to bargaining is one we commonly accept in the sphere of congressional relations. Every textbook states and every legislative session demonstrates that save in times like the extraordinary Hundred Days of 1933—times virtually ruled out by definition at mid-century—a President will often be unable to obtain congressional action on his terms or even to halt action he opposes. The reverse is equally accepted: Congress often is frustrated by the President. Their formal powers are so intertwined that neither will accomplish very much, for very long, without the acquiescence of the other. By the same token, though, what one demands the other can resist. The stage is set for that great game, much like collective bargaining, in which each seeks to profit from the other's needs and fears. It is a game played catch-as-catch-can, case by case. And everybody knows the game, observers and participants alike.

The concept of real power as a give-and-take is equally familiar when applied to presidential influence outside the formal structure of the Federal government. The Little Rock affair may be extreme, but Eisenhower's dealings with the Governor—and with the citizens—become a case in point. Less extreme but no less pertinent is the steel seizure case with respect to union leaders, and to workers, and to company executives as well. When he deals with such people a President draws bargaining advantage from his status or authority. By virtue of their public places or their private rights they have some capability to reply in kind.

In spheres of party politics the same thing follows, necessarily, from the confederal nature of our party organizations. Even in the case of national nominations a President's advantages are checked by those of others. In 1944 it is by no means clear that Roosevelt got his first choice as his running mate. In 1948 Truman, then the President, faced serious revolts against his nomination. In 1952 his intervention from the White House helped assure the choice of Adlai Stevenson, but it is far from clear that Truman could have done as much for any other candidate acceptable to him.[7] In 1956 when Eisenhower was President, the record leaves obscure just who backed Harold Stassen's efforts to block Richard Nixon's renomination as Vice-President. But evidently everything did not go quite as Eisenhower wanted, whatever his intentions may have been.[8] The outcomes in these instances bear all the marks of limits on command and of power checked by power that characterize congressional relations. Both in and out of politics these checks and limits seem to be quite widely understood.

Influence becomes still more a matter of give-and-take when Presidents attempt to deal with allied governments. A classic illustration is the long unhappy wrangle over Suez policy in 1956. In dealing with the British and the French before their military intervention, Eisenhower had his share of bargaining advantages but no effective power of command. His allies had their share of counter pressures, and they finally tried the most extreme of all: action despite him. His pressure then was instrumental in reversing them. But had the British government been on safe ground *at home,* Eisenhower's wishes might have made as little difference after intervention as before. Behind the decorum of diplomacy—which was not very decorous in the Suez affair—relationships among allies are not unlike relationships among state delegations at a national convention. Power is persuasion and persuasion becomes bargaining. The concept is familiar to everyone who watches foreign policy.

In only one sphere is the concept unfamiliar: the sphere of executive relations. Perhaps because of civics textbooks and teaching in our schools, Americans instinctively resist the view that power in this sphere resembles power in all others. Even Washington reporters, White House aides, and congressmen are not immune to the illusion that administrative agencies comprise a single structure, "the" Executive Branch, where presidential word is law, or ought to be. Yet we have seen in Chapter 2 that when a President seeks something from executive officials his persuasiveness is subject to the same sorts of limitations as in the case of congressmen, or governors, or national committeemen, or private citizens, or foreign governments. There are no generic differences, no differences in kind and only sometimes in degree. The incidents preceding the dismissal of MacArthur and the incidents surrounding seizure of the steel mills make it plain that here as elsewhere influence derives from bargaining advantages; power is a give-and-take.

Like our governmental structure as a whole, the executive establishment consists of separated institutions sharing powers. The President heads one of these; Cabinet officers, agency administrators, and military commanders head others. Below the departmental level, virtually independent bureau chiefs head many more. Under mid-century conditions, Federal operations spill across dividing lines on organization charts; almost every policy entangles many agencies; almost every program calls for interagency collaboration. Everything somehow involves the President. But operating agencies owe their existence least of all to one another—and only in some part to him. Each has a separate statutory base; each has its statutes to administer; each deals with a different set of subcommittees at the Capitol. Each has its own peculiar set of clients, friends, and enemies outside the formal government. Each has a different set of specialized careerists inside its own bailiwick. Our Constitution gives the President the "take-care" clause and the appointive power. Our statutes give him central budgeting and a degree of personnel control. All agency administrators are responsible to him. But they *also* are responsible to Congress, to their clients, to their staffs, and to themselves. In short, they have five masters. Only after all of those do they owe any loyalty to each other.

"The members of the Cabinet," Charles G. Dawes used to remark, "are a President's natural enemies." Dawes had been Harding's Budget Director, Coolidge's Vice-President, and Hoover's Ambassador to London; he also had been General Pershing's chief assistant for supply in the First World War. The words are highly colored, but Dawes knew whereof he spoke. The men who have to serve so many masters cannot help but be somewhat the "enemy" of any one of them. By the same token, any master wanting service is in some degree the "enemy" of such a servant. A President is likely to want loyal support but not to relish trouble on his doorstep. Yet the more his Cabinet members cleave to him, the more they may need help from him in fending off the wrath of rival masters. Help, though, is synonymous with trouble. Many a Cabinet officer, with loyalty ill-rewarded by his lights and help withheld, has come to view the White House as innately hostile to department heads. Dawes's dictum can be turned around.

A senior presidential aide remarked to me in Eisenhower's time: "If some of these Cabinet members would just take time out to stop and ask themselves, 'What would I want if I were President?', they wouldn't give him all the trouble he's been having." But even if they asked themselves the question, such officials often could not act upon the answer. Their personal attachment to the President is all too often overwhelmed by duty to their other masters.

Executive officials are not equally advantaged in their dealings with a President. Nor are the same officials equally advantaged all the time. Not every officeholder can resist like a MacArthur, or like Arnall, Sawyer, Wilson, in a rough descending order of effective counter pressure. The vantage points conferred upon officials by their own authority and status vary enormously. The variance is heightened by particulars of time and circumstance. In mid-October 1950, Truman, at a press conference, remarked of the man he had considered firing in August and would fire the next April for intolerable insubordination:

> Let me tell you something that will be good for your souls. It's a pity that you . . . can't understand the ideas of two intellectually honest men when they meet. General MacArthur . . . is a member of the Government of the United States. He is loyal to that Government. He is loyal to the President. He is loyal to the President in his foreign policy. . . . There is no disagreement between General MacArthur and myself. . . .[9]

MacArthur's status in and out of government was never higher than when Truman spoke those words. The words, once spoken, added to the General's credibility thereafter when he sought to use the press in his campaign against the President. And what had happened between August and October? Near-victory had happened, together with that premature conference on *post*-war plans, the meeting at Wake Island.

If the bargaining advantages of a MacArthur fluctuate with changing circumstances, this is bound to be so with subordinates who have at their disposal fewer "powers," lesser status, to fall back on. And when officials have no "powers" in their own right, or depend upon the President for status, their counter pressure may be limited indeed. White House aides, who fit both categories, are among the most responsive men of all, and for good reason. As a Director of the Budget once remarked to me, "Thank God I'm here and not across the street. If the President doesn't call me, I've got plenty I can do right here and plenty coming up to me, by rights, to justify my calling him. But those poor fellows over there, if the boss doesn't call them, doesn't ask them to do something, what *can* they do but sit?" Authority and status so conditional are frail reliances in resisting a President's own wants. Within the White House precincts, lifted eyebrows may suffice to set an aide in motion; command, coercion, even charm aside. But even in the White House a President does not monopolize effective power. Even there persuasion is akin to bargaining. A former Roosevelt aide once wrote of Cabinet officers:

> Half of a President's suggestions, which theoretically carry the weight of orders, can be safely forgotten by a Cabinet member. And if the President asks about a suggestion a second time, he can be told that it is being investigated. If he asks a third time, a wise Cabinet officer will give him at least part of what he suggests. But only occasionally, except about the most important matters, do Presidents ever get around to asking three times.[10]

The rule applies to staff as well as to the Cabinet, and certainly has been applied *by* staff in Truman's time and Eisenhower's.

Some aides will have more vantage points than a selective memory. Sherman Adams, for example, as The Assistant to the President under Eisenhower, scarcely deserved the appelation "White House aide" in the meaning of the term before his time or as applied to other members of the Eisenhower entourage. Although Adams was by no means "chief of staff" in any sense so sweeping—or so simple—as press commentaries often took for granted, he apparently became no more dependent on the President than Eisenhower on him. "I need him," said the President when Adams turned out to have been remarkably imprudent in the Goldfine case, and delegated to him even the decision on his own departure.[11] This instance is extreme, but the tendency it illustrates is common enough. Any aide who demonstrates to others that he has the President's consistent confidence and a consistent part in presidential business will acquire so much business on his own account that he becomes in some sense independent of his chief. Nothing in the Constitution keeps a well-placed aide from converting status into power of his own, usable in some degree even against the President—an outcome not unknown in Truman's regime or, by all acounts, in Eisenhower's.

The more an officeholder's status and his "powers" stem from sources independent of the President, the stronger will be his potential pressure *on* the President.

Department heads in general have more bargaining power than do most members of the White House staff; but bureau chiefs may have still more, and specialists at upper levels of established career services may have almost unlimited reserves of the enormous power which consists of sitting still. As Franklin Roosevelt once remarked:

> The Treasury is so large and far-flung and ingrained in its practices that I find it almost impossible to get the action and results I want—even with Henry [Morgenthau] there. But the Treasury is not to be compared with the State Department. You should go through the experience of trying to get any changes in the thinking, policy, and action of the career diplomats and then you'd know what a real problem was. But the Treasury and the State Department put together are nothing compared with the Na-a-vy. The admirals are really something to cope with—and I should know. To change anything in the Na-a-vy is like punching a feather bed. You punch it with your right and you punch it with your left until you are finally exhausted, and then you find the damn bed just as it was before you started punching.[12]

In the right circumstances, of course, a President can have his way with any of these people. Chapter 2 includes three instances where circumstances were "right" and a presidential order was promptly carried out. But one need only note the favorable factors giving those three orders their self-executing quality to recognize that as between a President and his "subordinates," no less than others on whom he depends, real power is reciprocal and varies markedly with organization, subject matter, personality, and situation. The mere fact that persuasion is directed at executive officials signifies no necessary easing of his way. Any new congressman of the Administration's party, especially if narrowly elected, may turn out more amenable (though less useful) to the President than any seasoned bureau chief "downtown." *The probabilities of power do not derive from the literary theory of the Constitution.*

III

There is a widely held belief in the United States that were it not for folly or for knavery, a reasonable President would need no power other than the logic of his argument. No less a personage than Eisenhower has subscribed to that belief in many a campaign speech and press-conference remark. But faulty reasoning and bad intentions do not cause all quarrels with Presidents. The best of reasoning and of intent cannot compose them all. For in the first place, what the President wants will rarely seem a trifle to the men he wants it from. And in the second place, they will be bound to judge it by the standard of their own responsibilities, not his. However logical his argument according to his lights, their judgment may not bring them to his view.

The men who share in governing this country frequently appear to act as though they were in business for themselves. So, in a real though not entire sense, they are and have to be. When Truman and MacArthur fell to quarreling, for example, the stakes were no less than the substance of American foreign policy, the risks of greater war or military stalemate, the prerogatives of Presidents and field commanders, the pride of a pro-consul and his place in history. Intertwined, inevitably, were other stakes, as well: political stakes for men and factions of both parties; power stakes for interest groups with which they were or wished to be affiliated. And every stake was raised by the apparent discontent in the American public mood. There is no reason to suppose that in such circumstances men of large but differing responsibilities will see all things through the same glasses. On the contrary, it is to be expected that their views of what ought to be done and what they then should do will vary with the differing perspectives their particular responsibilities evoke. Since their duties are not vested in a "team" or a "collegium" but in themselves, as individuals, one must expect that they will see things *for* themselves. Moreover, when they are responsible to many masters and when an event or policy turns loyalty against loyalty—a day by day occurrence in the nature of the case—one must assume that those who have the duties to perform will choose the terms of reconciliation. This is the essence of their personal responsibility. When their own duties pull in opposite directions, who else but they can choose what they will do?

When Truman dismissed MacArthur, the latter lost three posts: the American command in the Far East, the Allied command for the occupation of Japan, and the United Nations command in Korea. He also lost his status as the senior officer on active duty in the United States armed forces. So long as he held those positions and that status, though, he had a duty to his troops, to his profession, to himself (the last is hard for any man to disentangle from the rest). As a public figure and a focus for men's hopes he had a duty to constituents at home, and in Korea and Japan. He owed a duty also to those other constituents, the UN governments contributing to his field forces. As a patriot he had a duty to his country. As an accountable official and an expert guide he stood at the call of Congress. As a military officer he had, besides, a duty to the President, his constitutional commander. Some of these duties may have manifested themselves in terms more tangible or more direct than others. But it would be nonsense to argue that the last *negated* all the rest, however much it might be claimed to override them. And it makes no more sense to think that anybody but MacArthur was effectively empowered to decide how he, himself, would reconcile the competing demands his duties made upon him.

Similar observations could be made about the rest of the executive officials encountered in Chapter 2. Price Director Arnall, it will be recalled, refused in advance to sign a major price increase for steel if Mobilization Director Wilson or the White House should concede one before management had settled with the union.

When Arnall did this, he took his stand, in substance, on his oath of office. He would do what he had sworn to do in *his* best judgment, so long as he was there to do it. This posture may have been assumed for purposes of bargaining and might have been abandoned had his challenge been accepted by the President. But no one could be sure and no one, certainly, could question Arnall's right to make the judgment for himself. As head of an agency and as a politician, with a program to defend and a future to advance, *he* had to decide what he had to do on matters that, from his perspective, were exceedingly important. Neither in policy nor in personal terms, nor in terms of agency survival, were the issues of a sort to be considered secondary by an Arnall, however much they might have seemed so to a Wilson (or a Truman). Nor were the merits likely to appear the same to a price stabilizer and to men with broader duties. Reasonable men, it is so often said, *ought* to be able to agree on the requirements of given situations. But when the outlook varies with the placement of each man, and the response required in his place is for each to decide, their reasoning may lead to disagreement quite as well—and quite as reasonably. Vanity, or vice, may weaken reason, to be sure, but it is idle to assign these as the cause of Arnall's threat or MacArthur's defiance. Secretary Sawyer's hesitations, cited earlier, are in the same category. One need not denigrate such men to explain their conduct. For the responsibilities they felt, the "facts" they saw, simply were not the same as those of their superiors; yet they, not the superiors, had to decide what they would do.

Outside the Executive Branch the situation is the same, except that loyalty to the President may often matter *less*. There is no need to spell out the comparison with Governors of Arkansas, steel company executives, trade union leaders, and the like. And when one comes to congressmen who can do nothing for themselves (or their constituents) save as they are elected, term by term, in districts and through party structures *differing* from those on which a President depends, the case is very clear. An able Eisenhower aide with long congressional experience remarked to me in 1958: "The people on the Hill don't do what they might *like* to do, they do what they think they *have* to do in their own interest as *they* see it. . . ." This states the case precisely.

The essence of a President's persuasive task with congressmen and everybody else, *is to induce them to believe that what he wants of them is what their own appraisal of their own responsibilities requires them to do in their interest, not his*. Because men may differ in their views on public policy, because differences in outlook stem from differences in duty—duty to one's office, one's constitutents, oneself—that task is bound to be more like collective bargaining than like a reasoned argument among philosopher kings. Overtly or implicitly, hard bargaining has characterized all illustrations offered up to now. This is the reason why: persuasion deals in the coin of self-interest with men who have some freedom to reject what they find counterfeit.

IV

A President draws influence from bargaining advantages. But does he always need them? The episodes described in Chapter 2 were instances where views on public policy diverged with special sharpness. Suppose such sharp divergences are lacking, suppose most players of the governmental game see policy objectives much alike, then can he not rely on logic (or on charm) to get him what he wants? The answer is that even then most outcomes turn on bargaining. The reason for this answer is a simple one: most men who share in governing have interests of their own beyond the realm of policy *objectives*. The sponsorship of policy, the form it takes, the conduct of it, and the credit for it separate their interest from the President's despite agreement on the end in view. In political government, the means can matter quite as much as ends; they often matter more. And there are always differences of interest in the means.

Let me introduce a case externally the opposite of my previous examples: the European Recovery Program of 1948, the so-called Marshall Plan. This is perhaps the greatest exercise in policy *agreement* since the cold war began. When the then Secretary of State, George Catlett Marshall, spoke at the Harvard commencement in June of 1947, he launched one of the most creative, most imaginative ventures in the history of American foreign relations. What makes this policy most notable for present purposes, however, is that it became effective upon action by the 80th Congress, at the behest of Harry Truman, in the election year of 1948.[13]

Eight months before Marshall spoke at Harvard, the Democrats had lost control of both Houses of Congress for the first time in fourteen years. Truman, whom the Secretary represented, had just finished his second troubled year as President-by-succession. Truman was regarded with so little warmth in his own party that in 1946 he had been urged *not* to participate in the congressional campaign. At the opening of Congress in January 1947, Senator Robert A. Taft, "Mr. Republican," had somewhat the attitude of a President-elect. This was a vision widely shared in Washington, with Truman relegated, thereby, to the role of caretaker-on-term. Moreover, within just two weeks of Marshall's commencement address, Truman was to veto two prized accomplishments of Taft's congressional majority: the Taft-Hartley Act and tax reduction.[14] Yet scarcely ten months later the Marshall Plan was under way on terms to satisfy its sponsors, its authorization completed, its first-year funds in sight, its administering agency in being: all managed by as thorough a display of executive-congressional cooperation as any we have seen since the Second World War. For any President at any time this would have been a great accomplishment. In years before mid-century it would have been enough to make the future reputation of his term. And for a Truman, at this time, enactment of the Marshall Plan appears almost miraculous.

How was the miracle accomplished? How did a President so situated bring it off? In answer, the first thing to note is that he did not do it by himself. Truman had help of a sort no less extraordinary than the outcome. Although each stands for something more complex, the names of Marshall, Vandenberg, Patterson, Bevin, Stalin, tell the story of that help.

In 1947, two years after V-J Day, General Marshall was something more than Secretary of State. He was a man venerated by the President as "the greatest living American," literally an embodiment of Truman's ideals. He was honored at the Pentagon as an architect of victory. He was thoroughly respected by the Secretary of the Navy, James V. Forrestal, who that year became the first Secretary of Defense. On Capitol Hill Marshall had an enormous fund of respect stemming from his war record as Army Chief of Staff, and in the country generally no officer had come out of the war with a higher reputation for judgment, intellect, and probity. Besides, as Secretary of State, he had behind him the first generation of matured foreign service officers produced by the reforms of the 1920's, and mingled with them, in the departmental service, were some of the ablest of the men drawn by the war from private life to Washington. In terms both of staff talent and staff's use, Marshall's years began a State Department "golden age" which lasted until the era of McCarthy. Moreover, as his Under Secretary, Marshall had, successively, Dean Acheson and Robert Lovett, men who commanded the respect of the professionals and the regard of congressmen. (Acheson had been brilliantly successful at congressional relations as Assistant Secretary in the war and postwar years.) Finally, as a special undersecretary Marshall had Will Clayton, a man highly regarded, for good reason, at both ends of Pennsylvania Avenue.

Taken together, these are exceptional resources for a Secretary of State. In the circumstances, they were quite as necessary as they obviously are relevant. The Marshall Plan was launched by a "lame duck" Administration "scheduled" to leave office in eighteen months. Marshall's program faced a congressional leadership traditionally isolationist and currently intent upon economy. European aid was viewed with envy by a Pentagon distressed and virtually disarmed through budget cuts, and by domestic agencies intent on enlarged welfare programs. It was not viewed with liking by a Treasury intent on budget surpluses. The plan had need of every asset that could be extracted from the personal position of its nominal author and from the skills of his assistants.

Without the equally remarkable position of the senior Senator from Michigan, Arthur H. Vandenberg, it is hard to see how Marshall's assets could have been enough. Vandenberg was chairman of the Senate Foreign Relations Committee. Actually, he was much more than that. Twenty years a senator, he was the senior member of his party in the Chamber. Assiduously cultivated by F.D.R. and Truman, he was a chief Republican proponent of "bipartisanship" in foreign policy, and consciously conceived himself its living symbol to his party, to the country, and abroad. Moreover, by informal but entirely operative agreement with his colleague Taft, Vandenberg held the acknowledged lead among Senate Republicans in the whole field of international affairs. This acknowledgement meant more in 1947 than it might have meant at any other time. With confidence in the advent of a Republican administration two years hence, most of the gentlemen were in a mood to be responsive and responsible. The war was over, Roosevelt dead, Truman a caretaker, theirs the trust. That the Senator from Michigan saw matters in this light, his diaries make clear.[15] And this was not the outlook from the Senate side alone; the attitudes of House Republicans associated with the Herter Committee and its tours abroad suggest the same mood of responsibility. Vandenberg was not the only source of help on Capitol Hill. But relatively speaking, his position there was as exceptional as Marshall's was downtown.

Help of another sort was furnished by a group of dedicated private citizens who organized one of the most effective instruments for public information seen since the Second World War: the Committee for the Marshall Plan, headed by the eminent Republicans whom F.D.R., in 1940, had brought to the Department of War: Henry L. Stimson as honorary chairman and Robert P. Patterson as active spokesman. The remarkable array of bankers, lawyers, trade unionists, and editors, who had drawn together in defense of "internationalism" before Pearl Harbor and had joined their talents in the war itself, combined again to spark the work of this committee. Their efforts generated a great deal of vocal public support to buttress Marshall's arguments, and Vandenberg's, in Congress.

But before public support could be rallied, there had to be a purpose tangible enough, concrete enough, to provide a rallying ground. At Harvard, Marshall had voiced an idea in general terms. That this was turned into a hard program susceptible of presentation and support is due, in major part, to Ernest Bevin, the British Foreign Secretary. He well deserves the credit he has sometimes been assigned as, in effect, co-author of the Marshall Plan. For Bevin seized on Marshall's Harvard speech and organized a European response with promptness and concreteness beyond the State Department's expectations. What had been virtually a trial balloon to test reactions on both sides of the Atlantic was hailed in London as an invitation to the Europeans to send Washington a bill of particulars. This they promptly organized to do, and the American Administration then organized in turn for its reception without further argument internally about the pros and cons of issuing the "invitation" in the first place. But for Bevin there might have been trouble from the Secretary of the Treasury and others besides.[16]

If Bevin's help was useful at that early stage, Stalin's was vital from first to last. In a mood of self-deprecation Truman once remarked that without Moscow's "crazy" moves "we would never have had our foreign policy . . . we never could have got a thing from Congress."[17] George Kennan, among others, had deplored the anti-Soviet overtone of the case made for the Marshall Plan in Congress and the country, but there is no doubt that this clinched the argument for many segments of American opinion. There also is no doubt that Moscow made the crucial contributions to the case.

By 1947 events, far more than governmental prescience or open action, had given a variety of publics an impression of inimical Soviet intentions (and of Europe's weakness), and a growing urge to ''do something about it.'' Three months before Marshall spoke at Harvard, Greek-Turkish aid and promulgation of the Truman Doctrine had seemed rather to crystallize than to create a public mood and a congressional response. The Marshall planners, be it said, were poorly placed to capitalize on that mood, nor had the Secretary wished to do so. Their object, indeed, was to cut across it, striking at the cause of European weakness rather than at Soviet aggressiveness, *per se*. A strong economy in Western Europe called, ideally, for restorative measures of continental scope. American assistance proffered in an anti-Soviet context would have been contradictory in theory and unacceptable in fact to several of the governments that Washington was anxious to assist. As Marshall, himself, saw it, the logic of his purpose forbade him to play his strongest congressional card. The Russians then proceeded to play it for him. When the Europeans met in Paris, Molotov walked out. After the Czechs had shown continued interest in American aid, a communist coup overthrew their government while Soviet forces stood along their borders within easy reach of Prague. Molotov transformed the Marshall Plan's initial presentation; Czechoslovakia assured its final passage, which followed by a month the take-over in Prague.

Such was the help accorded Truman in obtaining action on the Marshall Plan. Considering his politically straightened circumstances he scarcely could have done with less. Conceivably, some part of Moscow's contribution might have been dispensable, but not Marshall's, or Vandenberg's, or Bevin's, or Patterson's, or that of the great many other men whose work is represented by their names in my account. Their aid was not extended to the President for his own sake. He was not favored in this fashion just because they liked him personally, or were spellbound by his intellect or charm. They might have been as helpful had all held him in disdain, which some of them certainly did. The Londoners who seized the ball, Vandenberg and Taft and the congressional majority, Marshall and his planners, the officials of other agencies who actively supported them or ''went along,'' the host of influential private citizens who rallied to the cause—all these played the parts they did because they thought they had to, in their interest, given their responsibilities, not Truman's. Yet they hardly would have found it in their interest to collaborate with one another, or with him, had he not furnished them precisely what *they* needed from the White House. Truman could not do without their help, but he could not have had it without unremitting effort on his part.

The crucial thing to note about this case is that despite compatibility of views on public policy, Truman got no help he did not pay for (except Stalin's). Bevin scarcely could have seized on Marshall's words had Marshall not been plainly backed by Truman. Marshall's interest would not have comported with the exploitation of his prestige by a President who undercut him openly, or subtly, or even inadvertently, at any point. Vandenberg, presumably, could not have backed proposals by a White House which begrudged him deference and access gratifying to his fellow-partisans (and satisfying to himself). Prominent Republicans in private life would not have found it easy to promote a cause identified with Truman's claims on 1948—and neither would the prominent New Dealers then engaged in searching for a substitute.

Truman paid the price required for their services. So far as the record shows, the White House did not falter once in firm support for Marshall and the Marshall Plan. Truman backed his Secretary's gamble on an invitation to all Europe. He made the plan his own in a well-timed address to the Canadians. He lost no opportunity to widen the involvements of his own official family in the cause. Averell Harriman the Secretary of Commerce, Julius Krug the Secretary of the Interior, Edwin Nourse the Economic Council Chairman, James Webb the Director of the Budget—all were made responsible for studies and reports contributing directly to the legislative presentation. Thus these men were committed in advance. Besides, the President continually emphasized to everyone in reach that he did not have doubts, did not desire complications and would foreclose all he could. Reportedly, his emphasis was felt at the Treasury, with good effect. And Truman was at special pains to smooth the way for Vandenberg. The Senator insisted on "no politics" from the Administration side; there was none. He thought a survey of American resources and capacity essential; he got it in the Krug and Harriman reports. Vandenberg expected advance consultation; he received it, step by step, in frequent meetings with the President and weekly conferences with Marshall. He asked for an effective liaison between Congress and agencies concerned; Lovett and others gave him what he wanted. When the Senator decided on the need to change financing and administrative features of the legislation, Truman disregarded Budget Bureau grumbling and acquiesced with grace. When, finally, Vandenberg desired a Republican to head the new administering agency, his candidate, Paul Hoffman, was appointed despite the President's own preference for another. In all of these ways Truman employed the sparse advantages his "powers" and his status then accorded him to gain the sort of help he had to have.

Truman helped himself in still another way. Traditionally and practically no one was placed as well as he to call public attention to the task of *Congress* (and its Republican leadership). Throughout the fall and winter of 1947 and on into the spring of 1948, he made repeated use of presidential "powers" to remind the country that congressional action was required. Messages, speeches, and an extra session were employed to make the point. Here, too, he drew advantage from his place. However, in his circumstances, Truman's public advocacy might have hurt, not helped, had his words seemed directed toward the forthcoming election. Truman gained advantage for his program only as his own endorsement of it stayed on the right side of that fine line between the "caretaker" in office and the would-be candidate. In public statements dealing with the Marshall Plan he seems to have risked blurring this distinction only once, when he called Congress into session in November 1947 asking both for interim aid to Europe *and* for peacetime price controls. The second request linked the then inflation with the current Congress (and with Taft), becoming a first step toward one of Truman's major themes in 1948. By calling for both measures at the extra session he could have been accused—and was—of mixing home-front politics with foreign aid. In the event no harm was done the European program (or his politics). But in advance a number of his own advisers feared that such a double call would jeopardize the Marshall Plan. Their fears are testimony to the narrowness of his advantage in employing his own "powers" for its benefit.[18]

It is symptomatic of Truman's situation that "bipartisan" accommodation by the White House then was thought to mean congressional consultation and conciliation on a scale unmatched in Eisenhower's time. Yet Eisenhower did about as well with opposition Congresses as Truman did, in terms of requests granted for defense and foreign aid. It may be said that Truman asked for more extraordinary measures. But it also may be said that Eisenhower never lacked for the prestige his predecessor had to borrow. It often was remarked, in Truman's time, that he seemed a "split-personality," so sharply did his conduct differentiate domestic politics from national security. But personality aside, how else could *he,* in his first term, gain ground for an evolving foreign policy? The plain fact is that Truman had to play bipartisanship as he did or lose the game.

V

Had Truman lacked the personal advantages his "powers" and his status gave him, or if he had been maladroit in using them, there probably would not have been a massive European aid program in 1948. Something of the sort, perhaps quite different in its emphasis, would almost certainly have come to pass before the end of 1949. *Some* American response to European weakness and to Soviet expansion was as certain as such things can be. But in 1948 temptations to await a Taft Plan or a Dewey Plan might well have caused at least a year's postponement of response had the "outgoing" Administration bungled its congressional, or public, or allied, or executive relations. Quite aside from the specific virtues of their plan, Truman and his helpers gained that year, at least, in timing the American response. As European time was measured then, this was a precious gain. The President's own share in this accomplishment was vital. He made his contribution by exploiting his advantages. Truman, in effect, lent Marshall and the rest the perquisites and status of his office. In return they lent him their prestige and their own influence. The transfer multiplied *his* influence despite his limited authority in form and lack of strength politically. Without the wherewithal to make this bargain, Truman could not have contributed to European aid.

Bargaining advantages convey no guarantees. Influence remains a two-way street. In the fortunate instance of the Marshall Plan, what Truman needed was actually in the hands of men who were prepared to "trade" with him. He personally could deliver what they wanted in return. Marshall, Vandenberg, Harriman, *et al.*, possessed the prestige, energy, associations, staffs, essential to the legislative effort. Truman himself had a sufficient hold on presidential messages and speeches, on budget policy, on high-level appointments, and on his own time and temper to carry through all aspects of his necessary part. But it takes two to make a bargain. It takes those who have prestige to lend it on whatever terms. Suppose that Marshall had declined the Secretaryship of State in January 1947; Truman might not have found a substitute so well-equipped to furnish what he needed in the months ahead. Or suppose that Vandenberg had fallen victim to a cancer two years before he actually did; Senator Wiley of Wisconsin would not have seemed to Taft a man with whom the world need be divided. Or suppose that the Secretary of the Treasury had been possessed of stature, force, and charm commensurate with that of his successor in Eisenhower's time, the redoubtable George M. Humphrey. And what if Truman then had seemed to the Republicans what he turned out to be in 1948, a formidable candidate for President? It is unlikely that a single one of these "supposes" would have changed the final outcome; two or three, however, might have altered it entirely. Truman was not guaranteed more power than his "powers" just because he had continuing relationships with Cabinet secretaries and with senior senators. Here, as everywhere, the outcome was conditional on who they were and what he was and how each viewed events, and on their actual performance in response.

Granting that persuasion has no guarantee attached, how can a President reduce the risks of failing to persuade? How can he maximize his prospects for effectiveness by minimizing chances that his power will elude him? The Marshall Plan suggests an answer: he guards his power prospects in the course of making choices. Marshall himself, and Forrestal, and Harriman, and others of the sort held office on the President's appointment. Vandenberg had vast symbolic value partly because F.D.R. and Truman had done everything they could, since 1944, to build him up. The Treasury Department and the Budget Bureau—which together might have jeopardized the plans these others made—were headed by officials whose prestige depended wholly on their jobs. What Truman needed from those "givers" he received, in part, because of his past choice of men and measures. What they received in turn were actions taken or withheld by him, himself. The things they needed from him mostly involved his own conduct where his current choices ruled. The President's own actions in the past had cleared the way for current bargaining. His actions in the present were his trading stock. Behind each action lay a personal choice, and these together comprised *his* control over the give-and-take that gained him what he wanted. In the degree that Truman, personally, affected the advantages he drew from his relationships with other men in government, *his power was protected by his choices.*

By "choice" I mean no more than what is commonly referred to as "decision": a President's own act of doing or not doing. Decision is so often indecisive and indecision is so frequently conclusive, that choice becomes the preferable term.

"Choice" has its share of undesired connotations. In common usage it implies a black-and-white alternative. Presidential choices are rarely of that character. It also may imply that the alternatives are set before the choice-maker by someone else. A President is often left to figure out his options for himself. Neither implication holds in any of the references to "choice" throughout this book.

If Presidents could count upon past choices to enhance their current influence, as Truman's choice of men had done for him, persuasion would pose fewer difficulties than it does. But Presidents can count on no such thing. Depending on the circumstances, prior choices can be as embarrassing as they were helpful in the instance of the Marshall Plan. The incidents described in Chapter 2 include some sharp examples of embarrassment. Among others: Eisenhower's influence with Faubus was diminished by his earlier statements to the press and by his unconditional agreement to converse in friendly style at Newport. Truman's hold upon MacArthur was weakened by his deference toward him in the past.

Assuming that past choices have protected influence, not harmed it, present choices still may be inadequate. If Presidents could count on their own conduct to provide them *enough* bargaining advantages, as Truman's conduct did where Vandenberg and Marshall were concerned, effective bargaining might be much easier to manage than it often is. In the steel crisis, for instance, Truman's own persuasiveness with companies and union, both, was burdened by the conduct of an independent Wage Board and of government attorneys in the courts, to say nothing of Wilson, Arnall, Sawyer, and the like. Yet in practice, if not theory, many of *their* crucial choices never were the President's to make. Decisions that are legally in other's hands, or delegated past recall, have an unhappy way of proving just the trading stock most needed when the White House wants to trade. One reason why Truman was consistently more influential in the instance of the Marshall Plan than in the steel case, or the MacArthur case, is that the Marshall Plan directly involved Congress. In congressional relations there are some things that no one but the President can do. His chance to choose is higher when a message must be sent, or a nomination submitted, or a bill signed into law, than when the sphere of action is confined to the Executive, where all decisive tasks may have been delegated past recall.

But adequate or not, a President's own choices are the only means *in his own hands* of guarding his own prospects for effective influence. He can draw power from continuing relationships in the degree that he can capitalize upon the needs of others for the Presidency's status and authority. He helps himself to do so, though, by nothing save ability to recognize the pre-conditions and the chance advantages and to proceed accordingly in the course of the choice-making that comes his way. To ask how he can guard prospective influence is thus to raise a further question: what helps him guard his power stakes in his own acts of choice?

4

Professional Reputation

A President's persuasiveness with other men in government depends on something more than his advantages for bargaining. The men he would persuade must be convinced in their own minds that he has skill and will enough to *use* his advantages. Their judgment of him is a factor in his influence with them. The final question posed in Chapter 3 was how a President protects his power stakes in his own acts of choice. This question can be set aside until we have examined what he has at stake in judgments made by others.

The men who share in governing this country are inveterate observers of a President. They have the doing of whatever he wants done. They are the objects of his personal persuasion. They also are the most attentive members of his audience. These doers comprise what in spirit, not geography, might well be termed the "Washington community." This community cuts across the President's constituencies. Members of Congress and of his Administration, governors of states, military commanders in the field, leading politicians in both parties, representatives of private organizations, newsmen of assorted types and sizes, foreign diplomats (and principals abroad)—all these are "Washingtonians" no matter what their physical location. In most respects the Washington community is far from homogeneous. In one respect it is tightly knit indeed: by definition, all its members are compelled to watch the President for reasons not of pleasure but vocation. They need him in their business just as he needs them. Their own work thus requires that they keep an eye on him. Because they watch him closely his persuasiveness with them turns quite as much on their informed appraisals as on his presumed advantages.

In influencing Washingtonians, the most important law at a President's disposal is the "law" of "anticipated reactions," propounded years ago by Carl J. Friedrich.[1] The men who share in governing do what they think they must. A President's effect on them is heightened or diminished by their thoughts about his probable reaction to their doing. They base their expectations on what they can see of him. And they are watching all the time. Looking at themselves, at him, at the immediate event, and toward the future, they may think that what he might do in theory, he would not dare to do in fact. So MacArthur evidently thought before he was dismissed. They may think that the President has tied his hands behind his back, as Faubus thought, apparently, before and after Newport. They may conclude with Arnall that the President has more to lose than they do, should he not support them. Or they may conclude, as Sawyer evidently did, that they risk more than he does if they do not support him. A Marshall and a Vandenberg may decide that the president can be relied upon to put his "powers" and his status at their service. A Charles E. Wilson, after Key West, may decide the opposite.

What these men think may or may not be "true" but it is the reality on which they act, at least until their calculations turn out wrong. As the steel crisis loomed in 1952 many Washingtonians took it for granted that should matters reach the strike stage, Truman had too many other troubles to risk anything so controversial as seizure. By April that year he and his party faced a wide-open contest for the presidential nomination; the Governor of Illinois whom he had wanted to proclaim as heir apparent would not serve. In Congress fights impended on half a dozen fronts. Downtown he was entangled in abortive efforts, highly publicized, to oversee a "cleanup" of "corruption." That at this point he could "afford" to seize the whole steel industry was heavily discounted in the industry itself, at the Capitol, and even by some members of his Cabinet. It was their thought that he would have "no choice" but resort to Taft-Hartley. This thought may have reduced management's incentive for a settlement; it almost certainly reduced the Pentagon's concern about the outcome.

Expectations often are much closer to the mark than were those views of Truman in the steel case. Ten months before the steel crisis, in June of 1951, he made an impassioned television plea to rally popular support for tighter price controls than Congress seemed about to grant as it renewed the authorizing legislation. Neither before his plea nor after were the anticontrol forces visibly impressed. A President's ability to "appeal to the people" may be chief among his vantage points, as all the textbooks say, but no one feared vast popular response to *Truman's* call for stiffer wartime regulation two months after his dismissal of MacArthur. In this instance, the expectation proved correct. "I never asked anybody to write to his congressman," Truman later told the press.[2] Hardly anybody did.

What other men expect of him becomes a cardinal factor in the President's own power to persuade. When men in government consider their relationships with him it does them little good to scan the Constitution or remind themselves that Presidents possess potential vantage points in excess of enumerated powers. Their problem never is what abstract Presidents might do in theory but what an actual incumbent will try in fact. They must anticipate, as best they can, his *ability* and *will* to make use of the bargaining advantages he has. Out of what others think of him emerge his opportunities for influence with them. If he would maximize his prospects for effectiveness, he must concern himself with what they think. To formulate his power problem in these terms is to illuminate the job of being President.

II

In a world of perfect rationality and unclouded perception it might turn out that Washingtonians could take the past performance of a President as an exact, precise, definitive determinant of future conduct, case by case. The known and open record, wholly understood, could be ransacked for counterparts to all details of each new situation. His skill, or lack of it, in using comparable vantage points for comparable purposes in like conditions, could be gauged with such precision that forecasting his every move would become a science practiced with the aid of mathematics.

In the real world, however, nobody is altogether sure what aspects of the past fit which piece of the present or the future. As the illustrations in this book suggest, particulars of time, of substance, organization, personalities, may make so great a difference, case by case, that forecasting remains a tricky game and expectations rest upon perceptions of a most imperfect sort. This can both help a President and hurt him. It can help in the sense that almost everyone in government discounts, to some degree, the flaws in his performance at a given moment. But it can hurt in the sense that over time these may lead to discounting, in advance, of his ability at any future moment.

In every move a President may make there are bound to be numerous aspects beyond his immediate control. So many things can go wrong that almost always some things do. Accordingly, the men who watch a President professionally, so to speak, cannot afford to ground their expectations on the slippages and errors in his every effort. But these accumulate, and as they do men seek for the appearance of a *pattern.* Lacking a better base, they tend to rest their forecasts of the future on such patterns as they find. The greatest danger to a President's potential influence with them is not the show of incapacity he makes today, but its apparent kinship to what happened yesterday, last month, last year. For if his failures seem to form a pattern, the consequence is bound to be a loss of faith in his effectiveness ''next time.'' The boy who cried ''wolf'' came to a sad end because nobody paid attention to his final cry.

The fine points of a President's ''technique'' in dealing with a given situation are not the only things men watch for signs of pattern. Whether he made the right phone call on the right day, or said the right words at the right time, or read the right report and drew the right conclusion may make all the difference at a given moment.

If the same thing seems to happen at successive moments it will make a mark on expectations of his future conduct. But in the present, looking toward the future, most men have more to think about than his apparent mastery of such techniques. So long as they must keep in mind continuing relationships while they consider what he wants from them, they also have to think about how hard, persistently, determinedly, he seems to *try*. With will enough, even the clumsiest technician might manage to hurt enemies somehow, sometime, and to provide some sort of cover for his friends. Signs of tenacity count quite as much as signs of skill in shaping expectations of a President's behavior.

Were Washington observers confined to the evidence of personal experience, a President would shape their expectations as he dealt with each in turn. But those who watch a President because their work requires it do not see only what he chooses to disclose to them. They see some part of almost everything he does with almost everyone, and what they cannot see they try to hear. Everything reported in the press adds to their field of vision. Whatever happens to their neighbors amplifies their view. They ask each other questions. They tell each other stories. They read with care the news reports, and newsletters, and syndicated columns circulating "inside dope" drawn from men like themselves. Theirs is a most incestuous community. In consequence, their outlook on a President at any given moment will be affected by impressions of his will and skill then currently in vogue among observers like themselves. If he wants influence, therefore, he must concern himself with more than *tête-à-têtes* in person or by proxy; his problem is no less than what all Washington may think of him. He has to be concerned with his professional reputation as a governor among the men who share in governing.

The general reputation of a President in Washington will not reflect the views of every Washingtonian. There usually is a dominant tone, a central tendency, in Washington appraisals of a President. If one wants echoes of that tone at any time one reads Krock, Lippmann, Reston, and Rovere, and half a dozen others. (One gains forewarnings also; these columnists are read with care by those from whom they draw their information.) However, no matter what the fashionable impression of the moment, some of the men on whom a President depends will always be discounting it in favor of what they perceive themselves, by light of their own loyalties, jobs, and first-hand observations. White House aides, Cabinet officers, legislative leaders, and the like will know more about some things than most commentators do (or know them differently) and will appraise the President in light of what they know. This may move their impressions far from those held by their less advantaged neighbors.

Nevertheless, differences in view between the better and the less informed tend to be self-adjusting. For one thing, the "insiders," or their aides, are looked to for the tips and "steers" and "dope" stories that help their neighbors read the public record. For another thing, their own appraisals are not always proof against appearances outside the range of personal observation. Besides, the men best placed to gain an independent view are duty-bound to take into account what others think, no matter how mistaken. Department heads or congressional leaders may see the President as pure in heart, but if their followers are sullenly convinced that he is not, this is a datum to be weighed in their own calculations. His general reputation may not be conclusive for the best informed, but it is almost sure to be a factor in their thinking.

A President who values power need not be concerned with every flaw in his performance day by day, but he has every reason for concern with the residual impressions of tenacity and skill accumulating in the minds of Washingtonians-at-large. His bargaining advantages in seeking what he wants are heightened or diminished by what others think of him. Their thoughts are shaped by what they see. They do not see alone, they see together. What they think of him is likely to be much affected by the things they see alike. His look in "everybody's" eyes becomes strategically important for his influence. Reputation, of itself, does not persuade, but it can make persuasion easier, or harder, or impossible.

Ideally, any President who valued personal power would start his term with vivid demonstrations of tenacity and skill in every sphere, thereby establishing a reputation sure to stand the shocks of daily disarray until he was prepared to demonstrate again. This is no more than Franklin Roosevelt did in his first term. It is the ideal formula for others. Unfortunately, F.D.R.'s successors have not held the combination of advantages that helped him make his first-term demonstration: the public memory of his predecessor, the crisis of the Great Depression, the easy escape from foreign affairs, the eagerness of intellectuals, the patronage for partisans, the breadth of his experience in government (unmatched in this century save by the other Roosevelt). Nor is there anything to indicate that while mid-century conditions last, a future President is likely to hold comparable advantages. Emergencies in policy with politics as usual can hardly favor an effective use of Roosevelt's formula.

A contemporary President may have to settle for a reputation short of the ideal. If so, what then should be his object? It should be to induce as much uncertainty as possible about the consequences of ignoring what he wants. If he cannot make men think him bound to win, his need is to keep them from thinking they can cross him without risk, or that they can be sure what risks they run. At the same time (no mean feat) he needs to keep them from fearing lest he leave them in the lurch if they support him. To maximize uncertainties in future opposition, to minimize the insecurities of possible support, and to avoid the opposite effect in either case—these together form the goal for any mid-century President who seeks a reputation that will serve his personal power.

How can a President accomplish this result? How does he build his reputation? How does he protect it? Let me begin consideration of these questions with a classic instance of the ways in which a reputation ought *not* to be guarded. This illustration deals with the first year of Eisenhower's second term.

III

Early in 1958 a technician from the Bureau of the Budget testified before a sub-committee of the House on the provisions of a pending bill within his field of expertise. As he concluded, he remarked for emphasis that what he recommended was essential "to the program of the President." Whereupon everybody laughed. The hilarity was general and leaped party lines; to a man, committee members found the reference very funny.[3] This incident occurred only fifteen months after Eisenhower's smashing re-election victory. Yet it is perfectly indicative, so far as can be judged from the outside, of an impression pervading all corners of the Capitol (and most places downtown), as a result of what had seemed to happen at the White House in the months between. This impression was to change somewhat with subsequent events. In 1959 a "new" Eisenhower emerged. Still, early in the second legislative session of his second term that laughter well expressed what most men thought. And why they thought it is an object lesson in how not to guard professional reputation.[4]

On election night in 1956, knowing the dimensions of his personal triumph, but perhaps not yet aware that he had carried neither House of Congress, Eisenhower told a national television audience:

> . . . And now let me say something that looks to the future. I think that modern republicanism has now proved itself. And America has approved of modern republicanism.
>
> And so, as we look ahead—as we look ahead to the problems in front, let us remember that a political party deserves the approbation of America only as it represents the ideals, the aspirations and the hopes of Americans. If it is anything less, it is merely a conspiracy to seize power and the Republican party is not that!
>
> Modern republicanism looks to the future. . . .[5]

For a few weeks thereafter old Washington hands of both political persuasions engaged in speculation about what, if anything, that comment might portend. They did not have to wonder very long. On January 16, 1957, the President sent to Congress his budget for Fiscal 1958, a document marked very generally by "modern" Republican touches reminiscent of the past campaign. These were evident, particularly, in the budget's relatively generous handling of resource development and welfare programs (among them general aid for school construction), in its moderate increases for defense and foreign aid, and in its bland acceptance of a spending total close to 72 billion dollars. The total was 12 billion dollars higher than the oratorical objective of the first Eisenhower campaign, four years gone but not forgotten; spending at this level heralded no further tax relief for at least two years more. Momentarily the budget seemed a clue to Eisenhower's views about the future of his party.

Then, the same day, Secretary of the Treasury George M. Humphrey held a press conference. His prepared statement struck a regretful note about the budget and its total but was mild compared to his response on being questioned. The *New York Times* account of that response is both accurate and concise:

> . . . if the government cannot reduce the "terrific" tax burden of the country, "I will predict that you will have a depression that will curl your hair, because we are just taking too much money out of this economy that we need to make jobs that you have to have as time goes on." . . . [Humphrey] said, "there are a lot of places in this budget that can be cut," and that he would be glad to see cuts "if Congress can find ways to cut and still do a proper job. . . ."[6]

"I may have gone overboard a bit this afternoon," Humphrey reportedly remarked, shortly thereafter, to the bemused Budget Director, Percival Brundage. To much of Washington that would have seemed an extraordinary understatement. Never in the history of executive budgeting since 1921 had there been anything to match the spectacle of a first-rank Cabinet officer publicly assailing the presidential budget on the very day it was sent down. Budget Bureau officials were furious; some of the aides within the White House were appalled. "Modern" Republicans in the Cabinet and their departmental staffs—and many a sharp-minded Pentagon official—took umbrage, as well they might, for obviously they were in the line of Humphrey's fire. At the Capitol and in the press corps, and among spokesmen for the private groups most vitally concerned, reactions were as unsure as the situation was unusual; everybody looked to see what Eisenhower would do.

Three days after his second inaugural, the President went before a packed press conference and, replying to the inevitable question, commented as follows:

> Well, in my own instructions to the Cabinet and heads of all offices, I have told them that every place that there is a chance to save a dollar out of the money that we have budgeted . . . everybody that is examining the many details . . . ought to find someplace where they might save another dollar.
>
> If they can, I think if Congress can, its committees, it is their duty to do it.
>
> So with the thought behind the Secretary's statements I am in complete agreement, even though he made statements that I don't believe have a present and immediate application because, indeed, the outlook for the next few months in the economic field is very good indeed.[7]

When these words came across the news tickers there were few laughs in Congress, or downtown, but many stricken faces, some delight, a great deal of suspicion, and considerable scorn. "Old Guard" Republicans and like-minded associates across the aisle sensed prospects brighter than they had thought possible so soon after the Eisenhower re-election. "Modern" Republicans felt the ground opening beneath their feet just when they had thought themselves secure. Democrats, both "liberal" and "moderate," sensed a deliberate squeeze-play with the middle place reserved for them. On the one hand (as they saw it) the President proposed a budget big with borrowings from their traditional stock-in-trade; on the other hand he joined in dramatizing the traditional Republican attack on Federal spending; with both hands he pointed at Congress where their party held a nominal majority. That "modern" Republicans might be caught in a comparable squeeze was insufficient recompense for many Democrats.

Right or wrong, all of these first impressions seemed to be borne out by happenings in the weeks after Eisenhower's press conference. For one, congressional in-boxes promptly became crammed with protests against spending (and demands for tax relief). "But two weeks later," wrote a Senator in retrospect, "the protesting tide swelled into an organized torrent . . . [which] gave the impression of being largely stimulated by corporations."[8] Behind these "corporations" numbers of Washingtonians thought they perceived a prompter in the Secretary of the Treasury. On March 6 he was reported by the *New York Times* (a paper read with care in Washington) to have informed Detroit Republicans that "specific and substantial [budget] reductions were possible if the people of the country continued their 'insistence'. . . . [This] 'would not only take . . . pressure off prices . . . but would also lead the way toward another tax cut.' . . . high spending for security would be required for some time, but that is all the more reason why expenditures in other areas must be curtailed and postponed. . . ."[9] Those last words were read with particular attention by proponents of school aid, the largest new domestic item in the budget.

Executive officials publicly identified with major spending programs did not go unnoticed as the mail campaign progressed. The Budget Director, for one, got more than letters. "Brundage wants the shirt off your back" became the slogan of some businessmen—and laundry, clean or dirty, flooded in to him by parcel post.

At the same time the Executive Branch was in the throes of one of the most hectic episodes in the whole history of central budgeting, the out-of-season "budget season" of 1957. To prove the President's sincerity the Budget Bureau spent the months of February and March extracting from the agencies reductions in his January budget. Contemporary accounts vary: budget aides counted "about" two "overall" revisions of the budget; some weary officials thought they counted five. On March 1, half in fun and half in anger, a House majority resolved that Eisenhower should inform the Congress where to cut.[10] A week later, the Budget Director told a subcommittee of the House that at the President's behest he was already doing all he could to get an answer for them (a response so astonishing to practical politicians that some of them swore off political readings of Administration behavior). "You would have thought," remarked a legislative aide in private conversation, "that they had just come into office and were trying to clean up the outgoing crowd's budget. It was 1953 all over again, only odder."

So numbers of observers thought when, in mid-April, Eisenhower formally submitted the results of Brundage's endeavor. In a letter to the Speaker of the House, the President then proposed or accepted reductions of 1.3 billion dollars in his January request for new appropriations. He warned, however, that these would not have much effect on 1958 *expenditures* and that a "multi-billion" saving in expenditures could be obtained "only at the expense of the national safety and interest." Taken alone, that warning spelled out a defense of the budget's central structure and the proffered cuts became no more than reasonable tidying by conscientious budgeteers. But in the light of what had gone before, the impact of this defense was diluted by the President's own opening remarks:

> I am sure many members of the Congress are as gratified as I am to note the growing awareness of private citizens that . . . Federal benefits are not free but must be paid for out of taxes collected from the people. It is good to see . . . widespread insistence that Federal activity be held to the minimum consistent with the national needs. . . .
>
> The evident responsiveness of the Congress to this attitude I find equally encouraging. I assure you . . . that the Executive Branch will continue to cooperate. . . .[11]

If his purpose was a defense of his budget—and a cover for the Congressmen who rallied to its cause—those remarks, as the saying goes, put Eisenhower's emphasis on the wrong syllable.

This letter of mid-April marked a late stage in White House equivocation after Humphrey's outbreak. When Eisenhower thus addressed the Speaker there were signs that he was concerned lest the assault on his budget go too far. Concern was certainly justified. By April, the Administration faced a real crisis of confidence in its own ranks and, simultaneously, a prospect of deep, indiscriminate appropriation cuts which would spare neither foreign aid nor national defense. Downtown the departmental staffs responsible for programs thought to be on Humphrey's "list," felt themselves victims of a backstairs *coup*. Under cover of the decorous behavior usual in Eisenhower's neighborhood their resentments ran deep, with the White House an object no less than Humphrey or Brundage. For Brundage's economy drive seemed to be strongly seconded at every turn by Sherman Adams and the President. At the Capitol, meanwhile, the sense of public pressure coupled to suspicions of Administration "strategy" left even friends of Pentagon programs— to say nothing of welfare or of aid abroad—increasingly inclined to show themselves more holy than the pope. Among the Democratic members of the House, especially, temptation grew to make a record out-economizing the economizers downtown. On April 11, no less a personage than Speaker Rayburn voiced the hope that by June revenue prospects and spending cuts, combined, would clear the way for tax relief. And on the Senate side Senator Byrd of Virginia, dean of the professional economizers, gained an unusually attentive audience for his retrenchment pleas which he embodied, late in March, in a 5-billion-dollar list of "feasible" appropriation cuts.

From the end of March until mid-April Eisenhower shifted back and forth between defense of his budget and good words for the economizers. On March 27, at his regular press conference, the President used stronger language on the budget's behalf than any since his January budget message. Stung, apparently, by Byrd's proposals and by talk of tax reduction, Eisenhower characterized as "futile" and as "fatuous" both sorts of claims. Without eliminating programs there could be no major savings, he asserted, and he entered a defense of programs such as foreign aid. In consequence, the claims for "piecemeal" cuts were fraudulent. ". . . to say you are going to save a few millions here and a few millions there, I think is the poorest kind of economy we can find."[12] As an acute observer noted at the time:

> The Congressional reaction to the President's strong attitude was unusually mixed. The "Eisenhower Republicans" were pleased and relieved . . . orthodox Republicans were glum and grumpy. The Democrats were not unhappy at the division . . . Sam Rayburn of Texas, Speaker of the House, pointed out that yesterday [March 26] House Republicans had passed a resolution unanimously calling for heavy budget cuts. The President's attack . . . "looks like a pretty good answer to what his own folks did up here yesterday."[13]

To concern over budget prospects, the White House had to add concern for the apparent disarray in Republican ranks. On two occasions in the week that followed, Eisenhower tried to formulate a budget stand that would both calm the "orthodox" and satisfy his "modern" followers.[14] The net effect was to reduce, somewhat, the force of his March 27 press statement. Then his letter in mid-April to the Speaker of the House blurred his position further. Shortly thereafter Congress recessed for Easter and the White House gained a chance to collect its thoughts.

In early May the White House announced that Eisenhower would deliver two nationally televised addresses rallying the country to his budget. Visits home in recess had convinced many Congressmen that calls to cut the budget, reduce taxes, were beginning to bite deep into the consciousness of usually inattentive publics. Though these are tricky things to gauge, there is considerable evidence that consonant with Humphrey's invitation "public opinion," organized and not, grew more aroused about those issues during 1957 than at any time in Eisenhower's first term (a matter no doubt bearing some relation to the climb in living costs that had begun in 1956). And whatever the facts, it is apparent that by May a wide variety of bureaucrats and politicians *thought* this was the case, which is what counts in Washington. The President's decision to address the country is a tribute to that thought.

The first of Eisenhower's "fireside chats," a general roundup on the budget, came on May 14. It was judged fairly ineffectual in Washington, a view held on the Hill and by the press corps, and quite evidently at the White House. Some notion of its public impact can be gleaned from the fact that the President's press secretary would not comment upon rumors of an adverse mail response. And its impact upon politicians was reduced materially by Eisenhower's own appearance of ambivalence at a press conference the next day:

> I don't think it is the function of a President of the United States to punish anybody for voting what he believes. . . . I don't see how it is possible for any President to work with the Republican group in Congress, the whole Republican group, except through their elected leadership. . . . When these large sums are involved, there comes a chance for both the Executive and the Congress to do a squeezing process . . . there is some squeezing possible and I have never kicked about that.[15]

As Senators Knowland and Bridges, Republican leaders both, were just then in the van of the congressional economizers, those words were noted throughout Washington and appropriate conclusions drawn.

A week later all conclusions were shaken. The President's second televised address on May 21, dealt with defense and foreign aid. It was generally thought "effective" and the White House happily announced a strongly favorable mail response. Moreover at his next press conference, again the following day, his tone was confident, his fielding fast and his words relatively tough:

> Well, as long as I am in a fight, I never rest until [I get] . . . what . . . I believe to be necessary for the operation of this Government. . . . I shall never stop until a decision is reached. . . . I do believe this: when a political party gets together and agrees upon a platform . . . they should remain true to it. I believe they should stick with it through thick and thin. . . . I have no right and no desire to punish anybody. I just say this: I am committed to the support of people who believe, as I do, that the Republican platform of 1956 must be our political doctrine.[16]

"In what have probably been the two most effective days of his second administration," James Reston wrote of Eisenhower's performance, "he has regained the initiative over the opposition in his own and the Democratic party."[17] Most members of the Washington community seem to have shared that view, and it grew stronger as the initiative, once taken, was sustained. On May 22 a presidential message went to Congress outlining the plans for foreign aid which were to be supported by the dollars in the budget. The Secretary of State, John Foster Dulles, followed with an elaborate personal presentation to the Senate Committee on Foreign Relations. Both the message and his testimony emphasized Administration sponsorship of program innovations previously advanced by congressional study groups. Chief among them was a Development Loan Fund as a source of capital assistance for the less developed countries, with the implication that eventually loans would replace most outright grants abroad. The upshot of the Dulles presentation was a heartening reception for the foreign-aid program in Senate offices and a more general cordiality than had seemed possible a week before.

Two days later Eisenhower spoke by telephone to a Republican Party conference in New Jersey and strongly urged the item veto as a way to "real" economies. His aim, apparently, was to turn the gaze of the economizers from his budget toward congressional initiatives on public works. At the same conference, his assistant, Sherman Adams, made a speech demanding party unity behind the President. Since Adams, twelve days earlier, reportedly had remarked on a television program that the budget could be cut 2 billion dollars without harm, his address in New Jersey seemed another sign in Washington of new determination at the White House.

Between the first and second presidential television talks, the Secretary of Defense, Charles E. (General Motors) Wilson, had held a press conference defending in detail the military budget which the House was threatening to cut by 1.2 billion dollars. Eisenhower in his second televised address had pressed the Secretary's case. A few days later, Minority Leader Martin was enabled to announce that as a party matter, House Republicans would now seek restoration of a fourth of the projected cut. When this was then attempted on the floor it was defeated by the Democrats. In the crucial roll-call all but eleven of them voted against the restoration, which three-quarters of the House Republicans supported.[18] Although this outcome seemed at first glance to repudiate the President's newly asserted leadership, the White House could take comfort from it nonetheless, and close observers gained from it a new respect for Eisenhower's potency. Congressional Republicans had closed ranks in a gesture to his cause, however short of his avowed objective. House Democrats had made a party record most embarrassing to defense-minded Senate colleagues. A base seemed surely laid for better fortune in the Senate and in conference.

Washingtonians quite generally responded with considerable respect to the "new" Eisenhower who had emerged in the month of May. Belatedly but definitely, he seemed to have accepted, now, the role reserved for Presidents in the time-honored play of legislative action on the budget. Downtown, men trying to rouse public support for their programs were encouraged. On Capitol Hill men trying to resist public pressure against spending were relieved. The President could now be praised or blamed for what they sought to do. Political interpretations of his conduct flourished once again, but these assigned him motives quite like those assigned in other years to other Presidents and the familiarity was reassuring to the politically minded. "Modern" Republicans were gratified. Democrats began to reassess. "Old Guard" Republicans prepared to give some ground. So far as I can ascertain, nobody laughed.

So matters stood by June of 1957. The President's own actions for the past five months, along with those of his associates, now seemed to show contrasting patterns, and the latest signs seemed to belie the relevance of what had gone before. Momentarily, a host of expectations throughout Washington were tempered or revised to suit.

In the month of June, however, there came some harbingers of new developments. For one thing, the Comptroller of the Pentagon testified on June 4 to a House subcommittee that military expenditures were running at an annual rate of 4 billion dollars above January estimates—the result of rising costs and (paradoxically) of improved paperwork—and that, in consequence, directives had come down from Wilson and from Brundage, late in May, to slow current spending to the rates originally projected. On the same day as this testimony, at the other end of Pennsylvania Avenue, the chairman of the Republican National Committee told the press that Eisenhower had been briefed on the adverse reaction of Republican contributors to current White House views about the budget. Three weeks later a Young Republican convention voted almost two-to-one, in Washington, against support for the Administration's proposed aid to schools. A week after that, the President in a letter to one of his most ardent House supporters said he could not "pass judgment on all the details" of the pending school aid bill, a response described by its recipient as "disappointing."[19]

Such miscellaneous occurrences as these gained pattern retrospectively for many Washingtonians when the Administration found itself embarrassed on three notable occasions in July. Early that month the Senate passed a military appropriation bill restoring most of the funds cut by the House, as Wilson and the President had urged. With confidence, the Senate conferees prepared to battle for their version. Then on July 18, while the conference committee was in session, a letter from the Secretary of Defense announced that to hold spending at the rate of January's estimate (under his May directive from Brundage) 100,000 men would be dropped by the army and a portion of the Senate increase would be saved. That announcement not only made senators look silly—and forced the Senate conferees to drop their base for bargaining—it also seriously hampered Senate advocates of foreign aid on which debate had just begun. Nine months later, Wilson's letter still caused scathing comment on the Senate floor, and there were no defenders in the chamber.[20]

On July 25 general aid for school construction came to a vote in the House. The measure as reported from committee compromised Administration plans for grants to states on grounds of need alone with plans by the bill's sponsors for grants proportional to school-age population. Eisenhower had not blessed the compromise, exactly. Although he had called repeatedly for action on the measure, he had evaded opportunities to put his own stamp of approval on its grant provisions. Even so, the Secretary of Health, Education and Welfare, Marion Folsom, had never ceased to represent the White House as firmly behind the bill. On the House floor, however, the Republican leadership failed to support it, even at the crucial moment when its Democratic sponsors offered to accept Administration terms for grants-in-aid. Thereupon the bill was killed in parliamentary circumstances so complex that this offer was scarcely mentioned by most press reports, while members made a record for each entry on which blame could be heaped from across the aisle.[21] But the interested lobbyists, officials, and reporters were aware, of course, that there had come a point in the debate when the Administration *might* have gained its grant provisions and secured the bill. In consequence the President was asked at his next press conference to comment on the lack of response from Republican leaders. He replied: "I never heard. . . . If that is true, why you are telling me something I never heard." [22]

The impact of that comment in the Washington community was heightened by the fact that just three weeks before the President had responded somewhat similarly on a matter even closer to the heart of his program. In the first week of July, Senator Russell of Georgia had charged the Administration with a tricky, hidden intent in provisions of the civil rights bill that it had sponsored and that the House had passed. The bill was in the front rank of Administration measures; its drafting had been done by the Department of Justice; those provisions were included from the first. Yet the President, on being asked about them in press conference had said:

> Well, I would not want to answer . . . in detail because I was reading part of that bill this morning, and I—there were certain phrases I didn't completely understand. So, before I made any more remarks on that, I would want to talk to the Attorney General and see exactly what they do mean. . . . Naturally I'm not a lawyer and I don't participate in drawing up the exact language of proposals. . . . [23]

These three occurrences in July furnished considerable food for thought to those who watch a President professionally, but it cannot be said that there was a consensus, all at once, on their interpretation. For during August Eisenhower led a renewed White House effort on behalf of foreign aid. Reportedly, he also intervened to assure enactment of a useful compromise on civil rights. By late August when Congress adjourned, its record, although mixed, seemed no disaster for the Administration, not even on the budget (when one sets aside the cuts that Eisenhower had endorsed). In light of that outcome there were numbers of Washingtonians, especially downtown, who thought they saw the likelihood of more consistency and more determination from the White House in the year ahead. For one thing, Humphrey had left office in July. For another, as one high official told me hopefully: "I think the President knows some things now he didn't have to learn in his first term." Again, as in late May, although less markedly, there was a tendency to read two patterns into Eisenhower's past behavior and to hedge, somewhat, the expectations based on either one of them.

Then, in September, came the Little Rock affair. Immediately afterward, the first Soviet sputniks went aloft. American egos were badly bruised, as all the world found out, and defense-minded citizens of every sort were jarred by contemplation of the thrust required to put Sputnik II in orbit. Moreover, as the sputniks rose there came the first sharp signs of a decline in the American economy, heralding the 1958 recession and rendered the more disturbing by continued increases in living costs. By December 1957 needs, lags, and lacks of national "preparedness" to meet the Russian "challenge" had become *the* Washington preoccupation, in terms ranging all the way from military hardware to science in our schools. As for the question posed by lessening production, many Washingtonians assumed that a response to sputnik held the answer.

The President's forthcoming budget and his legislative program thus became the focus of a new concern, at odds with—and in many quarters overriding, for a time—the "swollen" budget and high tax preoccupations of the spring. The congressmen who six months earlier had championed economy, the Pentagon officials who had worked throughout September to cut active forces to a level consonant with programmed spending rates; a whole array of experts, editorial writers, commentators, spokesmen for assorted interest groups—all these now called for governmental action, "leadership," "a sense of urgency," to meet the threats of Russian technological superiority and of American economic instability. And lest the presidential program fail to satisfy the urgent activists, the Senate leader, Johnson of Texas, made it plain that Democrats would do their utmost to make up the lack. As early as November he had convened a bipartisan Preparedness Subcommittee which gave the activists a forum in the weeks before Congress returned to Washington.

The President, himself, had spent much of November incapacitated by a cerebral spasm. Pushing his recovery, he had spent part of December in Paris at a post-sputnik rally of the North Atlantic Treaty Organization. The concern and curiosity about his coming program were heightened by his illness, by his absence, and by a long suspension of press conferences. He was, therefore, the center of attention in a transformed situation when his annual messages for 1958 went to the new session of Congress. The situation seemed so different that the patterns of the past appeared no guide; expectations, momentarily, were in suspense.

Eisenhower's State of the Union address in 1958 was strong in tone and vigorously delivered. It was also rather unspecific. But it won him a good deal of praise as Washington awaited the specifics of the budget. Speaker Rayburn, for one, called it the "strongest" speech the President had ever made to Congress.[24] This rendered all the more astonishing the Eisenhower budget (fiscal 1959) that Congress received on January 13. For congressmen and interest groups soon found, as department staffs already knew, that save for minimal response to sputnik, it was just the sort of budget Humphrey had desired but had failed to gain before his public outburst a year earlier.

On the domestic side, the new budget requested *program* changes to reduce the spending base in future years. Technically this was a realistic route toward major savings. Politically, it was a way of irritating interest groups of every sort and all at once. The President proposed a ban on all new starts for power, flood control, and reclamation. He urged a sharp downward revision of farm subsidies. He asked a narrowing of legal limits upon grants to states for hospital construction, urban redevelopment, and public welfare programs, among others. He hinted at reduction of the base for veterans' benefits and urged an increase in the interest rate on G.I. mortgages. He abandoned aid for school construction on the plea that funds were limited and aid for science training now deserved priority.

As Truman once used budgets to project his Fair Deal aims beyond his current prospects, Eisenhower presented an ideal projection for conservative Republicans. "Politically," as William S. White put it, "his domestic program involves an effort to return to the spirit of a traditional Republicanism never before seen in the current White House and not in years manifested in Congress itself, save by a comparative handful of beleaguered orthodox Republicans."[25]

The reaction among Democrats was sharp and scornful. "What does he want," one Senator is said to have asked an executive official, "every lobby in the country ganging up on foreign aid?" As for Republicans, to quote White once again, "They see the impact of the Eisenhower domestic policy as heavy all over the country for Republican members of Congress—damaging in urban areas . . . and simultaneously very bad news indeed in the farm belt. . . . Thus as not before in his Presidency has Eisenhower challenged the vital political interests of both wings of his congressional party at the same time."[26] As no one in Congress could forget, there would be an election in November.

Had the domestic policy been coupled to a massive build-up on the military side, it might have had a kindlier reception from the politically minded. Certainly they would have understood it better. But Eisenhower's budget for defense did little more than return Pentagon expenditures to rates achieved six months before (allowing for price changes in the interim), while increased emphasis on missiles and research was compensated, to a large degree, by reduced emphasis on active forces. The most striking of Eisenhower's own proposals in the defense sphere was not a budget increase but a Pentagon reorganization to "end" interservice rivalries. "America," he said in his initial address, "wants them stopped." Thereupon he pledged himself to find a way to do it: "Soon my conclusions will be finalized. I shall promptly take such executive action as is necessary and . . . present appropriate recommendations to the Congress."[27]

This pledge, at least, emerged unscathed from critical reactions to his budget. But in mid-January, when asked by the press how hard he meant to fight for Pentagon reform, his response struck a rather different note:

> . . . my personal convictions, no matter how strong, cannot be the final answer. There must be a consensus reached with the cab—with the Congress, with the people that have the job of operating the services . . . I am certainly hopeful that it goes in the direction of what I believe. But . . . organization has got to be effective after . . . [I have] passed from the scene. . . .[28]

A few days later, obviously mindful of reactions to this statement, Eisenhower announced that he "would participate personally" in the reorganization "until the job was done," and he journeyed to the Pentagon to emphasize the point.[29] But many Washingtonians were left unsure which Eisenhower to believe. Their puzzlement was not confined to this one issue.

Late in January 1958 there came the episode with which this story started: a

Budget Bureau aide evoked "the program of the President" in testimony on the Hill and all his hearers laughed. It is scarcely to be wondered why they did.

IV

The professional reputation of a President in Washington is made or altered by the man himself. No one can guard it for him; no one saves him from himself. His office has been institutionalized to a degree unknown before the Second World War, but as a reputation-builder he is no mere "office manager." On the contrary, everything he personally says and does (or fails to say, omits to do), becomes significant in everyone's appraisals regardless of the claims of his officialdom. For his words, his own actions, provide clues not only to his personal proclivities but to the forecasts and asserted influence of those around him. What Humphrey says gains weight as Eisenhower seems not to oppose him. What Folsom says becomes a joke as Eisenhower seems not to support him. Press secretariats and "chiefs of staff" and other aides aside, in fashioning his Washington reputation a President's own doings are decisive.

As these Eisenhower episodes make plain, a President runs risks by being personally responsible for his own reputation. In the fifteen months after his re-election Eisenhower managed to reverse the reputation-builder's goal: he increased the insecurities attendant on supporting him and lessened the apparent risks of openly opposing him. He managed this by seeming both unsure of his objectives and unwilling to persist, for long, in any given course. His words and actions cast increasing doubt not only on his skill but on his will. Both came to be discounted in the Washington community. The impact on his influence was marked.

Not all of Eisenhower's troubles were avoidable; some of them are native to the presidential job. In concrete cases any President may feel he must support, or rationalize, what his associates have done, as Eisenhower felt when Humphrey spoke out to the press. If he disavows their doings he may cast more doubt on his own will and capability than on theirs. And any President is judged in part by standards of behavior very different from his own. The impression that he makes by what he does depends not only on the content of his action but on the events surrounding it, as these events are understood by men who watch him work. Their notions of what they would do if they were in his place may count as much as what he does in shaping their impressions. When Eisenhower urged his program cuts in January 1958, politically minded members of the Washington community found his stand incredible in their terms of reference. Since they could not imagine themselves acting so, they would not take him seriously; what he meant to be decisive seemed instead to be equivocal or perverse. Yet there are so many different terms of reference in the Washington community that White House action rarely will be taken at face value by every part of Washington at once. Eisenhower suffered from a general lack of credit. This condition might have been avoidable. But nothing that he could have said or done would have made sense to every Washingtonian.

A President's decisive role in reputation-building is a source of opportunity as well as risk. In a government where Secretaries of the Treasury may go astray at press conference, where Secretaries of Defense may choose the poorest time to make announcements, where Presidents may not be briefed on legislative drafts— and ours is such a government no matter who is President—the fact that his own conduct will decide what others think of him is precious for the man inside the White House. He can steal scenes from his subordinates. He can switch roles or even open a new play. In May of 1957 when Eisenhower made and pressed a vigorous appeal for portions of his budget, he very nearly managed to switch roles himself. He also turned attention from what Humphrey, Brundage, Adams, and the like had seemed to say or do up to that time. A President can *change* his reputation. This is the essence of his opportunity. "I always must remind myself," a very senior bureaucrat once told me, looking at the White House from his office window, "that the power of that fellow over there is never the same two weeks in a row; it fluctuates almost from day to day." Had "everybody's" laughter in the early days of 1958 expressed a fixed, immutable impression, Eisenhower's own prospects for influence would have been less than actually became the case in the years after.

Few single actions on a President's part will either set or totally transform what Washington perceives of him. Eisenhower's program did not become laughable the moment he first seemed to sanction Humphrey's attack on his budget. The laughter followed a year later when that incident appeared the key to a whole pattern of equivocation. Nothing short of a contrasting pattern, equally substantial and sustained, could have transformed the view induced by the occurrences of 1957. In 1958 amidst recession difficulties, defense dilemmas, vicuna coats, hard desegregation problems, and a host of troubles overseas, Eisenhower managed no such transformation. But in 1959 the did achieve it; a "New Eisenhower" emerged that year. The newness was sustained for months on end. Impressions of equivocation were replaced by visions of tenacity and not a little skill. In his seventh year this President apparently won more respect from Washington on both these scores than he had been accorded since the time of his belated honeymoon in 1955, after the eclipse of Senator McCarthy and before the Denver heart attack. That Eisenhower could look "new" in 1959 despite his look in 1957 is a tribute to the opportunity presented by a President's own role in reputation.

How did Eisenhower manage to transform his reputation? He did it by defending a restrictive budget, of the sort he had proposed in 1958, against congressional attempts to add new programs of the sort he had endorsed in 1957. This oversimplifies to a degree: the Eisenhower budget for 1959 was rather more restrictive than had been the case before, and some of the congressional additions he disputed went beyond his own proposals two years earlier. But in education, housing, public works, and foreign aid, the parallels are close.[30] He changed his reputation by *consistently* opposing what he once had urged equivocally. He made his opposition manifest by threatening the veto and by using it. He made his purpose plain by his demeanor at press conference and he used the conference freely to expound his case in public. From the start of 1959 up to the time of writing (in July), Eisenhower's words and actions were consistent—and his vetoes were sustained. The public record in those months presents a striking contrast with the comparable period of 1957. His success was largely negative but it was still success. His reputation fed on his consistency and on accomplishment. The "new" Eisenhower was not universally approved by any means. Interpretations of his conduct were not always flattering. Both at the Capitol and near the White House some men saw him as the victim of an *idée fixe*. But those who held this view were all the more respectful of his will, at least within the range of his presumed fixation.

A President's opportunity to change his reputation is not unlimited. The circumstances of this Eisenhower transformation will suggest the limits. For one thing his display of will and skill was managed from the strongest ground a President can occupy late in his final term: the ground of opposition to congressional initiatives when Congress does not bear his party's label. Upon this ground his vantage points of "powers" and of status suffered nothing from the Twenty-second Amendment. For another thing, when Eisenhower occupied that ground his setting lent his actions weight in Washington. From early 1959 production and employment indices rose rapidly; his popularity appeared to move in train. By May he spoke and acted in a setting reminiscent of 1957. Psychologically, and in most economic terms, the recession was over. Sputniks had long since become routine. Popular concern about inflation and taxation reappeared as fears of a depression vanished. Eisenhower's legislative program had seemed laughable to congressmen in 1958; it was no laughing matter in 1959. The congressional elections of 1958 had produced heavy Democratic majorities, but with the economic upturn these majorities were as susceptible to pressures for economy as Democrats had been in 1957. Besides, throughout the spring of 1959 a threat of Soviet action in Berlin warned Washingtonians that they might have to rally around the White House on short notice. Eisenhower's critics grew relatively quiet as the year advanced. His new look was the product, partly, of the quietude around him. It left him free to stand on the offensive and it limited awareness of the flaws in his performance. A President can change the way he looks, but first he has to find some actions suited to the purpose, and then he has to hope that other men respect the change. His action does not dictate their reaction. His situation and their own, as *they* interpret both, decide what they will think of his new look. These are the limits on his opportunity.

Granting the limits, acknowledging the risks, how does a President exploit his opportunity? How does he make the most he can of his own reputation? The answer returns us to his choices. His general reputation will be shaped by signs of pattern in the things he says and does. These are the words and actions he has chosen, day by day. His choices are the means by which he does what he can do to build his reputation as he wants it. Decisions are his building-blocks. He has no others in *his* hands. The point we reached in Chapter 3 we reach again.

The President of the United States can rarely make a choice with nothing more in mind than his professional reputation. Franklin Roosevelt sometimes asked his aides for "something I can veto" as a lesson and a reminder to congressmen.[31] But chances for decision in these terms alone will not come often to a President. Most choices will involve him also in the institutional imperatives of being President, in the extensive duties of his clerkship. Through the first half of 1957 Eisenhower's troubles turned upon the fact that whatever he might want to be or seem, he could not escape authorship and advocacy of a budget. Both were required of the President-as-clerk in order that congressional and agency officials could carry on their jobs. Moreover, many choices will involve the President's own sense of right and wrong. Eisenhower, as we have seen, argued for economy amidst the outcry over sputniks and recession; Truman stuck to advocacy of his Fair Deal measures in the hardest months of the Korean War. Besides, each choice involves not only general reputation but particular relationships. The two considerations often clash. Although a President lacks other means to guard the way he looks, his choice-making involves him in *competing* considerations. The choice that started Eisenhower's reputation toward its downward slide in 1957 was his personal approval of a Treasury press conference on Budget Day. The grounds for that approval illustrate the competitions in a presidential choice. The story of that choice is told in Chapter 6.

At the start of this discussion of professional reputation I postponed consideration of choice-making. Now let me postpone it once again. The men who judge a President in Washington watch more than his performance and their neighbor's reaction. They also keep an eye upon reactions from his audience outside their own community; they watch the way he looks to that residual cross-section of constituents, his public at large. His power stakes are not confined to his relationships and reputation inside Washington; his influence depends, as well, on his apparent popular prestige. This factor in his influence remains to be explored.

CHAPTER 5

Public Prestige

The Washingtonians who watch a President have more to think about than his professional reputation. They also have to think about his standing with the public outside Washington. They have to gauge his popular prestige. Because they think about it, public standing is a source of influence for him, another factor bearing on their willingness to give him what he wants.

Prestige, like reputation is a subjective factor, a matter of judgment. It works on power just as reputation does through the mechanism of anticipated reactions. The same men, Washingtonians, do the judging. In the case of reputation they anticipate reactions from the President. In the instance of prestige they anticipate reactions from the public. Most members of the Washington community depend upon outsiders to support them or their interests. The dependence may be as direct as votes, or it may be as indirect as passive toleration. Dependent men must take account of popular reaction to *their* actions. What their publics may think of them becomes a factor, therefore, in deciding how to deal with the desires of a President. His prestige enters into that decision; their publics are part of his. Their view from inside Washington of how outsiders view him thus affects his influence with them.

A President's prestige is not a very precise thing to keep in view. "The" presidential public is actually an aggregate of publics as diverse and overlapping as the claims Americans and allied peoples press on Washington. Members of "the" public are divided not alone by differently felt needs and wants but by degrees of difference in attention paid a President. Some of them may make an avocation of the watchfulness vocationally imposed on Washingtonians. But the responses of the great majority shade all the way to general inattention broken only as a private share in public trouble makes men lift their eyes. Presidential standing outside Washington is actually a jumble of imprecise impressions held by relatively inattentive men.

This is a factor operating mostly in the background as a conditioner, not the determinant, of what Washingtonians will do about a President's request. Rarely is there any one-to-one relationship between appraisals of his popularity in general and responses to his wishes in particular. The Hundred Days of 1933 remain as exceptional as they were memorable. Even then, as careful commentators have made plain, both skill and energy were needed to maintain the link.[1] After Roosevelt's *second* inaugural came the legislative storms of 1937. After Eisenhower's re-election came the House revolt against his military budget. Yet the prevalent impression of a President's public standing tends to set a tone and to define the limits of what Washingtonians do for him, or do to him. In the background of Mac-Arthur's insubordination and the cheering that accompanied it on Capitol Hill was a prevailing view of Truman as decidedly unpopular. One finds this also in the background of the steel case, a year later. In 1958 the laughter heard in Washington became the louder as impressions spread that Eisenhower's popularity was falling. In 1959 the first signs of respect for the "new" Eisenhower coincided with reports that his prestige was on the rise again.

In conditioning responses to a President, the quality of his prestige can matter quite as much as any quantitative notion of his popularity. When men make judgments in the Washington community they are no less concerned with what he is liked *for,* than with how many like him. In 1949, to take a sharp example, Air Force and Navy "brass" fought openly, in turn, against the Truman budget for defense.[2] In 1954, armed with a technically better case, the Army swallowed hard and did not battle publicly against the "New Look" Eisenhower was presenting as his own.[3] Even in 1958, the year of Lebanon, when the Army's plight was worse but its case as good as ever, there came no "revolt of the generals."[4] Truman had been challenged within months of his surprise election. Eisenhower seemed less popular in 1958 than ever before. Truman, of course, had not gone to Annapolis; Eisenhower was a certified West Pointer. This may account for some part of the difference between Navy "revolt" and Army quiescence. But also Truman was not popularly thought to be among the country's greatest experts in military affairs; his successor was accorded that distinction. No doubt a factor in the Army's conduct was the difficulty of conceiving how to win a shouting match with *General* Eisenhower.[5]

The public standing of a President in the United States may be quite different from his standing with constituents abroad. Apparently, the President's position overseas was higher than at home in most of Truman's years and lower than at home in most of Eisenhower's. Those Washingtonians who are themselves dependent on a foreign public have to think about the quality of his prestige in both these spheres at once. But even Washingtonians whose publics are American will think, from time to time, of how he stands abroad. Members of Congress, for example, are increasingly aware that his position overseas can be a national asset and that their behavior toward him can enlarge it or diminish it. Their publics sometimes seem to be aware of this as well. Most men at the Capitol are anxious not to jeopardize American advantages, and no one wants the accusation flung at him from his own state or district. Except in Truman's final years, consideration for the President's prestige abroad has tended to inhibit congressional behavior ever since the Second World War. In 1959 the presence of Berlin, as an *impending* crisis through the whole length of the session, contributed to the respectfulness shown Eisenhower by a Congress that was advertised as certain to oppose him. However, even though a President's position overseas affects all sorts of judgments made in Washington, his standing with home publics is a matter of more moment to most Washingtonians most of the time. Accordingly, this chapter deals with the domestic side alone.

How do members of the Washington community assess a President's prestige with the American public? They talk to one another and to taxi drivers. They read the columnists and polls and news reports. They sample the opinions of their visitors and friends. They travel in the country and they listen as they go. Above all, they watch Congress. Generally speaking, only national party politicians, legislative leaders, congressmen in unsafe seats, and lobbyists in trouble wet their fingers every day to gauge winds blowing toward the White House from the public. Most others, and especially most bureaucrats, concentrate on the winds blowing from the Capitol. If an agency's careerists fail to challenge an Eisenhower, as in the Army case, their usual calculation is not that the public supports him but that Congress, fearing so, will not support them. Congressional sentiment tends to be officialdom's pragmatic substitute for "public opinion" because it is on Congress, not the general public, that officials must depend, day after day, for legislation and for funds to keep programs and personnel alive. And bureaucrats are not the only ones who make that substitution. For comparable reasons it is made, much of the time, by diplomats of many countries, officers of every state, representatives of private interests, local party leaders, and even congressmen themselves.

Congress is a distorting mirror for a President's prestige. Congressional constituencies differ from his own. What happens at the Capitol rarely will reflect the full extent of his apparent popularity. Eisenhower found this out in his first term. Neither is it likely to reflect the full extent of his unpopularity. Congressmen must live with presidential "powers." Truman's last Congress was often in an ugly mood; the mood of the country sometimes seemed uglier. Distortions are as likely to assist a man as hurt him.

Since the general public does not govern, presidential influence is shielded from the vagaries of shifting sentiment. Truman could not keep his Admirals from revolting in 1949, but as Commander-in-Chief he could retaliate and did: the Chief of Naval Operations was retired; other officers were transferred overseas. That year he could not keep the Air Force from demanding and obtaining an appropriation bigger than its budget but he could and did keep extra funds unspent, "impounding" them (by the device of not apportioning them) as statutes on the books allowed. When he seized the steel mills, press denunciations could not make him give them up, unless it can be said that the Supreme Court followed the newspapers. When he dismissed MacArthur, public outcries could not put the General back. With "powers" and with status—and sufficient show of will—a President of the United States can wield effective influence in many situations even though he has a balky Congress and seems short on popular appeal. Obviously, though, the less his demonstrated power at the Capitol, the more he is confined, downtown, to realms where sheer command proves workable. The weaker his apparent popular support, the more his cause in Congress may depend on negatives at his disposal like the veto, or "impounding." He may not be left helpless, but his options are reduced, his opportunities diminished, his freedom for maneuver checked in the degree that Washington conceives him unimpressive to the public.

Leeway is the term that best describes the presidential stake in Washington appraisals of prestige—leeway as opportunity, leeway in the sense of chances to be taken. This is what Truman gained from the prestige he borrowed during 1947 for the early, crucial stages of the Marshall Plan. This is what Eisenhower gained in 1959 when, contrary to expectations, Washington discovered that his popularity was rising. Leeway is no guarantee of governmental action. Popularity may not produce a Washington response. But public disapproval heartens Washington's resistance. Leeway guarantees one thing: avoidance of the trouble that can follow from its absence. Prestige counts in power by establishing some checks upon resistance from the men engaged in governing.

Not only does prestige check Washingtonians, it also often checks those members of the public who are called upon to act as agents for a President. Some chores of governing are not done in the Washington community. Some things are done directly by a portion of the public. Presidential influence on government becomes, in part, a matter of direct relationships with special-purpose publics. And the members of a special public, quite like Washingtonians, are often swayed by what they think the general public thinks of him.

What may a President desire from some portion of his public? One thing he may desire is an alteration of the Washington community to aid him in attaining policy objectives. In short, he may want votes. To be sure, votes are not a guarantee of any policy objective. But election outcomes obviously bear upon his chances to obtain his policy ends by other means. Since 1938 a consequence of each mid-term congressional election (with the possible exception of 1954) has been elimination, practically speaking, of prospects for some policy departures wanted by the White House. In 1952 the presidential election had the same effect on numbers of objectives urged by the retiring Administration.

Aside from votes, a President's objectives are affected by the willingness of special publics to use *private* means as substitutes for an official action. There are all sorts of concrete situations where a presidential policy or preference seems beyond accomplishment by acts of formal government, or would be better served by private action. Remember Truman's efforts to achieve a settlement in steel without a seizure. Recall that Eisenhower sent no troops to Little Rock until the mob had failed to heed his proclamation urging citizens to cease the obstruction of justice. On both occasions, failing private action, these Presidents were able to find official stop-gaps. But private action was what they required if their policy objectives were to be achieved. Moreover, in steel seizure, there was Sawyer's silent partner, the trade union. Even as a stop-gap, official action was contingent on collaboration from its members in the mills.

When a President appeals for votes or private action, the men whom he addresses will have more in mind than notions of his national prestige. As in the case of Washington, one rarely finds a one-to-one relationship between appraisals of his general popularity and responses from some public in particular. In 1954 and 1956 when Eisenhower was conceded to be high in public favor, he appealed in vain for a Republican Congress. In 1957 when he still seemed very popular, his unsupported word did not disperse the mob in Little Rock. Truman, on the other hand, was widely thought unpopular in 1952 when the men honored his call to stay at work in the steel mills. Yet the closer one looks at instances like these, the clearer are the signs that prestige was a factor in the background of behavior. Eisenhower did not get the Congresses he wanted, but the Democrats he got instead were pledged to treat him well, and Democratic leaders in both Houses had worked hard to lend those pledges substance in advance. At Little Rock he had to call upon the Army; bayonets dispersed the mob. It is notable, however, that mobs did not assemble elsewhere in the South and did not reassemble around Central High School. One cannot know to what extent the men who might have led such mobs were influenced by thoughts about the President's prestige. But had Eisenhower worn the look of Truman in the South, local leaders might have hastened to defy him. In the steel case the workers supported Truman when his course suited their purposes; they did not hesitate to overthrow his object, steel production, the moment that he ceased to be of concrete use to them.

With special publics as with Washingtonians, the President's supposed prestige can set a tone and may prescribe the limits of response to his appeals. Prestige can have great impact on behavior when the special public is self-consciously endeavoring to court "public opinion." On the other side of steel seizure were those most unhappy presidential "agents," the company executives. As an adjunct of their appeal to the courts they mounted an extraordinary attack on Truman personally. No doubt they were spurred on by a presumption of his lack of popularity. Had Truman worn the look of Eisenhower, one cannot conceive that they would have denounced him in such personal terms. Larger, looser publics than an industry's executives, and publics farther removed from the Washington community, may be much less concerned about the general public. For voters in a congressional district, or for workers in a steel mill, or for men on the streets of Little Rock, a sense of how the President is viewed outside their neighborhood may be a minor factor in deciding their behavior. But it rarely will be absent altogether from the thoughts of those who lead within the neighborhood.

A President's prestige is thus a factor in his influence of roughly the same sort as his professional reputation: a factor that may not decide the outcome in a given case but can affect the likelihoods in every case and therefore is strategically important to his power. If he cares about his prospects for effectiveness in government, he need be no less mindful of the one than of the other. Granting the importance of his popular prestige, how is a President to keep it under guard?

This question parallels my inquiry in the last chapter, but the two are not the same. Professional reputation is not popularity. Guarding the one, therefore, is not equivalent to guarding the other. Prestige will have a bearing upon reputation, certainly, and professional appraisals by attentive Washingtonians unquestionably trickle down to those outside. The interaction is continuous, but it is interaction between very different things. In Eisenhower's instance, for example, polls and press reports agree that his sharpest loss of popularity occurred in the recession year of 1958. But this loss corresponded neither in severity nor timing to the damage done his Washington reputation during 1957. Truman, on the other hand, undoubtedly got higher marks in Washington for capability and will than he obtained in public through his last two years of office, after Chinese intervention lengthened the Korean War. Like reputation, prestige is a matter to be judged, not "known." The judging, for the most part, will be done by Washingtonians. Judgments of prestige may be distorted inside Washington, but what is being judged remains outside. To question how a President can guard prestige is not to deal in disguise with his Washington reputation. Prestige must be guarded at its source.

II

If it were clear that publics outside Washington perceived a President in terms of personality alone, the guarding of prestige might be—as sometimes it is thought to be—a matter for Madison Avenue. But there have been sharp changes in the popularity of men whose public manners were substantially unaltered. The Truman of 1951 looked and sounded very much like Truman on Election Day in 1948. Allowing for age and illness (which millions of Americans were happy to do in 1956), Eisenhower seems to have projected the same human qualities throughout his time in office. To guard one's look in human terms is not enough.

Personality is a factor in prestige but not a very dynamic factor. Recent experience suggests that an impression of the presidential personality, a "public image" as the term is commonly, nontechnically employed, takes shape for most constituents no later than the time they first perceive him being President (a different thing from seeing him as candidate). And save within the Washington community where White House personalities are reassessed each day, such images, once formed, appear to change but slowly, if at all. Louis Harris, among others, has suggested that public perceptions of the Eisenhower personality shifted between 1952 and 1956 from "father" to "grandfather."[6] But this is to compare perceptions of the man as a *prospective* President with those of him in office. The "grandfather" image Harris traces as of 1956 seems in no way inconsistent with prevailing views reported by the press as early as 1954 and as late as 1959. In Truman's instance, an impression of the "little man" in Roosevelt's shoes, courageous and hard-working but not "big enough" was probably pervasive within days of his succession. Perhaps, for a time, he shared it himself; he certainly helped to spread it. "Boys, if you ever pray, pray for me now," he told the press with national attention focused on his takeover, ". . . when they told me . . . what had happened I felt like the moon, the stars, and all the planets had fallen on me."[7] Three years later, his campaign for election and his victory highlighted very different human qualities. The "little man" may not have disappeared, but now, in Jonathan Daniels's allusive phrase, he had become "The Man of Independence." Although we lack evidence on which to base conclusions about just whose views were changed by just how much, there seems no doubt that 1948 did have a marked effect on widely shared ideas about the Truman personality.[8] This is testimony rather to the impact of exceptional events than to the instability of public images. To judge from what occurred in his last years, the older image was not driven far below the surface.

An image of the office, not an image of the man, is the dynamic factor in a President's prestige. Impressions of the person will form early and last long, but the values men assign to what they see can alter rather quickly. "Decisiveness" may turn into irascibility; "cleverness" may come to seem deceitfulness; "openmindedness" to seem soft-headedness; "courage" to seem rashness. Truman, the "master-politician" of 1948 was the "mere" politician of 1951. The very sharpness of impressions driven home by his election made him suspect at the height of the Korean War. Two years after Eisenhower's smashing re-election, every poll behaved as though considerably fewer citizens welcomed what he represented at the White House. In his case, as in Truman's, the sense of what he *was* does not seem to have changed. Rather, the sense of what he *ought* to be had changed. Not personality perceptions but these "oughts" of office underlie most short-run shifts in popular prestige.

Why do the "oughts" of office vary as they do? Why are perceptions of the *job* so changeable? The answer, evidently, is that what a President should be is something most men see by light of what is happening to *them*. Their notions of the part a President should play, their satisfaction with the way he plays it, are affected by their private hopes and fears. Behind their judgments of performance lie the consequences in their lives. What threatens his prestige is their frustration.

For more than two decades the Gallup Poll has sampled nationally, at monthly intervals or thereabouts, "approval" of the President's performance on the job. The question asked has been almost unvarying: "Do you approve or disapprove of the way [the incumbent] is handling his job as President?" Unlike a pre-election poll, this inquiry does not relate to any concrete action by respondents. Unlike a query on specific issues, it does not relate to any concrete information. The question is unfocused; so is the response, which tells us anything or nothing about what respondents meant by what they said. The timing, however, provides a clue to what they saw around them when they said it. Approval figures in the poll results change almost every month. Minor variations and wild swings in narrow time-spans need be treated with reserve. But large and relatively lasting changes come at the same times as great events with widespread consequences. These major changes illustrate what threatens popularity.

Two of the largest changes ever traced by Gallup Polls came at the start of 1951 and in the spring of 1958. All through 1950 Truman's conduct was approved by a sample of his countrymen in proportions varying from 46 to 37 percent.[9] (His first-term "low" had been 32 percent in 1946.) After 1950 through the balance of his term, approval fluctuated in a range of 32 to 23 percent.[10] For almost a year following the 1956 election, approval of Eisenhower's conduct ranged above 62 percent; at the time of his inauguration it touched 79 percent. (His first-term "low" had been 57 percent in 1954.) In 1958, however, approval fell to 49 percent in one month, April, and only once, in August, rose as high as 58 percent; most of the year it moved within the narrow range of 52 to 56 percent.[11] In 1959 a rise began that brought approval up one point a month to 62 percent in June, the last figure available at this writing.[12] Assuming a continuation of the trend, Eisenhower's instance, unlike Truman's, will end with a recovery of range.

In looking at these figures, one can and probably should ignore the variations month by month; what cannot be ignored is the sharp shift of range. Such shifts do not disclose whose views were changed, in what direction, when. These figures may hide crosscurrents; they certainly hide regional differentials. But assuming an adequate sample, or at least a constant error, when Truman shifted from the "forties" to the "twenties," when Eisenhower shifted from the "sixties" to the "fifties," and when the figures stabilized for many months thereafter, public standing certainly had changed. And what must have contributed to changing it is not hard to discover.

In both these cases popular approval tumbled at a time when governmental action (or inaction) was associated with extraordinary disturbance in the private lives of millions of Americans. What happened between 1957 and 1958? "Prosperity" gave way to recession *and* inflation; "peace" gave way to an intensified cold war, with troops in Lebanon and fighting on the China Coast. A sense of social calm gave way before the struggles over school desegregation. "Complacency" in science, education, and defense was shaken, at the least, by outcries after sputnik. What happened between 1950 and 1951? Above all else, inflation and taxation and lost lives in "Truman's War," which had become interminable war with the Chinese.[13]

It scarcely is an accident that Truman's popularity, according to the polls, was never lower than in 1951. It scarcely is an accident that polls show Eisenhower more unpopular in 1958 than ever before or since. Such happenings as these are bound to threaten or upset the private prospects of great numbers of Americans. As these prospects are seen to change, the outlook on the Presidency cannot help but change. That marvelous rummage bag sometimes called our "belief system" is crammed with alternate and contradictory images of office ready for instant use. Eisenhower, once so satisfying as a "man above the struggle," apparently collided during 1958 with yearnings for a President who made his presence *felt*.[14] Truman, on the other hand, while very much in evidence some seven years before, seems to have run afoul of the twin notions that a wartime Chief Executive ought to be "above politics" and that he ought to help the generals "win." As private prospects are upset, men change their expectations of the President. As images of office change, appraisals of performance change to suit. It is no wonder that "approval" dropped in 1951 and 1958. Nor is it any wonder that there seemed to be recovery in 1959 but not in 1952.

This is not to suggest that members of the public act like Washingtonians, attending and reacting to a President at every stage of all proceedings. One never should underestimate the public's power to ignore, to acquiesce, and to forget, especially when the proceedings seem incalculable or remote from private life. Unless the shooting starts a Lebanon may be remote, a Berlin seems incalculable, sputniks overhead become routine. But paychecks, grocery bills, children's schooling, sons at war are quite distinctly matters of real life. No happenings in Eisenhower's whole first term brought him more public credit, it appears, than the truce in Korea and the "spirit of Geneva." Apparently, no happening in 1958 bit deeper than the juncture of recession with inflation.[15] One doubts, for instance, that the indiscretion of a Sherman Adams would have mattered much to voters (as the White House clearly thought it did) save for its symbolism at a time when "life" was not as advertised.[16] In 1951 there is no reason to suppose that lacking the hard, unexpected stretch-out in Korea either "communism" or "corruption" could have caused such deep frustrations as were evident when MacArthur came home.[17]

Personality is not without effect upon prestige. Impressions of the *man* can be a cushion and a prop. Judged by percentage points in Gallup polls, Eisenhower's lost approval during 1958 was not much less than Truman's after 1950. Still, one was left with better than majority approval and the other with approval half as large. Judged not in terms of figures but in terms of trend, these polls trace somewhat comparable patterns for both Presidents throughout their earlier years. But Truman's variations are much larger and much sharper, with much lower "lows" than Eisenhower's.[18] Such differences display the cushioning and bolstering effects of personality on expectations. Eisenhower was a hero *independent* of his office.

Truman was almost unknown apart from it. Personality alone cannot account for variations in each man's prestige, but as between them it left Truman far more vulnerable to the shock of private hopes belied by public happenings. Yet even Eisenhower, hero though he was, turned out to lack immunity. *His* lack, if anyone's, should serve to make the point. The moving factor in prestige is what men outside Washington see happening to *themselves*.

A President concerned to guard prestige must keep his eye on hopes and on what happens to those hopes in "life" as lived outside the Washington community. He need beware lest the outsiders look to him for pleasures he cannot provide, or lack preparedness for the pains he cannot stop. Either way, what threatens his prestige is popular frustration. "We will merchandise the hell out of the Eisenhower program," C. D. Jackson is supposed to have remarked in 1953. But "merchandising" only has its uses while events remain incalculable. Salesmanship cannot compete with "life." Merchandising is no match for history. A President who values power naturally will want his history productive of "good" response to him; he naturally will want to minimize the "bad" reactions. But wanting these results, what can *he* do about them? How, if at all, can *he* affect the hopes and happenings that generate frustration?

III

If a President were free to control happenings, to turn them on or off at his discretion, this would be the ideal way to safeguard his prestige. But he has no such freedom. The illustrations in preceding chapters make that plain. Outside the Federal government, events in which he plays no part set off what his constituents will see and feel as happenings. Inside the government courts, congressmen, executive officials act in ways that will contribute to or symbolize such happenings. They often act without recourse to him. The President is no mere spectator. His action also will contribute to and may become the highlight of what happens. What happened in Korea? Truman intervened. What happened when the war dragged on? He sent MacArthur home. But action of this sort is a far cry from control. No President can make most of what happens in his time occur or stop to suit his popularity. Had Truman held the option, Korea never would have been a happening at all.

Because he cannot control happenings, a President must do his best with hopes. His prestige is secure while men outside of Washington accept the hard conditions in their lives, or anyway do not blame him. If he can make them think the hardship necessary, and can make them want to bear it with good grace, his prestige may not suffer when they feel it. Had Truman's public thought interminable warfare-within-limits a necessity his prestige would have risen, not declined, in 1951. A President concerned for leeway inside government must try to shape the thoughts of men outside. If he would be effective as a guardian of public standing, he must be effective as a teacher to the public. Truman was an unsuccessful teacher in the midst of the Korean war. Some of his troubles will be traced in Chapter 6.

What kind of teaching job is this? It is no classroom exercise. Presidential teaching is instruction of a very different sort. It has at least four special features. First, it is instruction aimed at students who, by definition, are habitually inattentive to the teacher: his constituents *outside* the Washington community. These students only grow attentive when they notice public trouble pressing on their lives. Second, as a consequence, he can expect attention from them only when the things he need interpret to his benefit are on their minds for reasons independent of his telling. Third, again in consequence, he teaches less by telling than by doing (or not doing) in the context that his students have established in their minds. And fourth, what he has previously said and done will figure in that context. When the man inside the White House gains attention outside Washington, he finds two other teachers at his podium. Events themselves are there; so are the memories of his past performance. Under these conditions, presidential teaching is a formidable job. It is not to be confused with advertising.

The correspondence between popularity and happenings, as illustrated in "approval" polls, is matched by correspondence between popular attention and events. Let me illustrate this second correspondence with some radio program ratings in pretelevision years, when virtually all presidential broadcasts were rated by a single commercial source.[19]

From October 1945 (with the war over) through March 1948 (with electioneering not begun) there were eight occasions when Truman pre-empted *all* radio networks at an evening hour to take policy issues "to the country"; his subjects ranged from price inflation, welfare programs, strikes, to the Marshall Plan, and the Czech *coup d'état*. For those performances his Hooper ratings—estimating actual against potential auditors in homes—were successively 43.8, 49.4, 34.4, 31.8, 57.6, 30.7, 34.3, and 31.0 percent.[20] Whether accurate or not, the basis for these estimates remained the same in every case; this sequence is internally consistent. The shifts in size of audience on these occasions are due, in part, to time of year and choice of date or hour; listening habits, like more recent viewing habits, change with seasons, days, and times.[21] But factors of this sort are insufficient to explain the sharp peak in the middle of the sequence, the 57.6 percent that breaks the trend. And what was the occasion for that peak in Truman's audience? His subject was surrender on the price control of meat. He was announcing decontrol in the beef-hungry autumn of 1946, amidst the political campaign that terminated three weeks later in election of the 80th Congress.[22] Only once in his first term did Truman have a higher Hooper rating: 64.1 percent when he proclaimed V-E Day, shortly after his accession. Only six times during F.D.R.'s third term was *his* rating higher for a comparable evening address; all six came in a seventeen-month period, from May of 1941 to November 1942.[23] As an audience attraction, meat in 1946 ranks next to the Second World War.

When a President goes on the air the number of his listeners is obviously influenced by what Americans have on *their* minds. It also may be influenced by their sense of his relevance. When Truman vetoed the Taft-Hartley Act in 1947, his explanatory radio address received a rating of only 30.7 percent. It may be that the issue—union "power," labor "slavery"—mattered to fewer people than had "meat" the year before. Or, possibly, as many people cared, but fewer thought *his* explanation mattered. Decontrolling prices had been taken as a pledge of more supplies and he had the authority to decontrol. But vetoing Taft-Hartley offered no relief from strikes and Congress had the votes to override. At any rate the context of his address and its relevance to their concerns, as understood by radio-owning publics, presumably accounts for a great part of his lost listeners on that occasion—and of those gained on others.

In the early 1950's, the shift from radio to television "listening" casts doubt upon the meaning, in these terms, of ratings for both media. Not until 1956 did "television homes" start to compare in number and in distribution with their radio equivalents a decade earlier. As yet one cannot draw from Eisenhower's television ratings an internally consistent series on the order of those furnished by the older radio ratings.[24] But there is nothing in the scattered data now obtainable to controvert the Truman illustration just presented.

If a President's ability to gain a hearing voice-to-ear is so conditioned by "what happens," these same conditioners no doubt affect the prospect that his words will penetrate through news reports, opinion leaders, neighbors, and the like, to those who have not seen or heard (or anyway, not listened) for themselves. Without a real-life happening to hoist it into view, a piece of presidential news, much like the man's own voice, is likely to be lost amidst the noises and distractions of the day. Local news aside, most daily news reports in print or on the air are geared to wire service coverage and tempo; White House stories, classed with foreign news, are lumped together into factual and unaccented highlights of the day's events from everywhere, *that* day. The weekly magazines of "news" tend to blend commentary with reporting and summation in a mix so well homogenized that everything is equally accented and its impact uniformly predigested. As for word-of-mouth reports at third hand, or at fourth, the principle appears to be the same: events provide the emphasis required for attention.

A President is not in firm control of most events, but there are some that he can manufacture. He must depend on happenings for popular attention; with skill and luck he sometimes makes a happening. He then can ride it to a widened audience. Toward the close of 1953, six weeks of press build-up fed by meticulously staged White House and Cabinet actions, heralded the Eisenhower legislative program for 1954, his first since taking office.[25] By these means, apparently, his making of a program was established as momentous in the nation's life; his address to the country just before its presentation brought him an enormous television audience.[26] This surely was an instance of a self-made happening, and only one of several during Eisenhower's first term. Unfortunately, Presidents can rarely count for long on press cooperation of the sort available to Eisenhower in his early years. And often they will find what they contrive cast into shadow by outside events. Had the first bout of tension over Quemoy and Matsu come in the fall of 1953, instead of a year later, one doubts that the White House could have focused wide attention on its preparation of a *legislative* program. No matter how cooperative the press, a President needs quiet from competitive events if what he does is to be noticed as a happening.

Not only do outside events compete with self-made happenings, a President is frequently in competition with himself. That master of the art of mass communication, Franklin Roosevelt, once wrote an old associate:

> I know . . . you will be sympathetic to the point of view that the public psychology and, for that matter, individual psychology, cannot, because of human weakness, be attuned for long periods of time to a constant repetition of the highest note in the scale. . . . Whereas in this country there is a free and sensational press, people tire of seeing the same name, day after day, in the important headlines of the papers, and the same voice, night after night, over the radio. . . . if I had tried [in 1935] to keep up the pace of 1933 and 1934, the inevitable histrionics of the new actors, Long and Coughlin and Johnson, would have turned the eyes of the audience away from the main drama itself. . . .[27]

However, in most years since the Second World War, there has been no "main" drama like recovery-with-Roosevelt. Instead there have been half a dozen shows on stage at once, all running simultaneously and interminably and repetitively, act after act, with Presidents assigned a leading role in each, and everything relentlessly translated into headlines. Under mid-century conditions, prospects for the self-made happening secure from competition are not good.

Events determine audience attention for a President; they also make his actions more important than his words. When constituents grow conscious of his relevance to them they are already learning—from events. By then his telling will convey no lessons independent of the things he seems to do within the context of events. When Truman told of decontrolling meat, the act conveyed a meaning that the words, the look, the tone of voice could but embroider, not obliterate. Of course, the very telling is an action, and the words that linger in men's minds can have enormous educative influence. "We have nothing to fear but fear itself," said F.D.R. on March 4, 1933; the teaching he began with those eight words was as extraordinary as his chance, that day, to dwarf all other actors on the nation's stage. Still, what he said then conjured up a prospect not a meaning. It became a lesson learned when what he did thereafter and what happened in men's lives appeared to vindicate the confidence he had expressed. Had there not been the Hundred Days, and work relief, and a degree of real recovery, the lesson of those words would have been bitter for the country and his phrase would be remembered now with mockery not cheers.

What Roosevelt taught in 1933 was governed only by the future. He had no presidential past, nor had the nation a remembered precedent for the dark time when he took office. But for Presidents in other circumstances, talk and action may take meaning from "last time" as well as next, and teaching thus is placed in double jeopardy.

Let me illustrate the jeopardy of Presidents as teachers with an instance drawn from the domestic side of the Korean War. At the start of the Second World War civilian shortages had appeared just as buying power rose, but price inflation was suppressed for the duration by direct controls. When sharp price rises came after the war one antidote proposed by the White House was authority to reimpose controls. In 1947 and in 1948 Truman lost no opportunity to urge that course on an unwilling Congress. Yet when Korea came, and when he went to Congress for the funds and taxes to finance rearmament, he asked for war controls over production but *not* for price controls. By that act of omission Truman tried to stress what made the present different from the past. Economists had told him that rearmament need not cut deeply into civilian output. The Speaker of the House informed him (wrongly) that without the old, divisive price issue his other control measures would pass Congress in a week. And Truman was concerned, as well, lest friends or enemies abroad take a request for powers over prices as his forecast of an all-out war. He tried, therefore, by what he did, and by his statements as he did it, to convey the lesson that he was *not* playing politics; that this was *not* the start of the Third World War, that fighting did *not* promise short supplies and price controls.[28]

What followed? Through July and August 1950, prices rose precipitously in response to panic buying spurred by memories of 1942 and by the wide belief that government had no real remedy but price controls. Truman had not asked for them, but Congress gave him the discretion (and the onus) to impose them anyway. Only with September's great successes in the war did there come signs that buying publics might believe what Truman meant to teach. MacArthur's triumph, not surprisingly, was much the better teacher. But when the Chinese intervened— initially in late October, then with crushing force in late November—buying spurted once again and prices rose alarmingly. The Administration, caught unprepared, promised a general price freeze. The freeze, however, was not actually ordered until late January 1951. Thereafter, that year and the next, when Truman tried to rally public sentiment for strong controls he failed of much response.

A President's instruction is affected by his own performance both before and after. What Truman tried to teach in July 1950 was overborne by recollections of things past. What happened next taught an entirely different lesson than the one he had intended to convey. His own words and actions played a part in both these outcomes. His own doings contributed to public education of the sort he did not want. His past and future did not make him any less a teacher; they made him teach the opposite of what he meant to teach. That is the jeopardy of presidential teaching.

The President-as-teacher has a hard and risky job. If he wants to guard his

78 THE ORIGINAL STUDY

popular approval he must give real-life experience a meaning that will foster tolerance for him. But happenings create his opportunities to teach. He has to ride events to gain attention. Most members of his public grow attentive only as they grow concerned with what may happen in their lives. When they become attentive they will learn from what he does. And whether his own doings teach the lesson he intends depends on what he did before and on what happens next *as understood by them.* These are the terms and conditions of employment for the President who seeks to be a teacher in our time. It is not a scholar's job—or Madison Avenue's.

IV

Half a century ago, with Theodore Roosevelt still in office, Woodrow Wilson wrote that "more and more" the White House would be occupied by "men . . . of the sort of action that makes for enlightenment."[29] His prediction as to men can be debated; his description of their task cannot. At least, if his successors are concerned for their own power and would guard its every source, his formula describes what they must do. The enemy of their prestige is unreality: the groundless hopes, the unexpected happenings, the unaccepted outcomes that members of their public feel in daily life and relate, somehow, anyhow, to That Man in the White House. From such an enemy there can be no defense save better understanding on the public's part. And for the reasons I have now set forth, such light as Presidents can shed consists of meanings they convey by what they do. "Action making for enlightenment" is but effective teaching. Only as they teach effectively will they ward off the threats to their prestige. I have asked how men in office can protect that valuable commodity from lasting harm. The answer will be found in Wilson's formula.

The formula is sound enough; it ought to be engraved over the White House door. Yet there is no enlightenment in meanings given to the day's events that arouse hopes tomorrow cannot meet, or yesterday belies. And Presidents, no more than other men, can gauge the future with exactitude; far less than most can they expunge their past. Illuminating action is their only sure escape from the backlash of public inability to grasp or to accept what happens next. In the circumstances of mid-century, however, few things can be harder to accomplish. Truman's difficulties over price control were but one aspect of his greater difficulty in imparting a "good" meaning, from his point of view, to the Korean War. This was as hard a task as ever faced a President and one to which we will return in the next chapter. Nine years earlier Roosevelt's urgent educative problem was resolved to his entire satisfaction by the Japanese attack upon Pearl Harbor. His own sense of relief, that Sunday afternoon, is testimony both to the dimensions of the problem and to limits on what he himself could do.[30] In 1941 and 1950 there was no sustained crisis consensus in this country. There has been none since 1945. Without consensus everything conspires to complicate action and to dim illumination. So Wilson himself found in that year foreshadowing mid-century, 1919.

Although the outlook for enlightenment is cloudy, the means are clear. Our question has been how a President, himself, protects prospective leeway inside government by guarding his own prospects for approval outside Washington. The answer brings us to his choices once again. His prestige turns on what the members of his public think they want and think they get. He affects their thoughts by what he does. His choices of what he will do and when and how—his choices, also, of whom he will tell and in what way and words—are *his* means to protect this source of influence, just as they are his means to guard those other power sources: bargaining relationships and professional reputation. No more than in the instance of those others is a President at liberty to make prestige his sole criterion for choice. No more than in the case of the Washington community is what *he* does the sole determinant of public sentiment. But whether his choice-making actually is usable and whether it proves useful or does not, the fact remains that for the human being in the White House choices are the only means in his own hands by which to shield his sources of real power, prestige no less than the rest.

Beyond the reach of his self-executing orders, then, a President's own prospects for effective influence are regulated (in so far as he controls them) by his choices of objectives, and of timing, and of instruments, and by his choice of choices to avoid. Thus we now reach the question: what helps him guard his power stakes in his own acts of choice? Granting that his choices are his means to protect power, granting that these are imperfect means, how can he make the most of them? For the length of two chapters this question has been dangling in mid-air. Now we can deal with it.

CHAPTER 6

Two Matters of Choice

In January 1957 the Secretary of the Treasury, George M. Humphrey, warned of a "depression that will curl your hair" and called for cuts in Eisenhower's budget on the very day the budget went to Congress. The repercussions of this outburst are described in Chapter 4. The net result, as we have seen, was harm to Eisenhower's reputation and relationships in Washington. But colorful remarks were not the only cause of harm; Humphrey's status did more damage than his bluntness. His warning and his hope were voiced to members of the press immediately after he had read a formal statement on the budget. He then appeared to be a spokesman for the President. As Eisenhower told his own press conference a week later:

> Now, in the first place, you will recall there was a memorandum that was the basis of that [Humphrey's] discussion, a written memorandum, and that written memorandum I not only went over every word of it, I edited it and it expresses my convictions very thoroughly.[1]

Not only had the President approved the Treasury statement, he had authorized its presentation to the press on Budget Day. That statement on that day would have harmed Eisenhower even if there had been no harsh comments off-the-cuff. For the statement implied what the comments dramatized: that the President's spokesman had qualms about the President's budget. Eisenhower chose to put his Secretary of the Treasury before the press with such a statement on such a day; in choosing so he jeopardized his influence. The question now before us is how any President protects his stakes of influence when he makes choices. Eisenhower's failure to protect himself in Humphrey's case illuminates the question. A study of this instance starts us toward an answer.

To understand why Eisenhower made the choice he did, it is useful to begin by noting how he did it. Early in January 1957 the President engaged in a last, long discussion of the budget with his Cabinet. This was a post mortem, in effect, since dollar figures had been set and the document had gone to press. The narrow Cabinet room beside the Rose Garden was packed, on this occasion, as almost always during Eisenhower's time. (His Cabinet meetings customarily contained more White House and staff-agency officials than department heads.) By all accounts, the crowd was rather glum. Whatever was thought privately of items in particular, no one who spoke, the President included, showed any pleasure over budget totals. When Humphrey read a statement voicing his concern about tax implications of the spending trends in budgeted programs, no one demurred. When he suggested that he issue such a statement to the press, nobody disagreed; discussion turned, instead, to the best means for doing so. Initially, the Secretary had proposed that he should write a public letter to the President. Eisenhower, among others, thought a press conference preferable and approved that procedure on the spot, agreeing at the same time to review a final text.[2] Budget Director Brundage is said to have remarked that Humphrey need be careful lest the press insert a wedge between him and the President. Humphrey, reportedly, was vigorous in his assent that nothing of the sort should be allowed to happen. Other heads were nodded, the President's among them; on that amicable note discussion closed.

Considering what happened when the Secretary met the press, it may seem strange that nothing more was made of Brundage's remark. Treasury views about the budget were no secret in the Cabinet room. When Humphrey told the press "there are a lot of places in this budget that can be cut," he said no more in public than he often had said privately. Humphrey, reportedly, had fought both loud and long against a budget of the size submitted by the President. For two months past his opposition had been "bitter," "scathing," "vehement," "intense" (the terms in which it was described to me by various participants). This man was primed for an explosion and Eisenhower knew that when he chose him as a spokesman. But Eisenhower also knew, or thought, that Humphrey would restrain himself. As one White House advisor told me:

> Charlie Wilson would have been another story, but George had an *excellent* record of conducting himself with discretion, staying within bounds. He always had been brilliantly effective on the Hill. He never had got into trouble testifying there or talking to the press . . . and since he never had, nobody thought he would.

This may not have been the sole cause of seeming unconcern around the Cabinet table. Many inhibitions work on men in crowded gatherings of peers (and super-peers) and palace guards. Brundage, for one, was poorly placed to press his point of view in open meeting, no matter what he might have thought of Humphrey. But regardless of the reasoning of others, the President himself appears to have been satisfied by Humphrey's reputation for discretion.

Although Eisenhower was unworried lest his Secretary's private anger show itself in cautioning the public, his assurance on this point leaves unexplained why he should have assisted *anyone* to speak for him on Budget Day in terms that called his budget into question. Humphrey's "memorandum" was free of nasty words, but it amounted to a warning that our economic progress called for tax relief and tax relief depended on new standards of restraint in federal spending. As the *New York Times* reported:

> In a prepared statement Mr. Humphrey set the following conditions for a future tax cut:
>
> Restraint by Congress in appropriating funds beyond budget requests; efforts at savings by every Federal department and agency; planning for further reductions in government employment and spending. . . .
>
> He emphasized his hope that spending in the next fiscal year would be less, through government economy efforts, than the estimated total of $71.8 billion dollars. In each of the last two years, however, spending had surpassed the original estimates.[3]

Contrast this with the emphasis of Eisenhower's Budget Message:

> . . . the Budget must also reflect the general responsibilities of a Government which will be serving 172 million people. . . . In the face of continuing threats to world peace, our collective security must be strengthened. . . . Progress toward greater equality of opportunity for all of our people as well as toward a balanced development and conservation of our natural resources must go forward. . . .
>
> It is my firm belief that tax rates are still too high. . . . However, the reduction in tax rates must give way, under present circumstances, to the cost of meeting our urgent national responsibilities.[4]

If tax reductions "must give way," why have Humphrey apologize? If "urgent national responsibilities" were now at stake, why have him emphasize how much they hurt? If Eisenhower was preparing to accentuate the positive, why send Humphrey to do the opposite? Or, putting it the other way, if Humphrey on the President's behalf urged "planning for further reductions," why have budget estimates include new programs, new commitments, sure to swell expenditure in future years?

Eisenhower's Message struck a different note than Humphrey's text; a look at budget items makes the difference seem the greater. The President was asking more funds for the Pentagon, and for atomic energy, for housing, and for public health, and public works. He was projecting an increase in foreign economic aid. His current school-aid scheme involved a whole new category of expenditure, and he was urging half a dozen other new commitments in domestic welfare spheres. On information programs overseas, where Cohn and Schine once romped, he was proposing to bestow both larger sums and Arthur Larsen. Yet having raised this monument to ''Modern Republicanism,'' Eisenhower chose that Humphrey should preside at its unveiling. The Treasury press conference took place at the hour that the Budget Message formally reached Congress, in time to share most headlines with the budget itself. And not only was Humphrey's text at hand, his timing seems to have been understood when Eisenhower told him to proceed. Why, then, tell him to do so? Above all else, whey have both statements made at the same time on the same day?

No matter how discreet the Secretary might have been, this curious procedure risked the power of the President. What was Eisenhower's risk in Humphrey's statement? Let me digress to answer that before I turn to why the risk was run. A budget presentation is among the cardinal services the President-as-clerk performs for Congressmen and bureaucrats and lobbyists, alike. Without it they would be hard put to do their jobs. Its money estimates and legislative program are the nearest things available to an agenda for their struggle over scope and shape of government. By fixing the position of a chief participant, it gives the rest a reference point in judging their own interests, risks, and tactics. As a device for organizing struggle and for giving strugglers something to respond to or react against, this agenda is perhaps the biggest labor-saver known to Washington. In the degree to which it saves their labor, those who use it are dependent on the President who makes it. In the degree to which his own endorsement helps or hurts their causes, they depend upon his choice of what to ask. In the degree that they may gain protection or publicity by helping (or opposing) him, they depend on his asking. As always, *their* dependence means some leverage for *him*. His clerkship may be onerous, but services like these yield bargaining advantages to him. However, the advantage in this instance turns upon one working premise: that the presidential budget is the President's; that what he says he wants will be supported, within reason, by his ''powers'' and his influence so long as it is asked. Unless this premise works in practice nobody is served, there is no labor saved, dependence vanishes, the leverage is lost. And Humphrey's statement as approved and timed was bound to call this premise into question.

To cast doubt on this premise would be risky for a President in any year, but never more so than in 1957. For Eisenhower then was at the outset of a four-year term with Congress in the opposition from the start, for the first time since 1849. He was certain not to run again, thanks to the Twenty-second Amendment. His party, patently, was not in shape to substitute for his own popularity. The outcome of the 1956 election guaranteed that politicians of both parties, interest groups of all descriptions, members of the press corps would be specially alert for signs of Eisenhower's response to his ''lame duck'' status and his party's plight. Here was a novel, central challenge to his influence, a challenge highly advertised in Washington. How did he mean to meet it? Naturally, his postelection budget would be searched for clues. The risks of Humphrey's statement rose accordingly. That statement preached what Eisenhower's budget failed to practice. To sponsor such a statement would make Eisenhower seem a man who had turned heat upon himself. Inevitably, Washingtonians would wonder why. He might be thought the victim of an inadvertence, or naiveté, or ignorance, or sabotage, or clumsy execution of some devious design. He even might be thought the man he was, a man in doubt about his own direction. Eisenhower's choice was bound to put such thoughts into the minds of agency officials fresh from "firm" agreements with the Budget Bureau, and of congressmen awaiting "firm" proposals to react to, and of commentators seeking portents for the second term. Some damage to his reputation and his trading stock in Washington was almost certain from the moment he said "go ahead" to Humphrey.

The prospect, naturally, was for less damage, more easily repaired, than actually became the case when Humphrey failed to show restraint. But there was never likelihood that Eisenhower could escape scot-free if Humphrey's press conference received publicity commensurate with White House sanction and its timing. Inattention would have spared the President embarrassment, but headlines were encouraged by the course he chose. The folkways of Washington assured him trouble in proportion to attention gained. How much attention, how much trouble, Humphrey and the press corps would decide. Eisenhower left it up to them. Among the risks he ran, his delegation, in effect, of that decision was the greatest. Humphrey had *carte blanche* to magnify the rest.

Given the risks why make the choice? Why choose to put the Secretary of the Treasury before the press with such a text on Budget Day? This is the question to which I would now return. Abstractly, one might suppose the answer lay in judging these risks less than risks of other sorts, on conscious calculation of all aspects of the case. Actually, the answer seems to be that power in these personal terms was not assessed at all; not anyway by Eisenhower as he made his choice. He certainly had many things in mind—among them power factors of some sorts—but safeguarding his personal position seems not to have been one of them. He was preoccupied, reportedly, by matters of a rather different order. The key to his behavior is the glumness in the Cabinet Room. When he heard Humphrey's statement read, the President was deep in second-thoughts about his budget. Most of what he heard from others added to his doubts. He "bought" that statement, basically, because he was in doubt. His doubts obscured his risks.

Eisenhower's doubts revolved around the budget's size and trend. Its spending total bothered him. Program commitments mortgaging the future bothered him still more. In 1956 he had sent down a 69 billion-dollar budget; now the total would be nearly 72 billion dollars. Brundage's projections showed that even without price rises and even though there were no further growth of public services, the cost of Federal programs *now* established or approved might outrun 80 billion dollars before Eisenhower left the White House. (New weapons systems, among other things, made that a likely prospect.) Prices, moreover, had been rising for months past; their rate of climb appeared to be accelerating; the current boom was taking an inflationary turn. And Congress, still controlled by Democrats, could not be counted on to keep commitments down to size as specified in Republican budgets. Brundage's projections looked conservative.

Seen thus, in terms of totals and of trend, the pending budget seemed to belie almost everything that Eisenhower personally believed in and was told concerning the requirements of proper fiscal policy. On economic grounds not only orthodox Republicans but the more "modern" men around him (with differences regarding "what" and "when") were anxious to see Federal spending stabilize on some plateau so that tax revenues enlarging with the growth of the economy could furnish surpluses to check inflation, cut the public debt, and bring nearer the day of tax reduction. On grounds of party politics the President did not lack for advisers who thought this a very practical necessity; prolong the combination of high taxes with inflation and the party in the White House would be punished at the polls. The reasoning, both economic and political, was scarcely a Republican invention; seven years earlier, in pre-Korean days, Truman had held military spending down for roughly comparable reasons.[5] But numbers of Republicans saw an ideological corollary which had not troubled Truman. Appealing for economy and tax relief some thirty years before, a President of the United States had stated:

> We are testing out the success of self-government. . . . We require no property qualifications for voters . . . it has too often been found that democratic institutions tend to confiscate property to such an extent that economic progress becomes impossible. . . . This is the test which America must meet and meet constantly and unless it is met successfully, the strength, progress and prosperity of our country will cease.[6]

So Calvin Coolidge put it, and his words, I gather, would have evoked warm response from Eisenhower's Secretary of the Treasury.

On any of these grounds, or on them all, the logical response to Brundage's projections was an effort to check spending at its source, the statutory mandates that invoked it. As Eisenhower was to tell the press, quite rightly, in March 1957: "If you are going to save . . . money you have got to look at programs . . . think of what programs you want to eliminate."[7] Without cuts in the program base, mere budgeting could have but marginal effect in cutting budgets. Curb spending at its source, however, and if not this budget then the next, or the one after, might show major savings in the cost of present programs and make room for new necessities (like military hardware) without overall increases in expenditures. Here ran the path to a plateau. This was the reasoning, implicitly, of Humphrey's formal statement to the press, and quite explicitly of his explosive comments off-the-cuff. This was the course that he had urged upon the budget-makers. Ironically, it was the course the President himself would espouse just a year later, and the year after that. But in January 1957 it was not the course—or rationale—of Eisenhower's budget. The whole "modern" Republican appearance of that budget was a consequence of choices which inclined the other way. There lay the difficulty, and the doubts.

The President had acted in good faith when he approved the items that enlarged his budget. Individually, all these were things he then thought proper for the country and in keeping with the tenor of his fall campaign. Each item had its share of departmental advocates, its grounds of public policy, its political claims for his support. In sanctioning more spending and new programs, case by case, he had not lacked for signs of Treasury displeasure. Nor had he lacked for data on the trend of his approvals. All through budget season, from late August 1956, the Budget Bureau's "target" for expenditures had been near 71 billion dollars, a figure corresponding to the current rate of spending plus 2 billion dollars for defense. Because increases for other programs pushed above that target, trial balances had gone to Eisenhower with each major estimate for his approval. Although it grew plain, before December, that he would exceed the target by a billion, this was not a great departure, overall, from prior plans. The budget would be balanced still; some surplus would remain; the total rise in spending would be less than increased revenues from economic growth; compared to the economy, expenditures still would be lower than they had been when he first took office. From the start of budget planning, little more had been expected by the planners or, so far as they knew, by the President. With reassurances like these his Budget Message, as they drafted it, and as he sent it, was to minimize the consequences of more spending.

But this had been a budget planned in *1956*. Those "targets" had been set in a convention summer full of promise—and of promises—when prices, it was hoped, would level off and Congress, it was thought, would go Republican. Those estimates had come before the President while he campaigned for re-election or presided over conferences on Hungary and Suez. Whatever Eisenhower may have felt about the budget in September, or October, or November, it is clear that when he looked at final totals in December he did not like what he saw. And neither did assorted White House aides who only then became sharply aware of what impended; their concern heightened his own. Humphrey's warnings now were voiced in chorus.

As always happens in election years, a number of the President's associates who normally would play an active part in budget season had been concerned with other things before December. Budget totals came to them as something of a shock, suggestive of a Budget Bureau fumble while their backs were turned. Reportedly, the President, himself, was not immune to those sensations when he turned from his campaigning and from crises overseas to face the final choices on his budget. However that may be, some members of his circle were decidedly affected by the sense that Budget bureaucrats had let them down.

There remained men around the President whose ideology and preferences were echoed by the Budget Message, not by Humphrey. But with inflation threatening and Congress Democratic, few of them, reportedly, were ready to defend the tactics of so high a budget total. The whole Administration now would be aligned with every congressman and lobbyist who wanted more from government; how could they be held to 72 billion? With spenders on the march, where were the troops to counter them? The President would be in the parade. "We have to create countervailing power," a White House aide would tell me later, rationalizing February's budget-cutting drive, "the military thing will go right through the roof unless there's enough public heat on Congress for economy." But while Eisenhower's theme was confident expansion, how could his Administration rouse and guide that "countervailing power?" These were the sorts of questions that hung, unanswered, in the Cabinet Room at the turn of the year. Even the men who liked the budget as it was were willing to concede a general problem. Even its major beneficiaries confined themselves, for the most part, to guarding their own bailiwicks. The views of the more "orthodox" among them squared with Humphrey's on all points except particulars. Even the most "modern" of department heads were disinclined to argue abstract principles with him. (Their reticence, reportedly, bore some relation to the fact that at preceding meetings there had been no more articulate defender of the budget than the man whose kiss was death in this Administration, Harold Stassen.[8])

As for Eisenhower, personally, let me quote the private recollections of a man much in his confidence who was not at the Cabinet meeting but saw him before and after:

> Pressure to freeze the budget [in time] for [deadlines set by] the Government Printing Office meant that ideological differences and programmatic ones were dangling *unresolved* and the President was left feeling "one more week, one more day to work this over could have made it better, tighter, smaller." That was the frame of mind he carried into Cabinet meeting. . . .

There, in this context, the Secretary of the Treasury advanced his proposition and the President accepted it, forthwith.

II

When Eisenhower made that choice, not even witnesses agree which of the arguments and circumstances sketched above affected him the most. Precisely what he hoped to gain remains uncertain. At the very least, presumably, he meant to ease his conscience, to conciliate a faction, and to please a trusted counselor; at the most, perhaps, he meant to take a step toward "countervailing power." By all accounts, however, something else is plain enough: so far as words and manner show, he made his choice without a thought of what he stood to lose. How could he have done otherwise? A President can only think about the things he is aware of. His awareness can come only from the face the issue turns to him, or from the words of others, or from promptings in his mind. On this occasion, all three sources evidently failed him.

The issue wore a face that featured 72 billion dollars, upward trend, inflation-ary pressure, Democratic Congress, Republican discomfiture—and Humphrey's reputation for discretion. The latter's proposition showed no flaws upon its surface; neither substantively nor procedurally did its terms proclaim what Eisenhower risked by its endorsement.

The words of others told him no more than the issue did. Few means of consultation were less likely to point up his risks than Cabinet meetings of the Eisenhower sort, especially a meeting timed as this one was and in the given context.[9] Quite apart from inhibitions native to such gatherings, it is an open question whether those who might have argued were aware, themselves, of reasons for resisting Humphrey's course. At most, no one but Eisenhower would look foolish; disproportions between departmental risks and his were great. Except perhaps for Brundage it does not appear that any Cabinet member saw much trouble for himself in carefully phrased cautions from the Treasury (and some, no doubt, saw positive advantage). Without qualms on their own account it is by no means certain that they thought to fear for Eisenhower or, at any rate, to voice concern to him while he showed none. As for Brundage, it suffices to record that after Hum-phrey's unforeseen explosion his advice was tendered to the President through White House aides; this was no man to urge, unasked, that Humphrey should be stopped before he started.

Which left it up to Eisenhower, and his state of mind was calculated to ob-scure, not clarify, the risks he ran as President. For these were risks in personal terms, risks to his personal power, risks to his reputation and relationships in Washington's community. But Eisenhower was not thinking in these terms. He saw himself, apparently, as one man in a group with a collective reputation, conscious of a common problem, trying to resolve it, trapped by time. In this perspective Hum-phrey was his friend and annual budgeting the cause of his entrapment. That Secre-taries of Departments *also* are "a President's natural enemies," that "clerical" endeavors like the budget *also* are a source of White House influence, Eisenhower's outlook evidently blurred beyond recognition. In power terms the one thing he most needed to remember was that budgeting brings Presidents advantage. In his cir-cumstances, understandably enough, this seems to have been one thing he forgot. The clarifying question in those terms was, "how may Humphrey's presentation make mine (and me) look when I have endorsed both?" That question Eisenhower had to ask himself since no one else was asking. I find no indication it occurred to him. Why should it have? He viewed *his* presentation with distaste, and trusted Humphrey.

This does not mean that power was no object when the President approved a press show at the Treasury, but merely that he laid hold of the wrong end of the stick. Some of his aides were to discourse on "countervailing power"; something of the sort was very likely in his mind. Yet in the circumstances, this would not be power he could wield or could control himself. His Secretary's move might boost the bargaining position of respectable Republicans in Congress and the country, but not Eisenhower's own; not when it would seem aimed, with his connivance, at "his" program. Unquestionably power did flow from that press conference as it turned out in practice; accidentally (or on purpose?) Humphrey gained a lot, but not for Eisenhower. And the relative gains and losses would have been the same, though probably far smaller in amount, had Humphrey bit his tongue and stuck to text.

The distinction between one man's power and another's may be fine, but it is crucial. Eisenhower missed it and because he did, his own choice worked against, not for, his influence. I began by asking why make such a choice; here lies the answer, and the answer points a moral: *Influence adheres to those who sense what it is made of.*

If choices are a President's own means to guard his power, he is likelier to hurt than to help himself unless he knows what power is and sees its shape in what he does. Before power can be served, it must be seen. That certainly ranks high among the lessons of this case. Had Eisenhower realized he was courting real embarrassment, presumably he would have answered "no" or "wait" when Humphrey urged a statement to the press. What makes this case so useful as an illustration is precisely the simplicity and ease of such an option. Nothing but lack of realization barred the way to a "stop-order" of a self-executing sort. (The President's approval, after all, was what enlarged his risk.)

It does not follow that because a risk is seen, a President can choose in its terms only. Almost always there will be competing risks in other terms of power, or of policy. When problems stem from substance, personalities, outside events, the choices they impose upon a President have numerous dimensions, each involving risks of different sort. If Eisenhower saw a need in policy and politics for "countervailing power" against spenders, he was dutybound to further it by every means he could. Saying "no" to Humphrey hardly satisfies. But had Eisenhower thought to answer so, the very sense behind that thought would have alerted him to some alternatives. Humphrey's press show certainly was not the only way to approach "countervaillance" in this situation. To quote again the informant last quoted:

> Sure, there was a need for the President to appear decisive, knowing about everything, knowing all the answers, defending every penny of his budget—it's ridiculous, but that's the way government works. . . . And then he could have turned around and amended it equally forcefully!

So he could. He also could have picked a fight with Congress on some "raid upon the Treasury" that overran his budget. Many variations are conceivable. It was not written in the book of fate that he must burn himself in order to light fires for economy.

Issues may arise, and do, where none of the alternatives appears less risky than the course at hand. But even so, to see the risk one takes is to be cautioned for the future. In the circumstances of the case it can be argued, for example, that once Humphrey had exploded, Eisenhower risked more by a show of irritation than by speaking softly, as he did. But full awareness of the risks he ran in doing so should have sufficed to warn him away from a subsequent, gratuitous display of indecisiveness in public. The whole handling of February's budget-cutting drive showed precious little feel for what I have called "pattern-setting." Had Eisenhower grasped his danger at the start that feel would have been stronger, and among his later choices several, certainly, allowed him scope to use it. There may be arguments, in power terms, for softness toward one's Secretary of the Treasury gone wrong, but none for equal softness toward a taunting resolution by the House of Representatives that asked, with tongue in cheek, where it should cut the budget.[10]

If not as the determinant "right now" then as the means of opening alternatives and posting caution signs "next time," a President's perception of his power stakes (and sources) in each act of choice conditions every chance to make his saying and his doing serve his influence. What choices are to power, these perceptions are to choice: the means in his own hands. To ask how he can guard his power stakes in acts of choice is thus to ask how clearly he perceives. To ask how he can help himself to power is to ask how he can sharpen his perceptions. The question now becomes what helps him see?

The Humphrey story would suggest that nobody and nothing helps a President to see save as he helps himself; that neither issues nor advisers as they reach him are a substitute for sensitivity to power on his part. It follows that in answering this question one must look to his resources for self-help. To ask what helps him see is really to inquire what he can do for himself. That follows from this case, but does it always follow? My own response is "Yes." An incident like Eisenhower's "go ahead" to Humphrey is distinctly *not* unique in this regard. What it suggests applies to every case of which I am aware.[11] The indication of them all is that no man who sits where Eisenhower sat can count on reading his own risks upon the face of issues brought before him; none is safe in counting on subordinates to remedy the lack. Outcomes may be happier by far than in this case; the likelihoods are not.

To demonstrate the point, and test it, let me turn from Humphrey's statement to some choices of a very different sort, involving different policies and personalities, a different order of importance and a different set of risks. These are the choices underlying alteration of American objectives in the third month of the Korean War and leading to the end-the-war offensive that was turned into a rout by Chinese intervention two months later. This new example shifts the scene from 1957 to 1950, from Eisenhower to Truman, from quasi-peace to limited war, from fiscal policy to foreign policy and military tactics. It returns us to the cast of characters encountered in MacArthur's firing (which followed five months after); it affords a context as unlike the Humphrey case as I can find—the better to distinguish common ground.

On its surface, this new case is far more complex than the last, involving choices made not at one moment but by stages. That is why the Humphrey story was put first. Because of its complexity this second story must be told in rather more detail. But I would hope the editorial difference leads no one to believe that I see Truman's problem of self-help as differing *essentially* from Eisenhower's just discussed. Essentially, they seem to me the same.

III

On October 7, 1950 the General Assembly of the United Nations, "recalling that the essential objective was the establishment of a unified independent and democratic Korea," recommended that "all appropriate steps be taken to assure stability" throughout the country, North as well as South. That same day the first non-Korean units of MacArthur's forces crossed the thirty-eighth parallel in pursuit of the enemy so nearly (but not quite) entrapped by the end-run of Inchon three weeks earlier.[12] The General Assembly's words sanctioned this military move, of course, but they did more; they set the "war aim" of the member governments whose troops were under MacArthur's command: a unified, noncommunist Korea. This aim had long been a secondary objective of American foreign policy, pursued by peaceful means. It now became the policy objective of the war. Thus "victory" was now defined for the armed forces and the public of the United States, which never yet—as every school child knew—had failed to "win" a "War."

Three months before, when North Korean armies had invaded South Korea, a less ambitious aim had been envisaged by the authors of American intervention.[13] As Truman, in his *Memoirs,* paraphrases National Security Council minutes of June 29, 1950:

> I stated categorically that . . . I wanted to take every step necessary to push the North Koreans back behind the 38th parallel. But I wanted to be sure that we did not become so deeply committed in Korea that we could not take care of such other situations as might develop.
>
> . . . I wanted it clearly understood that our operations were designed to restore peace there and to restore the border.[14]

The United Nations Resolution of June 27, which both justified and authorized those operations, was drafted in the American State Department. It recommended "such assistance to the Republic of Korea as may be necessary to repel the armed attack and to restore international peace and security in the area." The last phrase was ambiguous, but its inclusion in the draft cannot be said to have reflected any conscious purpose at top departmental levels different from that stated by the President. And in the early weeks of fighting, as our forces were committed and pushed back to the Pusan perimeter, nothing he or Cabinet members said in public contravened the emphasis of his remarks just quoted.

The United Nations resolution of October 7 thus embodied and expressed a real shift in the foreign policy objective of hostilities, a shift made possible by transformation of the military situation in the last half of September, after Inchon. The new policy objective was no less a war aim of Americans for being an expression of the General Assembly. The United States was in the war as UN agent. In form, not Washington but UN Headquarters then temporarily at Lake Success, New York, was properly the source of such objectives. In fact, the General Assembly's words on this occasion were of Washington's selection. Reportedly, the Secretary of State, Dean Acheson, chose most of them himself. At any rate, the State Department's draft of what became the UN resolution had his personal approval, and the President's. Truman knew its terms before it was proposed at Lake Success. Despite its UN form, the resolution was American in roughly the degree that UN aid to South Korea was American, that is to say in all essentials. Many other governments concurred, of course, the British chief among them. Despite a popular impression to the contrary, this shift of policy objectives was no Washington *diktat*. But the decision was a Washington decision; in that he assented, it was Truman's. Thereby he took a personal risk of such proportions as to make Eisenhower's risk in Humphrey's instance trifling by comparison.

What was Truman's risk? Let me begin by mentioning what it was not. In and of itself, announcement of the new war aim did not *create* a military risk. To be sure, military risks were run by the troop movements that accompanied the announcement (other risks were avoided by abandoning that very poor defense line, the thirty-eighth parallel). But the decision to attempt destruction of the North Korean forces on home grounds preceded the decision on what war aim to announce. The same thing can be said of diplomatic risks. No allies were estranged *by the announcement* of a new war aim. As for potential enemies, it is improbable that their intentions were affected one way or the other. To judge from what the Chinese said, and later did, Peking's concern was with MacArthur's military progress, never mind its foreign policy objective. Chinese concern was not confined to anything so simple as a buffer zone along the border; an entity called North Korea, not the border, was the stake (perhaps in roughly the same sense that South Korea, under reverse circumstances, was for Washington). Even had the UN promised restoration of an independent North once all resistance ceased—which, naturally, no one proposed—I know of nothing to suggest that Peking would have withheld intervention. The communist world does not take kindly, it appears, to the dismantling of a member state's facilities for governance: the party and the army. MacArthur's military progress threatened both, no matter what came after. In short, the military risks and diplomatic dangers usually associated with MacArthur's march across the parallel existed independent of the words used in the UN resolution. MacArthur's march was authorized before the words were seen, much less approved, at Lake Success.

Truman's risk when the UN announced its new war aim was of another sort.

The risk was to his own prospective influence in every facet of his work as President. His risk was not the same as Eisenhower's in the Humphrey case. It did not bear directly on his Washington relationships or reputation. What he endangered, rather, was that other power source, his prestige with his public outside Washington. In the terms of Chapter 5, what Truman risked was leeway. He gambled with his own ability to get done many things far more important to him than the unification of Korea. His risk was that worst risk for Presidents in public: the teaching of a lesson that rebounds against himself, the rousing of expectancies in conflict with his policies, the risk of action making for confusion not enlightenment. "Korea," as a series of events, was bound to be a foremost "happening" in public consciousness, arousing hopes and fears that could not but affect the look of Truman and his policies. In the degree he needed leeway to accomplish what he wanted, he depended on the lessons that this happening would teach. In the degree he needed national attention, he depended on the focus it provided. Only as Korea could be made to point *his* moral could he foster acquiescence in his regime and his aims. Only by his actions could he influence its teaching. Yet that UN resolution risked imparting to "what happened" the least fortunate of meanings from his point of view: the meaning his opponents compressed into two words, "Truman's War," the bloodletting "he" started, would not "win," and could not stop.

Had the unification of Korea been Truman's dearest object, its announcement as a war aim would have been another matter. But it was among the least of the objectives on his mind. In July and August 1950, in December after Chinese intervention, in his struggles with MacArthur, and thereafter through his last two years of office, his behavior leaves no doubt about the many things he wanted more than that. He wanted to affirm that the UN was not a League of Nations, that aggression would be met with counter-force, that "police actions" were well worth their cost, that the "lessons of the 1930's" had been learned. He wanted to avoid "the wrong war, in the wrong place, at the wrong time," as General Bradley put it—and any "War," if possible. He wanted NATO strengthened fast, both militarily and psychologically. He wanted the United States rearmed without inflation, and prepared, thereafter, to sustain a level of expenditure for military forces and for foreign aid far higher than had seemed achievable before Korea. He also wanted to get on with the Fair Deal, keep Democrats in office, strengthen his congressional support from North and West, and calm the waters stirred by men like Senator McCarthy.

None of these aims *required* unification of Korea (however helpful at sufficiently low cost), and all of them took precedence with Truman. One need but read the "minutes" from Wake Island, where he met MacArthur on October 15, to sense Truman's relative disinterest in Korea save as a symbol of UN success and as a source of seasoned troops for Europe. One need but read between the lines of his address at San Francisco, two days later, to recall that war or no war he retained the hopes for November's congressional election which had brought him "whistle-stopping" West in May, before the war began.[15]

Indeed, Korean unity was so low in Truman's order of priorities that it was off his list within three months of its adoption. It went off London's list on first sight of the Chinese in Korea; Truman was somewhat slower, to his cost. But once the Chinese demonstrated that a widespread war in Asia and a risk of World War III would be the lowest price for unification, he showed firm unwillingness to pay it. By December 1950, as the enemy poured south, his object became merely to hang on. By February 1951, with the lines stabilized and an advance in prospect, he reverted to his aim at the beginning of the war: a restoration of the border and cessation of hostilities. By March, he was preparing to dismiss MacArthur. By June, with the Chinese in full retreat (and with NATO Commander Eisenhower in full cry for troops), Truman was prepared to make a truce on the first strong defense line north of the thirty-eighth parallel, and to dismiss as "real estate"—not his term but the Pentagon's—the territory stretching to the next line north of that, the "waist" of the peninsula where London unsuccessfully had urged a halt some seven months before.

If Truman thus retreated from the war aim of October 1950, rather than pay cash for it in coin of other policies, he did so with the full support of Washington advisers, military, diplomatic, and political alike. And their retreat in chorus was a decorous performance next to the stampede at the UN. Within eight weeks the resolution of October 7 had not only dropped from sight but out of mind and, save for twinges of regret and of embarrassment, seems to have figured further in the thoughts of few, indeed, at Lake Success.

Unfortunately, the new war aim was not so easily expunged from public consciousness in the United States, or from the mind of the commander in the field, General MacArthur. What for Washington and Lake Success was but a passing fancy, taken and abandoned as the war news changed, MacArthur seems to have regarded as the only proper outcome of hostilities, at least of those in which *he* was engaged (scarcely an unreasonable notion for the man who had accepted the surrender of Japan). He had not forced this war aim on his government, but very willingly became its instrument with no sign of the mental reservations hedging its choice by his superiors. When they abandoned it, the consequences of that difference grew severe indeed, and I have dealt with some of them in Chapter 2. But even in the weeks before the great Chinese attack, while Truman and MacArthur proclaimed a common aim, the difference in intensity of feeling for that aim contributed to the impending tactical disaster.

Long after the event I once asked Mr. Truman if he had not grown concerned while UN troops, dividing as they went, moved toward their fatal "end-the-war" offensive. His answer, though a retrospective one, reflects, I think, the essence of his viewpoint at the time:

What we should have done is stop at the neck of Korea right here [pointing to a globe]. . . . That's what the British wanted. . . . We knew the Chinese had close to a million men on the border and all that. . . . But [MacArthur] was commander in the field. You pick your man, you've got to back him up. That's the only way a military organization can work. I got the best advice I could and the man on the spot said this was the thing to do. . . . So I agreed. That was my decision—no matter what hindsight shows.

This raises a nice question about how to get advice and whose to take—a question I will leave for the next chapter—but what requires emphasis just now is that a "man on the spot" no more committed to the terms of "victory" than Truman proved to be would have been much less likely to take military risks of such proportions as MacArthur did. The Pentagon's discomfort as his isolated columns moved to north and east is most suggestive on the point.

Thus by choosing unification as a war aim the President not only tied Korea's meaning and his prestige to an easy occupation of the North, but he also added something to the likelihood that he would have no benefits to show by way of substitute. The halting of MacArthur short of "victory" might have been troublesome enough, once victory had been defined as unification. Instead, because that was its definition, Truman let MacArthur risk and lose the tangible advantages of ground and of diplomacy gained from five months of fighting. The lessons that Korea taught might not have been as pleasant with a stalemate at the "waist" as with a victory. The actual outcome made those lessons sad, indeed, for Truman and his causes—the sadder since his war aim meant so little in his scheme of things.

These are the terms in which to measure Truman's power risk when he endorsed his State Department's words for the UN. The many things he wanted more than North Korea's conquest called for leeway from his public. To foster public tolerance of him and his aims he needed object lessons that would demonstrate the worth of what he wanted. To make Korea's teaching turn on unification was to risk the opposite result. Korea was the teacher at the center of the stage. To reach and teach his public any President must ride events; he teaches by his doing in the context of events; he teaches as his actions attach meaning to "what happens." The publicizing of a new war aim invited Truman's "students" to attach "wrong" meaning in precisely the degree it should turn costly of accomplishment. Truman gave MacArthur, of all people, the initiative in calculating costs. MacArthur is the Humphrey of this case. The greatest risk that Truman ran lay in MacArthur's capability to magnify all other risks.

However, these were not the terms in which the issue came to Truman. The clarifying questions would have been: What should the outcome of this war convey to men outside the Washington community? How may this war aim color what they come to see and feel? Few Presidents, presumably, much less their State Departments, would formulate such questions so precisely; to do so puts an instinct into words. The formulation, though, is not in point. What matters is that nothing of the sort, however stated or implied, seems to have reached the President. Instead, the issue of a new war aim wore the disguise of military choices; the risks that showed themselves were military risks. The danger in the issue was political, but this was not apparent on its face or in the words of Truman's chief advisers.

How did Truman come to choose a new war aim? The question can be answered only by a chronological account. The story starts in August 1950. In early August after some hesitation, not without some doubts, the President and the Joint Chiefs of Staff approved MacArthur's daring plan to crush the North Koreans: a landing at Inchon, behind them, simultaneous with an offensive at their front on the Pusan perimeter. The date then set (and met) was September 15; as it approached, MacArthur was supremely confident; the White House and the Pentagon were not. But it was clear to Washington that if MacArthur should succeed, even in part, the war would be transformed and he would need some new directives. "What next?" was put to the Departments of State and Defense, and their response eventually became a National Security Council paper, initialled by Truman on September 11. His paraphrase of its conclusion will suggest the hopes and fears—and the uncertainties—involved in the discussions that preceded his approval:

> General MacArthur was to conduct . . . military operations either to force the North Koreans behind the 38th parallel or to destroy their forces [south of it]. If there was no *indication or threat of entry of Soviet or Chinese Communist elements in force* . . . [he] was to extend his operations north of the parallel and to make plans for the occupation of North Korea. . . . no ground operations were to take place north of the parallel in the event of Soviet or Chinese Communist entry. [Italics added.][16]

The first part of the foregoing was turned into a directive for quick dispatch to MacArthur; the balance was left to await allied consultations and the outcome of Inchon.

MacArthur's purpose, as reported to the Pentagon in August, was destruction of the North Korean forces before they could get behind their border. This he did not manage, as the National Security Council discussions had foreseen he might not do. With this exception (a momentous one), his Inchon operation was a triumph, transforming not the war alone but the emotions felt in Washington and Lake Success. Appetites rose as the troops went forward. On September 26 the UN army from the south made contact with the units from Inchon. On September 28 Seoul was finally liberated. On October 1 some South Korean units crossed the parallel without much opposition.

The North Koreans, though, had crossed ahead of them. The communist troops were battered, disorganized, but still a force in being. And from no quarter did there come the faintest sign that they were ready to surrender or even to negotiate. On September 21, Senator Knowland of California, gave it as his opinion that to leave them in that state behind the parallel would be "appeasement." For once his views were shared by the Administration and by friendly governments. The border, at the parallel, had proved its insufficiency as a defense line. To break off when it was reached was to invite a new attack across it, when and as the North Koreans chose.

Short of pursuing and destroying their field forces, there seemed no effective way to meet that threat. No one around the President proposed to live with it.

Within a week of Inchon all Truman's advisers were agreed upon pursuit, if nothing else turned up to simplify (or complicate) the problem militarily. In consequence, and after some amount of inter-allied consultation, the Defense and State Departments urged and he approved a second missive to MacArthur; approval seems to have been given on or about September 24; the directive was dispatched September 27. To quote from Truman's *Memoirs:*

> . . . [MacArthur] was told that his military objective was "the destruction of the North Korean Armed Forces." In attaining this objective he was authorized to conduct military operations north of the 38th parallel . . . provided that at the time of such operation there had been no entry into North Korea by major Soviet or Chinese Communist forces, no announcement of an intended entry, *and no threat by Russian or Chinese Communists to counter our operations militarily.* . . . [Italics added.][17]

Had Truman (and his Chiefs of Staff) been fully confident of Inchon from the first, or had a measure of success not come so fast thereafter, forethought might have counseled hedging the military objective for MacArthur even further than was done in this second directive. (Within two days of its dispatch he had submitted and gained approval for a plan committing him to moves beyond the waist of the peninsula.) But flat refusal to attempt *some* military exploitation of his sudden, great advantage was not to be expected, in the circumstances, from governments with troops engaged; from Washington and London and the rest it certainly was not forthcoming. There is no evidence that any of the governments with forces under his command were in the least reluctant to pursue the North Koreans.[18]

Strictly speaking, the decision to pursue the North Koreans did not call for UN action; strictly speaking, its approval was already on the books. Destruction of the enemy's armed forces, whether on home grounds or not, was well within the terms of that vague, early-summer phrase: "the restoration of peace and security in the area." But in practice Truman's chief advisers, and the President himself, seem to have taken as a matter of course the need for something more from Lake Success, once it had been decided that MacArthur should go north. In theory Washington might have authority, but the fine print of prior resolutions had been little publicized. Before Inchon, repelling the aggression had meant getting North Koreans out of South Korea in the emphasis of news dispatches generally. Although the Administration might conceive "what next" in terms of how to liquidate the enemy, the press and congressmen and certain UN delegates now posed the issue publicly in terms of the thirty-eighth parallel. To cross or not to cross might seem irrelevant inside the Pentagon and State, but most insiders were aware that on the outside it was being called *the* question.

From the President on down, responsible officials wanted to avoid a look of "going it alone," or putting something over, or relying on fine print, especially

.

when such a look was undeserved. In the circumstances some specific UN sanction seemed to follow logically from the dispatch of new orders to MacArthur. "That is, a matter for the UN to decide," said Truman on September 21, when queried at press conference about crossing the parallel; thereafter, UN action was not only logical, it had to happen.[19]

Besides, no one in Washington was now disposed to doubt MacArthur's power to make daring pay. Once he was ordered north it was assumed that he would go there in a hurry. So he did—by October 10 the east coast was in his hands up to Wonsan, just below the waist of the peninsula; on the west, Pyongyang, the North Korean capital, was taken October 19; before the month was out he would control the whole peninsula, and with it the great bulk of North Korea's population ("mainland" Korea to the north and east was mostly barren ground). Foreseeing this in late September both State and Pentagon thought UN guidelines indispensable for occupation of a territory that did not belong to Syngman Rhee. The South Koreans claimed their government, by rights, embraced the North. This belied the UN's declaration of intent, dating from 1947, that a united government should stem from free elections. The issue had been academic for three years; now it would be joined within three weeks, and with it other issues, reconstruction and the like, which went beyond American authority as UN military agent. Psychology aside, these seemed reason enough for something new from Lake Success.

What that something should be does not seem to have taken a great deal of time or long attention from the President's advisers, to say nothing of the President. The desired General Assembly resolution was formally presented by eight UN delegations, *not* including the United States, on the last day of September.[20] Initial drafting must have been completed well before the Joint Chiefs of Staff dispatched their new directive to MacArthur. In line with the instructions given him, what Washington proposed through friends at Lake Success contained no mention of the parallel— Assembly action, in itself, would settle that—and phrased policy objectives briefly and obliquely (quoted on p. 123). The cautions to MacArthur about Russians and Chinese might not embody likelihoods; it was not thought they did. But just in case, there were to be no highly charged, unbreakably committing words upon the record. Instead, the resolution was devoted, mainly, to machinery or intentions for political and economic reconstruction of the country. What I have called a new war aim was conveyed less by the specific words than by the clear assumption underlying all the words: that military action would produce a unified, noncommunist Korea.[21]

Except from UN delegates in Moscow's sphere there was little disposition at Lake Success to argue against prompt endorsement of what Washington proposed. Only the Indians strongly urged delay. Their suggestion was put forward in the interest of a further search for some way to negotiate (which they themselves were not sure how to find). Only the Yugoslavs distinguished sharply between military tactics and policy objectives, while decrying shifts in both. But Tito's delegation, which had chosen to abstain three months before, could not claim much attention

TWO MATTERS OF CHOICE 99

from the friends of South Korea. At any rate, the partners in the fighting were agreed, most other delegations willing, votes available, and Washington committed to its own proposal. On October 4 the resolution passed the Political Committee; three days later it went through the General Assembly by a vote of 47 to 5 with 7 abstentions.[22]

It will be clear from this account what face that outcome and its preparations showed to Truman: a tying up of loose ends in his choice of a new target for the troops, a choice that merely set their prior target on new ground. It also will be clear what sort of word he had from his advisers in the circle of the National Security Council and on the day he saw the drafted UN resolution. If other words were heard from other sources, as of course they may have been, they left no traces I can find. In all events, with Acheson and the Joint Chiefs agreed, it is unlikely that he would have listened very hard. Of course, he read five newspapers; no doubt he saw expression of concern about the UN's move. But what the press conveyed were pros and cons couched mostly in the language of a crossing of the parallel. That emphasis, itself, had a significance and held a warning for him. But the language was so academic, from where Truman sat, as to dilute his interest and divert attention. I have no doubt it did. From where he sat the crossing of the parallel had already "occurred," and for good reason, on the day *he* chose to send MacArthur north, two weeks (or more) before the vote at Lake Success.

One difficulty with the press as an adviser to a President is that he has enough to crowd his calendar and mind without attending closely to debate on prospects which for him are past (unless, of course, a trial balloon is up; this was no trial balloon). Not even readers of the *New York Times*—not even its columnists—move in precisely the same time-dimension as the man who sits where Truman did in the days after Inchon.

Had something tangible occurred during those days to emphasize the diplomatic risks of moving north, one can assume that Truman's advisers would have changed their tune, the State Department, Pentagon, and press alike. But unless one took as tangible the casual word of Chinese generals or the phrasing of a Peking speech—which no one in authority inclined to do—nothing of the sort developed in the interval between Inchon and the last stages of UN proceedings.[23] Not until the first week of October did there come the sort of threat presumably envisaged in September's two directives to MacArthur. Then it came from such a source, in such a way, as to invite discounting by Americans.

On October 3 the Indian ambassador to mainland China, K. M. Panikkar, advised his government—which passed the word abroad—that Chou En-lai, the Chinese Foreign Minister, had told him:

> . . . if the United Nations forces crossed the 38th parallel China would send in troops to help the North Koreans. However, this action would not be taken if only South Koreans crossed the 38th parallel.

I quote the paraphrase in Truman's *Memoirs,* where he also sets forth, faithfully, the gist of the appraisal he received from his advisers:

> . . . the problem . . . was that Mr. Panikkar had in the past played the game of the Chinese Communists. . . . It might . . . be no more than a relay of Communist propaganda. There was also then pending in . . . the General Assembly . . . a clear authorization for the United Nations commander to operate in North Korea. The key vote on the resolution was due the following day, and it appeared quite likely that Chou En-lai's "message" was a bald attempt to blackmail the United Nations. . . .[24]

Besides, since the directives to MacArthur, Moscow not Peking had been the Pentagon's great worry. Now that the UN was on the march, an intervention by Chinese, alone, seemed relatively easy to withstand and *therefore* most unlikely to occur (an interesting exercise in logic). "They have no air," as Truman was to be told, wrongly, at Wake Island; further comfort was derived from the reflection that their ground attack had not come when it could have been decisive, near Pusan. In Washington no less than at MacArthur's headquarters there was some lack of readiness "to take seriously a country which up until this time had been notorious for its political and military weakness."[25]

Even had Peking appeared more formidable, more in earnest, less a mere blackmailer; even had the British say, not Panikkar, been chosen to transmit Chou's threat, it is improbable that Truman's chief advisers would have counseled abandoning MacArthur's broad advance or putting off the General Assembly action. It is equally improbable that Truman would have accepted such advice if offered. A threat of intervention *in Korea* could but stress the military need for rapid movement north; only there would troops find strong defense lines. And by that late date, October 3, the UN's pending action had become identified in press accounts as the "clear authorization" Truman later called it. By that time, to proceed without it would have caused immense embarrassment both at home and abroad. Not to proceed at all would have meant overturning every tactical consideration and diplomatic assumption on which policy had rested for three weeks with no more reason than a verbal warning, given second-hand, and such evaluation as could be obtained in one or two days after its receipt. Before Chou's warning, Truman's power risk was called to his attention neither by the terms of what he was deciding nor by what he learned from his associates. When the warning came, he scarcely could have chosen *not* to take the risk, no matter how aware he might have been.

This chronological account explains why Truman acted as he did in making unification the aim of the Korean War. He chose his aim because it seemed to follow from the military movement at virtually no diplomatic risk. With the military opportunity before them and with diplomatic dangers out of sight, the men he leaned on for advice saw little risk of any sort. There is nothing in the record to suggest that he saw more than they did. In June it had been clear to him that restoration of the border was worth fighting for. In August when he sanctioned plans for Inchon he evidently saw no need to take an early stand on what should happen if the enemy escaped destruction south of the border. When the contingency arose, he met it in the way that then appeared most opportune. Chou's warning challenged the perspective of the moment, but the warning was too suspect and arrived too late to affect choices taken ten days earlier. The President incurred his power risk without seeing it, or at least without assessing it, when he made the choices put to him in August and September.

Having incurred the risk before Chou's warning came, why make it worse thereafter? The question arises because Truman spent October adding to his power risk with every choice he made. The new war aim had been announced by the UN in cautious words; Truman promptly and repeatedly restated it himself without equivocation. MacArthur's northward march had been approved with qualifications; Truman promptly waived the major qualification. The President's own course throughout October heightened every danger of "wrong",meaning for Korea if there should be some substance in Chou's warning. And it cannot be said that an alternative approach was urged on Truman by his circle of advisers. Unhappily for him he chose as they advised.

The President's own choices in October consisted of words addressed to MacArthur and of other words addressed to public audiences. On October 8, the second day of general advance past the parallel, Truman approved new instructions to MacArthur in the words proposed by the Joint Chiefs of Staff and endorsed by General Marshall, now the Secretary of Defense, with Acheson's concurrence:[26]

> In light of the possible intervention of Chinese Communist forces in North Korea the following amplification of our directive [of September 25] is forwarded for your guidance:
>
> "Hereafter in the event of open or covert employment anywhere in Korea of major Chinese Communist units, without prior announcement, you should *continue the action as long as, in your judgment, action by forces now under your control offers a reasonable chance of success.*" [Italics added.][27]

"Success" as thus unqualified could not now be expected to mean anything but enemy destruction for the sake of unification. "Reasonable" now was delegated to the judgment of MacArthur with no other qualifier than a limit on his forces. In the weeks to come he would misjudge with tragic consequences, but it cannot be charged that he exceeded his instructions. Nothing said by anybody at Wake Island on October 15 qualified this delegation to MacArthur; indeed, it was confirmed by the prevailing atmosphere of confidence in him. Nothing said in public on the President's return diluted the commitment to a unified Korea. Rather the Wake Island communique, the San Francisco speech, a presidential address to the UN (at its birthday celebration on October 24), all added weight and definiteness to the war aim, publicized it further, promised its achievement cheap, and made it Truman's own. The discretion given to MacArthur in October contributed directly to disaster in November. When disaster came, the White House bore the brunt of popular frustration with the consequences of MacArthur's judgment. Truman's public statements of October contributed to this result.

Why was the President so optimistic in October? His optimism was the product, mainly, of MacArthur's confident assurance at Wake Island. The General had told Truman flatly (as the latter recollects their private conversation), "that if any Chinese were to enter Korea they would face certain disaster, but he did not expect them to try anything that foolish."[28] The President had this to match against Washington estimates that Peking *could* mount an effective intervention but probably *would* do no more than covertly assist the North Koreans. Intervention of the sort suggested by Chou's warning was discounted on all grounds of logic (Washington's) as buttressed by some diplomatic inquiries in other capitals (including Taipei, naturally, but not, of course, Peking). These estimates were scarcely worrisome; they were made less so by the General's reassurance. For Truman and his speech writers MacArthur's word sufficed—and so it seems to have done for the others at Wake Island, the Chairman of the Joint Chiefs of Staff, the State Department's Ambassador-at-Large, the Secretary of the Army, and assorted lesser lights.

Chou's warning of October 3 thus faded out of sight, and everything looked as it had before: a military victory assuring in its train a gratifying policy objective. Perhaps it is more accurate to say that the look of things by mid-October was not as it had been, it was more so. Victory was closer, the war aim was embraced in public by the President, and privately in government Korean unification grew weightier each day. In White House memoranda and in papers for the National Security Council, in intelligence evaluations, and the like, repeated use of such terms as "the UN objective," "the decision of the UN," "the UN's purpose to unify," soon dulled awareness that the new war aim was nothing but a target of opportunity chosen rather casually (and at first provisionally) by the very men who read these words. The tendency of bureaucratic language to create in private the same images presented to the public never should be underrated. By the middle of October, I would say, in their minds no less than in public, Truman and the rest were thinking of the UN aim not as a mere convenience but as a cause.

When Truman spoke at San Francisco and at Lake Success he had no inkling that the Chinese had begun a massive, hidden move across the Yalu. Two weeks after Wake Island some five Chinese armies were established in the mountainous terrain directly north of the peninsula. Reinforced, by stealth, for four weeks more, that striking force was almost to destroy MacArthur. Even before November 1 it made a mockery of his existing orders. We know that now, but Truman did not know it then. The location of the Chinese striking force remained unknown to the Americans until it struck, November 28.

Truman did learn early in November that the war would not end on the pleasant note his government had sounded. Two weeks after his address at the UN he knew the outcome could not be successful in the way he had defined success. By late

October Chinese presence in Korea was confirmed from contacts on the battlefield. In the first week of November MacArthur insisted upon bombing Yalu bridges because troops "pouring" south threatened "ultimate destruction of the [UN] forces. . . ."[29] Before November 10, Truman's advisers had informed him, in effect, that military action limited to present forces, confined to Korea, could not achieve the military target set September 27: destruction of the enemy's armed forces. Everyone agreed that no more troops could be spared for MacArthur and that he should not enlarge the boundaries of the war. But he now faced a new enemy with airpower and troops massed north of the Yalu and with several tens of thousand men already south of it. So Washington believed when UN aircraft were employed against the Yalu bridges. Washington was wrong about proportions north and south, but it was no secret that the river probably would be a bridge of ice before MacArthur could complete his occupation of North Korea. At the least, negotiation would be necessary to that occupation; necessary to its maintenance and probably to its achievement. At the most, if Peking meant the worst, unification would no longer be a viable objective; Chinese *capabilities* were not in doubt.

Thus within a month of MacArthur's march past the thirty-eighth parallel, it became plain that the policy objective, the war aim, once supposed to follow from the military action, now could only follow from a diplomatic deal with the unrecognized, avowedly hostile claimants to Formosa—or be given up entirely. That these were the alternatives of policy, and that there were no others short of risking general war, was clear from the intelligence available to Washington in the first week of November. As Truman's *Memoirs* show, the policy dilemma was implicitly *accepted* by all parties to a National Security Council discussion on November 9. The President was not among the parties on that day. He got a briefing afterwards, however, and acceded to the views he heard expressed. Truman has recorded Acheson's summation of those views:

> . . . [Acheson] pointed out that it was agreed that General MacArthur's directive should not now be changed and *he should be free to do what he could in a military way,* but without bombing Manchuria. At the same time, the State Department would seek ways to find out whether negotiations with the Chinese Communists were possible, although one problem was that we lacked any direct contacts with the Peiping regime . . . . [Italics added.][30]

In other words, MacArthur's opportunity, once the *occasion* for a new war aim, now was reduced to "doing what he could" in aid of diplomatic efforts no less dubious than those urged by the Indians six weeks earlier. So far as this had the discussion wandered from assumptions—and from preconditions—voiced in mid-September.

With Washington's assumptions changed, why were MacArthur's orders left unaltered? Why was he still to pursue the objective of September 27 with the discretion of October 8? Why was the man whom Truman had considered firing in

August now left the discretion to attempt what Washington no longer thought he could achieve? The National Security Council discussion of November 9 suggests an answer. To quote again from Truman's *Memoirs:*

> General Bradley stated that . . . [if] the Chinese desired only to set up a buffer area . . . negotiations might be fruitful . . . [but if not] . . . *we should be able to hold in the general area of our present positions* . . . [with] . . . increasing question of how much pressure we could stand without attacking Manchurian bases.

> . . . Marshall pointed out . . . that our eastern front in Korea was widely dispersed and thinly spread and that this represented an added risk. . . . Bradley replied that of course General MacArthur had done this in order *to carry out his directive that he was to occupy the whole country and hold elections.*

> . . . Acheson asked . . . if there was any line that was better from a military point of view than the *present* one, and Bradley replied that . . . the farther *back* . . . the easier it would be to maintain. . . . however, he realized that *any backward movement . . . might lose us the South Koreans' will to fight.* [Italics added.][31]

In terms of foreign policy, to halt MacArthur or to pull him back would not have clarified Chinese intentions; neither would it aid the diplomatic bargaining. In military terms to call a halt seemed overcautious, given *policy* objectives and the chance these could be salvaged by diplomacy. In fact there was no chance, but Truman's National Security Council advisers did not know that. Instead, they knew, or rather thought, that Peking very likely wanted only a buffer zone. They reasoned, it appears, that mainland China was dependent on the Russians and that more ambitious wants would mean *Russia* was courting war. As Bradley put it to the National Security Council, Peking's alternative intentions might be either "to force us into a war of attrition . . . where we might be in danger of losing if the Soviets decided to start a global war," or "to drive us completely off the Korean peninsula . . . [which] would mean World War III because [the Chinese] would be unable to do it alone, and Soviet entry would inevitably extend the fighting. . . ." But Moscow, it was thought, did not want general war; the Chinese, then, would have to show restraint.

Why these Americans, who had proclaimed *their own* aversion to world war, should have thought Stalin would assume that *he* risked general war if Peking acted, I will not endeavor to explain. It is enough to see that this is how they reasoned; thereby they discounted what they knew on November 9. Besides, there was the thing they did not know: that Peking's striking force was on the *south* side of the Yalu.

With Chinese aims misunderstood, with Moscow's risks misread, with this one fact unknown, Truman's advisers focused on the diplomatic prospects as intently as they once had done on military opportunities. While they sought to assess the chances for diplomacy, MacArthur should "do what he could." This was the course they urged upon the President after their meeting of November 9. This was the course he followed. The issue as it reached him wore a diplomatic face which fatally obscured the military risk, a reversal, in effect, of late September's situation. But this time, in contrast with the other, the issue's look cannot be said to have obscured the risk to his own influence. On the contrary, its diplomatic features bore a strong family resemblance to those of his prestige. By then United States prestige, UN prestige, were quite as much committed in the world as his at home. By then his problem in relation to his public had become how best to back away from his October promises without harming the many things that made retreat worthwhile. His problem had become how best to make some outcome short of "victory" teach tolerance for him and for his aims. His problem had become how best to *act* in order to *enlighten*. And with but a change of pronoun this conveys his country's problem in relation to its enemies and its allies.

There is no reason to believe that Truman's chief advisers, or the President, himself, considered his prestige apart from issues of diplomacy. Had they done so in these circumstances it is probable that their course would have been much the same. In essence the considerations were alike on either score. Both counseled a postponement of decision. While it was thought that Peking might negotiate, why halt MacArthur before bargaining began? If the Chinese intended otherwise, there was all the more reason for allowing them to demonstrate, so everyone could see, that their aggression, not timidity in Washington, had thwarted the UN and stopped MacArthur. Besides, he had done better at Inchon than his superiors expected; conceivably he might do so again. Thus ran the logic, it appears, beneath the surface of discussion in the National Security Council, a logic quite as good in prestige terms as in those of diplomacy.

This was good logic if Peking's forces were where they were thought to be and if MacArthur's generalship was as infallible as Inchon had suggested. In the fifteen days between November 9 and MacArthur's march into an enemy trap, Washington learned little more of Chinese dispositions. Indeed, their forward elements now broke off contact, which encouraged the opinion that their purpose was defensive and their show of force intended but to emphasize the border. Meanwhile MacArthur, seeming confident again after his scare about the Yalu bridges, hurried preparations for a victory march with scattered forces fanning out to occupy the country. His troops began to move November 25; within three days the Chinese struck, not from beyond the Yalu but from mountains to the south of it, between MacArthur's columns and behind them. What then occurred, in military terms, was "one of the major decisive battles of the present century, followed by the longest retreat in American history." [32] The Chinese did not demonstrate mere power to deny the UN victory; they demonstrated power to deprive MacArthur of his whole success since Inchon—a power his deployment placed into their hands.

It was one thing to leave MacArthur's orders unchanged on November 9; it was quite another to leave them unchanged day by day thereafter while he prepared and began his victory march. On November 9 the National Security Council had agreed that directives to MacArthur should be "kept under review," pending "clarification" of Peking's intent. In accepting this agreement Truman had postponed a change of orders; he had not intended to decide the issue for all time. Yet this postponement of decision proved to be one of the most decisive actions Truman ever took. So far as I can ascertain his National Security Council advisers did not raise with him, nor he with them, the question of concluding that postponement. In the two-week interval before MacArthur's march the General, not the President, became the judge and arbiter of White House risks. Action in October had heightened Truman's personal risk; inaction in November heightened every danger, military, diplomatic, and personal alike. Why, then, did Truman passively await the outcome of MacArthur's plans for victory? I have explained why orders to the General went unchanged in the second week of November. But why were they not altered in the third week or the fourth?

Poor intelligence, or poor evaluation, may account for MacArthur's conduct, but it does not suffice to explain Washington's behavior in the days before his victory march. Although no one there *knew* where the Chinese were, the Pentagon, as least, included men who could read maps and knew where they *might* be. By mid-November some of these men felt virtually certain of the real Chinese location and were becoming worried lest MacArthur fail to concentrate his forces. Before those forces marched, the worry had touched Truman's chief advisers. In the last days, reportedly, it was intense in Bradley's mind and Marshall's and in Acheson's. The British, whose diplomatic fears had outrun Washington's kept urging that the troops be stopped and forward columns pulled back to the "waist." The American Joint Chiefs of Staff were not prepared to sacrifice MacArthur's plans on London's say-so, but Pentagon unhappiness about those separate columns grew apace, and he was practically implored to show more caution. When he demurred, as under his instructions he had every right to do, the Chiefs of Staff lacked courage (lacking certainty) to seek their alteration from the President. Despite the worry, no one went to Truman—and that outcome turns on matters more complex than poor intelligence.

No one went to Truman because everyone thought someone else should go. Before November 25 the men who had concluded two weeks earlier that Truman should not change MacArthur's orders were agreed, it seems, in wishing that he would. The diplomatic emphasis of earlier discussion ceased to obscure military risks; when those grew sharp enough, it reinforced them. The logic of November 9 led to an opposite conclusion some days later, in the light of what these men had come to fear. On November 9 the Chairman of the Joint Chiefs, Bradley, had waived military risks in deference to foreign policy; his words appear on p. 141. But policy had not envisaged tactical disaster; policy suggested its avoidance at all costs. When worry grew, the military chiefs deferred to State; let Acheson, as guardian of "policy," ask Truman to reverse MacArthur. But Acheson, already under fire from the Capitol, was treading warily between the Pentagon and that inveterate idealist about generals, Harry Truman. In immediate terms the risk was "military"; if it justified reversing the commander in the field, then the Joint Chiefs must make the judgment and tell Truman. So Acheson is said to have insisted, understandably enough, and there the matter rested.[33] On a "military" issue the Chiefs of Staff were loath to balk the victor of Inchon, whose tactics might be better than they seemed 8000 miles away. As for the Secretary of Defense, he had preceded Acheson in State and had been Army Chief of Staff when Bradley was a subordinate commander. Since his return to government Marshall had leaned over backwards not to meddle with the work of his successors in *their* jobs. He also had leaned over backwards not to revive the old Army feud between him and MacArthur. What Acheson and Bradley were not ready to initiate, Marshall evidently felt he could not take upon himself.

For Cabinet members and for military chiefs, a decision to go to the President is something like a government's decision to go to war; it is not something done each day on every issue. When the issue is reversal of established plans on grounds of sheer conjecture, men of prudence and responsibility may pause, and no wonder. In this instance, moreover, the plans were MacArthur's, and Truman was a man who liked to deal in the concrete.

The President, meanwhile, had little thought of overriding, on his own, the tactical decisions of a qualified commander. That seems to be the face the issue wore for Truman, personally, just before the win-the-war offensive: "You pick your man, you've got to back him up. That's the only way a military organization can work." If he perceived the policy and power risks beneath this surface, these were outweighed by fidelity to military doctrine. That weighting his advisers did not urge him to reverse. Instead, they all kept up the search for clarification. They still were seeking it on November 28.[34]

IV

By hindsight it is tragic that MacArthur did not halt along a line on which he might have blunted or withstood attack—tragic in human terms as well as in the worldly terms of policy and politics. But the elements of tragedy were not produced from nowhere in November; they were seeded before Inchon and matured at Wake Island. By November only the precise amount of loss remained in question. By then the answer rested with a government that Washington knew least of any in the world, and with a general Truman had considered firing in August. The essence of the tragedy, though not its outside shape, is that a President should have walked into such a corner facing front; he was not pushed, he chose. September's choices, and October's took him there.

Truman walked in step with his advisers; on numbers of occasions he could hardly have done otherwise; now and then, however, he might have changed the pace or the direction. In August 1950, when he approved plans for Inchon, Truman might have nailed down publicly his aim of June: a restoration of the South Korean border. If he had done so then, success at Inchon would have achieved "victory" and Truman could have called on the UN to guard the border. In September 1950, after he approved a crossing of the parallel, he might have justified MacArthur's northward march on other grounds than unification. Eight months later, as UN troops were marching north again, their target came to be the first good natural defense line past the border. In October 1950 it might have been the "better" line above the waist of the peninsula. This line was north of the most populous, productive part of North Korea. More realism and less appetite in Washington might have suggested this as victory enough. But Truman did as his advisers urged and tied himself to unification. He tied himself tighter by his statements in October; MacArthur's confidence erased Chou's threat. This is quite understandable but scarcely seems inevitable. And early in November when Washington deferred a change of orders to MacArthur, Truman might have taken steps to let the General know that his directives now meant something rather different than they had been thought to mean when they were issued. In mid-November, a few Pentagon officials talked among themselves about a Marshall visit to MacArthur. Nothing came of this. Something like it—or a new directive—might have cut the costs of Chinese intervention. Truman could have taken the initiative; he did not take it. These might-have-dones are not presented as suggestions of what should have been. Truman, after all, proceeded without benefit of hindsight. These speculations have no other purpose than to demonstrate that he had *some* control of his direction.

This story of choice-making was preceded by another, where a different President in other circumstances also strode face-forward to a corner. By comparison, that Eisenhower instance may appear a "simple" matter, almost comic in its momentary setting and results. But with a longer view it takes on a complexity, even a tragic quality, to match this example from the Korean War. For Humphrey's press explosion was the first of many episodes in a domestic war of interests and of policies foreshadowing the future of our politics. What caused the doubts in Eisenhower's mind were durable dilemmas we shall carry with us through the 1960's. By letting Humphrey speak for him in different words than his, Eisenhower merely publicized the fact that he was forced to seek opposed objectives which had torn the patchwork holding them together through his earlier years: stability *and* growth, defense *and* welfare, funds for public services *and* funds in private hands. At the moment he was re-elected Eisenhower faced the job of reconciling these anew, or of opening the way toward reconciliation by a successor of his choosing. This proved to be a harder job than he was prepared for. Within a year he virtually abandoned it and jettisoned his tentative approach to reconciliation, "Modern Republicanism." Taken alone, his approval of the Humphrey press conference is a minor incident. Perspective dignifies it as a sign of things to come.

Despite their surface differences, my two examples are alike in what they have to show: how *not* to extract power out of choice. The Presidents in both these cases failed to make their choices serve their influence. They failed because they left out of account the stakes for them, in person. They did not reckon their own risks because they saw the issues through the eyes of their advisers. And personal stakes were not the terms in which they got advice. What Eisenhower saw around his Cabinet table in January 1957 was gloom upon the faces of the men he most respected in the spheres of economics and finance and *party* politics. The choice before him featured fiscal policy; accordingly he took those spheres of expertise as relevant, and worried as he watched the experts worrying. What Truman heard in late September and the first weeks of October 1950 was a confident discounting of the military-diplomatic dangers in Korea. The choices then before him wore the guise of military orders backed by diplomatic action; expertise in those two spheres he took to be controlling, and he acted as his experts recommended.

In both these instances the net result was a neglect of the one sphere of expertise where "experts" were laymen: the sphere of personal power for the President himself. It can be said of Truman's instance that the experts went astray on their home grounds; in Eisenhower's case their views diverged. But error or division is to be expected among experts. Amidst the revolutions of our time expert misjudgments are the norm, and experts regularly differ with each other. It also can be said of both these cases that the President, as layman, would not challenge his own experts on *their* grounds. But this should be expected from most Presidents, the more so as the issues grow remote from their experience. In democratic systems—and in modern life—a Winston Churchill is a rarity. The lesson of these cases does not come down to the fact that experts often will be wrong, or to the further fact that Presidents may balk at second-guessing them. Those facts but underscore the perils of neglecting personal power.

The lesson of these cases is that when it comes to power, nobody is expert but the President; if he, too, acts as layman, it goes hard with him.

Expertise in power terms is not a substitute for expertise in policy; it offers some protection, though, from errors and from bafflements in policy appraisal. From those a President needs all the guarding he can get, as the examples of this chapter have made plain. And he, himself, the layman in most areas of policy, has no better protector than concern for his own power. A sense of Truman's power stakes could not have clarified Peking's intent, but what it could have done was shift the weight assigned Chou's threat. A small risk militarily or diplomatically was a big risk in terms of Truman's influence, considering his order of priorities. Once Panikkar's report was seen, if not before, a firm appreciation of the *presidential* risk would have suggested caution, militarily, and moves to qualify, not boost, the new war aim. Similarly, a sense of Eisenhower's personal stakes could not have eased his policy dilemmas, but it could have changed the weight assigned to Humphrey's sense of urgency. The latter might be trustworthy, but why entrust to anyone the blurring of the President's own budget presentation? The moment Humphrey's text was read at Cabinet meeting, sensitivity to Washington reactions would have prompted doubts about a Treasury press conference on Budget Day. To compensate for deficiencies in other sorts of counsel, expertness on power has some obvious advantages.

It may be, in a given situation, that counsels both of power and of policy point in the same direction. I have suggested that this could have been the case when Truman, in November 1950, agreed to a postponement of decision on changed orders for MacArthur. Even so, a consciousness of power stakes apart from policy affords a President protection toward the future. I think it highly likely that had Truman been more mindful of his personal risk when he postponed decision on a change of orders, he would have been insistent, day by day thereafter, that his chief advisers justify renewed postponement. Had he pushed them hard they scarcely could have done so.

In other situations it may be that an event or policy leaves no room for maneuver, regardless of the risk in personal terms. I have suggested that this might have been the case with Eisenhower in the days just after Humphrey's press conference. It certainly appears the case with Truman in the days just following Chou's statement to the Indian Ambassador. Yet here again the service of a power sense in posting *caution* signs could have helped both these Presidents to side-step later pitfalls in the paths laid out for them by their advisers.

No doubt there can be quite as much uncertainty, as much misjudgment, in the expert use of power as in a specialty of any other sort. *A sensitivity to power's stakes and sources is no cure-all.* Oversensitivity to any one aspect at any time might wreck the very things a President most wanted and leave him beneath the ruins. To speculate, it appears possible that in the spring of 1951 a full-scale war with China would have heightened, momentarily, the response of home publics to the man then in the White House. But its net effect on Washington, on publics overseas, and on his own priority objectives could have been disastrous. Ultimately, one supposes, so would have been popular reaction in this country. Truman never put that sort of stock in popularity; it was as well for him that he did not.

Appearances can be no less deceptive in the sphere of personal power than in spheres of diplomacy, or military tactics, or economics, or party politics, or any other. The sources of a President's own influence are various; his stakes in any act of choice are multiple and changeable. At given times he may misread the face of power no less than of policy. At some times he may be unable to affect his situation even though he reads them both aright. My point is *not* that he can guarantee against those fates, but merely that his chance to ward them off improves as he impresses on his choices expertise from *every* sphere of relevance, his own sphere with the rest: the sphere of personal power.

But if he is to bring his own sphere into play, *he* has to do it. If he is to do it, he must overcome the difficulty that his personal stakes may not show on the surface of the issues put before him or be stressed in the advice of his advisers. The likelihoods, indeed, are that those stakes will be obscured. This chapter's two examples merely indicate the likelihoods. What occurred in these cases is what always tends to happen. While experts in all spheres except his own advised the President from where they sat, their judgments hid from him the need for personal perspective. They did not take his own look for him (how could they?), but neither did their presentations prompt him to start looking. Presumably, there was in this no "sabotage," no bad intent. In neither instance is there much indication that advisers acted "irresponsibly." Each seems to have performed his duty as he saw it; none sat where the President did. Truman's choices were more serious and his own risks less obvious than Eisenhower's. But both men were the victims of reliance upon issues and advisers to do more than any President can count on them to do—to clarify his stakes of personal power.

I prefaced the account of Truman's war aim for Korea with assertions drawn from Eisenhower's "go ahead" to Humphrey: if choices are the means by which a President builds power, it is only as he sees his power stakes in what he does that choices become building blocks *for him*. To see may or may not be to decide, but at the least it is to be forewarned. *Yet nobody and nothing helps a President to see, save as he helps himself.* Those are the words my second story was to test. The question still remains, how can he help himself?

CHAPTER 7

Men in Office

"The President needs help," wrote the Brownlow Committee of 1936 in its famous report on administrative management.[1] Since then "help" has been heaped upon his office in the form of staff facilities of every sort.[2] The visibility of this development has been so high that scholars have a name for it: the "institutionalized Presidency." Some of its advantages have been so obvious that competent observers are unstinting in their praise. "It converts the Presidency," writes Clinton Rossiter, "into an instrument of twentieth century government; it gives the incumbent a sporting chance to stand the strain and fulfill his constitutional mandate . . . . "[3]

As Rossiter suggests, the Presidency's clerkship could no longer be performed without the staff support provided now to Presidents. In that sense the great growth of staff since 1936 is an undoubted help to White House occupants who seek effective power for themselves. Shorn of the possibility of actual performance, formal powers would confer few practical advantages and Washington relationships would cease to be a source of influence for Presidents in person.

However, only in that sense can it be said that modern staffing has helped Presidents hold power. A "sporting chance" to do the chores of office will not automatically turn doing into influence. Helping a President perform his chores is a far cry from helping him see personal stakes in his own acts of choice. The question now before us is how help in this second sense can be obtained. By way of answer, it is not sufficient to gesture toward the "institutionalized Presidency." A Budget Bureau and a Cabinet secretariat were little help to Eisenhower in the Humphrey case. The absence of a National Security Council did not harm Truman's handling of the Marshall Plan. Its presence did not help him in Korea.

A President is helped by what he gets into *his* mind. His first essential need is information. No doubt he needs the data that advisers can provide. He also needs to know the little things they fail to mention. To illustrate, it is reliably reported that by mid-December 1956 the Secretary of the Treasury was declining to take phone calls from the Director of the Budget. In effect, Humphrey had broken off diplomatic relations with Brundage. This is a little thing and an affair of "personalities"; a thing of just the sort that Eisenhower seemingly disliked to hear and his associates disliked to tell him. But what could be more useful for a President to know while those two personalities conversed at Cabinet table? If nothing else aroused his sense of danger to himself, this knowledge might have done it. In January 1957, immediately after Humphrey's press explosion, Brundage was prepared to-argue strongly for the rightness of the Eisenhower budget as it stood, and for the practical necessity of rallying to its defense in public. Brundage went so far as to prepare a White House press release for issuance that very afternoon. But he got no encouragement from White House staff officials, and he did not feel he could appeal over their heads. Within a week he had lost heart and changed his tune. Eisenhower, it appears, was spared the knowledge that his Budget Director once had thought it right as well as politic for him to disassociate himself from Humphrey's stand. Yet few things could have helped as much as this to give the President a sense that *he* was playing in a hard game for high stakes. No matter what he might have done with Brundage's advice, the very force of Brundage's reaction was a warning sign.

It is not information of a general sort that helps a President see personal stakes; not summaries, not surveys, not the bland amalgams. Rather, as these illustrations will suggest, it is the odds and ends of tangible detail that pieced together in his mind illuminate the underside of issues put before him. To help himself he must reach out as widely as he can for every scrap of fact, opinion, gossip, bearing on his interests and relationships as President. He must become his own director of his own central intelligence. For that directorship two rules of conduct can be drawn from the case studies in this book. On the one hand, he never can assume that anyone or any system will supply the bits and pieces he needs most; on the other hand, he must assume that much of what he needs will not be volunteered by his official advisers.

To fill one's mind with odds and ends is only the beginning. What helps is not the information, merely, but its meaning. Not only need a President know tangible details, he also needs to have a frame of reference. The information that a Brundage wanted White House disavowal of a Humphrey might mean no more than "parochialism" to a President unless he grasped the workings of the budget process well enough to sense that every agency and scores of congressmen were treasuring commitments which they took to be from *him*. Yet sensitivity to processes, to who does what and how, is hard to gain except by joining in the doing. The same thing can be said of sensitivity to substance; one gains by joining in the argument.

Presidents are always being told that they should leave details to others. It is dubious advice. Exposure to details of operation and of policy provides the frame of reference for details of information. To be effective as his own director of intelligence, a President need be his own executive assistant.[4] He need be both, that is to say, *if he would help himself*.

This is the help that starts a man along the road to power. Information in his mind and rightly understood alerts him to his personal stakes when choices come before him. By taking his own stakes into account he does what he can do to make a choice contribute to his influence. By choosing he builds power in the only way he can. If power is his object, to inform himself is help indeed. By the same token, though, it is not help enough.

A President in search of power cannot rest content to be informed. Along with data in his mind he needs the choices in his hands. But power-laden choices may not reach him; others may pre-empt them or foreclose them. Or they may reach him so late that personal perspective has no bearing on his options. Situations of both sorts will be familiar to the readers of case studies in this book. In theory, any President, informed enough and sensitive enough to what he knew, could make such situations go away, at will, by reaching out and down for just the choices that he wanted. In practice, though, he rarely has the time. However much he knows, however sharp his senses, his time remains the prisoner of first-things-first. And almost always something else comes first.

A President's own use of time, his allocation of his personal attention, is governed by the things he *has* to do from day to day: the speech he has agreed to make, the fixed appointment he cannot put off, the paper no one else can sign, the rest and exercise his doctors order. These doings may be far removed from academic images of White House concentration on high policy, grand strategy. There is no help for that. A President's priorities are set not by the relative importance of a task, buy by the relative necessity for him to do it. He deals first with the things that are required of *him* next. Deadlines rule his personal agenda. In most days of his working week, most seasons of his year, he meets deadlines enough to drain his energy and crowd his time regardless of all else. The net result may be a far cry from the order of priorities that would appeal to scholars or to columnists—or to the President himself.

What makes a deadline? The answer, very simply, is a date or an event or both combined. The date set by MacArthur for a landing at Inchon, or the date set by statute for submission of the budget, or the date set by the White House for a press conference, these and others like them force decisions on a President, pre-empt his time. And statements by MacArthur, or a Humphrey press explosion, or a House appropriations cut, or sputniks overhead, may generate such pressure inside government or out as to affect him in precisely the same way. Dates make deadlines in proportion to their certainty; events make deadlines in proportion to their heat. Singly or combined, approaching dates and rising heat start fires burning underneath the White House. Trying to stop fires is what Presidents do first. It takes most of their time.

The rule of first things first is a decided drag upon a President who seeks to make his choices serve his power. The choices lacking dates or heat may end in others' hands or be precluded by events; the choices he takes first may be distorted by their urgency. And even though he knows an issue he should reach for, even though he senses one escaping from his hands, the knowledge will not help him if the rule of first things first gets in his way. To sense what he should do if he had time is not enough. The most informed and most alert of Presidents needs something more: he needs the means to make himself take time. He needs means of putting pressure on himself, of imposing new deadlines on himself, to come to grips with those things he would want to make his own if he were free to interfere and pick and choose at will. Deadlines self-imposed are no less helpful to a President than tangible details. The one informs his mind, the other arms his hand. Together they contribute what he needs when he seeks power.

No President has been more conscious of those needs or more adroit in meeting them than Franklin Roosevelt. Roosevelt can be criticized on many grounds, but least of all for failure to protect his personal power stakes in his own acts of choice. As Arthur Schlesinger reports:

> The first task of an executive, as he evidently saw it, was to guarantee himself an effective flow of information and ideas. . . . Roosevelt's persistent effort therefore was to check and balance information acquired through official channels by information acquired through a myriad of private, informal, and unorthodox channels and espionage networks. At times he seemed almost to pit his personal sources against his public sources.[5]

His personal sources were the product of a sociability and curiosity that reached back to the other Roosevelt's time. He had an enormous acquaintance in various phases of national life and at various levels of government; he also had his wife and her variety of contacts. He extended his acquaintanceships abroad; in the war years Winston Churchill, among others, became a "personal source." Roosevelt quite deliberately exploited these relationships and mixed them up to widen his own range of information. He changed his sources as his interests changed, but no one who had ever interested him was quite forgotten or immune to sudden use. Roosevelt's search for information was an extraordinary, virtuoso performance. Besides, it was effective. Through his long tenure F.D.R. had more grasp of the details that can help a man build power than most Presidents before or either President since.

The essence of Roosevelt's technique for information-gathering was competition. "He would call you in," one of his aides once told me, "and he'd ask you to get the story on some complicated business, and you'd come back after a couple of days of hard labor and present the juicy morsel you'd uncovered under a stone somewhere, and *then* you'd find out he knew all about it, along with something else you *didn't* know. Where he got his information from he wouldn't mention, usually, but after he had done this to you once or twice you got damn careful about *your* information.''

Roosevelt was as much a master of the self-created deadline as of self-directed networks of intelligence. Here, too, his method centered on the fostering of competition. To quote Schlesinger again:

> His favorite technique was to keep grants of authority incomplete, jurisdictions uncertain, charters overlapping. The result of this competitive theory of administration was often confusion and exasperation on the operating level; but no other method could so reliably insure that in a large bureaucracy filled with ambitious men eager for power the decisions, and the power to make them, would remain with the President.[6]

Not only did he keep his organizations overlapping and divide authority among them, but he also tended to put men of clashing temperaments, outlooks, ideas, in charge of them. Competitive personalities mixed with competing jurisdictions was Roosevelt's formula for putting pressure on himself, for making his subordinates push up to him the choices they could not take for themselves. It also made them advertise their punches; their quarrels provided him not only heat but information. Administrative competition gave him two rewards. He got the choices and due notice, both.

As a result he also got that treasure for a President, time to defer decision. By and large, his built-in competitions forced the choices to him early, or at least made him aware that they were coming. He, not others, then disposed of time to seek and to apply his own perspective. Schlesinger provides a sharp, insightful sketch of F.D.R.'s approach to a decision:

> He evidently felt that clear-cut administrative decisions would 'work only if they expressed equally clear-cut realities of administrative competence and vigor. If they did not, if the balance of administrative power would not sustain the decision, then decision would only compound confusion and discredit government. And the actualities of administrative power were to be discovered, not by writing—or by reading—Executive orders, but by apprehending through intuition a vast constellation of political forces. His complex administrative sensibility, infinitely subtle and sensitive, was forever weighing questions of personal force, of political timing, of congressional concern, of partisan benefit, of public interest. Situations had to be permitted to develop, to crystallize, to clarify; the competing forces had to vindicate themselves in the actual pull and tug of conflict; public opinion had to face the question, consider it, pronounce upon it—only then, at the long, frazzled end, would the President's intuitions consolidate and precipitate a result.[7]

But this approach was only possible if he held the decision in *his* hands. It may seem paradoxical, but deadlines self-imposed helped him employ the technique of postponement. Delay then helped him see and weigh his stakes of personal power. Sometimes he miscalculated, but he rarely failed to make the calculation and he rarely lacked for time.[8]

These Rooseveltian devices are almost literally the opposite of those employed in Eisenhower's Presidency. Eisenhower often was reported in the press to have transformed the White House into an Army Headquarters. That he did not do—nobody could—but he did manage to impart more superficial symmetry and order to his flow of information and of choices than was ever done before. Thereby, he became typically the last man in his office to know tangible details and the last to come to grips with acts of choice. His one-time chief assistant in the White House, Sherman Adams, is reported to have told a close associate: "I count the day lost when I have not found some new way of lightening the President's load." This but suggests the spirit of the "staff system," so called, in Eisenhower's time. The aims of that system were of the best. Within its limits it was reasonably well-designed and rather more than reasonably effective. In Eisenhower's instance there is no disputing that it may have been essential to his health and peace of mind. But its workings often were disastrous for his hold on personal power.

What was pernicious about all the staffs and inter-agency committees and the paper-flows around this President was not their mere existence. Many of them had been there before; others no doubt will go on long after. The difficulty, rather, was that they became almost his only source of information and of issues to decide. This was the case particularly, and quite understandably, after his heart attack in 1955. Thereafter for at least three years the "staff system" came to be, in fact, almost as much in charge of Eisenhower's business as it always was in theory. The only great exception seems to have been foreign relations; there, at least while Dulles was alive, the Secretary of State in person took the "system's" place.[9]

The Humphrey case in Chapter 6 and many of the incidents described in Chapter 4 attest to details or to choices spared the President, until too late, by staff work aimed at lightening his load. And there is reason to believe that his dependence on such staff work grew the greater as it served him so. In the words of one official close to White House operations and decidedly in sympathy with Eisenhower:

> The process has been cumulative since the heart attack. Then there were massive delegations which simply followed the existing lines to Adams and on down. Those delegations were administered by men who told each other (and themselves), "don't bother the boss," "can't do this to him now." But the less he was bothered, the less he knew, and the less he knew, the less confidence he felt in his own judgment. He let himself grow stale. . . . That made the delegations irreversible. It made him cling the tighter to the judgments of the people already around him. The less he trusted himself, the more he *had* to trust them. And they thought the way to help him was to "spare" him. A lot of this was very well intentioned.[10]

The process of cumulative delegation seems to have been reversed by Sherman Adam's resignation in the fall of 1958 and by the loss of Dulles some months later. Reportedly, more issues and more detail reached the President in 1959 than at any time since 1955. Apparently, however, these still reached him through his "system." The change lay not in his methods but in partial relaxation of the system's vast protectiveness upon departure of the prime protectors. Even so, the relaxation helped him. Within the White House, Adams was replaced by not one man but a group of former subordinates who now gained equal access to the President. Most members of this group were more experienced in government than Adams had been. The "new" Eisenhower of 1959 is attributable partly to this new arrangement. The irony is that Eisenhower had been loath to let Adams resign.

An Eisenhower fully fit, much less a cardiac case, could not have been expected to assist himself in quite the Roosevelt way. The government he headed in the Fifties was far bigger, more impersonal, than Roosevelt's in the Thirties. No President can spread himself across the whole of *post*-Rooseveltian government. Roosevelt, for his own part, took the first steps toward the "institutionalized Presidency." But Roosevelt rarely let himself become its prisoner. Few persons or procedures ever got exclusive license to secure his information or to time his choices for him. None held such a license very long. That is the essential difference. Eisenhower did not merely alter Roosevelt's methods; Eisenhower's methods often left him helpless. The contrast goes considerably deeper than the presence or the absence of a "staff system." The crucial thing is that effective competitions were not built into the system.

Eisenhower had no need to foster competition by confusing jurisdictions. Cold war and welfare programs automatically confused them; policies and operations cut across the boundaries marked on organization charts. Yet Eisenhower evidently made no conscious effort to turn these confusions to his own account by mixing in competitive personalities. To be sure there were men of different temperaments and views around him. But a Stassen does not guarantee much competition for a Humphrey if the one is merely a Disarmament Assistant while the other holds that massive post of institutional authority, the Treasury Department. And even though their institutional positions seem to match, a Budget Director scarcely offers competition to the chief White House assistant when the one man is a Brundage and the other an Adams. Eisenhower's use of men tended to smother, not enhance, the competition roused by overlapping jurisdictions. Apparently this was intentional; the Roosevelt formula was not misused, it was rejected. Eisenhower, seemingly, preferred to let subordinates proceed upon the lowest common denominators of agreement than to have their quarrels—and issues and details—pushed up to him.

The contrast between Roosevelt's way and Eisenhower's way suggests a further question: why does one man give himself the help he needs; why does the other man deny it to himself? I have outlined what a President can do to help himself. But what brings him to do it?

II

Roosevelt's methods were the product of his insights, his incentives, and his confidence. No President in this century has had a sharper sense of personal power, a sense of what it is and where it comes from; none has had more hunger for it, few have had more use for it, and only one or two could match his faith in his own competence to use it. Perception and desire and self-confidence, combined, produced their own reward. No modern President has been more nearly master in the White House.

Roosevelt had a love affair with power in that place. It was an early romance and it lasted all his life. Behind his sensitivity there lay a long and relevant experience: seven years of bureaucratic free-wheeling as *the* Assistant Secretary of the Navy, four years as the Governor of New York State, a quarter-century in party politics, and with it all, an "Uncle Ted." Experience informed a temperament precisely suited to absorb what it could teach about the nature and uses of real power in high office. For Roosevelt, this was fun. Experience also informed a fixed *intention* to possess the power of the highest office. Roosevelt always wanted the Presidency and mastery was what he wanted from it.

He wanted power for its own sake; he also wanted what it could achieve. The challenge and the fun of power lay not just in having, but in doing. His private satisfactions were enriched by public purposes and these grew more compelling as more power came his way. Political experience and private life created in him not an ideology but a decided feeling for what government should be and where its policies should lead. In terms of fixed commitments to particular solutions he was neither a "New Dealer" nor an "internationalist." But he shared with men in both of these camps a feeling of direction. And happily for him, his own sense of direction coincided, in the main, with the course of contemporary history. His purposes ran with and not against the grain of what was going to happen in his time. His sense of power thus was reinforced by his sense of direction. Unlike a Herbert Hoover he was not caught in the trap of fighting history. But neither was he caught asleep and left behind.

Roosevelt had another ground for wanting to be President: it seemed to him so fitting. The White House was for him almost a family seat and like the other Roosevelt he regarded the whole country almost as a family property. Once he became the President of the United States that sense of fitness gave him an extraordinary confidence. Roosevelt, almost alone among our Presidents, had no conception of the office to live up to; he was it. His image of the office was himself-in-office. The memoirs left by his associates agree on this if nothing else: he saw the job of being President as being F.D.R. He wanted mastery, projected that desire on the office and fulfilled it there with every sign of feeling he had come into his own. Self-confidence so based was bound to reinforce his sense of purpose and to guarantee reliance on his sense of power. His methods of self-help in seeking power were precisely what one would expect from such a combination of interior resources. Where Roosevelt let his channels and advisers become orderly he acted out of character.

With Eisenhower, seemingly, the case is quite the opposite. Apparently he had a sense of power and a source of confidence as unlike Roosevelt's as were the two men's methods. For Eisenhower the promotion of disorder was distinctly out of character. When he could not work through a set procedure, or when channels failed

him, or when his associates quarreled openly, he grew either disheartened or en-
raged. As Robert Donovan attests, reactions of both sorts were characteristic of this
President from his first days in office.[11] All indications are that they remained in
character throughout the following years. If Eisenhower's "system" did not help
him see his power stakes, the reason, basically, is that this help was not the sort he
wanted. His sensitivities did not prompt him to want it and his confidence was
highest when he could assure himself that *personal* advantage had no place among
his aims. So, at least, it seems.

One cannot assess Eisenhower's motives with the same assurance one can
bring to F.D.R.'s. Roosevelt had an entourage of diarists and note-takers; most of
them have published what they wrote. Members of his family circle write and speak
with candor. He, himself, was a prodigious correspondent and a most revealing
talker to the press. And he has fascinated the historians. In a few years when Frank
Friedel and Arthur Schlesinger are done with him, he will have had more serious
attention than has been accorded yet to four-fifths of his predecessors. Eisenhower,
on the other hand is only to be known, as yet, by what he has said publicly and by
what men around him will say privately. Appraisal on the basis of such sources calls
for caution. It may turn out that he was not the man they make him seem. But at the
present everything suggests that with his motivations as with methods, Eisenhower
has been a sort of Roosevelt in reverse.

Through Eisenhower's first six years his power sense was blunt in almost the
degree that F.D.R's was sharp. As late as 1958 he had not quite got over "shocked
surprise" that orders did not carry themselves out. Apparently he could not quite
absorb the notion that effective power had to be extracted out of other men's
self-interest; neither did he quite absorb the notion that nobody else's interest could
be wholly like his own. And he seems to have been unaware of all his natural
advantages in turning different interests toward his own. By 1959 he certainly had
learned to use the veto as a vantage point, but other points less obviously "constitutional" appear to have eluded him; the Humphrey case and its long aftermath bear
witness.

This relative insensitivity can be explained, at least in part, by Eisenhower's
background. He lacked Roosevelt's experience. Instead he had behind him the
irrelevancy of an army record compiled for the most part outside Washington. As a
member of his entourage once told me:

> In the Army—at least in the old Army, Eisenhower's Army—everybody knew every-
> body, and knew what kind of job the other fellow had, and how he was supposed to do
> it. . . . Responsibility was a two way flow, with the lower echelons acting in terms of
> what the boss wanted as laid down in his master plan—and with the boss out in the field
> making inspections. Here [in civil government] there's no master plan, no two way
> flow, and no inspections. Besides, nobody fathoms the boss's job and he's never done
> theirs. And they haven't been together since West Point. They don't expect to stay
> together, either. The Army was full of politics, sure, but it was personality politics;
> everybody knew the game and knew who he was playing with and for what—and it was
> all inside the *family*. Here, there's no family.

Coming to the White House from that background, Eisenhower also lacked Roosevelt's enjoyment. At least until his seventh year the politics of power in the Presidency never was his sport; not recreation for him; certainly not fun. Like most politically inexperienced Americans, he seems to have thought party politics a "dirty" business (which may explain why his campaigning sometimes was so disingenuous). And the politics of self-aggrandizement as Roosevelt practiced it affronted Eisenhower's sense of personal propriety. Besides, the General seems to have had mental reservations about politicians as a class, mistrusting not alone their business but their characters. To quote the private comment of another of his aides:

> It really surprises me how mad he gets and the things that upset him. . . . He won't say anything personal against a member of Congress in public, but in private he can get much madder than any "pro" would. . . . And it isn't just the Democrats; deep down I think he feels the same way about Republicans.

Robert Donovan supplies us Eisenhower's answer when it was suggested to him a few weeks before his heart attack that Congress might be called back for a special session in the fall of 1955:

> He slowly twisted his head around to [Arthur] Burns and told him painfully that the cost of a special session might be the sanity and possibly the life of one Dwight D. Eisenhower.[12]

Such comments simply strengthen the suggestion of the Humphrey case that this man neither liked the game he was engaged in nor had gained much understanding of its rules.

Yet Eisenhower was not dragged protesting to the White House and he was not kept there against his will. In 1952 he actively sought nomination; in 1956 he actively sought re-election. By the time of his first campaign his candidacy had been debated publicly and privately for some five years.[13] By the time of his second campaign he had been President for almost a full term. By then he was no longer "inexperienced." His fingertips, however, remained blunt. Every Eisenhower illustration in this book is taken from his *second* term.

What kept experience from sharpening his sense of power and his taste for it? The answer, seemingly, turns on a single point: Eisenhower wanted to be President, but what he wanted from it was a far cry from what F.D.R. had wanted. Roosevelt was a politician seeking personal power; Eisenhower was a hero seeking national unity. He came to crown a reputation not to make one. He wanted to be arbiter, not master. His love was not for power but for duty—and for status. Naturally, the thing he did not seek he did not often find.

The most inhibiting effect of Eisenhower's past career lay not in its irrelevance for presidential politics but its influence upon his image of himself as President. He genuinely thought himself the hero others thought him. In Marquis Childs's chilling words, "his view of himself was the official view of the Eisenhower personality, the view seen through channels."[14] And he genuinely thought the Presidency was, or ought to be, the source of unifying, moderating influence above the struggle, on the model of George Washington—the Washington, that is to say, of legend, not of life. As Eisenhower told the press in 1955:

> . . . in the general derogatory sense you can say that, of course, I do not like politics.
>
> Now on the other hand, any man who finds himself in a position of authority where he has a very great influence in the efforts of people to work toward a peaceful—a peaceful world—toward international relationships that will eliminate or minimize the chances of war, all that sort of thing, of course, it is a fascinating business. . . .
>
> There are in this office thousands of unique opportunities to meet especially interesting people, . . . leaders in culture, in health, in governmental action, and from all over the world.
>
> There are many things about the office and the work, the work with your associates, that are, well, let's say at least intriguing, even if at times they are very fatiguing. But they are—it is a wonderful experience.
>
> But the word "politics" as you use it, I think the answer to that one, would be, no. I have no great liking for that.[15]

What drew him to the Presidency and held him there, it seems, was a conception of the good man above politics, emulating the Father of his Country.

With this image before him his self-confidence was high when he took office; higher still, perhaps, when he acceded to a second term. With this to guide him he could not dispute the arguments of all his friends that his "place in the world was unique," that he had "a God-given ability for reconciling differences among . . . nations," and for "healing divisions among the American people"—and, inferentially, that he fulfilled the Presidency just by being there.[16] But the reverse side of the coin was a diminished confidence when he dealt with the hard, divisive issues forced upon a President by dates and by events. His heightened confidence in 1956, after three years of office, suggests no change of image but a trick of history. When he decided on a second term the signs abounded that to be there was enough: "peace" in Korea, prosperity at home, the "spirit of Geneva," the censure of McCarthy, all these signs and others made beneficence appear its own reward. But precisely at the moment of his re-election, history caught up with him in giant jumps: Hungary, and Suez, and George Humphrey. Others followed after.

So long as he could play the statesman and the moderator, Eisenhower's sense of fitness for his job seems to have been no less than F.D.R.'s. His confidence, like Roosevelt's, was rooted in a sense of being naturally equipped to match his image of the office. But quite unlike the Roosevelt image, Eisenhower's, seemingly, did not delineate the politician and initiator in that lonely place where no one else's interests are one's own and no one else's expertise is expert. Thus the source of his self-confidence was frequently *an enemy of his power sense* and not, as with Roosevelt, a constant ally. Only in Eisenhower's seventh year, with his last congressional campaign behind him and his re-election barred by Constitutional Amendment, did his image of himself enhance his sensitivity to power in one sphere, the sphere of congressional relations. By then he could assure himself—reportedly he did—that "politics" played no part in his reach for personal influence.

Had Eisenhower been more purposeful as President his own sense of direction might have come to the rescue of his power sense. Occasionally this seems to have occurred, but not often. His purposes were not well suited to the task. His public statements, taken altogether, show he very much desired peace-with-honor both at home and abroad. He was more or less committed to the aims of foreign policy he had inherited, and more or less committed to maintain the welfare heritage from the New Deal. He was committed, also, to his party as the safest source of leadership for the United States; he hoped to see Republicans in office after he was gone. Taken on their face, such goals as these might have sufficed a man with a keen sense of power. Eisenhower's purposes seem tangible enough to have kept such a man in motion without being so precise as to impel him down blind alleys or to turn him against history. Their very imprecision, though, made them unsuitable to sharpen a dull power sense. If anything, they dulled it more. Eisenhower often seemed to mistake generalities for concrete undertakings; when he did pursue a concrete aim he often seemed to lose sight of his broad objectives.

Throughout Eisenhower's years of office there can be no doubt that peace, in the sense of a fundamental easing of the threat of war, was the broad objective he had most in mind, the one that stirred and interested him most, the one for which he felt himself particularly fitted. The thought that he, uniquely, could contribute to the cause of peace may have decided him upon a second term. As Robert Donovan reports in tracing that decision, "Constantly Eisenhower heard this appeal repeated, sometimes expressed in terms of duty to which he seemed peculiarly responsive. 'It was this advice,' an intimate said later, 'that he took to bed with him when he was making up his mind.' "[17] Yet both before and after 1956, this personal commitment seemed to guide him only on the mountaintop of general goals; down in the valley of specific applications he often appeared lost. In 1955 he personally was at great pains to create and to gain credit for the "spirit of Geneva." But in the weeks between the summit conference and his heart attack he gave no sign of knowing what he meant to do with either the creation or the credit. In 1957, during the London disarmament talks, Eisenhower backed Dulles over Stassen on approaches to the Russians without disallowing Stassen's premises. At the same time Eisenhower moved toward a Treasury view on defense budgeting that did not square at all with Dulles's premises. That year—among others—foreign policy disputes in his Administration found the President committed and uncertain on both sides, a situation reminiscent of the Humphrey case. Results were somewhat similar. Even in the sphere of peace which mattered to him most, Eisenhower's purposes were frequently too general to provide a guideline for him on specific undertakings.

It is no wonder that in other spheres of policy and politics which meant far less to Eisenhower than did peace, there should have been still greater gaps between his advocacy of a general goal and his sense of direction on particulars. When broad objectives were inapplicable or in conflict—as broad objectives usually are—he was inclined to throw the issue to the experts and to follow where the men he thought most expert chose to lead. He had enormous respect for successful businessmen, the more so as their manner matched the layman's expectations; if he did not equally admire politicians, he accorded them a layman's deference in what he took to be *their* line of work. When Eisenhower dealt with the particulars of home affairs and party politics, these were the experts he inclined to follow. They took him rather far, sometimes, from his avowed objectives.

It would be a distortion of the Eisenhower record to suggest that he invariably acted in this fashion. Intermittently, specifics came to interest him, even the political specifics. Sometimes his energies and personal enthusiasm fastened upon very concrete aims. Particularly in the months before his heart attack and, again, after the Democratic landslide of 1958, one senses that his own assertiveness about specific aims was definitely on the rise. His aides report that when and as this happened he was frequently quite capable of being his own guide, of taking his direction on particulars from his own sense of where and how to go. But it appears that these excursions to the realm of the specific often disengaged his mind from general aims. The classic instance seems to be his concentration on the budget in the seventh year of his Administration.

In part, perhaps, because his time was running out; in part, perhaps, because the Democratic victories of 1958 roused his combative instincts, Eisenhower turned his mind to budget-balancing with the enthusiasm once reserved for peace alone. By 1959 he was as purposeful about his budget aim as Humphrey had been two years earlier. What Humphrey then had advocated, Eisenhower made his own: an effort to keep *future* budgets balanced by resisting new commitments and reducing those on hand; in long-run terms an effort to keep spending down so that the rising revenues from economic growth could be applied to debt and tax reduction without adding to inflationary pressures. As we have seen in Chapter 4, the President pursued this negative objective with a fervor—and a skill in utilizing vantage points—which made him seem a "changed man" from the hesitant performer of 1957. By the same token, though, the positive objectives that had caused his hesitations in the first year of his second term seem almost to have vanished from his mind.

Eisenhower did not change the labels on his broader aims. In 1959 he still avowed the goals of 1956: peace, prosperity, and Modern Republicanism. But the meaning of those goals was altered rather markedly when each became identified with holding down the budget. Whether he was conscious of that alteration is an open question. And whether the new meanings were compatible with Soviet containment, with American advance, and with Republican advantage is decidedly in doubt. The answer will be given in the 1960's. Meanwhile, an affirmation of compatibility is only credible on the assumption that the Eisenhower program at the outset of his second term was based on faulty premises in almost every sphere—and that the reports of the Rockefeller Brothers Fund are fantasy. To assume otherwise is to conclude that Eisenhower's campaign for a balanced budget, with its pressure wholly on the spending side, involved a risk not only to his other goals of policy but also to the power prospects *after* 1960 of the Republican he hoped would follow him into the White House. For if Eisenhower's budgeting promoted expectations that the future could not meet, his political legacy was likely to be popular frustration in the time of the next President. Reportedly, the moral was not lost on either Rockefeller or Nixon. But there are no reports that Eisenhower saw the risk he ran, if not for himself then for them, in anything like these terms. On the contrary, by 1959 he seems to have been satisfied that Humphrey's aim was not merely good policy but quite sufficient as a base for White House power politics.

Conceivably, the "new" Eisenhower of 1959 bespeaks a change of outlook more profound than the foregoing analysis suggests. Conceivably, this President in his last years came to perceive his office and his power very differently than he had done before. It is conceivable but unlikely. A sympathetic member of his Administration told me:

> This is the Eisenhower of North Africa and Normandy, motivated by the same belief: that the only battle that counts is the last battle. After 1958 he knew the war was nearly over and the time was now or never for the final fight.

But in political warfare, the outcome for a President depends as much or more on the *first* battles. These are the battles that decide his public image and create a pattern for his Washington reputation. A President who makes himself a "new" man in his *seventh* year must be presumed a stranger, still, to politics and power.

With Eisenhower as with F.D.R., performance on the job reflected qualities inside the man which shaped his whole approach to personal power. In Roosevelt's case a striking sensitivity to power was heightened by vast confidence in using it, and by his sense of what to use it for. In Eisenhower's case a relative *in*sensitivity was reinforced by a self-confidence that wavered least when "politics" was farthest off, and by a set of purposes that either raised his eyes too high or cast them down too low to see the middle ground where strategy and tactics meet. It is no wonder that an F.D.R. on most occasions seemed acutely conscious of his power risks, whereas an Eisenhower frequently seemed unaware of them. Nor is it any wonder that the one man's methods helped him see his stakes of power, while the other man worked in a manner likely to obscure them. Roosevelt always knew what power was and always wanted it.

III

In his reach for personal power Harry Truman differed both from Roosevelt and from Eisenhower. Truman's methods of self-help were different. So were his insights, his incentives, and his image of himself as President. In these respects he neither forecast his successor nor proceded like his predecessor. However, Truman's own behavior will confirm what theirs suggests: that there exists the closest of connections between self-help in the Presidency and three aspects of a President's interior resources: his power sense, his confidence—which turns on his self image—and his sense of direction.

Truman's methods in the White House followed forms somewhat like Eisenhower's to results somewhat like Roosevelt's. In theory Truman was as much committed as was Eisenhower to straight lines and tidy boxes on the organization chart, and to "completed staff work." But in practice Truman had more feel for personalities than jurisdictions, and his instinct was to improvise arrangements around problems rather than to work through fixed procedures. In dealing with his staff he set no precise lines of demarcation or of hierarchy; those he did establish he was likely to ignore. As best he could he saw whoever wished to see him, whether congressmen or private persons or department heads or staff assistants, and he listened to their talk and read their documents. Truman theorized like a reserve officer impressed with Army doctrine; he acted like a Senator. His office was decked out with many of the trappings of what later became known as a staff system, but he, himself, remained incurably informal and accessible. Besides, in Truman's practice there was one ingredient which cannot be described as senatorial: he loved to make decisions. Unlike Eisenhower he was not disposed to keep away from them and unlike Roosevelt he had little inclination to defer them once he got them. On the contrary, his own initial impulse when an issue came before him was to make a firm decision then and there; his staff and State Department were forever clinging to his coattails. Although Truman rather frowned on Roosevelt's methods and would not have dreamed of fostering disorder for its own sake, his accessibility and personal decisiveness combined to furnish him—under the table, so to speak—with information in his mind and choices in his hands on a scale more like Roosevelt's than like Eisenhower's.

However where Roosevelt was instinctively an intelligence operative, Truman was instinctively a judge. Details reached him, ordinarily, as a by-product of his listening and reading, case by case. He did not seek as avidly as F.D.R. had done for bits of information unrelated to the day's affairs. Although he relished gossip when he got it, Truman did not often try to fit the pieces into patterns, or to speculate about their implications, or to make connections between something learned in one context and something done in another. Characteristically, he concentrated on the "here" and "now" in terms befitting a decision-machine, looking for what was to be decided, looking at what bore directly on the case, and tending to dismiss all else as interesting but irrelevant. Moreover, while he dealt with the decision next in line, the ones already processed and the ones that might come after were not often on his mind. No more than in the case of tangible details was Truman prone to fit his choices into patterns or to visualize the one at hand outside of its own context. And just as in the case of information, Truman usually let other men's initiatives time his decisions for him. The issues that existed were the issues on his desk. Because his door was open and he listened and he read, details piled in upon him; because he was so willing to decide, decisions piled in, too. But Roosevelt had pursued these things with power as an object; Truman rather welcomed them in line of duty. The difference is significant. Information in his mind and choices in his hands were not the help to Truman they had been to F.D.R.

Truman's sensitivity to power was no match for his predecessor's. Truman's past experience had been less relevant and he lacked Roosevelt's instinct for the uses of *Executive* position. Truman's instincts ran another way. He had been ten years a Senator, beginning at a time when Roosevelt's emissaries were both blunt and curt with new men at the Capitol. Truman never did like White House meddling in legislative *tactics;* indeed he entered office with his mind set on restoring "proper" balance between President and Congress. Moreover, Truman shared with many senators a sense of the Executive as "they," conceiving it much more an entity and much more an extension of the Chief Executive than it looks from within. Roosevelt seemed to him a poor administrator—as Roosevelt seemed, of course, to many others—and Truman entered office with his mind set on administering by and through the Cabinet. As the first volume of his *Memoirs* shows (a volume based in part on notes written in 1945), Truman carried to the White House certain of the preconceptions commonly identified with Eisenhower.[18] The experience of senators like that of generals can be far removed, it seems, from life as lived at 1600 Pennsylvania Avenue. And Truman had not only been a Senator, he had been the Kansas City organization's candidate and office holder for a quarter century. He reached the Presidency possessed of that great virtue in an organization politician, loyalty up and loyalty down. Truman had remained a Roosevelt Democrat, loyal to his party's leader in the White House, even after F.D.R. tried to unseat him from the Senate in the primary campaign of 1940. When Truman took the leader's place, when *he* became the boss, he gave an equal loyalty to his followers. He sensed—indeed he could not help but know—that Roosevelt had been loyal above all else to F.D.R. In this respect as in some others Truman entered office with his mind set on revising the procedure of his predecessor.

Truman learned by doing; to a marked degree he rid himself of his illusions about government administration, notably with regard to the Cabinet, and in practice if not theory he changed many of his views about congressional relations. The unpublished diary of his holdover Budget Director, Harold Smith, does much to trace the education—on the job and by it—of a very educable man.[19] Truman often learned a great deal more than he articulated and his *Memoirs* scarcely show the sweep of his self-education; but in fact, if not in memory, it was vast. Yet never having been an agency official, Truman never did acquire Roosevelt's intimate awareness of just how the work got done (or stopped) around him and beneath him in the bureaucratic world. And never having let ambition for the White House shape his code of loyalty, Truman, once he got there, had no motive to reshape the code by which he had been living all his political life. Throughout his Presidency, Truman's lack of bureaucratic "feel," in combination with his loyalty down, left him decidedly less sensitive than F.D.R. to stakes of personal power. The way these two men chose and dealt with appointees is most instructive on the point.

Truman, it must be remembered, had not aimed at the Presidency; his own aims reached no farther than a lifetime in the Senate. Before his unsolicited vice-presidential nomination, thoughts of being President had scarcely crossed his mind, and by his own account they scarcely crossed it afterward, until the day that Roosevelt died. Until then Truman had been hungry neither for the Presidency's power nor its status. Nothing in his life had been planned around visions of himself as boss; Roosevelt was the boss, and after Roosevelt there would be another. In 1948 Truman fought to get himself *elected* President; he did so for the record's sake, for vindication, for his pride's sake, as a man who made good on his own and always faced a fight. But even then he had no notion of himself as fit above all others to be President. As late as 1952 he was quite capable of saying, and believing, "There are a great many people, I expect a million in the country, who could have done the job better than I could, but I had the job and I had to do it."[20] In that remark one finds the essence of his image of himself in office.

Truman's image of the Presidency and of himself as President kept job and man distinct to a degree unknown in Roosevelt's case or Eisenhower's. Truman built his image of the office out of his perceptions as a politician, as a Democrat, as a young worshipper of Woodrow Wilson, as a mature follower of F.D.R. and as a constant reader of political biography, who found a lot to like in Jackson, Polk, and Johnson. Truman saw the Presidency as the place "where the buck stopped"; he saw the President as man-in-charge of government, as maker of a record for his party, and as voice for the whole body of Americans. The job he had to do, as Truman saw it, was to make decisions and to take initiatives; those were the duties of the boss-and-spokesman; so his perceptions told him. Mixed into those perceptions, perhaps guiding them, were Truman's private values; decisiveness was high upon his list. But never in his tenure does he seem to have conceived that he fulfilled the Presidency by being Harry Truman. He saw himself not as a man for whom the job was made, but as a man who had the job to do. He drew his confidence from seeing himself do it.

The source of Truman's confidence was his ability, in his own mind, to live up to that image of the President as man-in-charge. His confidence was highest when he saw himself deciding and initiating. Rarely was he calmer or more certain of himself than when he had to act amidst a crisis. Few things made him more uncomfortable than mulling over "ifs" and "buts" with nothing to decide. But Truman's confidence required more than sheer decision-making. It required that he see himself deciding in terms worthy of a *President*. His image of his office made it seem to him the focal point of governmental policy, of national politics, and of American history. He could not feel that he had done his job if he let personal proclivities or personal self-interest outweigh what he took to be a presidential duty. His own sense of the separateness of man and office made him more self-conscious than most Presidents about each shift of role among the six or eight or ten into which modern writers split the Presidency. He played "Chief of State" like a gracious host, "Chief of Party" like an organization politician, "Chief of Foreign Policy" like a career official anxious to obey his own injunction that "politics stops at the water's edge." When he was not playing one role or another he saw nothing inappropriate in being Harry Truman, but he rarely thought that Truman's likes or dislikes had a warrant to determine what he did in any role.

Truman's kind of confidence was capable of offsetting the weakness in his power sense, but it was also capable of rendering the weakness all the worse. Everything depended on the given situation. As Chapter 3 records, he was enormously successful in his handling of the Marshall Plan. As Chapter 6 records, he got into deep trouble with his handling of Korean war aims. And these two results were products of the same approach. In both these instances the President remained intensely loyal to his subordinates and did his personal best to smooth *their* way as they conducted their share of Administration policy. In both instances he shunned ideas and interventions which might lay him open, *in his own mind*, to the charge that he "played politics with national security." In both cases he deferred to the counsel of the men he least suspected—as a rule—of partisan motivation, generals above all. (His lay regard for their career line more or less matched Eisenhower's faith in businessmen.) And in both instances he made decisions willingly and fast, whenever his advisers brought him some to make. The political adroitness and the look of calculation in the case of the Marshall Plan can give a false impression. Truman was not being subtle; he was simply doing what he thought a President should do from day to day. As Jack Redding has written in another connection:

> What so many people failed to understand was that the President [Truman] rarely used circumlocution to gain his ends. He meant what he said. That is why so many pundits failed in trying to analyze the President's actions. They were always looking behind what he said and did, looking for an explanation other than the obvious.[21]

Truman's sense of personal direction was cut from the same cloth as his self-confidence and had a like effect upon his power sense, sharpening it or dulling it in different situations. He came to office very conscious of his heritage from F.D.R. In policy terms he saw himself as heir to the New Deal and internationalism; in political terms he saw himself as heir to Roosevelt's coalition of the Democratic South and the Progressive West with Northern ethnic and religious minorities. Truman was not only mindful of this heritage, but also he felt obliged to guard it and refurbish it and pass it on. In combination with his image of his office that feeling quite sufficed to give him all the purposes a man can carry while he tries to cope with an eight-year supply of modern history. Indeed the combination spurred this man toward fixed positions of a sort not easily abandoned in the face of changed events, and made him, very often, most reluctant to retreat. Where Roosevelt had shunned fixed positions, Truman staked them out. As Roosevelt characteristically kept fire-exits open, Truman characteristically slammed doors. When Eisenhower went "all out" to hold down Federal spending, his stance, if not his object, reminded one of Truman.

"The President's got to set the sights," was Truman's comment in a conversation after leaving office. To him the task included dotting "i's" and crossing "t's." Advocacy in specific terms was his conception of appropriate initiative. If the specifics were ignored, or if they later rose to haunt him, he would still have done his duty as a President. In his words: "What the country needed in every field . . . was up to me to say . . . and if Congress wouldn't respond, well, I'd have done all I could in a straightforward way." Sometimes this approach directed him toward power as it certainly did in 1948. But sometimes his specifics left him small room for maneuver when events produced a shift in his priorities or altered public expectations of his office. In 1943 a Roosevelt could drop "Dr. New Deal" for "Dr. Win-the-War," and seem in character and make a point. The indications are that Truman could have managed no such thing in 1950-1951. Besides, he would have thought it wrong to try.[22]

The help that Truman gave himself in calculating power stakes was help of an uneven sort; his power sense was equally uneven. His methods in the Presidency brought him into contact with details and with decisions more consistently than Eisenhower, but the timing of those contacts was not on a par with Roosevelt's from the standpoint of protecting personal power. As in his predecessor's case and his successor's also, Truman's methods bear an obvious relationship to his own "feel" for power and its purposes and to his source of confidence. His methods were the methods of a man who loved the Presidency less for what he could get out of it, by way of personal power or of status, than for what he saw in it as an embodiment of government and party and of history apart from him. Truman loved his image of the institution. When stakes of power for the office—in his image of it—coincided with his stakes of personal influence, his sensitivities were quick to be aroused. But when there was no obvious coincidence he could be quite insensitive to personal stakes, or even deprecate them, if he saw them as beneath a President's dignity. His dealings with MacArthur provide classic illustrations on both scores.

Truman's distaste for the "merely" personal was not much less than his successor's. Eisenhower also deprecated personal advantage as a guide in presidential choice-making. But Truman's image of the office made him sensitive to anything that challenged his position as decider and proposer. His feeling for the Presidency's clerkship was so strong that often he was led to self-protection in the process of protecting what he took to be his duties. Eisenhower's image offered no such compensation. Eisenhower's sensitivities were reserved, in the main, for what he took to be his place above the struggle. Paradoxically, his instinct for the Presidency's honorific element often made his own reactions seem intensely personal. But rarely did they seem "political." In Eisenhower's image, "politics" defined the merely personal. In Truman's image "politics" was duty.

In Roosevelt's image, unlike both of these, "politics" and all else was a vehicle for *him*. Roosevelt, of the three, was much the most effective in protecting personal power.

IV

These observations on our recent Presidents conclude a line of argument begun in Chapter 2. Let me restate it briefly. Governmental power, in reality not form, is influence of an effective sort on the behavior of men actually involved in making public policy and carrying it out. Effective influence for the man in the White House stems from three related sources: first are the bargaining advantages inherent in his job with which to persuade other men that what he wants of them is what their own responsibilities require them to do. Second are the expectations of those other men regarding his ability and will to use the various advantages they think he has. Third are those men's estimates of how his public views him and of how their publics may view them if they do what he wants. In short, his power is the product of his vantage points in government, together with his reputation in the Washington community and his prestige outside.

A President, himself, affects the flow of power from these sources, though whether they flow freely or run dry he never will decide alone. He makes his personal impact by the things he says and does. Accordingly, his choices of what he should say and do, and how and when, are his means to conserve and tap the sources of his power. Alternatively, choices are the means by which he dissipates his power. The outcome, case by case, will often turn on whether he perceives his risk in power terms and takes account of what he sees before he makes his choice. A President is so uniquely situated and his power so bound up with the uniqueness of his place, that he can count on no one else to be perceptive for him. Yet he can scarcely see and weigh his power stakes himself unless he is alerted by significant details and deals with his decisions in good time. Useful information, timely choices may not reach him; he must do the reaching. To do so is to help himself enhance his personal influence. This is the sort of help he needs the most. But he will neither feel that need nor fill it if his image of his office keeps him faced away from power.

It is natural that Franklin Roosevelt, hungry for the Presidency's power as his birthright, should exemplify the man who helps himself. It is ironic that a Truman, who felt no such hunger and laid claim to no such birthright, still created from his background, and his heroes, and his reading, an image of the office that impelled him toward self-help. It is an equal irony that Eisenhower, hailed by commentators and by voters (and by many intellectuals) as quite uniquely qualified for power in the Presidency, was turned away from self-help by his very qualifications. Only an extraordinary politician could have managed to exploit the opportunities for influence created by the presence of a hero in the White House. But had Eisenhower been a man of politics he never would have come there as the hero that he was. And being what he was, he looked upon his presence there through the eyes of an *anti*-politician. There can be little doubt that he exchanged his hero's welcome for much less than its full value in the currency of power. But how could Eisenhower have done otherwise? His image of himself in office dictated the terms of that exchange.

One never can be sure that when a man becomes the President of the United States his sense of power and of purpose and his own source of self-confidence will show him how to help himself enhance his personal influence. But there is every reason to believe that he will be shown nothing of the sort if he has made the White House his first venture into politics. The Presidency is no place for amateurs.

CHAPTER 8

The Sixties Come Next

To make the most of power for himself a President must know what it is made of. This book has treated power in the sense of personal influence and influence in the sense of effectiveness *prospectively,* looking toward tomorrow from today. That look conveys the essence of the task before a man who seeks to maximize his power. If he wants it for the future, he must guard it in the present. He mounts guard, as best *he* can, when he appraises the effects of present action on the sources of his influence. In making that appraisal he has no one to depend on but himself; his power and its sources are a sphere of expertise reserved to him. But the issues that present themselves for action day by day rarely show his personal risks upon their surface. His expertise must first help him to see beneath the surface if it is to help him weigh what may be there. The President as expert does himself a double service. Without the expertise he cannot do it.

The Presidency, to repeat, is not a place for amateurs. That sort of expertise can hardly be acquired without deep experience in political office. The Presidency is a place for men of politics. But by no means is it a place for every politician.

There is no reason to suppose that politicians, on the average, have the where-withal to help themselves build *presidential* power. The men of politics who specialize in organization work and party office scarcely qualify at all; governmental office is the relevant experience. For present purposes we can regard as politicians only those who build careers in public office. Yet skillful use of presidential power does not follow automatically from such experience. No post in government at any level necessarily equips a man to recognize the Presidency's peculiar sources of influence. Those sources have as many parts as a President has constituencies, foreign and domestic; the posts that furnish insights into one part often obscure others. Besides, past officeholding is no guarantee that any man brings with him to the White House the degree and kind of feeling for direction that can help him once he gets there. Former Commerce Secretary Hoover had a sense of purpose so precise as to be stultifying. Former Senator Harding seems to have had none at all. And mere experience, however relevant, is no assurance that a President will find the confidence he needs just when he needs it most. Such confidence requires that his image of himself in office justify an unremitting search for personal power. But it requires, also, that his image of himself allow for failures and frustration in the search.

F.D.R. is said to have remarked that Lincoln "was a sad man because he couldn't get it all at once. And nobody can."[1] If a President is to assist himself through the vicissitudes of four long years or eight, *his source of confidence must make him capable of bearing Lincoln's sadness with good grace.* The power-seeker whose self-confidence requires quick returns and sure success might make a mess of everything including his own power. Grace calls for humor and perspective. Political experience does not assure those qualities. Indeed, it may diminish them in the degree it brings a taste for power. The officeholder who combines them with an insight into presidential influence and hunger for it is no average politician.

Expertise in presidential power seems to be the province not of politicians as a class but of extraordinary politicians. What sets such men apart? Mr. Justice Holmes once characterized Franklin Roosevelt as a "second-rate intellect but a first-rate temperament." Perhaps this is a necessary combination. The politics of well-established government has rarely been attractive to and rarely has dealt kindly with the men whom intellectuals regard as first-rate intellects. Temperament, at any rate, is the great separator. Experience will leave its mark on expertise; so will a man's ambitions for himself and his constituents. But something like that "first-rate" temperament is what turns know-how and desire to his personal account. The necessary confidence is nourished by that temperament. It is a human resource not discovered every day among American politicians.

II

If skill in maximizing power for himself served purposes no larger than the man's own pride or pleasure, there would be no reason for the rest of us to care whether he were skillful or not. More precisely, there would be no reason except sentiment and partisanship. But a President's success in that endeavor serves objectives far beyond his own and far beyond his party's. For reasons I will come to in a moment, an expert search for presidential influence contributes to the energy of government and to the viability of public policy. Government is energized by a productive tension among its working parts. Policy is kept alive by a sustained transformation of intent into result. Energetic government and viable public policy are at a premium as we begin the seventh decade of the twentieth century. Expertise in presidential power adds to both. A President's constituents, regardless of their party (or their country for that matter), have a great stake in his search for personal influence.

In the American political system the President sits in a unique seat and works within a unique frame of reference. The things he personally has to do are no respecters of the lines between "civil" and "military," or "foreign" and "domestic," or "legislative" and "executive," or "administrative" and "political." At his desk—and there alone—distinctions of these sorts lose their last shred of meaning. The expectations centered in his person converge upon no other individual; nobody else feels pressure from all five of *his* constituencies; no one else takes pressure in the consciousness that *he* has been elected "by the Nation." Besides, nobody but the President lives day by day with *his* responsibility in an atomic age amidst cold war. And he alone can claim unquestionable right to everybody's information on the mysteries of that age and that war. His place and frame of reference are unique. By the same token, though, his power is mercurial. Since no one shares his place, nobody is committed to uphold what he may do there. The consequences are described by every illustration in this book.

The things a President must think about if he would build his influence are not unlike those bearing on the viability of public policy. The correspondence may be inexact, but it is close. The man who thinks about the one can hardly help contributing to the other. A President who senses what his influence is made of and who means to guard his future will approach his present actions with an eye to the reactions of constituents in Washington and out. The very breadth and sweep of his constituencies and of their calls upon him, along with the uncertainty of their response, will make him keen to see and weigh what Arthur Schlesinger has called "the balance of administrative power."[2] This is a balance of political, managerial, psychological, and personal feasibilities. And because the President's own frame of reference is at once so all-encompassing and so political, what he sees as a balance for himself is likely to be close to what is viable in terms of public policy.

What he sees in terms of power *gives him clues in terms of policy* to help him search beneath the surfaces of issues.

Viability in policy has three ingredients. First is a purpose that moves with the grain of history, a direction consonant with coming needs. Second is an operation that proves manageable to the men who must administer it, acceptable to those who must support it, tolerable to those who must put up with it, in Washington and out. Timing can be crucial for support and acquiescence; proper timing is the third ingredient. The President who sees his power stakes sees something very much like the ingredients that make for viability in policy.

Our system affords nobody a better source of clues. Presidential expertise thus serves effective policy. Deciding what is viable has grown more critical and more complex with almost every turn of world events (and of home politics) since the Second World War. Substantive considerations have become so specialized that experts in one sphere lose touch with expertise in any other. Substantive appraisals have become so tricky that the specialists in every sphere dispute among themselves. In consequence the viability of policy may be the only ground on which a substantive decision can be reached. When that ground is itself inordinately complicated by the tendency of policies to interlock, and overlap, and to leap national boundaries, it becomes a sphere of expertness as specialized as others. In the sphere of viability our system can supply no better expert than a President intent on husbanding his influence—provided that he understands what influence is made of.

The more determinedly a President seeks power, the more he will be likely to bring vigor to his clerkship. As he does so he contributes to the energy of government. In Congress and the agencies and in the national parties, energy is generated by support or opposition. But first there must be something to support or to oppose. Most Washingtonians look to the White House for it. There often is no other place to look. The need of others for a President's initiatives creates dependence on him. Their dependence becomes his advantage. Yet he can only capture the advantage as he meets the need. An energetic clerk will energize all government; the man intent on influence will be that sort of clerk. (So may a man intent on history, provided that he has the heroes of a Harry Truman. But one cannot expect that many men will know their history as well as he, and those who know it may choose other heroes.)

The contributions that a President can make to government are indispensable. Assuming that he knows what power is and wants it, those contributions cannot help but be forthcoming in some measure as by-products of his search for personal influence. In a relative but real sense one can say of a President what Eisenhower's first Secretary of Defense once said of General Motors: what is good for the country is good for the President, and *vice versa*. There is no guarantee, of course, that every President will keep an eye on what is "good" for him; his sense of power and of purpose and the source of his self-confidence may turn his head away. If so, his "contributions" could be lethargy not energy, or policy that moves against, not with, the grain of history. The way he sees his influence and seeks it will affect the rest of us, no matter what becomes of him.

III

There is reason to suppose that in the years immediately ahead the power problems of a President will remain what they have been in the decades just behind us. If so there will be equal need for presidential expertise of the peculiar sort this book has stressed. Indeed, the need is likely to be greater. The President himself and with him the whole government are likely to be more than ever at the mercy of his personal approach.

What may the Sixties do to politics and policy and to the place of Presidents in our political system? The Sixties may destroy them as we know them; that goes without saying. But barring deep depression or unlimited war, a total transformation is the least of likelihoods. Without catastrophes of those dimensions nothing in our past experience suggests that we shall see either consensus of the sort available to F.D.R. in 1933 and 1942, or popular demand for institutional adjustments likely to assist a President. Lacking popular demand, the natural conservatism of established institutions will keep Congress and the party organizations quite resistant to reforms that could give him a clear advantage over them. Four-year terms for congressmen and senators might do it, if the new terms ran with his. What will occasion a demand for that? As for crisis consensus it is probably beyond the reach of the next President. We may have priced ourselves out of the market for "productive" crises on the pattern Roosevelt knew—productive in the sense of strengthening his chances for sustained support *within* the system. Judging from the Fifties, neither limited war nor limited depression is productive in those terms. Anything unlimited will probably break the system.

In the absence of productive crises, and assuming that we manage to avoid destructive ones, nothing now foreseeable suggests that our next President will have assured support from any quarter. There is no use expecting it from the bureaucracy unless it is displayed on Capitol Hill. Assured support will not be found in Congress unless contemplation of their own electorates keeps a majority of members constantly aligned with him. In the Sixties it is to be doubted—for reasons to be mentioned in a moment—that pressure from electorates will move the same majority of men in either House toward consistent backing for the President. Instead the chances are that he will gain majorities, when and if he does so, by *ad hoc* coalition-building, issue after issue. In that respect the Sixties will be reminiscent of the Fifties; indeed, a closer parallel may well be the late Forties. As for "party discipline" in English terms—the favorite cure-all of political scientists since Woodrow Wilson was a youth—the first preliminary is a party link between the White House and the leadership on both sides of the Capitol. But even this preliminary has been lacking in eight of the fifteen years since the Second World War. If ballot-splitting should continue through the Sixties it will soon be "un-American" for President and Congress to belong to the same party.

Even if the trend were now reversed, there is no short-run prospect that behind each party label we would find assembled a sufficiently like-minded bloc of voters, similarly aligned in states and districts all across the country, to negate the massive barriers our institutions and traditions have erected against "discipline" on anything like the British scale. This does not mean that a reversal of the ballot-splitting trend would be without significance. If the White House and the legislative leadership were linked by party ties again, a real advantage would accrue to both. Their opportunities for mutually productive bargaining would be enhanced. The policy results might surprise critics of our system. Bargaining "within the family" has a rather different quality than bargaining with members of the rival clan. But we would still be a long way from "party government." Bargaining, not "discipline," would still remain the key to congressional action on a President's behalf. The critical distinctions between presidential party and congressional party are not likely to be lost in the term of the next President.

Our parties are unlikely be revolutionized as instruments of government because they are unlikely to be altered fundamentally as voter coalitions differently aligned for different offices in different places. The long awaited "nationalization" of our parties, breaking the old sectionalism, may be on its way despite the current setback in the South. But even if each party's voting base were nationalized tomorrow, the issues of the next few years hold out no prospect that the partisans in one place will stay put on the same terms as those in every other. In the next years we face a snarly sort of politics with party followings more likely to be brittle and unstable than secure and likely to shift differently in different locations. Nationalization may be coming, but if we find it with us in the Sixties we should not expect to find that it has brought us those clean cleavages so dear to advocates of "party realignment." Our history suggests that only sustained crises, striking deep into the private lives of voters everywhere, will produce *stable* partisan alignments; crises on the order of the Civil War and of the Great Depression. But a comparable crisis in our time would strike so deep that there might well be nothing left of our contemporary party system. Again we probably have priced ourselves out of the market for the useful products of an old-style crisis. Assuming no catastrophe, the Sixties, like the Fifties, probably will be a time of changeability without great change in terms of party preferences. The alterations now foreseeable will not be of the sort to promote unanimity among a party's congressmen.

This is not to argue that our politics will be as tepid in the next decade as in the middle Fifties. The Sixties, it appears, will be a fighting time. Our politics in the next years are likely to revolve around at least four overlapping areas of controversy; these are visible in 1959, others may emerge. One of the four can be identified, though imprecisely, as a shift in capital resources from private use to public purposes; the issues of inflation, and taxation, and of economic growth are bound up with the issue of a larger public "take." How much shift of resources there should be, and whether absolute or relative, and for what ends, and by what means, and at whose cost, need not detain us here. It is enough to note that these will be the subjects of hot argument, politically, throughout the next decade, perhaps long after. No one who looks squarely at "competitive coexistence," or at population trends, or at our cities (and their suburbs), or at subsidy and service needs of private enterprise, and then considers that a ceiling on the public sector has been advertised as *the* cure for inflation and a key to growth, can doubt what the late Fifties are bequeathing to the Sixties by way of heat in politics. The heat will be proportional to a great lack of light.

Debate over the sources, size, and distribution of the public "take" may raise as many issues in the sphere of foreign policy as in domestic spheres. Indeed, this is the likely way in which foreign relations will be linked directly and continuously to domestic politics. Among the pressing claims upon our Treasury will be the claims of those who do not vote in our elections. We face substantial bills for capital development. We are not done with paying bills for military forces. And all these bills will come due while we fight about expansion of domestic public services. The competitions between claims abroad and claims at home will affect every sphere of policy from military deterrence, to arms control, to economic aid, to foreign trade, to political relations in our system of alliances. The pressure of competing claims is certainly not new, but the intensity of pressure may make foreign policy more controversial in our politics than it has been for many years. And while it grows more controversial it will also grow more critical. What happens in the Sixties may decide the long-term outcome of "competitive coexistence."

A second area of controversy can be described in simplest terms as when, and where, and how to squeeze farm subsidies. While agricultural employment shrinks to a small fraction of the American labor force, and rural population drops proportionately, the present scale of subsidies will come under attack by every other claimant known to Washington. But between those rival claimants and the money stands the legislative influence of the farm organizations, buttressed by the rural gerrymander, helped by our inheritance of rural values. Clamorous attack and powerful resistance make for heat in politics; this second area becomes a likely source of it.

If agriculture's place in our society is likely to be challenged in the Sixties, so is the place of organized labor. This is a third area of controversy; conceivably it may produce as much heat as the others, or still more. For there are signs in 1959 of something deeper than a relatively generalized distaste for certain trade unions. There now are signs that we may be approaching a distinct deterioration in industrial relations. During the Fifties, management concern about union prerogatives found principal expression on the front of politics—with limited effect—while economic pressure was suspended rather generally wherever the trade unions were entrenched. The Sixties, though, may bring us warfare on both fronts. A struggle on the economic front will sharpen every struggle on the other; it will also sharpen rank-and-file allegiances in both the warring camps. But Labor's camp is shrinking in proportion to the labor force, and it is far from clear that this would be "class" war. Much depends on management approaches to unorganized or loosely organized industrial and service workers. If we have warfare on the economic front there is no knowing how it will turn out. But clearly, if and as it comes it will add heat to politics.

There will be a fourth area of controversy in the Sixties, and it ranks with all these others put together: the integration of nonwhite Americans. This is so plainly in our future that to name it is enough. The future features Northern housing quite as much as Southern schools; it also features economic *and political* opportunity. No domestic issues are more likely to bring heat into our politics; none are more inflammable and none may turn more critical in the years just ahead.

These four are merely the most readily foreseeable as areas of controversy in the Nineteen-sixties. A hint of other issues can be found in a variety of present signs. Among them, for example, are the signs that Soviet production and trade policy (and markets) may become a serious factor in the near-term outlook for some major segments of American industry. Other signs suggest that in our legacy of foreign policy and posture from the Fifties are some fixed positions which will have to change but cannot without turning into issues in our politics. As a further source of issues there are dozens of contingencies abroad which might arise at any time to complicate home politics. And finally, there are matters like the spread of nuclear weapons, or radiation hazards, or the race for the moon, matters too arcane to heat our politics consistently but capable of flaring into issues overnight if sparked by a conjunction of events.

The purpose here is not to be exhaustive but indicative; this list should indicate why party politics in the next years can hardly bring us "party government." It does not matter whether the list covers every issue or describes it as it may appear in retrospect. What matters is that in so far as one can see ahead our politics will be made out of *issues with disparate local impacts*, impacts bound to alter rather suddenly depending on the way the issues mix. In combination with the timing of elections and the localism of electorates in party primaries, those disparate impacts almost guarantee that no congressional party will provide assured support, day in and out, to any President, and that no President will be the passive instrument of those who claim his party's name in Congress. Older sectionalisms may be fading (or may not); disparate local impacts are at hand to take their place. Until there is a marriage between presidential and congressional electorates, particularly at the stage of nomination, there will be no marriage between President and Congress. Until then Presidents will have to seek support as best they can from case to case. While this holds true on Capitol Hill, it will hold true along Pennsylvania Avenue. The reverse side of the coin is that a President's position and perspective will remain unique in the American political system.

The issues of the Sixties will be fought out in a system that keeps Presidents uniquely placed and gives them no assurance of sustained support. "Emergencies in policy with politics as usual" was my introductory characterization of the fifteen years just passed. Everything suggests that these mid-century conditions will persist into the new decade. But policy is likely to grow still more difficult, and politics is likely to grow hotter. Conditions will not be just what they were, they may be more so. It follows that our need will be the greater for a presidential expert in the Presidency.

IV

We are confronted by an evident necessity for government more energetic, policies more viable, than we have been enjoying in the Fifties. The areas of controversy, just described, are also fields for governmental action. But every path to action

leads through controversy. Effective policy can only be created out of the material our politics provides. It is not very promising material. If policy is to be viable, ways must be found in every field to reconcile all sorts of things now called irreconcilable. This is the special province of the President-as-expert whose concern for power brings him face to face with the ingredients that make for viability in policy.

A President who knows what power is and wants it has to face irreconcilables whenever he considers his own stakes in acts of choice. The sources of his influence are such that one may suffer from whatever serves another. The move that gains him ground on some particular may scar his general Washington reputation. The move that brightens Washington impressions may raise public hopes the future cannot meet. And moves that seem imperative for reasons of high policy may threaten all three sources of his power. The essence of his expertise is an awareness that these are irreconcilable and that they must be reconciled. Viability in policy calls for the same awareness.

A President-as-expert is no cure-all. The illustrations in this book suggest his limitations. Power cannot be his sole criterion for choice, nor will his choices be the only regulators of his influence. They are the only levers in *his* hands, but other hands hold other levers. And his influence, at most, is only one of many factors shaping what eventuates as governmental action; events and men beyond his personal control are much the greater shapers. One cannot look around the world in the late Fifties with any special confidence in men or in events throughout the Sixties. It is not easy, after such a look, to quarrel with those who think that science and technology have pushed our social competence too far. Yet it seems premature to write off the adaptability and the inventiveness of American public policy. Admitting that the future is not wholly in our hands, our policy responses may make a substantial difference. Despairing views could have been voiced—and were—in 1950, or in 1940, or in 1930. At a time and in a world where rates of change accelerate, the Sixties may be the decade that finally proves too much for us. But on the record of the past, the policy responses of our political system give us grounds for hope. (In the whole perspective of this century so far, our recent pause seems relatively brief; besides, it was a pause, not a regression.) We might as well enjoy the hope; there is no present prospect that we soon shall change the system. Nor is there any prospect that a change of system would eliminate our policy dilemmas.

An expert in the White House does not guarantee effective policy, but lacking such an expert every hope is placed in doubt. If past experience is reassuring, its assurances are conveyed with that caveat. The responses of our system remain markedly dependent on the person of the President. "As matters have stood," Edward Corwin writes, ". . . presidential power has been at times dangerously *personalized*," and with unerring instinct for an expertise in influence he distrusts Franklin Roosevelt only less than Abraham Lincoln.[3] But if one wants effective policy from the American system, danger does not lie in our dependence on *a* man; it lies in our capacity to make ourselves depend upon a man who is inexpert. Any human judgment is worth fearing nowadays, but save for this the expert is a boon. His expertise assures a contribution to the system and it naturally commits him to proceed within the system. The system, after all, is what he knows. The danger lies in men who do not know it.

A dangerous dependence on the expertise of the top man—dependence on his "feel" for power in the going system—is not confined to the United States. It seems to be a feature of all democratic governments (presumably of communist regimes as well) though sometimes, as in Britain, it is so disguised that numbers of Americans may not have noticed it. The British cabinet system tends to cover up the weaknesses and to show up the strengths of the top man; ours tends to do the opposite. English politics does not place amateurs on top, while ours has put an amateur in office very recently. But Britain, in this century, has not lacked for inexpert heads of government, albeit quite professional, and British policy has paid a heavy price for them; most recently in Eden's case, to say nothing of Chamberlain's. With the English, as with us, structure and conventions and traditions count for everything *within* the system since the top man's expertise is wedded to them. But the English seem to be no less dependent than Americans upon the contributions of an expert at the top. If we were to import the British system overnight, power at the White House would be personalized still—and the person might turn out to be a Ramsay MacDonald. Some dangers in political society are not escaped by structure.

One of those dangers is the yearning in our national electorate for political leaders "above politics." Eisenhower, to be sure, is *sui generis*. But part of Stevenson's appeal was that he had not been in politics for long and did not seem to be a "politician." Currently, contenders for the 1960 nomination are doing all they can, each in his way, to take the curse off their political careers by assertions of amateur standing. Desire for an amateur is not new in American politics; Wendell Willkie's instance makes that plain. Now we have had Eisenhower. Significantly, to the limited extent that Eisenhower has been criticized in public his detractors, for the most part, deal in arguments *ad hominum*. Much of the criticism is unjust. Little of it makes allowance for the words attributed to Speaker Rayburn in the spring of 1952: "No, won't do. Good man. Wrong profession." But this is the heart of the matter.

The striking thing about our national elections in the Fifties was not Eisenhower's personal popularity; it was the genuine approval of his candidacy by informed Americans whom one might have supposed would know better. A sizeable majority of voters twice elected him. And save for one brief interval, his conduct as a President has always had commensurate approval on the showing of the Gallup Poll. Why not? The popular hero in a genuine sense, the man who is both great and friend, has never been in long supply with us. In the later Forties and throughout the Fifties, Eisenhower was the only one we had. To place him in the White House without losing him as hero seems both reasonable and prudent on the part of average citizens, no matter what their general view of politics or Presidents. The same thing can be said of the Republican professionals who managed Eisenhower's nomination in 1952; their action appears reasonable and prudent in *their* terms. They twice had tried a leading politician as their candidate; this time they wanted most of all to win. But when it comes to journalists, and government officials, and business leaders, and professors, who joined in the parade or urged it on, one deals with a phenomenon decidedly less reasonable. Some of Eisenhower's sharpest critics at the present time were once among his most articulate admirers. What was their understanding then—what is it now—of our political institutions? His virtue was supposed to be that he was above politics, and disenchantment with him rarely seems a disenchantment with this odd criterion. Instead it is all Eisenhower's fault that he is not what temperament and training never equipped him to be. When one finds attitudes of this sort in the circle of articulate observers, one wonders at the meaning for American society.

Before he reached the White House Woodrow Wilson once remarked: "Men of ordinary physique and discretion cannot be Presidents and live, if the strain be not somehow relieved. We shall be obliged always to be picking our chief magistrates from among wise and prudent athletes—a small class."[4] In the perspective of this book his formula needs some revision. The strain is vastly greater now, with no relief in sight. If we want Presidents alive and fully useful, we shall have to pick them from among experienced politicians of extraordinary temperament—an even smaller class.

PART TWO

LATER REFLECTIONS

9

Appraising a President

Those last paragraphs conclude the text of *Presidential Power* as it first appeared in April 1960. When a French edition of the book was prepared eight years later, its editor suggested I append an "afterword" appraising John F. Kennedy as President by light of the book's analysis. Having agreed to do so I discovered that its terms, being prospective, do not lend themselves to retrospect without some adaptation. The same ideas take somewhat different form when somebody's performance is reviewed, after the fact, from what is wanted to elaborate his needs before he chooses. Without changing concepts I endeavored to restate them in a form befitting retrospect, the form of questions to be asked about a Presidency—as one person in a vast machine—after it ends. Here are the results, now offered for convenience in a chapter, not an afterword. This I hope suggests what might be done with *Presidential Power's* frame of reference if one wishes to look retrospectively at any President.[1]

In appraising the personal performance of a President it seems useful to ask four questions. First, what were his purposes and did these run with or against the grain of history; how relevant were they to what would happen in his time? Second, what was his "feel," his human understanding, for the nature of his power in the circumstances of his time, and how close did he come in this respect to the realities around him (a matter again of relevance)? Third, what was his stance under pressure in office, what sustained him as a person against the frustrations native to the place, and how did his peacemaking with himself affect the style and content of his own decision making? This becomes especially important now that nuclear technology has equipped both Americans and Russians with an intercontinental capability; stresses on the Presidency grow apace. Fourth, what was his legacy? What imprint did he leave on the office, its character, and public standing; where did he leave his party and the other party nationally; what remained by way of public policies adopted or in controversy; what remained as issues in American society, insofar as his own stance may have affected them; and what were the American positions in the world affected by his own diplomacy?

To answer these four questions, the outside observer must look for certain clues.

1. Regarding purpose, clues are found in irreversible commitments to defined courses of action. By "purpose" I mean nothing so particular as an endorsement for, say, "Medicare," or anything so general as a pledge to "peace." (All Presidents desire peace.) By "course of action" I mean something broader than the one but more definable than the other: Harry S. Truman's commitment to "containment," so called, or Dwight D. Eisenhower's commitment to what he called "fiscal responsibility." By "commitment" I mean personal involvement, in terms of what the man himself is seen to say and do, so plain and so direct that politics—and history—will not let him turn back: Truman on civil rights, or Eisenhower on the Army budget, or Lyndon B. Johnson, alas, on South Vietnam where turning even slightly was rendered credible only by his promise to leave office.

2. Regarding feel for office, sensitivity to power, clues are drawn from signs of pattern in the man's own operating style as he encounters concrete cases, cases of decision and of follow-through in every sphere of action, legislative and executive, public and partisan, foreign and domestic— Truman seeking above all to be decisive; Eisenhower reaching for a place above the struggle.

3. Regarding pressure and its consequences, clues are to be drawn again from cases; here one examines crisis situations, seeking signs of pattern in the man's response—Truman at the time of the Korean outbreak, or of Chinese intervention; Eisenhower at the time of Hungary and Suez, or of Little Rock—times like these compared with others just as tough in terms of stress.

4. With regard to the man's legacy, one seeks clues in the conduct of the *next* Administration. Roosevelt's first New Deal in 1933 tells us a lot about the Hoover Presidency. Truman's troubled turnabout in postwar foreign policy casts shadows on the later Roosevelt Presidency. And Kennedy's complaint at Yale in 1962 about the "myths" regarding economic man-

agement is testimony to one part of Eisenhower's legacy: the part identified with the redoubtable George Humphrey.

To list these sources of the wherewithal for answers is to indicate the folly of pursuing my four questions when the object of the exercise is Kennedy-in-office. He was President for two years and ten months. If one were to assess Franklin Roosevelt on the basis of performance before January 1936, or Harry Truman on his accomplishments before enactment of the Marshall Plan, or Eisenhower if he had not survived his heart attack, or LBJ before the 1966 Congressional elections—or Lincoln, for that matter, if he had been assassinated six months after Gettysburg— one would be most unlikely to reach judgments about any of these men resembling current judgments drawn from the full record of their terms. We cannot know what Kenndy's full record would have been if he had escaped assassination. Still more important, we can never know precisely how to weigh events in his truncated term.

Truman's seven years and Eisenhower's eight years suggest a certain rhythm in the modern Presidency. The first eighteen months or more become a learning time for the new President who has to learn—or unlearn—many things about his job. Regardless of his prior training, nothing he has done will have prepared him for all facets of that job. Some aspects of the learning process will persist beyond the first year and a half. Most Presidents will go on making new discoveries as long as they hold office (until, at last, they learn the bitterness of leaving office). But the intensive learning time comes at the start and dominates the first two years. A President's behavior in those years is an uncertain source of clues to what will follow. It is unreliable in indicating what will be the patterns of performance "on the job" once learning has been done. Yet the fourth year is also unreliable; traditionally it brings a period of pause, dominated by a special test requiring special effort—the test of re-election. The way that test is taken tells us much about a President, but less about his conduct on the job in other years. The seventh year is the beginning of the end—now guaranteed by constitutional amendment—as all eyes turn toward the coming nominations and the *next* Administration.

Thus, in the search for signs of pattern, clues to conduct, the key years are the third, the fifth, and the sixth. Kennedy had only one of these.

Moreover, in this presidential cycle, retrospect is an essential aid for sorting evidence. What a man does in his later years sheds light on the significance of what he did in early years, distinguishing the actions that conform to lasting patterns from the aspects of behavior that were transient. The man's early performance will include a host of clues to what is typical throughout his term of office. But it also will include assorted actions that turn out to be unrepresentative. Looking back from later years these become easy to distinguish. But in the second or third year it is hard indeed to say, "This action, this behavior will be dominant throughout." That is the sort of statement best reserved for retrospect. Kennedy's case leaves no room for retrospect; he was cut off too early in the cycle.

No scholar, therefore, should have the temerity to undertake what follows.

II

Turning to an appraisal of this President in office, I come to my first question, the question of purpose. This is not a matter of initial "ideology," fixed intent; far from it. Franklin Roosevelt did not enter office bent upon becoming "traitor to his class." Truman did not swear the oath with any notion that he was to take this country into the cold war. Lincoln certainly did not assume the presidency to gain the title of "Great Emancipator." Johnson's massive victory of 1964 surely was not *intended* as a prelude to the Vietnam war we know today.

The purposes of Presidents are not to be confused with their intentions at the start; these are a matter, rather, of responses to events. Nor should these purposes be confused with signs of temperament, with "passion." Whether Kennedy was "passionate" is scarcely relevant. Truman certainly deserves to have the cause of civil rights cited among his purposes, but if he were to be judged in temperamental terms according to the standards of, say, Eastern liberals, he scarcely could be called a man of passion on the point. And FDR is considered historically as "Labor's friend," although his coolness toward the great show of that friendship in his time, the Wagner Act, remained until he sensed that it was sure to be enacted. What counts here is not "passion," but the words and acts that lead to irreversible *commitment*.

In Kennedy's three years of office, what were his commitments? Never mind his private thoughts at twenty or at forty; never mind his preferences for one thing or another; never mind his distaste for a passionate display—taking the real world as he found it, what attracted his commitment in the sense that he identified himself beyond recall?

The record will disclose, I think, at least three purposes so understood. First, above all others, most compelling, most intense, was a commitment to reduce the risk of holocaust by *mutual* miscalculation, to "get the nuclear genie back in the bottle," to render statecraft manageable by statesmen, tolerable for the rest of us. He did not aim at anything so trite (or unachievable) as "victory" in the cold war. His aim, apparently, was to outlast it with American society intact and nuclear risks in check. Nothing, I think, mattered more to Kennedy than bottling that genie. This, I know, was deeply in his mind. It also was made manifest in words, among them his address at American University on June 10, 1963. That speech is seal and symbol of this purpose. But other signs are found in acts, as well, and in more private words accompanying action: from his Vienna interview with Khrushchev, through the Berlin crisis during 1961, to the Cuban missile crisis and thereafter—this commitment evidently deepened with experience as Kennedy responded to events.

Another speech in June of 1963 stands for a second purpose: the speech on civil rights, June 11, and the message to Congress eight days later which launched Kennedy's campaign for what became the Civil Rights Act of 1964. Thereby he undertook an irreversible commitment to Negro integration in American society, aiming once again to get us through the effort with society intact. He evidently came to see the risks of social alienation as plainly as he saw the risks of nuclear escalation, and he sought to steer a course toward integration that could hold inside our social order both impatient Blacks and reactive Whites—as tough a task of politics as any we have known, and one he faced no sooner than he had to. But he faced it. What Vienna, Berlin, and Cuba were to his first purpose, Oxford and then Birmingham were to this second purpose: events that shaped his personal commitment.

A third speech is indicative of still another purpose, a speech less known and a commitment less apparent, though as definite, I think, as both of the others: Kennedy's commencement speech at Yale on June 11, 1962, soon after his short "war" over steel price increases. He spoke of making our complex economy, our somewhat *sui generis* economy, function effectively for meaningful growth, and as the means he urged an end of ideology in problem solving. His speech affirmed the notion that the key problems of economic growth are techincal, not ideological, to be met not by passion but by intellect, and that the greatest barriers to growth are the ideas in people's heads—"myths" as he called them—standing in the way of reasoned diagnosis and response. Kennedy, I think, was well aware (indeed, he was made painfully aware) that only on our old-style Left is ideology defunct. Elsewhere it flourishes, clamping a lid on applied intelligence, withholding brainpower from rational engagement in the novel problems of our economic management. He evidently wanted most of all to lift that lid.

Failing a response to his Yale lecture, Kennedy retreated to the easier task of teaching one simple economic lesson, the lesson the tax bill carried through after his death: well-timed budget deficits can lead to balanced budgets. This, evidently, was the most that he thought he could manage in contesting "myths," at least before election. But his ambition, I believe, was to assault a lot more myths than this, when and as he could. That amibtion measures his commitment to effective growth in the economy.

Stemming from this third commitment (and the second), one discerns a corollary that perhaps would have become a fourth: what Kennedy's successor named "the war against poverty." During the course of 1963, Kennedy became active in prompting plans for an attack on chronic poverty. His prospective timing no doubt had political utility, but it also had social utility that evidently mattered quite as much. Historically, the "war" is Lyndon Johnson's. All we know of Kennedy is that he meant to make one. Still, for either of these men the effort, if sustained, would lead to irreversible commitment. So it has seemed to be for Johnson, even though he let another such commitment take priority for energy and funds.

Each purpose I have outlined meant commitment to a course of action that engaged the man—his reputation, *amour propre*, and sense of self in history— beyond recall. The question then becomes: how relevant were these, historically? How relevant to Kennedy's own years of actual (and of prospective) office? Here I can only make a judgment (tentative, of course) devoid of long perspective. These purposes seem to me entirely relevant. In short perspective, they seem precisely right as the preeminent concerns for the first half of this decade.

What of Vietnam? The worst thing one can say of Kennedy's decisions in that quarter is that these were offhand, intermittent, and discontinuous—in short, the reverse of "committal." No doubt there was a frightful lapse in management, but not in purpose. By way of purpose, small attention to Vietnam, a low priority, seems *right* for this decade. Consider the results of high priority after Kennedy left the scene!

III

So much for Kennedy as a man of purpose. What about the man of power?

He strikes me as a senator who learned very fast from his confrontation with the Executive establishment, particularly after the fiasco at the Bay of Pigs which taught him a great deal (see Chapter 11). On action-issues of particular concern to him he rapidly evolved an operating style that he maintained consistently (and sharpened at the edges) through his years of office. If one looks at Berlin, or Oxford, Mississippi, or the Cuban missile crisis, or at half a dozen other issues of the sort, one finds a pattern: the personal command post, a deliberate reaching down for the details, hard questioning of the alternatives, a drive to protect options from foreclosure by sheer urgency or by *ex parte* advocacy, and finally a close watch on follow-through. Even on the issues that were secondary to the President and left, perforce, primarily to others, Kennedy was constantly in search of means and men to assure that those others used this personalized pattern with its stress on open options and on close control. Numbers of outsiders—Hans Morgenthau and Joseph Alsop for two— sometimes viewed the pattern with alarm and saw this man as "indecisive." But that was to consult *their* preferences, not his performance. Kennedy always seemed keen to single out the necessary from the merely possible. He then decided with alacrity.

Not everything was always done effectively, of course, and even the successes produced side effects of bureaucratic bafflement, frustration, and irritation, which were not without their costs. Even so, the pattern testifies to an extraordinary feel for the distinction between President and Presidency, an extraordinary urge to master the machine. This took him quite a way toward mastery in two years and ten months. We shall not know how far he might have gone.

Kennedy's feel for his own executive position carried over into that of fellow rulers everywhere. He evidently had great curiosity and real concern about the politics of rulership wherever he encountered it. His feel for fine distinctions among fellow "kings" was rare; it was comparable to the feel of Senate-Leader Johnson for the fine distinctions among fellow senators. And, with this, Kennedy apparently absorbed in his short time a lesson Franklin Roosevelt never learned about the

Russians (or de Gaulle): that in another country an *effective* politician can have motives very *different* from his own. What an advantageous lesson to have learned in two years time! It would have served him well. Indeed, while he still lived I think it did.

The cardinal test of Kennedy as an executive in his own right and also as a student of executives abroad was certainly the confrontation of October 1962 with Khrushchev: the Cuban missile crisis. For almost the first time in our foreign relations, the President displayed on that occasion both concern for the psychology of his opponent and insistence on a limited objective. Contrast the Korean War, where we positively courted Chinese intervention by relying on Douglas MacArthur as psychologist and by enlarging our objective after each success. "There is no substitute for victory," MacArthur wrote, but at that time we virtually had a nuclear monopoly and even then our government hastened to find a substitute. Now, with mutual capability, the whole traditional meaning has been taken out of "victory." In nuclear confrontations there is room for no such thing. Kennedy quite evidently knew it. He also knew, as his performance demonstrates, that risks of escalation lurk in high-level misjudgments *and* in low-level momentum. Washington assuredly was capable of both; so, probably, was Moscow. Accordingly, the President outstripped all previous efforts to guard options and assure control. His operating style was tested then as not before. It got him what he wanted.

Unhappily, another, subtler, seemingly less pressing test came his way a year later with the Buddhist agitation in Vietnam. That test he flunked. Diem's assassination may have made this plain to him three weeks before his own demise.

In confrontations with Congress, quite another world than the Executive, the key to Kennedy's congressional relations lay outside his feel for power, beyond reach of technique; he won the Presidency by a hair, while in the House of Representatives his party lost twenty of the seats gained two years earlier. The Democrats *retained* a sizeable majority as they had done in earlier years, no thanks to him. With this beginning, Kennedy's own record of accomplishment in Congress looks enormous, indeterminate, or small, depending on one's willingness to give him credit for enactment of the most divisive, innovative bills he espoused: the tax and civil rights bills passed in Johnson's Presidency. Certainly it can be said that Kennedy prepared the way, negotiating a bipartisan approach, and also that he took the heat, stalling his whole program in the process. Equally, it can be said that with his death—or by it—the White House gained advantages that he could not have mustered. Johnson made the most of these. How well would Kennedy have done without them? My own guess is that in the end, with rancor and delay, both bills would have been passed. But it is a moot point. Accordingly, so is the Kennedy record.

Whatever his accomplishment, does it appear the most he could have managed in his years? Granting the limits set by his election, granting the divisiveness injected after Birmingham with his decisive move on civil rights, did he use to the fullest his advantages of office? The answer may well be "not quite." Perhaps a better answer is, "This man could do no more." For Kennedy, it seems, was not a man enamored of the legislative way of life, and legislators knew it. He was wry about it. He had spent fourteen years in Congress and he understood its business, but he never was a "member of the family" on the Hill. "Downtown" had always seemed his native habitat; he was a natural executive. They knew that, too. Besides, he was a young man, very young by Senate standards, and his presence in the White House with still younger men around him was a constant irritant to seniors. Moreover, he was not a "mixer" socially, not, anyway, with most members of Congress and their wives. His manners were impeccable, his charm impelling, but he kept his social life distinct from his official life and congressmen were rarely in his social circle. To know how Congress works but to disdain its joys is an acquired taste for most ex-congressmen downtown, produced by hard experience. Kennedy, however, brought it with him. Many of the difficulties he was to encounter in his day-to-day congressional relations stemmed from that disdain.

But even if he had been a man who dearly loved the Congress, even if that feeling had been reciprocated, nothing could have rendered their relationship sweetness and light in his last year, so long as he persisted with his legislative program. As an innovative President confronting a reluctant Congress, he was heir to Truman, and to Roosevelt after 1936. Kennedy's own manner may have hurt him on the Hill, but these were scratches. Deeper scars had more substantial sources and he knew it.

In confrontations with the larger public outside Washington (again a different world), Kennedy made a brilliant beginning, matched only by the start in different circumstances of his successor. The "public relations" of transition into office were superb. In three months after his election, Kennedy transformed himself from "pushy," "young," "Catholic," into President-of-all-the-people, widening and deepening acceptance of his presidency out of all proportion to the election returns. The Bay of Pigs was a severe check, but his handling of the aftermath displayed again superb feel for the imagery befitting an incumbent of the White House, heir to FDR *and* Eisenhower. That feel he always had. I think it never failed him.

What he also had was a distaste for preaching, really for the preachiness of politics, backed by genuine mistrust of mass emotion as a tool in politics. These attitudes are rare among American politicians; with Kennedy their roots ran deep into recesses of experience and character where I, as an outsider, cannot follow. But they assuredly were rooted in this man and they had visible effects on his public style. He delighted in the play of minds, not of emotions. He doted on press conferences, not set performances. He feared "overexposure"; he dreaded overreaction. Obviously he enjoyed responsive crowds, and was responsive to a sea of cheering faces, but I think he rarely looked at their reaction—or his own—without a twinge of apprehension. He never seems to have displayed much fondness for the "fireside chat," a form of crowd appeal without the crowd; television talks in evening hours evidently struck him more as duty than as opportunity, and dangerous at that; some words on air-raid shelters in a talk about Berlin could set off mass hysteria—and did. At the moment when he had his largest, most attentive audience, on the climactic Sunday of the Cuban missile crisis, he turned it away (and turned attention off) with a two-minute announcement, spare and dry.

Yet we know now, after his death, what none of us knew before: that with a minimum of preaching, of emotional appeal, or of self-justification, even explanation, he had managed to touch millions in their private lives, not only at home but emphatically abroad. Perhaps his very coolness helped him do it. Perhaps his very vigor, family, fortune, sense of fun, his manners, taste, and sportsmanship, his evident enjoyment of his life and of the job made him the heart's desire of all sorts of people everywhere, not least among the young. At any rate, we know now that he managed in his years to make enormous impact on a world-wide audience, building an extraordinary base of public interest and affection (interspersed, of course, with doubters and detractors). What he might have made of this or done with it in later years, nobody knows.

IV

So much for power; what about pressure? What sustained this man in his decisions, his frustrations, and with what effect on his approach to being president? For an answer one turns to the evidence of crises, those already mentioned among others, and the *surface* signs are clear. In all such situations it appears that Kennedy was cool, collected, courteous, and terse. This does not mean that he was unemotional. By temperament I think he was a man of mood and passion. But he had schooled his temperament. He kept his emotions under tight control. He did not lose his temper inadvertently, and never lost it for long. He was observer and participant combined; he saw himself as coolly as all others—and with humor. He always was a witty man, dry with a bit of bite and a touch of self-deprecation. He could laugh at himself, and did. Often he used humor to break tension. And in tight places he displayed a keen awareness of the human situation, human limits (his included), but it did not slow his work.

Readers beyond the age of forty may recognize this portrait as "the stance of junior officers in the Second World War''; Elspeth Rostow coined that phrase and, superficially at least, she is quite right. This was the Kennedy stance, and his self-confidence, his shield against frustration, must have owed a lot to his young manhood in that war.

This tells us a good deal but not nearly enough. At his very first encounter with a crisis in the Presidency, Kennedy's self-confidence seems to have been severely strained. The Bay of Pigs fiasco shook him deeply, shook his confidence in methods and associates.[2] Yet he went on governing without a break, no change in manner, or in temper, or in humor. What sustained him? Surely much that went beyond experience of war.

What else? I cannot answer, I can only conjecture. His family life and rearing have some part to play, no doubt. His political successes also played a part. In 1952 he bucked the Eisenhower title to reach the Senate; in 1960 he broke barriers of youth and of religion which had always held before; on each occasion the Conventional Wisdom was against him: "can't be done." Beyond these things, this man had been exceptionally close to death, not only in World War II but ten years after. And in his presidential years his back was almost constantly a source of pain; he never talked about it but he lived with it. All this is of a piece with his behavior in a crisis. His control, his objectivity, his humor, and his sense of human limits, those were but expressions of his confidence; its sources must lie somewhere in this ground.

Whatever the sources, the results were rewarding for this President's performance on the job. In the most critical, nerve-straining aspects of the office, coping with its terrible responsibility for use of force, Kennedy's own image of himself impelled him neither to lash out nor to run for cover. Instead, it released him for engagement and decision as a reasonable man. In some of the less awesome aspects of the Presidency his own values restrained him, kept him off the pulpit, trimmed his guest list, and made him shy away from the hyperbole of politics. But as a chief *executive*, confronting action-issues for decision and control, his duty and his confidence in doing it were nicely matched. So the world discovered in October 1962.

V

Now for my last question. What did he leave behind him? What was the legacy of his short years? At the very least he left a myth: the vibrant, youthful leader cut down senselessly before his time. What this may come to signify as the years pass, I cannot tell. He left a glamorous moment, an engaging, youthful time, but how we shall remember it depends on how we shall remember Lyndon Johnson. He left a broken promise, that "the torch has been passed to a new generation," and the youngsters who identified with him felt cheated as the promise, like the glamor, disappeared. What do their feelings matter? We shall have to wait and see (although the evidence will be ambiguous at best).

May this be all that history is likely to record? Perhaps, but I doubt it. My guess is that when the observers can appraise the work of Kennedy's successors, they will find some things of substance in his legacy. Rashly, let me record what I think these are.

To begin with, our first Catholic President chose and paved the way for our first Southern President since the Civil War. (Woodrow Wilson was no Southerner *politically*; he came to the White House from the State House of New Jersey.) Although Texas may be suspect now in Southern eyes, it certainly is of the South in Northern eyes, as Johnson found so painfully in 1960. Kennedy made him President. How freely he chose Johnson as vice-presidential candidate is subject to some argument. But what appears beyond dispute is that, once chosen, Johnson was so treated by his rival for the White House as to ease his way enormously when he took over there. Johnson may have suffered great frustration as Vice-President, but his public standing and his knowledge of affairs were nurtured in those years. From this he gained a running start. The credit goes in no small part to Kennedy.

Moreover, Kennedy bequeathed to Johnson widened options in the sphere of foreign relations: a military posture far more flexible and usable than he himself inherited; a diplomatic posture more sophisticated in its whole approach to neutralists and Leftists, markedly more mindful of distinctions in the world, even among allies. In European relations and in dealings with the Soviets, LBJ built on this diplomatic legacy. In Vietnam he departed from it, squandering his military legacy. Unhappily it must be recorded that without the military posture Kennedy left behind, the officials whom he also left behind would not have had the wherewithal to offer Johnson the disastrous option of a full-scale intervention in Vietnam.

The most dubious thing Kennedy left Johnson was American involvement with Saigon. Rashly, this had been enlarged in Kennedy's last months of life by acquiescence in the overthrow of Diem, which transferred to that abstract entity, "the Government of South Vietnam," an undertaking hitherto identified with Diem. Involvement might have been conditioned upon Diem's regime and dropped as he departed, or devolved as his associates dealt with the North. The reverse happened. Kennedy's decisions made it so. By hindsight these were mistaken. Johnson took the consequences. Thereupon he made still less fortunate decisions, which produced a war more costly and more futile than Korea.

Would Kennedy have done the same? We cannot know. My guess is that he would have done quite differently. Given his age, experience, and temperament, given the priorities emergent from three years of office, given the advantages in our domestic politics accorded to a man who had faced down Khrushchev—given all these, I think he would have kept his bombers and his combat troops away, leaving the Saigonese of 1965 to fashion such accommodations as they could. "It's their war, they have to win it," he declared two months before he died. Presumably he would have stood so as they lost it. But the point is moot.

On the domestic side, Kennedy left a large inheritance of controversies, opened by a youthful, Catholic urbanite from the Northeast, which his Southwestern, Protestant successor might have had more trouble stirring at the start, but now could ride and maybe even "heal." Vietnam aside, this might have been a productive division of labor. Even if not, Kennedy lived long enough to keep at least one promise. He got the country "moving again."

In American politics, the *sine qua non* of innovative policy is controversy. By 1963 we were engaged in controversy with an openness that would have been unthinkable, or at least "un-American," during the later Eisenhower years. Events, of course, have more to do with stirring controversy than a President. No man can make an issue on his own. But Presidents will help to shape the meaning of events, the terms of discourse, the attention paid, and the noise level. Eisenhower's years were marked by a pervasive fog of self-congratulation, muffling noise. The fog machine was centered in the White House. Perhaps there had been need for this after the divisive Truman years. But by the late 1950's, it fuzzed our chance to innovate in time. Kennedy broke out of it. This gave his successor an initial opportunity.

Finally, JFK set a new standard of performance on the job, suitable to a new state of presidential being, a state he was the first to face throughout his term of office: the state of substantial, deliverable, nuclear capability in other hands than ours. Whatever else historians may make of Kennedy, I think they probably will begin with this. Eventually they may ask in horror what could justify risking the northern hemisphere, and find an insufficient answer in the Cuban missiles. But given the then climate those would have sufficed for anyone within range of the Presidency in 1960. There can be little doubt that Kennedy's successors have a lighter task because *he* pioneered in handling nuclear confrontations. During the Cuban missile crisis and thereafter, he did something that had not been done before, did it well, and got it publicly accepted. Innovation was on our agenda; technology had put it there. But also, in his reach for information and control, his balancing of firmness with caution, his sense of limits, he displayed and dramatized what Presidents must do to minimize the risk of nuclear war through mutual miscalculation. This may become the cardinal risk confronting his successors. If so, he made a major contribution to the Presidency.

VI

What a President now lives with is the consequence of a nuclear second-strike capability acquired by the Soviet Union as well as the United States. It is the mutual capability that pushes our choice-making—and theirs, too, of course—into a new dimension of risk. In previous writings I have termed this the risk of "irreversibility," the risk that either bureaucratic momentum in a large-scale undertaking or mutual miscalculation by atomic adversaries, or both combined, may make it infeasible to call back, or play over, or revise an action taken in our foreign relations, at least within the range of the cold war. But the term "irreversibility," standing alone, does not really suffice to convey what is new in this dimension. Bureaucratic momentum and multiple miscalculations made a German Emperor's snap reaction after Saravejo "irreversible" as long ago as July 1914. Therefore, to amend the term: what is new since the Soviets acquired their missiles is the risk of *irreversibility become irreparable*. Unlike the problems facing Kaiser Wilhelm then—or those of FDR in World War II, or even those of Truman in Korea—a possible result of present action is that nothing one does later can ward off, reduce, repair, or compensate for costs to one's society.

The Cuban confrontation seems to me a relatively simplified affair, geographically, in the issue raised, in the number of contestants, and in duration. What if there were two or three such issues simultaneously, or stretched over two months instead of two weeks? What if there were a multiplicity of nuclear powers, a multiplicity of possible miscalculators, each capable of setting off irreparable consequences? Consider the next President's risk-taking, let alone Kennedy's or Johnson's. This new dimension deepens year by year.

The consequences for the Presidency are profound.

One consequence is that the sitting President lives daily with the knowledge that at any time he, personally, may have to make a human judgment—or may fail to control someone else's judgment—which puts half the world in jeopardy and cannot be called back. Many of us recognize his burden intellectually, he actually experiences it emotionally. It cannot help but set him and his needs sharply apart from all the rest of us, not least from the officials who have only to advise him. As Kennedy remarked in his year-end television interview for 1962: "The President bears the burden of the responsibility. The advisers may move on to new advice."

A second related consequence is that now, more than ever before, his mind becomes the only source available from which to draw politically legitimated judgments on what, broadly speaking, can be termed the political feasibilities of contemplated action vis-à-vis our world antagonists: judgments on where history is tending, what opponents can stand, what friends will take, what officials will enforce, what "men in the street" will tolerate—judgments on the balance of support, opposition, and indifference, at home and abroad. Our Constitution contemplated that such judgments should emanate from President *and* Congress, from a combination of the men who owed their places to electorates, who had themselves experienced the hazards of nomination and election. *The democratic element in our system consists essentially of reserving these judgments to men with that experience.* But when it comes to action risking nuclear war, technology has modified the Constitution: the President, perforce, becomes the only such man in the system capable of exercising judgment under the extraordinary limits now imposed by secrecy, complexity, and time.

Therefore, as a matter not only of securing his own peace of mind but also of preserving the essentials in our democratic order, a President these days is virtually compelled to reach for information and to seek control over details of concrete plans, of actual performance, on "small" operations (to say nothing of large ones), where there often is a fleeting chance—sometimes the only chance—to interject effective judgment. And it is at this level that risks of the gravest sort are often run. "Irreversibility become irreparable" is not to be considered something separate from details of operation. If, as reported, Kennedy kept track of every movement of blockading warships during the Cuban crisis of October 1962, this is but a natural and necessary corollary of the new dimension of risk shadowing us all, but most of all a President.

The net effect is to restrict if not repeal a hallowed aspect of American military doctrine—the autonomy of field commanders—which as recently as Truman's time, as recently as the Korean War, was thought to set sharp limits on White House intervention in details of operation. The conduct of diplomacy is comparably affected. So, I presume, is the conduct of intelligence. Also, we now rediscover that age-old problem for the rulers of States: timely and secure communications. The complications here are mind-stretching.

The only persons qualified to give a full appreciation of the President's needs in such a situation are Eisenhower, keeping his last years in view, and Johnson, who watched Kennedy in 1962 and now sits there himself. Nikita Khrushchev might be equipped to offer some contributory evidence. The situation is so new and so unprecedented that, outside the narrow circle of these men and their immediate associates, one cannot look with confidence for understanding of their prospects or requirements *as these appear to them*.

Thus we encounter, at least for the time being, a new source of differences between the President and most executive officials, the former cannot fail for long to see what he is up against; the latter have not seen enough of men so placed to have much sympathy or a sure sense for how it feels these days, in these conditions, to be President. What they see with assurance is what they in their jobs want of him in his—a very different matter. These differing perceptions of the presidential task are bound to widen differences between the White House, where responsibility is focused, and officialdom, where it is not.

The same phenomenon of differing perceptions seems to play a part in other presidential relationships. No doubt it has some bearing on the current difficulties of relationship between the White House and its counterparts in certain allied capitals where political leaders, in their own capacities, have not experienced the risk to which our President is heir because they lack the power that produced it. Presumably, some of the sore spots in congressional relations have a comparable source. Certainly this is the case with some of the complaints voiced against Eisenhower and Kennedy by private groups intent upon particular action programs.

The lack of common outlook increases the Presidency's isolation and thus reinforces the dictates of common prudence for a man who bears the burden of that office in our time, namely, to stretch his personal control, his human judgment, as wide and deep as he can make them reach.

From now on, everything asserted in this book must be transposed into these terms. The President remains our system's usual initiator. When what we once called "war" impends, he now becomes our system's final arbiter. He is no less a clerk in one capacity than in the other. But in the second instance those he serves are utterly dependent on his judgment—and judgment then becomes the mark of "leadership." Command may have a narrow reach but it encompasses irreparable consequences. Yet persuasion is required to exercise command, to get one's hands upon subordinate decisions. With this so-nearly absolute dependence upon presidential judgment backed by presidential skill, we and our system have no previous experience. Now in the 1960's we begin to explore it.

We can only hope that citizens and Presidents will do so without fear, or histrionics, or withdrawals from reality, or lurches toward aggression. Regardless of the dangers, presidential power, even in this new dimension, still has to be sought and used; it cannot be escaped. We now are even more dependent than before on the mind and temperament of the man in the White House.

10

Reappraising Power

In March 1976, on the invitation of the University of Michigan Law School, I gave three lectures entitled "Presidential Power Revisited." These were responsive to the frequent question thrust at me—sometimes accusingly—by light of Vietnam and Watergate, "what do you think of it now?" I had no choice but to respond "about the same," and did so at length, with refinements, as follows.

In 1900 Woodrow Wilson, then at Princeton, did an admirable thing, displaying rare forthrightness as an author. Fifteen years before he had published his first book, *Congressional Government*—a *tour de force*, worth reading still—which located the center of our public life in Congress and looked to the House Speaker as a likely source of governmental leadership. By 1900, in the aftermath of Grover Cleveland's Presidency, William McKinley's election, and the Spanish-American War, Wilson was prepared to change his tune and did. He introduced a new edition of that book with a discussion of the Presidency's unlooked-for emergence, responsive to events, from the subordinate role he had assigned it in the Eighteen-eighties. Writing on the eve of Theodore Roosevelt's Presidency, Wilson's reading of events was prescient, making up for faulty foresight in his earlier appraisal.[1]

I am admiring and envious, eager to emulate him but unable to do so. For I do not see a comparable change. Since April 1960, when *Presidential Power* first came out, there have been events aplenty, not alone Vietnam and Watergate, but assassinations, riots, inflation, recession, even a nuclear confrontation, to say nothing of changes in our world relationships, political *and* economic. Still, these do not appear to have altered very much the general character of presidential power. Nor do they disclose to me a likely shift of central role from President to Congress or the courts, or elsewhere, of the sort that Wilson found emergent in a turn from Congress to the Presidency.

Not seeing it I cannot report it. Thereby I may have lost my chance for prescience. But in my view the power of a President today derives from roughly the same sources as a generation ago, is comparably limited, similarly frustrating, more changeable than ever, yet as central to our system as before, a far cry still from congressional government. If so, this book's characterization of a President's dilemmas and its notions about how he helps himself to cope still remain relevant at least in general terms. So I think they are.

This does not mean that I would now dot every "i," cross every "t" just as before. In six respects the intervening years, and Presidents, suggest to me a need for altered emphasis or reinterpretation. Let me identify these six, then deal with each in turn.

First are two factors that we now know can affect in striking ways the sources of a President's potential power: perceptions of legitimacy and sentiments of loyalty.

Second are changes of institutional detail, the "fine print" of our system, that cumulating over time affect the relative advantages of Presidents in seeking what they want from others. Below I offer eight such changes, representative I think of all since 1960.

Third are changes in the policy environment—the prominent issues and the actors they bring center stage—which can affect a President's advantages as much as institutional details, or more, and often differently.

Fourth are the human qualities with which a President confronts what history deals out to him, his temperamental fitness for the place, and the enormous consequences of a lack of fit. Witness Johnson and Nixon.

Fifth are the difficulties these men had with power as a source of clues to policy. In crucial instances their power calculations seem to have moved them toward the very policies that later dragged them down. It is precisely against inexpert performances like these that *Presidential Power* tried to warn. Yet failures so spectacular cast doubt upon the adequacy of the warning!

Sixth are developments in the "institutionalized Presidency," the widening array of agencies and aides across the street, or up the block, or literally at the White House, evolving under Franklin Roosevelt and his six successors, four of them *since* 1960.

These six points are examined in successive sections of this chapter. Running through them all is an assumption carried over from the original book, found in every chapter, namely that Americans cannot escape an active federal government because so many of them want so much from it, and that activity in Washington calls for an active President: like it or not, the governmental system will impel him to take initiatives and to render judgments. He may try to lead the system; he is bound to be its clerk. In 1898, two years before Wilson's *apologia*, a scholarly observer who may well have influenced him wrote a deeper book than *Congressional Government*. This was Henry Jones Ford, his book *The Rise and Growth of American Politics*. Correctly, in my view, he even then put the Presidency at the system's center:

> The agency of the presidential office has been such a master force in shaping public policy that to give a detailed account of it would be equivalent to writing the political history of the United States.

> The evidence . . . history affords seems conclusive of the fact that the only power which . . . define[s] issues in such a way that public opinion can pass upon them is that which emanates from presidential authority. . . .

> The rise of presidential authority cannot be accounted for by the intention of presidents; it is the product of political conditions which dominate all the departments of government, so that Congress itself shows an unconscious disposition to aggrandize the presidential office. . . .[2]

Eighty years later the trend seems the same. The question then becomes what next: what lies ahead? That question is addressed in the last section of this chapter.

II

In 1960 I traced presidential influence to three related sources. One was formal powers, often termed authority, vested by the Constitution, laws, or customs in the Presidency, along with the status they conferred upon a President, and sometimes—as in Eisenhower's case—the sparkle his own aura lent to them. These were a source of power for a President insofar as he was able and willing to use them. A second source was professional reputation, amounting to impressions in the Washington community about the skill and will with which he put those things to use. A third source was prestige, his public standing, amounting to impressions in the country generally about how well or badly he was doing as its President.

I see no need to change that formulation now. I would, however, tinker with its emphasis in two respects. The first concerns legitimacy as a link between prestige and formal powers; the second concerns loyalty as a source of influence (and as a trap).

A president's prestige I once regarded as important mainly in the minds of Washingtonians—the actual, direct participants in governance—attempting to anticipate reactions from *their* publics when they dealt with him. Prestige like reputation was a factor in his influence by virtue of their calculations. Unlike reputation, prestige entered indirectly as a sort of limitation, enlarging or restricting their perceived room for maneuver, their "leeway" as I termed it. For their calculations were presumed to be not general but particular, and quite professional, turning on their readings of their own responsibilities by light of his requests, his public mattering only as it affected theirs, hence them.

In the aftermath of Watergate, however, we have seen occasions where distinctions between reputation and prestige seemed to dissolve, where Washingtonians seemed quite like members of the general public, reacting to a President in almost the same terms, conducting themselves accordingly.[3] One such occasion was the "Saturday night massacre" of 1973 when Nixon fired the Watergate Prosecutor, forcing resignations from the Attorney General and his Deputy, all of whom responded on TV. This dramatic sequence—televised and thus "firsthand" in all parts of the country—seemed so to contradict the President's contentions as to drain them of credibility, enlarging what we now label a credibility "gap," indeed extending it so wide as to cast doubt on his legitimacy and with it his authority as President. Nixon seemed to be engaging in a cover-up of criminal activity. He seemingly was fighting law enforcement. But he had sworn an oath of office encompassing the "take-care" clause. Hence the cloud on his legitimacy. The "massacre" tripped off impeachment proceedings.[4] It is easy to see why.

What was striking then is that inside the government or near it, in the watchful circle of the Washington community, reactions against Nixon seemed to have so much in common with the popular impressions outside government. Citizens at large were swept into a "firestorm" of protest and suspicion. But so were commentators, congressmen, and civil servants. Apparently the President's behavior planted the same question in all minds. Some Washingtonians, waiting upon evidence, were slower than others to draw ultimate conclusions, and slower by far than some citizens, but he was treated henceforth with reserve throughout the Washington community. Diplomacy aside—there was a crisis in the Middle East—he turned away from governing and focussed on the prospect of impeachment. Had Nixon tried to be assertive in domestic spheres, I take it that he would have been ignored or resisted. All over town officials shook themselves free of the White House, released by suspicion from deference, distancing their programs from his person. This occurred within one year of his triumphant re-election, three years before expiration of his term. For Washingtonians it was a most uncharacteristic reaction, especially so early in the term. Calculations about possible impeachment played a part, no doubt. But so did outraged feelings about Nixon's performance. There was precious little rallying around him. Instead, so far as I can judge, there was a widespread sense, even in some quarters of the White House, that he had compromised his right to be there and should go, impeached or not.

In 1951 when Truman fired General MacArthur, public indignation did not echo so widely in official Washington, nor did the echo last so long. The President's specific act was plainly constitutional (as Nixon's *may* have been). Moreover it was backed by Truman's Pentagon advisers including the Joint Chiefs of Staff. There were no resignations, nothing to suggest a criminal conspiracy. On Capitol Hill a comprehensive inquiry ensued; those advisers held firm; criticism quieted; the General faded away. Truman's public standing, measured by the Gallup Poll, which had bottomed out six weeks before at 23 percent, rose no more than nine points in his ensuing years of office. But his professional standing, his repute with Washingtonians—as I observed it then and now recall—shot up, responding to the firmness and the calm with which (belatedly) he put MacArthur down, something even FDR had never dared to do.[5]

It must be said that television played a lesser part on this occasion than in 1973, lesser because new both in technique and distribution. But it also must be said—as a pure speculation—that had the dismissal been available to TV with contemporary coverage, MacArthur no doubt hearing and acknowledging his orders on a stage superbly set, then *both* the public outcry against Truman and the Washington respect for him might have been heightened, thus enlarging the disparity between them, rendering them more not less distinct.

The immediacy of television messages and the availability of television screens combine today to complicate all aspects of our politics, not least presidential public relations. But if I am right about Truman and MacArthur, television as such cannot account for the close correspondence between reputation and prestige in 1973.

What then distinguishes Nixon's dismissal of the Prosecutor from Truman's of the General? The answer is suggested by the current connotation of a term not yet in use as late as 1960, "credibility" combined with "gap." Truman-watchers often found disparities between his words and acts, intentions and results, along with inconsistencies in conduct. Gaps of these sorts got him into public trouble, reducing confidence and lessening attention. Control of prices during the Korean War is a case in point outlined in Chapter 5; there it illustrates some of the troubles of a President-as-teacher trying to instruct his general public.[6] These gaps, however, seem to have been generally regarded, save rhetorically by some extreme opponents, as products of misjudgment, or misfortune, or mismanagement—dumb perhaps but not deliberately deceptive—chargeable against his lack of vision, luck, or competence, but not against his candor. Truman took as much abuse as any President before or since, but not for being disingenuous. Nixon, on the other hand, so spoke and acted in the Watergate affair as to assure that he would look like a deceiver.

The distinction between Truman's case and Nixon's is a presidential stance suggestive of deception on a massive scale, substantial and sustained, directed at associates and citizens alike. No wonder that in Nixon's instance they reacted alike. To deal with Americans in this way is to breach the assumptions of representative government, interfering also with the Presidency's service as the nearest thing we have to a human symbol of our nationality and continuity, in short our form of kingship. Disappointed hopes for a good king cut deep, but no deeper than fears of a bad one. A "Saturday night massacre" induces both from all concerned.

A gap in credibility so large as to cast doubt upon the king's legitimacy threatens the throne precisely because commoners and court perceive it and react in the same terms. Were I rewriting *Presidential Power*, risks attendant on such gaps would figure in discussions of prestige and reputation, with the impact on legitimacy underlined in treating formal powers. For even the advantages a President derives from his authority now seem to be at risk if Washingtonians disdain him in the same terms and time as citizens at large. Nixon at the end is said to have experienced a virtual coup d'etat.[7]

The term "credibility gap" was widely used by the Washington press corps well before Watergate. Its original target was not Nixon but Johnson whose deceptiveness on small things and one big one, Vietnam, alienated portions of his public, and infuriated journalists, hence that usage. But members of the press aside, most Washingtonians seem to have been unmoved by Johnson's troubles with the truth except as these impaired his press relations and his popularity, thereby constricting his prospective power. Most Washingtonians, in short, reacted to him, lies and all, with relatively cool professionalism, judging him in terms like those applied to Truman, very much along the lines of this book's chapters on professional reputation and public prestige. In 1968 Johnson suffered not from lack of credibility impinging on legitimacy, as in Nixon's case, but rather from a plain, old-fashioned lack of leeway, after Tet, to pursue a piece of policy, his war, on the same terms as before.

In her brilliant study of LBJ's political career, Doris H. Kearns describes the Tet offensive's impact first on television viewers nationally (with filmed news stories every night) and then on calculations in the Washington community:

> . . . the enemy's sudden attack . . . suddenly exposed the falsity of the Administration's optimistic progress reports . . . What happened at Tet taught the American public an entirely different lesson from the one Johnson intended to convey. . . . In the space of six weeks the percentage of Americans who approved of Johnson's handling of the Presidency dropped from 48 to 36 percent. . . . This decline in public support was both father and child of an equally dramatic decline in media support . . . it also affected Congress, the Democratic Party, the Cabinet, and the White House staff . . . Even the members of the Senior Advisory Group. . . .[8]

What seems to have occurred here was a puncturing of prestige much like Truman's after Chinese intervention in Korea, followed by a widespread understanding among Washingtonians that Johnson lacked the wherewithal to reverse public sentiment and thus lacked the capacity to shield them (or indeed himself) from the opposition attendant on continuing his policy. Many of them soon began to press him to change course. Support for the war sagged in Congress and bureaucracy—also in the law firms of New York and Washington—while key subordinates began opposing and obstructing as never before. Deference to Johnson declined, not only among Democrats in states with early primaries, but also in

official circles at the Pentagon. Thereupon he did change course, at least cosmeti-
cally in Vietnam where bombing was restricted, and decisively in politics where he
gave up the presidential race.[9]

What mattered then in Washington was not Johnson's lack of candor three
years earlier, when he had gradually Americanized the war without acknowledging
its likely scope or character. To Washingtonians that was old hat, a gamble on good
fortune overseas, long since acknowledged and discounted, a mark against his skill,
no doubt, denting his reputation, but buried under three years worth of intervening
acts more relevant to current calculations. What mattered, rather, was the sense that
adversaries in Vietnam were still too strong and popular approval in this country
now too weak to justify continued warfare on the present scale, or higher, and if we
were not going up the scale, we must come down. Johnson may have wished to
disagree, but tactically, at least, took stands that were responsive. He, of course,
knew how to count and, having looked about him, evidently felt he had no other
option.

Johnson was brought to this pass by a progressive failure of his own devising
(although many others helped). Through three years of a worsening war he failed to
shield himself, and thus his chosen policy, from the backlash of disappointed
expectations in the private lives of millions of Americans. Indeed in 1964 and 1965
he positively built up expectations sure to be frustrated by a war of long duration,
while at the same time making it "his" war—enlarged without acknowledgement
on his authority—and then in 1966 and 1967 he seemed to promise what Tet would
belie, a victory of some sort soon. Looking back on Truman's troubles during the
Korean war, I wrote in Chapter 5:

> Because he cannot control happenings a President must do his best with hopes. His
> prestige is secure while men outside of Washington accept the hard conditions in their
> lives, or anyway do not blame him. If he can make them think the hardship necessary,
> and can make them want to bear it with good grace, his prestige may not suffer when
> they feel it. Had Truman's public thought interminable warfare-within-limits a necessity
> his prestige would have risen, not declined, in 1951. A President concerned for leeway
> inside government must try to shape the thoughts of those outside. If he would be
> effective as a guardian of public standing, he must be effective as a teacher to the
> public. Truman was an unsuccessful teacher in the midst of the Korean war. . . .[10]

So it was with Johnson in the Vietnam war. Looking at *his* troubles I find nothing
new to say about the guarding of prestige, no precepts I can add to those set forth
in earlier chapters.

Prestige seems to have been always on the mind of at least one modern
President, Eisenhower. In the light of subsequent events, this is an aspect of his
Presidency which I, among others, find more attractive now than I did then. As a
national hero from the Second World War, he lent the Office his own aura, and was
conscious that he did so, and considered that the loan was badly needed after

Truman's years. Eisenhower found it hard to understand how government could be sustained if three-fourths of the country disapproved a President's performance. He shunned the sorts of controversy that in his opinion had contributed to Truman's low ratings in the polls. He also shunned compatriots who jeopardized his standing as the good man above politics. Years later Nixon, Eisenhower's Vice-President, complained about the latter's stance toward Sherman Adams, then the White House chief of staff, when it turned out that Adams had accepted gifts he ought to have refused:

> . . . He shouldn't have been sacked, he shouldn't have been . . . It's unfair . . . Eisenhower, that's all he cared about—Christ, "be sure he was clean". . . .[11]

Even though the term was not in use, what Eisenhower cared about was his own credibility. He gave it his first loyalty, which was sensible of him, as Nixon probably now knows.

To write in Eisenhower's time after serving under Truman was to writhe with impatience at the President's concern for his extraordinary public standing, his hero's prestige, hoarding not risking it, being not doing. Especially during his second term, after the divisiveness of Truman's years had calmed, Eisenhower's quietude seemed more conservative in terms of policy than I, for one, deemed prudent. So I still think it was. We paid a price for damming up reform until the flood of the mid-Sixties. Still, it also was conservative in institutional terms, identifying man and office to the office's advantage. Looking back after Nixon, that seems a more impressive contribution than it did before.

Now let me turn to the matter of loyalty. When he deprecated Eisenhower's treatment of Adams, Nixon was weighing what he owed his own chief of staff, H. R. Haldeman. The time was early 1973. Haldeman soon would be sacked in his turn, but Nixon was deeply reluctant. He felt he should reciprocate loyalty received, and Haldeman had given him devoted service. That Presidents attract such service is an attribute of office, not peculiar to Nixon. This tells us a good deal about the status of the Presidency. It suggests still more about the yearnings of Americans to serve a cause outside themselves and to rise at the same time. Since 1960 I have frequently been told that *Presidential Power* underestimates such service as a source of influence for Presidents: "do this, do that . . ." and these liegemen will try to do it, no *quid pro quo* required, no implicit bargains struck.[12] Until Nixon's time I grant that while I understood the mechanism, having once been part of it, I never thought it could achieve significant results in matters of great moment to a President. For matters of that sort by definition would engage those separate sharers in a President's authority, officials owing loyalty to others besides him—to Congress, or subordinates, or clients, or themselves—and would thus impel a process more like bargaining than service. But if loyalty cannot manage to move mountains it certainly can produce catastrophic side effects. So Watergate has shown. My critics thus were right for the wrong reasons.

In negative respects, I did indeed underestimate loyalty. A Haldeman or Ehrlichman or aides like Egil Krogh may not be able to dispose of Daniel Ellsberg but, in trying, they can dig a hole so deep as to dispose of Nixon.[13] If there is such a thing as negative influence, misguided loyalty—up *or* down—can be a major source of it. This is something Eisenhower evidently knew; Nixon, it appears, did not.

III

It is the need to bargain that keeps presidential power as uncertain as in most respects I find it. And the need to bargain is the product of a constitutional system that shares formal powers among separate institutions. Of these the Presidency is only one. Checks and balances are with us still, as Nixon's fate reminds us.

But the details of that sharing, the precise terms of those checks, have changed in many ways since 1960. Some of the changes are statutory, some—a very few— reflect court orders, most are far less formal, running not to laws but to accustomed practices or widespread expectations. Details are of the essence in the exercise of power, day by day, and changes of detail foreshadow institutional development, they cumulate and thus suggest the system's future character. These changes are my next concern.

I cannot deal with every alteration of detail since Eisenhower's time, but offer eight that seem to me indicative of all. These eight affect the following activities: appointment schedules, press relations, cabinet contacts, congressional relations, bipartisan consultations, warmaking, impoundments, and renominations. The first five rather lessen the restrictions on a President, the last three add at least procedural constraints. After dealing with each one I will take up their net effects.

First are a President's appointments, by which I mean not jobs but rather time in the man's schedule. In 1960 after his election Kennedy was warned (to his discomfort) that he would be expected to resume the Truman practice, a long peacetime tradition, of granting fifteen-minute interviews to congressmen and other high officials at *their* option, if possible within a day of their request. Eisenhower had stopped most of this, interposing White House aides, a change nobody questioned after 1955 when he suffered his heart attack. Kennedy's transition team did not expect such tolerance for him—relatively young and in good health—but they turned out to be wrong: he got it. Washington had grown accepting of the Eisenhower custom. Kennedy found himself relatively free to see or put off whom he chose. So was Johnson. Their freedom to choose paved the way for Nixon, the most reclusive President in modern times. Ford by conscious contrast has been more acccessible, especially to cabinet members (see below), but again as a matter of choice. The change that has occurred is this: A generation ago, Nixon's practice would have seemed almost an abdication, and Ford's a grudging restoration. Now they are considered matters of style, and the next man can do as he likes.[14]

Second are presidential press relations. From Roosevelt's time through Kennedy's these centered on what then seemed an established institution, the regularly scheduled press conference, where White House correspondents questioned the President on subjects of their choice without advance notice or censorship. Since FDR, the schedule had been cut from two to one a week; since Eisenhower, schedule changes and postponements had ceased to be rarities. And as early as Truman's time the conference had been moved—to accommodate more correspondents—out of the Oval Office, becoming less a briefing for the press than a performance for the public. Live television coverage, a Kennedy device, completed that transition. Television fatally eroded journalism's case for regularity, which rested on the needs of newspapers and wire services. Johnson soon balked at being regularly televised in conference format. He reacted against risks to his own image and his programs inherent in a medium, an *entertainment* medium, where many things besides words are conveyed to many publics viewing as a passive audience. Endowed with different style and temperament, Kennedy had faced these risks with relish. Not Johnson and not Nixon. They did quite well, but they hated the doing. LBJ held conferences at unexpected times and increasingly long intervals. Nixon virtually dispensed with them. Under Ford they have been revived. Indeed they now are flourishing as not since Johnson's early months. Still, there is no commitment to be regular, and but an early promise to be frequent. Again the choice is Ford's, and with a freedom that would have seemed fanciful a generation ago.[15]

Third are a President's relations with the heads of Federal departments, members of his Cabinet, so called. Ford like Eisenhower has been holding regular cabinet meetings (at longer intervals) while his aides, like Eisenhower's, seek agendas that induce team spirit but not boredom, a hard task. And again like Eisenhower—at least before his heart attack—Ford, reportedly, is prompt to honor the request of any cabinet member for a separate interview on any subject. He naturally sees some more than others, as events compel, the Secretary of State most of all. On principle, however, he is ready to see all of them; none is supposed to be in the predicament of Nixon's Interior Secretary, Walter Hickel.[16] The same thing could have been said of the early Eisenhower and his cabinet members, or of Truman and his people. On the surface all is "as was" twenty years ago. There is, though, one small change which, if it lasts, makes a substantial difference. Ford's cabinet members are expected to be grateful for the courtesy. (In Truman's time it was conceived to be a right.) This is a general White House expectation, I am told. They are supposed to know a privilege when they see one. And indeed it is one. For until Ford's accession, many of their predecessors were shut out. By Johnson's time, still more in Nixon's, most principal advisers to the President were concentrated at the White House, with department heads becoming, for the most part, second (or third) stringers. Two or three exceptions usually were made from among State, Defense, Treasury, and Justice. For the rest entrée was rare and status relatively low. As compared even with Eisenhower's early years domestic cabinet members in the Sixties seemed far more dependent on the President's support and services than he on theirs. This came to pass presumably because in program formulation and in legislative liaison the White House had amassed its own resources.[17] It still has them. Cabinet officers do well to be appreciative. What Ford gives he can take away.

Fourth are a President's relations with the leadership of Congress, the Speaker of the House, the House and Senate floor leaders, the key committee chairmen. After 1954, Eisenhower had formal relations with none of them, since they were Democrats; instead he presided regularly over meetings with Republican floor leaders and the White House legislative liaison staff (his innovation) to canvass their combined prospects in opposition. At the same time, however, he kept alive warm personal relations with an old friend from his years of military leadership, the Speaker, Sam Rayburn, whose protégé was the new Senate leader, Johnson. Thereby Eisenhower managed both to become the "new Eisenhower" of 1959—wielder of the veto against Democratic spending—and to keep in foreign policy, as well as in key domestic spheres, an ambiance of good will, above party. The Ford of 1975, with his old friends on Capitol Hill, did very much the same thing for a while, then yielded to the new conditions of campaigning (see below).[18] Their precursor was Truman in 1948, when Republicans held the congressional majorities, denouncing Congress, "terrible," "do-nothing," while embracing foreign policy enactments—like the Marshall Plan—that he himself had nurtured through collaboration with the Republican Chairman of the Senate Foreign Relations Committee, Arthur Vandenberg.[19] Presidents so circumstanced are relatively free to face both ways at once.

Where is the change? In terms of personalities it is enormous. Rayburn and Johnson are gone, while Ford, the career Republican, replaces the hero, Eisenhower. Otherwise, institutionally, there is no change. This, however, is an accident of time-frame. Were we comparing the mid-Seventies with the mid-Sixties, say, or 1950, 1940, even 1930, we would find the President and "his" majority leadership relating to each other in a very different way. Truman could not have turned as sharply on an institution led by Rayburn. Nor would he have wanted to. Nor did he, in fact, during the six years that he was President with Democratic Congresses. Family quarrels are internal affairs, unlike conflicts with the rival clan. But that is just the question. Is there still a family?

The answer may well turn out to be "no," not in the sense of HST and Rayburn. Were a Democratic President in office, the Senate and House leadership again could treat the White House as their meeting ground. Relations with the President might also boost their status on the Hill, at least if they were heeded more than others. But he, looking at them, might find they had still fewer troops behind them than before. Seniority is cracking, constitutents are calling, even safe seats must be worked for, everybody's into his own thing. The fewer troops the more obscure the kinship. Cousins with the same name, to be sure. But colleagues? More like poor relations putting up a front. And he, perhaps, in their eyes looks the same.

Fifth are a President's consultations at times of gravity and stress with the bipartisan Establishment, in Congress and out, that since the start of World War II has buttressed foreign policy, supporting the historic turn from traditional isolation. Eisenhower, who embodied the Establishment himself—at once a hero to it and a symbol of it—used his connection with Rayburn and Johnson as his main means of acknowledging congressional and Democratic elements outside his own official family. One instructive instance among many was his handling of emergency support for France in Vietnam at the time of Dien Bien Phu: he deferred to them and they dragged their feet as he must have expected.[20] Kennedy reached wider, impelled by youth and rendered prudent by the Bay of Pigs affair in the third month of his Administration. At his climactic time of stress, the Cuban missile crisis, he drew into his topmost circle of advisers Dean Acheson, Robert Lovett, Douglas Dillon, Lyndon Johnson, and Adlai Stevenson. These men had been, respectively, Truman's Secretaries of State and Defense, Eisenhower's Under Secretary of State, Rayburn's former colleague in the legislative leadership, and Kennedy's own predecessor as the Democratic nominee for President. They were, in short, a set of surrogates for elder statesmen and their backers in both parties. Acheson was much consulted by key Senators, many of them Johnson men, Lovett much respected by his fellow bankers, Dillon too stood well in the financial world, and Stevenson had won the hearts of Democratic liberals—all this was to the good. That three of these men currently held government positions, Dillon as Secretary of the Treasury, Johnson as Vice-President, Stevenson as Ambassador to the United Nations, tells much about Kennedy's concerns when he appointed them but little about why he brought them into consultation when he faced a national crisis. As far as I can find, it was not their positions that attracted him—or entitled them—but rather their perspectives and their prominence as surrogates.

This I found so striking that I took it for a time to be the sign of a new check upon a President's discretion to make war, a pragmatic substitute for the old check of a constitutional, that is congressional, war declaration.[21] In 1970, however, Nixon proved me wrong, as Arthur Schlesinger noted more tactfully than I deserve.[22] No circle of such surrogates, to say nothing of Congress, was consulted in advance of our Cambodian incursion or our other acts of war there. Nixon seems to have consulted nobody outside the National Security Council's Washington Special Action Group, which neither had members who qualified nor was enlarged to suit.[23]

At this writing, Ford has yet to be heard from. The most that can be said is that he has before him, on the one hand, Kennedy and Eisenhower precedents and, on the other hand, Nixon's (with Johnson cases tending first one way and then the other). Again, the choice is Ford's.

Sixth is the continuation of hostilities once forces are engaged without a declaration of war. During Eisenhower's years the occasion never actually arose, but the contingency was met by seeking in advance from Congress a "blank check"

(Rayburn's terms for it) known generically, from the first time it was used, as a "Quemoy-Matsu Resolution." This was an expression of support for a contingent use of force within a given geographic area, requested when some palpable disturbance in the area jeopardized American interests (that is, when Congress could not readily refuse). Thereby Eisenhower undertook to spare himself his predecessor's troubles during the Korean War, "Truman's War," which Congress had supported but not sanctioned (not having been asked).[24] Eisenhower sought such resolutions twice, once for East Asia, once for the Middle East; in each case forces were deployed but not engaged, time passed, and prospects brightened. Johnson then applied the same device to Southeast Asia and so overloaded it as to destroy it, with warfare on a scale neither imagined nor endorsed by most congressional supporters of the Tonkin Gulf Resolution. Nixon then reverted to Truman's stance, having no other recourse, and stood on his authority as commander-in-chief. The upshot was new legislation, the War Powers Resolution of 1973, a reaction to Vietnam by light of Watergate.

Under this Resolution a President who starts hostilities must first report his reasoning to Congress and then stop them after sixty days unless Congress approves.[25] Previously, once fighting had begun Congress could have stopped it only by denying funds, or by limiting force levels, or restricting deployment. These are actions which originate in the appropriations and armed services committees of both Houses. Now the Foreign Relations Committee of the Senate and the International Affairs Committee of the House have gained a role they craved and lacked. And now within the White House, legislative aides, political advisers, speechwriters, can claim a share—as experts on reporting to the Hill—of staff work once monopolized by national security advisers. Whether these complications of procedure make a President more cautious or more forceful, and Congress more or less inclined to rally to the flag, remains uncertain. What the Resolution puts beyond dispute is that he does possess precisely the initiative asserted by Truman and Nixon. Congress of course can intervene with a specific ban, as on Vietnam and Cambodia after 1973. Congress always could.

Seventh are the changes set in motion by that other legislative monument to Watergate, the Congressional Budget and Impoundment Control Act of 1974. Its provisions on impoundment sanction an old presidential practice—orders to stop spending appropriated funds—but make each order subject to congressional approval. Committee jurisdictions again are key. Until the Nineteen-fifties the appropriations committees had so clear a role in Congress as to almost guarantee that Presidents would not impound funds without their knowledge. Informal consultation was the order of the day. In Eisenhower's second term, however, and thereafter, parts of every chapter of the Federal budget became eligible for funding only after annually renewed authorizations. These brought the substantive committees into play. Their presence stretched out the appropriations process while diminishing the role of the appropriations committees, which by Nixon's time no longer could command to be consulted. Nixon then proceeded at the outset of his second term to impound funds more widely and more substantively than ever before, not after consultation but despite demurrers from all quarters of the Democratic Congress. Federal courts have since struck down a number of his orders on the grounds that they lacked a sufficient statutory base. The new Act fixes that, but at the price of flexibility.[26] Congressional approval now becomes a formal matter, which assures some sort of voice to every interested committee.

The budgetary provisions of the new Act may prove vastly more important to the White House in the long run than impoundment. Everything depends on whether Congress can create and will sustain new institutions of its own, including a coherent budget of its own to which it actually adheres with some fidelity. If it does not a President is no worse off than now. If it does, he may well find himself among the principal beneficiaries: of this more later.

Eighth are a President's decision and announcement for another term, his willingness, or not, to take his party's nomination. Presidents have always considered timing in these matters as important to their influence. Their usual calculation if preparing *not* to run has been to defer the announcement that could tag them a lame duck. Truman in 1952 (the Twenty-second Amendment exempted him) and Johnson in 1968 held off announcing their decisions until late March. If their intention is to run, traditional timing also points to spring of the election year. Even Eisenhower, after his heart attack cast doubt on his capacity to serve, announced his candidacy only at the start of March in 1956, while in 1940 FDR, breaking the two-term tradition, never announced at all; he simply avoided the word "no." And organizational arrangements for campaigning also have traditionally been left to spring or summer. Indeed, one of incumbency's most advertised advantages has been the flexibility to deal with these things later than a nonincumbent.

Behind that advantage there once lay the presumption, taken as fact for most of this century, that in each major party some 50 to 100 men—state leaders, local bosses, elder statesmen, big contributors—decided nominations, most of them too clever or conservative to launch a national campaign by dumping their incumbent. These party barons actually controlled and could deliver delegates at national conventions, campaign services and workers, money, sometimes even votes. Incumbents bent on running could afford to wait because they knew with whom they had to deal in planning a campaign. Incumbents bent on quitting knew with whom they had to deal in choosing a successor.

Yet Ford announced his candidacy and his campaign manager, along with an elaborate organization, in July 1975, thirteen months before his party's national convention, seven months before the first primary election, six months earlier than *non*incumbent Kennedy had moved in 1960, with what was then regarded as unprecedented haste. The immediate cause of Ford's announcement was the Federal Election Campaign Act Amendments of 1974, another Watergate-related measure, so complex in its requirements for financial reports and so rewarding in its formula for public funds as almost to rule out delay.[27] Nixon's successor had to be above suspicion in the matter of campaign finance. Early organization was his means. But deeper causes run beneath the surface of that Act. Its provisions reflect partly an extraordinary change in nominating processes since 1960, doubling the number of state primary elections for the delegates to national conventions. This upsurge in primaries is partly a response of hard-pressed state officials to the Democratic Party's complex rules for representative state conventions, the alternative to primaries, adopted after 1968 in reforms associated with Senator George McGovern. Those reforms, together with his candidacy in 1972, reflect the virtual demise of old-style party barons, while encouraging new-style competitiveness in primaries and conventions alike. What McGovern's nomination signified for Democrats, the Barry Goldwater convention eight years earlier had meant to the Republicans, the passing of the old order.

While the Republicans kept their new order to themselves the Democrats have hastened to entrench theirs in both parties by means of state laws binding on both. Along with federal campaign funds, the new provisions in the states for delegate selection do more than encourage competition among Democrats. They also seem to have encouraged Ronald Reagan. As this is written, other Republicans wait in the wings. Ford's early start owes much to the prospective force of his Republican competitors. Their timing and procedures owe a lot, in turn, to laws accommodating the reforms of Democrats.

We have left the age of barons and entered the age of candidates. Its hallmarks are management by private firms, exposure through television, funding through direct-mail drives, and canvassing by zealous volunteers.[28] That an incumbent President becomes an avowed candidate a year before his party meets in national convention seems a sure and fitting sign of the new age.

These eight are not the only changes since the Fifties in the fine print of our check-and-balance system. There are many others, some well known, as with executive privilege where a right that previous Presidents had not asserted— withholding evidence from courts in criminal cases—was denied by the Supreme Court to Nixon and his successors (at least unless they find a better excuse than he did).[29] But these eight are representative, I think, of what has happened since the Eisenhower years. I offer them as such.

What then are net effects upon a President's position in the system? Plainly there has been no revolution. The landmarks stand. He still shares most of his authority with others and is no more free than formerly to rule by sheer command. Persuasion in a sense akin to bargaining remains for major purposes the order of his day. But at least some of those with whom he deals appear less formidable than before. Despite the legislative aftermath of Watergate, his own advantages, while dented here and there, may have suffered relatively less than theirs, over the years. And this shows up in his autonomy from them, his freedom, relatively speaking, to deal with them on his terms, not theirs.

The leadership of Congress and its key committees, the departments, the Establishment, the party, once afforded any President some men who came as near to being "colleagues" in the British sense as separate institutions (and elections) can allow. With them he had to deal continuously, day by day, on somewhat equal terms, inviting their opinions, taking counsel in advance, because their services were so important to him in his business, mattering to him at least as much as he to them in their business. The balance evidently has been tipping against them. The details I have cited now suggest that they may need him rather more than he needs them. If so, to that extent, they are less colleagues now than customers, whom he by the same token has to "sell" but not consult—not on those terms.

IV

If Ford or his successor were to deal with the same policy environment as Eisenhower twenty years ago, my sense of an imbalance in our governmental system might be strong; the President's advantages essentially intact, the Cabinet compliant, the Congress at bay and the parties collapsed. In the mid-Seventies however, other actors crowd onto our governmental stage, propelled there by historical developments. One such development is the inheritance of Johnson's Great Society, a tangled mass of programs, federal, state, and local. A second development is the conjunction of inflation with recession in the context of emergent resource problems. A third development is the decline of bipolarity abroad accompanied by nuclear proliferation. These three developments—and these are not alone—confront a President with other chief executives, public and private, abroad and at home, each of whom presides over a "governmental" system of his own. Those other chieftains are in a quite different category from cabinet members, congressmen, and bureaucrats, neither potential colleagues nor mere customers for Presidents but rather separate sovereigns, monarchs all, at best potential allies and at worst warlike opponents. In Eisenhower's time, of course, they sat upon their thrones just as now, but a particular conjunction of historical conditions, economic and political, made their mutual interaction and dependence rather less than now. Ford is deeply dependent. So will he or his successor be for years to come. The reasons are embedded in those three developments. Let me take them in turn.

First are the social programs legislated in the Sixties. These meant a quantum jump of Federal oversight and funding for public services that have the most direct effects on private lives, services traditionally in state and local—or in private—hands, now subsidized and supervised from Washington. Consider education, health care, human rehabilitation. These spheres and others suddenly were opened up to Federal aid and oversight, and on a scale approaching highways in the Fifties, or suburban housing in the Forties, or social security in the Thirties. This movement in the Sixties was the biggest jump on the domestic side of Federal undertakings since the New Deal, not entirely unlike the alliances and force levels on the foreign side that followed the Korean War.[30] And after this outburst of social legislation, there came problems of administrative management that are hardly to be compared with anything before, except perhaps consolidating the New Deal. These problems were the fruits of substantive complexity, limited technology, and tangled jurisdiction—all at once and on every hand. In Johnson's time and since the White House has tried alternately to embrace and to escape these problems and the onus. Either way a President will find upon his doorstep men with whom he has to deal on relatively equal terms. If he escapes a fellow chief executive, he does so at the price of giving plenipotentiary powers to an intermediary with whom he then must deal. If Ford for instance hopes to keep his distance from those problems, interposing his department heads, then courtesies to cabinet members soon will become rights he has to honor as a form of compensation. Otherwise, he honors his assistants in their stead, or finds himself confronted with the governors and mayors. In the fall of 1975, reportedly, one consequence of standing off the Mayor of nearly-bankrupt New York City and the Governor of New York State was increased status at the White House for the Secretary of the Treasury who took their calls.

Second are the economic issues of the Seventies, inflation, and recession, and resources. These underline a President's necessitous dependence on performance in the private sector, outside government as such. Oil companies become for Ford or his successor what steel companies once were for Truman, the direct executants of presidential purposes which cannot be achieved without them or despite them. The same thing can be said of many other companies, along with banks, trade unions, and the like. If not executants, then vetoers: wheat sales to Moscow are dependent, for example, on assent from the AFL-CIO. Here is another set of separate institutions, indeed another executive branch, walled off by the Bill of Rights, protected by the courts, in charge of the decisions on investment, on production, prices, wages, and employment which make or break Administration policy. Formal choices can be regulated, to be sure, Congress willing, but their actual execution all too often cannot. And Presidents may hate to regulate, or fear to, or Congress may not have the will, or regulators lack the skill. What then does a President do? Truman's *ad hoc* answer, governmental seizure, was ruled out by the Supreme Court, at least for him. Chapter 2 tells the story.[31] His plight suggests prospective problems.

Third are events abroad that bear upon nuclear risks. One striking aspect of the cold war years after Korea, still more after Suez, is the degree to which a President of the United States stood on a lonely eminence, removed both from enemies and allies by his government's preponderance of power in the world. Among other chiefs of government he sometimes had old friends evoking sentiment, Macmillan to Eisenhower, or Dutch uncles proffering advice, De Gaulle to Kennedy, or clients wielding vetoes, Thieu to Johnson, but not allies in the sense of the "Big Three"—Roosevelt, Winston Churchill, Joseph Stalin—during World War II, or even in the sense of Neville Chamberlain before the war, infuriating but conceived to be the key to Roosevelt's hopes for containing Hitler. After the war, Britain although weakening progressively remained the nearest thing available, and Londoners held status long after losing power because Washingtonians so wanted "somebody to talk to in the world." I quote Dean Rusk. In Johnson's time, however, they were sent away from table for ambivalence about Vietnam. Nixon, starting fresh, but building on beginnings made by Kennedy and Johnson, found somebody more powerful to talk to, the Russians.

Detente in current practice is expressive of a trend that can be traced to mutual shock in 1962, the shock of nuclear confrontation. From the Cuban missile crisis both sides seem to have drawn an abiding mutual interest in the avoidance of destruction by mutual miscalculation. Since then they also may have been discovering a shared distaste for the potential risks of nuclear proliferation in a multipolar world. If so they have not yet been moved to act effectively, or found a way, but seem at least aware of a community of interest. A comparable awareness is made manifest in space by astronauts and cosmonauts together, the "haves" of high technology distinct from the "have-littles" or "have-nots." That is the distinction at the root of detente.

In a world where income and wealth are unevenly distributed while manufacture of atomic weapons spreads across all continents, the rich (having the most to lose) may face egregious risks as time goes on, risks from governments, guerrillas, gangsters, brandishing the bomb. The risks run not only to what such bombs could do but also to the strains on Washington trying not to mutually miscalculate with Moscow. Thus Moscow is indeed a source of allies for a President, essential in the most compelling aspect of his business, aiding and constraining and potentially destroying, all at the same time.

In Chapter 9, appraising John Kennedy, I noted that a nuclear second-strike capability, available to Moscow and Washington alike, had pushed the risk of war for both into a new dimension, one of "irreversibility become irreparable." By this I meant not only that some choices were beyond recall once made—an old dimension—but worse, that nothing later could "ward off, reduce, repair, or compensate for costs to one's society."[32] What became clear with Kennedy and has remained so since is that this new dimension pushes Presidents of the United States into a new degree of isolation: no other American lives daily with so much responsibility for just that sort of choice. In a peculiarly uncomfortable way, the new dimension is theirs personally, setting them apart both intellectually and emotionally. Jonathan Schell brilliantly evokes that isolation and its cause to run a thread of explanation through Vietnam and Watergate, tying them together, possibly too neatly, in a fashion that cannot be lightly set aside.[33] If such events as these have been affected in the past by isolated thoughts about atomic risks, then how much more significant a President's responses in the worsened circumstances of proliferation.

And a President now faces isolation not only in these terms of mind and heart but operationally as well. He may be checked and balanced by a set of rival chieftains either allied or opposed, but still less than the old colleagues from party, Cabinet, Congress do these other chief executives afford a President the prospect of sustained support. Few of them are likely to feel themselves bound to him by common class or ethnic origin, or education, training, or experience, or even aspirations, save in the most general sense, to say nothing of party. If he can sustain loyalty in his Cabinet, he will have more luck than most Presidents before him. If he sustains reliable relationships with governors, mayors, businessmen and labor leaders, and the Russians too, he will be a miracle worker. Viewed thus, the cumulative changes of detail in institutions, lessening restraints upon a President, are being countered by historical developments in policy. This leaves a lot of balance in our system; indeed it may be balanced to the point of immobility. The burden on the President is in no way diminished, rather the reverse. Governance remains as much as ever, or still more, dependent on his human qualities.

V

Chapter 7 dealt with human qualities in terms of three things that a President brought with him to the job: a sense of purpose, a feel for power, and a source of confidence. I argued that the first two were conditioned by the third, and that self-confidence was fashioned from experience and temperament. I traced the connections briefly in three cases, those of Roosevelt, Truman, and Eisenhower, later adding Kennedy, but drew from them no other pointers for the future than two widely quoted, singularly unhelpful generalizations: "The Presidency is no place for amateurs . . ." and needs ". . . experienced politicians of extraordinary temperament." After Johnson and Nixon, experienced both and beyond doubt extraordinary, I no longer can leave it at that!

Those two—Johnson and Nixon—were unlike in many ways, in regional affiliations, party loyalties, human sympathies, political aspirations, policy approaches, and notably in operating styles: Johnson, for example, was addicted to the face-to-face (or voice-to-voice) encounter; Nixon was fearful of surprises, and mistrustful of his own responses, much preferring paper. In two respects however they seem similar. Each was a driving man and driven, tending to excess, compulsive in seeking control, taking frustration hard.[34] At the same time, perhaps for the same reasons, each presided over a Royal Court, writ large. George Reedy, after a short, unhappy stay in Johnson's time described it as:

> . . . a mass of intrigue, posturing, strutting, cringing, and pious "commitment" . . . the conspiracy of . . . the untalented, the unpassionate, and the insincere . . . .[35]

Reedy was right in thinking he had stumbled unexpectedly into a new Versailles, but wrong in his description of the problem. It is not that his colleagues were the sycophants he makes them out to be, for most were not (neither of course were men like Nixon's Haldeman). Those adjectives are mostly misapplied. The problem, rather, is that LBJ and Nixon both indulged themselves in office, drawing from the White House and the smoothness of its workings a false sense of security and mastery. Self-indulgence took the form of an illusion of omnipotence, not in the large but worse, in the small (which indeed became the essence of the old Versailles). Johnson ceased to respect other people's mealtimes. Nixon stopped seeing most associates. In these and myriad other ways they "rose above" the courtesies and duties of American public life as practiced by most politicians, including previous Presidents. It may have been a good thing for FDR that White House food in his time was as awful as accounts suggest. It surely was a bad thing for Johnson and Nixon that in their time every sort of service worked superlatively well. From air conditioning to carpentry to helicopters, all was at hand and in order. This was the seduction, not the flattery of staff, that led these men into extraordinary self-indulgence.

All Presidents since Coolidge have had drive and all since Hoover have been surrounded by a set of aides somewhat resembling courtiers. Some have lived official life quite lavishly like Eisenhower, the General, and Kennedy, the man of inherited wealth. But none seems to have been so driven, so surrounded, or so self-indulgent in the small as LBJ and RMN. In those respects these two appear distinct from Roosevelt, Truman, Eisenhower, Kennedy—and Ford at least in his first year.

That Ford can be included with those others, even provisionally, keeps his two immediate predecessors from looming as a trend, but their peculiarities continue to be damaging to hopes placed in experience. Nixon, to be sure, had had a limited experience of *government* before becoming President: four years in the House, two in the Senate, and eight in the Vice-Presidency sitting on the sidelines. But Kennedy's was rather comparable: six years in the House and eight in the Senate of which four were largely taken up by illness or campaigning. And LBJ had had immeasurably more experience: three years on a House staff, three as an administrator, eleven as a Congressman, twelve as a Senator—six as Majority Leader—and then three as Vice-President. Among modern Presidents none but FDR—with two years in a legislature, eight in Wilson's sub-Cabinet, and four as Governor of New York State—had previous careers remotely comparable in their variety. None, again save Roosevelt with those four years in New York, came close to wielding comparable power.

Perhaps the quality of experience counts more than the quantity. Roosevelt's experience though less than LBJ's was far more relevant to *presidential* power. Kennedy's informed a mind already open to experience-at-one-remove, his father's and grandfather's. He also came to office as a "winner," alike in his encounters with elections and with illness, and in his family's climb toward the heights of our society. Nixon, relatively speaking, entered office as a "loser," nursing the resentments of a lifetime. Johnson, we are told by Kearns, brought with him a besetting fear of loss. Quality may count; in all of these respects I think it did. But the variety of experience is such that none of it can be applied predictively with confidence. Theodore Roosevelt had but two years as a governor; Abraham Lincoln was something of a loser.

What then of temperament? Lincoln's ambition, his law partner wrote, was "an engine that knew no rest."[36] The same thing could be said of all but two men in our modern list, Truman and Ford, the two who never aimed at being President. And even they, once there, promptly became ambitious to remain, to vindicate themselves, to enter history in their own right. Ambition evidently counts, along with drive, or more precisely as a part of drive, the part that chooses personal goals. And drive amounts to energy so strong that it can bring a Roosevelt back from polio, a Nixon back from limbo, or a Truman into office relishing his work. By all accounts Johnson had superabundant energy, and Nixon a sufficiency. But this, like the ambition woven through it, scarcely renders them distinct from others. It is not their drive but their drivenness that sets them apart from the rest. Its mark is their reaction to frustration: a striking out succeeded by a closing in, angry suspicion leading to sulky isolation.

I touched, too lightly, on frustration in Chapter 7:

> FDR is said to have remarked that "Lincoln was a sad man because he couldn't get it all at once. And nobody can." If a President is to assist himself through the viscissitudes of four long years or eight, his source of confidence must make him capable of bearing Lincoln's sadness with good grace. . . .[37]

This is a test Johnson and Nixon flunked, each in his way. Johnson experienced immense frustration with Vietnam and his own countrymen. By 1967 it had made of him a mean and fearful man. He regained a measure of self-satisfaction only when he convinced himself that his withdrawal from the presidential race would help achieve his aims and serve the country. Nixon, at the end, bereft of comparable comfort, unable to believe his aims were served by his disgrace—as indeed they were not—froze into immobility, then for a while fell apart. In this he was the victim less of his acute frustration with events than of the events themselves. Yet those were matters he himself had set in motion out of earlier frustration with such relatively trivial things as leaks of information.

Back of their bad grace when things went wrong lay insecurity, or so it seems, a stressful inner turmoil that would go away only when things went right. Apparently both men were in the grip of human hungers they endeavored to appease by being President: Johnson always seeking to assure himself that he had performed wonders and won love, Nixon always demonstrating to himself that he had retained mastery and kept cool. Nothing in the Presidency guaranteed them constant satisfaction, rather the reverse. Yet they were constantly in need.

The source of their self-confidence was a performance on the job beyond their reach in their circumstances. Johnson might conceivably have managed to live up to his immense conception of the job (that is, his huge demands upon himself) if he had come to office earlier or later and escaped Vietnam. But his is the easier instance for he seems the more solid personality. Nixon, self-made in every sense, watching himself, mastering himself, hating improvisation, almost surely would have found his Presidency hard to take, a torment, even without Watergate. Both men, in all events, drew confidence from images of office they were fated very often not to meet, falling short. It is no wonder that they took frustration badly. For they took it altogether personally.

David Barber, in his pioneering effort to derive predictive lessons from political biography, has classed Johnson and Nixon with Wilson and Hoover as "active-negative" Presidents, a reference to their characters not their avowed positions.[38] This sweeps too far for me. I admire but am doubtful of a scheme that crowds these four into a single square. However that may be, Barber's view of what is common in their characters helps to delineate two temperaments at least, the two that now concern us:

> The contradiction here is between relatively intense effort and relatively low emotional reward . . . The activity has a compulsive quality, as if the man were trying to make up for something or to escape from anxiety into hard work . . . Active-negative types pour energy into the political system, but it is energy distorted from within.[39]

And that distortion seems to me a profound insecurity reflected in their images of office. Truman and Eisenhower both projected on the office images they could live up to, and derived security from doing so. Roosevelt and Kennedy approached the office as their natural habitat and drew security from being themselves. Johnson, still more Nixon, on the other hand, imposed upon themselves demands they often could not meet, and suffered accordingly.

The simple lesson then, is to beware the insecure. But how are we to know them? Senate Leader Johnson, job fitting like a glove, seemed wholly in command both of himself and of its resources. So he did again, remarkably, in the transition after Kennedy's assassination, to say nothing of his own campaign for election and the dazzling early months of his new term. New York lawyer Nixon, California left behind, was generally reported to have broadened, mellowed, calmed, and shed the tension of his gubernatorial campaign. And the President-elect who asked Americans to "lower our voices," while placing on his staff a Rockefeller Republican along with a Kennedy Democrat—Henry Kissinger and Daniel Patrick Moynihan, both from Harvard to boot—seemed more of the same.

Some clues might have been found in the operating styles of Senator Johnson and Candidate Nixon. The tension that would characterize their staffs in later times had some precursors. Johnson's Senate staff is said to have been dominated by him, and his will and whims, far beyond the norm in Senator-to-aide relations. It was often fascinating, rarely comfortable. Nixon's campaign staff, by all accounts, was never comfortable once Haldeman came aboard; his was the personality that domineered thereafter, and by Nixon's choice. More important, there is nothing to suggest that either Nixon or Johnson ever took himself less than seriously. I hear and read no reminiscences about their laughing at themselves. Johnson was a marvelous storyteller, full of tales about himself, including stories on himself, self-critical indeed, but not self-deprecating. He had a gift for ridicule, but seems not to have turned it on himself. His personal pretensions were not fit subjects for humor. Nixon, though not gifted in that special Texan way, seems to have been equally inhibited. The contrast between them and Kennedy is sharp. The sharpness is instructive. Kennedy was frequently the butt of his own jokes. He watched himself with wry detachment; his sense of humor was a sign of his perspective. Perspective is precisely what those others lacked. Their solemnity about themselves was of a piece with their intensely personal reactions to frustration.

How then might I improve on my assertion that the Presidency needs "experienced politicians of extraordinary temperament?" Two points emerge; neither is world-shaking. First, enjoyment of the job, and on it, and an ease in it, together with enjoyment of one's self, seem of the essence. Roosevelt's sense of fun combined with Roosevelt's sort of confidence remain for me what they were sixteen years ago: a target at which to aim. The need is for a temperament that nurtures these ingredients. One external sign of it sometimes is a man's humor, as with Kennedy. Another sign sometimes is unpretentious self-assurance as with Eisenhower. Still another, sometimes, is an unselfconscious rootedness, a sturdy sense of "home," like Truman's for Kansas City. Alas, such signs can all be feigned. This brings me to my second point: we—and he—are well advised to seek signs independent of his campaign (and its merchandising). The search should encompass his previous employment. Since nothing he has done will be precisely like the Presidency, nothing in his past can be conclusive. But the nearer the comparisons the more suggestive. Hence the relevance for him—and us—of previous experience, its prime utility, overshadowing acquired skills: it tests his temperament, with luck it strengthens his perspective on himself (and gives us some on him). Kennedy's case illustrates both points, and the forever-mooted argument about his future conduct will suggest their limits: external signs are not infallible; experience may prove irrelevant.

Had Johnson's case and Nixon's been like Harding's—victimized by faithless friends—their human qualities would not now give us pause. But quite the contrary, these recent Presidents were men who victimized themselves, men of intelligence and acuity, determinedly pursuing a great cause which they themselves endangered by their moves in its defense, moves prompted by their insecurities. Johnson's cause—the thing for which he hoped to be remembered—was the Great Society, his effort to outpace the New Deal, outflank group conflict, override class structure, and improve the lot of everybody in America. Nixon's equivalent, more coolly calculated if perhaps no less romantic, was a generation of peace achieved by carefully maneuvering American armed forces and diplomacy and economic resources to bolster and adjust a world balance of power. These were the things they cared for, and these were what they jeopardized, Johnson trying simultaneously to safeguard South Vietnam, Nixon trying to entrap his real and fancied enemies, then covering up.

Their causes being notable, their failures are lamentable. It matters that they left the goals they cared for in distress: Johnson's stalemated, Nixon's at the least somewhat distorted, both in doubt. There is in Nixon's drama so much evil that his cause and the reality of his commitment are disputed. I am prepared to take them at face value. Doing so sets him alongside Johnson as a figure worth attention and compassion. Comparatively speaking, Nixon fell far lower, but the terrible dimensions of the fall seem much the same. For Johnson fell from higher. Unmatched as Senate Leader he came within sight of an unparalleled Presidency and a political career unique in American annals. What happened to him then? What happened to the two of them? How could they fail so signally to serve those causes?

VI

What Presidents do every day is make decisions that are mostly thrust upon them, the deadlines all too often outside their control, on options mostly framed by others, about issues crammed with technical complexities and uncertain outcomes. The technicalities may be no less mysterious to Presidents than the uncertainties, yet they must choose, even if only to defer. Choice-making on these terms is high among their functions in our government. It is indeed the essence of what I have called their clerkship.

In Chapters 7 and 8 I endeavored to advise on what a President could do, himself, regardless of all others, to bring something of his own to bear upon those mysteries, not so much dispelling them as compensating for them with a guidance system he himself could use and check. I fastened on the likelihood that, rightly understood, his personal stakes of power in a given act of choice, its bearing on his own prospects for influence, could readily suggest to him key questions about policy, questions of relevance, effectiveness, and timing, in any course of action he considered:

> The things a President must think about if he would build his influence are not unlike those bearing on the viability of public policy. The correspondence may be inexact but it is close. The man who thinks about the one can hardly help contributing to the other. . . . The very breadth and sweep of his constituencies and of their calls upon him, along with the uncertainty of their response, will make him keen to see and weigh . . . political, managerial, psychological and personal feasibilities. And because the

President's own frame of reference is at once so all-encompassing and so political, what
he sees . . . in terms of power *gives him clues in terms of policy* to help him search
beneath the surfaces of issues. . . .

Our system affords nobody a better source of clues. . . .[40]

At the center of converging expectations from five sources—from officialdom,
from congressmen, from partisans, from citizens at large, and from abroad—a
President's advantage as a seeker after clues turns on the very fact that no one else
has such diverse "constituents," who in their collectivity decide alike his future and
the fate of national policy. Therefore, I argued, every President can make a special
contribution to development of policy, asking questions prompted by concern for
his own prospects. And the better his perception of what lies behind his prospects,
the more "expert" he is about the sources of his influence, the more likely he is to
seize upon key issues in a policy's prospects for requisite support, both at the start
and as conditions change. "Presidential expertise thus serves effective policy." So
ran my argument in 1960.

But in 1965 Johnson launched his Great Society, sending Congress a stream of
bills, and almost simultaneously Americanized the Vietnam War, bombing the
North while sending troops to Saigon. (He also seized Santo Domingo for a time,
temporarily adding to the din.) By July, Congress was enacting social legislation
with a speed and scope unprecedented since the Hundred Days of 1933. Johnson
had another year's worth of legislation to feed in, and urged against the slightest
slacking off. At the same time he committed 175,000 troops to fight for South
Vietnam, aware that his advisers believed twice that number would be needed for
some two-and-a-half years to secure Saigon's hold upon the country, breaking the
resistance of guerrillas and their allies from the North.[41] We now know that those
estimates of men and time were ludicrously low compared to subsequent, still
insufficient efforts. But Johnson and his aides knew then that their estimates were
inordinately high, compared to congressional and public expectations. Johnson's
Pentagon advisers urged him to fill that gap by calling up reserves, calling for new
taxes, and inviting congressional approval of his aims. Johnson refused. He tried
instead to wage the war without acknowledging its scale to Congress, or the public,
or indeed his own economic advisers.

LBJ chose not to risk his legislative program by a war, but chose at the same
time to have a war and, thus, to be deceptive. Thereby he paved the way for an
inflationary upsurge, turned colleges into pressure cookers, diverted energies, not
least his own, from the administrative challenge in his Great Society, and moved
decisively toward his later loss of public standing. Eight months after an extraordinary election in 1964 had given him the congressional votes for domestic reform, he
plunged toward the conjunction of events and sentiments that three years later
forced him to withdraw from re-election with the war un-won, the Great Society
unraveling, the Democrats in disarray, and Nixon, back from the political grave,
well on his way to the Presidency.

Where then was Johnson's expertise in power when he made his choice for unacknowledged war? Did he see what he risked himself? And seeing did he probe the implications for effective policy? Alas for my argument, the answer seemingly is "yes" on both these scores. Perhaps he did not see completely and he almost surely failed to probe enough, but see and probe he did.[42] The trouble is that what he saw cut both ways on the issue. Every source of power yielded insights into policy. But these diverged.

Many of Johnson's insights helped to steer him toward deception. In terms of the advantages he drew from his authority, a formal partnership with Congress on the war would crimp his freedom to keep hostilities limited, or to negotiate a peace, while at the same time giving congressmen excuses to slight legislation for the Great Society. In terms of his professional reputation, an acknowledged need for taxes—which had just been cut at his urging the year before—would suggest that he was less than omnipotent, less than the Master Politician of Senate legend and the 1964 campaign. Alternatively, calling for a War Tax would suggest that times and his priorities had changed; he wanted none of that. Yet failing in Vietnam would seem to violate his pledge after Kennedy's death ". . . let us continue." Worse still it could bring down on Johnson's head (so he believed) an outcry from the man he humanly feared the most: Robert F. Kennedy. And failure would also court trouble from traditional hard-liners on the Hill, conservatives from West and South, who once in Nixon's fashion had lambasted Truman for the "loss" of China. Finally, in terms of prestige, popular approval, acknowledging the war could promise Johnson nothing that he wanted. For that matter, neither could withdrawal from the war. A rally to the flag might spur demands for a still wider war, "no substitute for victory," shades of MacArthur, while South Vietnam's defeat as we departed might set off an orgy of recrimination.

These were not Johnson's only insights into influence, but these apparently impressed him most. Each one conveyed a short-run risk to his prospective power. Every risk was easily discerned. Each was tangible, partaking readily of concrete images like votes in Congress, headlines in the press, slogans in elections, names, dates, places. All these I think he saw. In terms of his prestige—and with it reputation—there was besides a long-run risk, less tangible since less immediate: the risk of wide frustration stirred by disappointed expectations, with the disappointment blamed on him; the risk, in short, of something like what actually occurred. I think he saw this too.[43] But since it was a long-run risk he chose to gamble that the two-and-a-half years he had been told about would be the maximum duration of his war. He thought this was a gamble on our military hardware, on the capacity of guns and bombs to stop Hanoi and stiffen Saigon. Knowing as he did a lot about our weaponry, he conceived it a good gamble and he took it. But in fact it was a gamble on Vietnamese psychology about which he knew nothing. He mortgaged his prestige to their regimes, both North and South, and suffered accordingly. In this he rather resembled Truman during the first phase of the Korean War, who mortgaged his prestige to MacArthur and Mao Tse-tung, strangers both. Chapter 5 tells the Truman story.[44] It is as sad as Johnson's although not as long.

As for Nixon in the cover-up of Watergate, some aspects of his own psychology will not come clear at least until he publishes his memoirs, if then, but on the public record as it now appears—unprecedented in the detail of his tapes—the short-run tangibles again seem to have overshadowed long-run risks. Indeed the latter scarcely seem to have been seen at all, obscured by arrogance, or ignorance, suspiciousness, or fear, or all of these, until too late. That was the pattern from stage to stage.

In June 1972, when Nixon seems to have first learned of the break-in at the Democratic National Committee (in the Watergate office building, hence the term), he evidently feared not only the immediate embarrassment to his campaign if the involvement of his close associates came out but also the incitement to opponents of the war if there should be revealed, as well, the burglaries and buggings done directly for the White House in a "do-it-yourself" effort to plug leaks of information. That effort Nixon had himself brought into being by successive worries about momentary matters, risks to his diplomacy (and politics) attendant on specific acts of opposition, leaks included. In 1970 and 1971, he and his aides had been frustrated by what seemed to them foot-dragging in the duly constituted counterintelligence agencies, notably the Federal Bureau of Investigation. "Do-it-yourself" ventures were the fruits of that frustration. Thereby Nixon mortgaged every aspect of his influence—prestige, reputation, ultimately formal powers—to the judgment exercised by Haldeman and others in directing a scratch team composed of misfits and incompetents, the so-called White House "plumbers." Then, in order to protect them from disclosure, he took out a second mortgage, this time on the loyalty of a counsel he had scarcely met, John Dean, who handled the initial cover-up. In 1973, as Dean grew restive and afraid, Nixon tried to put in place through Haldeman and Ehrlichman a cover of the cover-up. After their forced departure he continued it himself, hiding some things even from their replacements. And all this time his conversations were recorded by an automatic system, Haldeman's device, that Nixon had accepted for the sake of history.

The ultimate custodian of Nixon's power came to be his tapes which he—whether through prudence, confidence, short-sightedness, or indecision—left intact for the most part. Not surprisingly, except perhaps to him, their existence became public and the Supreme Court in time insisted upon treating them as evidence. Their record of his words then brought him down.[45]

Meanwhile, for sixteen months, from April 1973 to August 1974, the foreign and domestic policy initiatives once confidently planned for Nixon's second term fell by the wayside, victims of the President's enforced preoccupation with the complicated aftermath of Watergate. The so-called "Year of Europe," then billed as a fresh approach, soon faded out of sight. Soviet grain purchases drove up American prices, so did Middle Eastern oil producers after the Yom Kippur War. Washington, once vigorous in combating inflation, now was flaccid. The war itself severely complicated our approaches both to Europe and the Middle East. Complications were compounded by a Greek-inspired uprising in Cyprus and its aftermath of Turkish intervention. A President riding the crest at home might have been useful; Nixon was already drowning. Shortly before scandal overtook him, he had got our forces out of Southeast Asia "with honor." Thereafter Congress forbade him to put them back and also started squeezing military aid to Saigon and Pnom Penh. Nixon, it appears, had meant to react sharply, using aid or bombs or both, against untoward military pressures on those governments.[46] Congress struck the instruments out of his hands.

This setback to his policy, like those in Europe and the Middle East, and energy dilemmas and inflation (and the onset of recession) and the linkage of them all with prospects for detente now won from Nixon's White House but minimal response, intermittent when not inattentive. His mind reportedly was fixed for the most part upon his vanishing reputation, plummeting prestige, and possible impeachment. Thus loss of time as well as lost momentum—and the foregone opportunities that momentum seemed to promise—were prices Nixon paid in coin of policy for his involvement with those plumbers.

From one stage to the next in his entanglement with them there is no doubt that Nixon thought about his own prospects for power. Indeed he may have thought of little else. But every move he made to guard some aspect of his influence exposed another aspect that was often more important. And in contrast to Johnson (or Truman) the aspects Nixon neglected were as tangible as those he sought to serve. Before him I would have asserted confidently that no President in his right mind could let those plumbers near *his* House, or delegate to aides like Dean a massive obstruction of justice, much less do such things lightly in side comments to an Ehrlichman or Haldeman. Nixon was remarkably inept about a key aspect of power and that the most concrete of all, whom to trust. He also was remarkably insensitive about a cardinal aspect of his formal powers, the most traditional aspect of all, the status of his office as a "chief magistracy," representing all Americans to carry out their laws. Still, knowing that he failed to see important things we also know that what he saw—and feared and fought—bore no less on his influence. He seems to have been woefully inexpert in distinguishing the crucial from the irritating. He also seems inexpert in distinguishing the implications over time from effects of the moment. For present purposes, however, his expertise, or lack, is of less interest than the evidence in his case as in Johnson's that the insights power offers into policy diverge, pointing many ways at once, thus limiting their usefulness as guides to viability. From start to finish of the Watergate affair, Nixon chose courses of action that turned out to be unviable.

Where does this leave my argument? Still valid, in my view, but not nearly as helpful as I once had hoped.

A President remains as much in need as ever of some sources he can call his own for questions to illuminate the judgments and criteria served up to him by others. I would not for a moment cease my advocacy of his power-stakes as such a source. Applied by men more skillful than Nixon, this might suffice. But greater skill than Johnson's is not met with every day, even though marred by temperament, and his instance leads me to think that something else is needed as a safeguard and a check.

What might it be? I would suggest that Presidents might try, never as a substitute but often as a supplement, to reverse my original procedure, looking into policy for clues to power problems they might otherwise miss. The aspect of a policy at which to look is its requirement for implementing action, in a word its "do-ability" (or if already implemented its adaptability). The way to look at do-ability is first to visualize the outcome, the societal effect, at which a given option aims, and then to specify the last act—whether or not sufficient in itself—of whatever members of whichever organizations will be ultimately necessary to produce that outcome. If the outcome Nixon wanted was a regime without leaks, the final act had to be self-denial on the part of all officials in the national security sphere, especially up top where leaks are likeliest. Once that last act is identified, in this instance no talking, then the next step is to ponder its prerequisites, looking from the end toward the beginning. No talk by anyone requires in its turn a set of sanctions impelling all. Such potency, in turn, requires that careers be broken, quite consistently, on an enforceable no-leak criterion. Such a criterion implies both standards and surveillance, spread across a dozen personnel systems. And so forth, stage by stage, back to Nixon at the White House, giving an initial order. No President need try to think about the whole sequence. Approximating just the later stages should suffice. For these provide a handy standard, easily devised in a few minutes of hard thought, with which to gauge the usefulness of options framed by others, as for instance those extraordinary plumbers. So measured their inadequacy might have given pause even to a man unconscious of their incongruity.

"Backward mapping," as some of my colleagues call it, is one method—not the only one—to make a start on estimating what if any gap exists between the way an institution works, on average, and the way that it would have to work in order to contribute to a given outcome.[47] Forward planning, step by step, becomes another method—far more usual—for sizing up a gap of this sort, while at the same time thinking how to fill it. Inching forward is what most people do: with some sort of an aim in mind one thinks about the obstacles, especially those nearest, pondering one's resources for getting over, under, or around them, formulates a first step, tries it, looks and listens, reassesses, and then formulates another step (or maybe another aim). Not unreasonably, this is how most bureaucrats and politicians in our public life—and the three Presidents that I myself have seen—appear to plan. It is a piecemeal process, and an iterative process, and decidedly dependent upon feedback. It is a far cry from mapping backward. But I often urge on students headed toward the public sector that when they get into government they try to mix the two, working backward every now and then, enough to notice where their forward motion takes them and how far off course. My students, I presume, will have no option but to try their hands at some such implementation estimates. Unlike a President they scarcely can expect—at least for a long time—to treat their power as a useful guide for policy. Yet Presidents, I take it, find this hard enough to do, so I can justify a bit of backward mapping for them too.

Students aside, this is no academic exercise. Shifting illustrations to a more substantial level, less bizarre than Nixon's, let me now return to Johnson and his choices on Vietnam in 1965. The outcome Johnson evidently wanted was a separate South Vietnam with popular support enough and forces strong enough to keep guerrillas down, while North Vietnam restrained itself from large-scale intervention, and both Vietnams boomed economically on massive doses of American aid. So matters were to stand by 1968. The date was part-and-parcel of the outcome he desired. Translated into final acts of organizations this meant, presumably, for North Vietnam a string of standing orders in the army and the party, commanding restraint, constantly maintained and faithfully obeyed at every level from year to year. For South Vietnam it evidently meant a long list of reforms, effectively translated into daily work by civil servants and by army officers with villagers, refugees and troops, as well as with the monied men of Saigon. Backing up one stage, in North Vietnam there seems to be no doubt—democratic centralism working as it does—that Hanoi's leadership could give and gain obedience for orders of the sort, if wanted. But save in strictly tactical and temporary terms these evidently were precisely what the leaders were agreed they did not want. In South Vietnam by contrast, leaders of all factions in the government and army could agree when times were desperate to reforms of every sort, without the capability, to say nothing of will, for steering them to ultimate fruition through the maze of factional and bureaucratic politics. So at least it seems after ten years from far away.

And what did LBJ's associates urge him to do in order to secure the outcome he desired? Bomb the North indefinitely on a rising scale, within limits, and take over the fighting in the South along with full support of its economy (to which he added dollars for the North as well once it issued those orders). Yet history does not suggest, nor did it then, that bombing of the sort proposed and tried can break the will of governments or make them reverse course. If anything, the evidence available suggested, and still does, that bombing stiffens popular support and renders a regime the more determined.[48] As for running the war in the South, this was managed only with enough of our own men to take the brunt of it, and even when we shouldered both their war and their economy we found ourselves unable to reshape to our content the operating methods of their government and army. But anyone familiar with the workings of our State and Defense departments, our military services, our aid missions, our intelligence stations, and our embassies could well have known that these were all blunt instruments, all big machines, each with its own momentum, not in the least likely so to interlock with Saigon's counterparts as to produce at secondhand a fundamental change in someone else's public services, to say nothing of hearts and minds.

A saddening aspect of our intervention is that ample evidence on this score—as indeed on bombing—was available in Washington to anyone who cared to look about him and take thought, never mind what he could glean from Saigon. Yet few gave such things thought. Most were beguiled by faith in the capacity of our bureaucracies, when pushed by the right people, to do anything they wanted. Some comforted themselves with strained analogies to Greece or to Korea, neither of which in fact was very comparable. The activists at State who pressed political reform were more heedless than most about American capabilities. But as the Pentagon Papers suggest the level of sophistication on this score was low, even from opponents of the intervention.[49]

Yet had Johnson ever had the issues posed to him in terms like these, suggesting the strong likelihood of gaps between desired ends and recommended means, his well-developed senatorial skepticism might have led him at the least to ask hard questions about executive capabilities. Had he done my bit of backward mapping he would have come upon those terms himself. He then could have more readily demanded from associates—because he could so easily have shot holes in their arguments—a richer set of options than the fatal three they gave him in July 1965.

Had Johnson then been willing to think seriously about alternatives to an enlargement of the war, he needed arguments that rested not on matters in his own discretion—not policy priorities, emphatically not politics—but rather on technology or something very much like it. He needed such arguments to ease the crowding of his short-run risks about him, and to arm himself against them, and to help him turn the minds of his advisers toward his long-run risk. He evidently felt that he could not afford—or could not bear—to be seen "playing politics with national security," not by the press or public, not by Congress, not by his foreign policy advisers, all Kennedy men. That sight may well have been repulsive in his own eyes too. He was convinced, apparently, that all of them, himself perhaps included but emphatically including his advisers, would see any lessening of our concern for South Vietnam, any narrowing of our commitment, any casting off, even if gradual, as an appeasement for the sake of domestic objectives, thus inherently political. "Politics stops at the water's edge" had been Truman's motto and belief as he built bipartisanship on the foundations dug by Roosevelt during World War II. Now, in a reverse twist, not doing something that had gained the imprimatur of the bipartisan Establishment was *ipso facto* "politics." And LBJ's advisers, pillars of bipartisanship all, gave just that imprimatur to enlargement of the war. He could stall them on a partnership for Congress in the war, for that was this side of the water's edge, but he could not reject or modify their call for bombs and troops unless his grounds demonstrably were nonpolitical, hence technical. Arguments of operational infeasibility could have come close. Had these but cast doubts on all methods short of wiping out the North combined with full colonial administration for the South— feasible indeed in strictly operational terms—such prospects might themselves have changed the tune of his advisers, most of whom would surely have preferred retreat.

Alternatively, had Johnson then been minded only to enlarge the war within limits, as he did, what he needed were strong arguments, pressed hard, to help him meet his long-run risk: the risk that in hostilities enlarged by him alone, anything short of success on schedule courted popular frustration aimed at him. What he got instead, I gather, was a set of muffled arguments pressed weakly. His Secretary of Defense and others urged candor with Congress and clear signals to the country. In doing so they seem to have been mindful, generally if not precisely, of that long-run risk. But since it was preeminently a political risk, and he the master politician in their eyes and they rank amateurs in his, they couched their argument in terms of constitutional proprieties rather than political imperatives. Yet it was of the latter that he needed most to hear to make him face up to the likelihood of failure. Had he done so, given his mind-set at the time, he might conceivably have opted for more bombing, sooner, rather than commit himself in public to protracted war. But rather than accede to all-out bombing, those advisers very probably would have preferred retreat (again). If not his mind then theirs might have been opened by that interchange. In their respectfulness, however, it did not take place.

As these remarks suggest, the help that Johnson needed then was not self-help alone, not only what he failed to bring to his own acts of choice but also what his own advisers failed to offer him by way of close analysis as well as aid and comfort. I think they served him in this instance very poorly but their sins grow pale compared to those of Nixon's Watergate advisers. The 1960 edition of *Presidential Power*, with its focus on the personal, gave little space to presidential staffing. On the evidence of intervening years that lack of emphasis was a mistake.[50] A President's associates can so contribute to his personal destruction that the staffing of the Presidency ought to be discussed in its own terms.

VII

Earlier I commented on eight details in institutional development since 1960; now for a ninth: In 1959 the full-time senior members of the White House staff—those who held commissions from the President with titles signifying some direct relation to him—numbered 24, up from 12 during Truman's last year. In 1963 the corresponding number was 17, and so again in 1967. By 1972, Nixon had let it rise to 52, then set a pattern for his second term at 40. (For him, of course, most of those titles signified what was not so.) Three years later, Ford's figure was under 30 and drifting down, a reassuring contrast although high for a first year. Truman, following a pattern set by FDR, began with 11. These numbers leave out junior staff—assistants to assistants and the like—of whom Truman, Eisenhower and Kennedy each tolerated about 10, and Johnson a few more at times, while Nixon had dozens. Ford, coming down from Nixon's high, still has at least one dozen. Administrative service staffs and household help account for hundreds more, of course, but are beside the point.[51]

The White House staff traditionally is presidential in a special sense distinct from other agencies associated formally with the Executive Office of the President. Such units as the Office of Management and Budget (once styled Bureau of the Budget), the Council of Economic Advisers, the staff of the National Security Council, and now the staff of the Domestic Council are one step removed from White House status, although their chiefs may claim it: for the most part they have separate switchboards, letterheads and carpools, mostly separate buildings, separate histories and futures, and in OMB substantial career staff. Some agencies have come and others gone in the Executive Office since 1960. For those with continuity, like three of the four above, the ups and downs numerically are far less interesting than in the case of White House aides. One agency waxes, another wanes, but numbers are the least of it.

What makes those White House variations interesting is not only the oddity of Nixon—or perhaps more accurately Haldeman—but the fact that running back to Roosevelt they are classifiable by party: Democrats fewer, Republicans more. I think this is no accident; behind it there lie different sensitivities about the presidential office and its duties and its uses. Strictly speaking these are not partisan differences. For forty years, however, they appear to have been mixed and weighed quite differently depending on which party held the White House. The essence of the difference is in attitudes toward management and what it means at presidential level in our government.

The institutions that surround the Presidency now have thus been stitched together from two rather different patterns alternately favored in successive Administrations. No doctrine of what staffs are there to do, or how, or why, has ever been pursued without encountering and being countered by a different doctrine. No wonder that a President gets less help than he needs. From institutions built in such a way it is remarkable that Ford, or anybody else, can get as much help as he does.

The Democratic Presidents from FDR through Kennedy had some instincts in common. LBJ shared most of these, though less perhaps in his last years. One was a veritable passion for the White House as *their* House, its budget theirs to dole out, and its staff to serve them personally. No one was to work there who did not deal quite directly with some aspect of the President's own work from day to day. "This is the White House calling" was to mean him or somebody reliably in touch with him, able to gauge his feelings and intentions at first hand, not by report. White House stationery was on the same footing. So were offices and cars, mess privileges, and other signs of status. Senior aides with titles ending in those key words ". . . to the President" could have the rank when it matched the reality, not otherwise (allowing an exception now and then for charitable cases such as especially deserving former congressmen). And junior staff assistants to those seniors would be tolerated only if they too had work that brought them often into contact with the President, enough so they could gauge his attitudes and he their judgment. If they were regularly exposed to him less than once or twice a week, they had no business serving in "his" House, however junior. That was a Truman rule of thumb which appealed to Kennedy. Had it applied in Eisenhower's White House, most of the juniors would have gone and some of the seniors too. Had it applied in Nixon's, he would have had a smaller staff than Truman.

In the outlook of a Truman or a Kennedy the place for any aide who did not meet those rules was outside the charmed circle, off his telephone, on someone else's letterhead. Where else? Roosevelt's favorite place became the Bureau of the Budget. Truman for a time toyed with perpetuating the Office of War Mobilization and Reconversion. Kennedy tried dumping extra duties on the Council of Economic Advisers, and was stoutly resisted, Johnson contemplated for his third term a new Office of Program Coordination. Whatever the solution these men improvised, their answer to "where else" always began with "not here."

That viewpoint as initially expressed by FDR when modern staffs were first developing in the late Nineteen-thirties, sparked a once-sharp distinction between "personal" and "institutional." Executive Office agencies outside the White House were conceived to be the place for institutional staff, in short the place for everybody else. In this there was a politician's sense of self-protection from the second-string subordinate at work for himself. There also was a sense of self-protection from the second-string activity on someone else's impulse. Joined to these, however, was a strong belief in separate points of view which should be staffed and cultivated separately so that the President could be assured of both. Institutional advisers had a mandate to think broadly, nondepartmentally, in terms as wide as the Executive Branch, as high as the national polity, as deep as Congress, but *not* personal or partisan terms, cultivating "neutral competence" in Hugh Heclo's phrase.[52] The White House staff would think about the man's own stakes and purposes, including *party* politics, while he could weigh both views and choose between them.

Forty years ago this gospel guided Harold D. Smith, the builder of the modern Budget Bureau.[53] Well into the sixties the distinction held within the Bureau and with Democratic Presidents. Truman and Kennedy followed pretty much in Roosevelt's footsteps. So did LBJ, at least in his first years. But Eisenhower seems to have had little feel for the distinction, and Nixon none at all. The line they drew reflected hierarchy not perspective, separating those with immediate access from those who had to apply for it; in Eisenhower's practice the former came to be a handful of White House aides and a few department heads, while the latter comprised other cabinet members and his whole Executive Office, the rest of the White House included. For all he knew or cared, I gather, junior White House aides could be as much or little "institutional" as an Associate Director of the Budget was "personal." These terms soon lost their bite: "career" and "noncareer" are not the same. Neither are "political" and "nonpolitical." Former Eisenhower aides are simply puzzled by the old distinction. Former Kennedy aides are not, but while his practice temporarily revived it, Nixon's practice interred it, perhaps for good. Smith had disclaimed cabinet rank, emphasizing his nondepartmental status, and he shunned White House emoluments to emphasize his institutional role. Eisenhower's Budget Director took a seat at cabinet table; Nixon's took an office in the White House and a title too. Smith's point was lost, but it was really FDR's.

For Roosevelt, the President was not the Presidency, both ought to be staffed, the President should weigh advice from both. He sought advice as well from everybody else that he could get his hands on: cabinet members, congressmen, and columnists, interest groups and partisans, citizens and friends. Roosevelt never thought that staffs had a monopoly on judgment or on information either. Nor did he rely on aides alone for programmatic ideas, "happy thoughts."

This had a corollary in Roosevelt's practice, which again appealed more to his Democratic successors than to the Republicans. He shied away from fixed assignments of a programmatic character which let his aides grow specialized. Why tempt them into business for themselves? Why layer the Executive branch? Instead, most of the fixed assignments he gave out dealt with his daily work. They usually were couched in terms of helping him to handle some specific and recurrent stream of action-forcing deadlines he himself could not escape: manning his schedule, nursing the press corps, guarding his signature, drafting his speeches, framing proposals and polishing vetoes or, in the war, dealing with Churchill and Stalin, commanders abroad, and the Joint Chiefs of Staff. Assignments like these were organized around recurrent presidential obligations, not functional subject matters. They were differentiated by particular sorts of actions, not by program areas. The men on such assignments were impelled to be generalists, with a perspective almost as unspecialized as the President's own. If somebody's activities did not encourage this, he usually got a second assignment. In wartime, Harry Hopkins dealt with allied governments and also helped to write political speeches.[54] Moreover their assignments mixed them up with one another. Presidential actions interlocked and overlapped. These men knew what their jobs were but they could not do them without watching, checking, jostling one another. Roosevelt liked it so.[55]

All this applied not only to assignments in the personal staff but also to Budget Director Smith, heading the main unit in the then institutional staff, with his work wrapped around that notable stream of deadlines for a President, the budget process. Smith would jostle everybody else, and vice versa.

In 1960 Kennedy found those arrangements to his taste and consciously restored Rooseveltian assignments in a White House altered out of recognition under Eisenhower. Along with press relations and appointment scheduling—invariant assignments by all Presidents—JFK put back together under Theodore Sorensen a bundle of activities that Roosevelt had given Samuel Rosenman, his Counsel both in Washington and Albany.[56] These activities encompassed drafting all the public documents through which the President defined and pressed his program: speeches, messages to Congress, drafts of legislation, statements on enrolled bills, executive orders. This put the Counsel at the center of domestic affairs. At the same time Kennedy made McGeorge Bundy a limited peacetime equivalent for Hopkins, assisting with the stream of presidential actions in diplomacy and defense: approvals, and instructions, and requests for information.[57] After the Bay of Pigs affair, Kennedy brought Sorensen—as well as Robert Kennedy—into the circle that reviewed options with Bundy, and Bundy into the review of major speeches. This was a salutary mixing of assignments. Alas for LBJ, it did not outlast Kennedy.

As FDR had done, and Truman also, Kennedy put nobody between himself and men on such assignments. In the catch phrase, he had no chief of staff. More precisely, less well understood, Roosevelt's pattern left no room for one. The President's advisers were assigned to work he had to do himself; they helped him do it; he superintended them. And if they did not help in such a way, they did not belong in the White House. Roosevelt may not have objected to a chief outside the House for institutional staff. Indeed he sometimes may have thought of Smith as such; Smith certainly encouraged the conception. However that may be, none but the President could run the White House staff because it was by definition personal to him, doing *his* work, filled with *his* people.

In a White House on Roosevelt's pattern, senior aides were called upon to do two things at once: to help their President put his concerns in personal perspective and to help him keep his work informed by other perspectives also. These two are somewhat contradictory; to manage both a man needs empathy and loyalty and self-discipline, all three. For these qualities in combination, Roosevelt looked to old associates from politics and government, a Hopkins, a Rosenman, earlier a Louis Howe. Truman followed suit as best he could. Lacking at the start enough reliable associates, he picked most of his best aides young and grew them on the job, Clark Clifford for example who succeeded Rosenman.[58] In time this method worked quite well outside the sphere of national security. There Truman never had a continuing personal staff. Kennedy, who did, chose men for the assignment from outside his intimate circle; all the rest, however, had been with him in the Senate or in campaigning or both, mostly both. Eisenhower, coming fresh to politics, estranged from his associates in Truman's government, and bent upon a different pattern for his staff, brought to the White House mostly men with whom he had but brief acquaintance. Adams, his chief of staff, had been a stranger to him, save by reputation, a year earlier. It was not very different with John Foster Dulles, his "Adams on the foreign side" as Secretary of State. Yet by the time of the "new Eisenhower," late in his second term—personalities smoothed down, or out, Adams and Dulles departed, the survivors grown accustomed to each other and to him—Eisenhower's White House although differing in form and size became in substance much more personal, more nearly like a Democrat's. It fitted him more closely than before. By then, of course, his time was running out.

This brings me to Johnson and Nixon, our two men who needed help so badly in the instances I note above, yet neither gave it to themselves nor got it from advisers. Each of their cases had curious features. Johnson the Democrat, well versed in Roosevelt's ways, not all of which he liked, spent his first year conciliating the aides he had inherited from Kennedy and running, in effect, two White House staffs at once. He spent his second year in happy symbiosis with one part of his inheritance, the legislative aides around Lawrence O'Brien, and in edgy, on-again-off-again relations with another part, Bundy's part, which Johnson alternately used and by-passed.[59] Meanwhile he lost one of the ablest men who had come with him from the Hill, disciplined and empathetic to a fault, Walter Jenkins.[60] By the time Bundy went, there was no one of Jenkins' weight on Johnson's staff to play Sorensen, much less RFK, with Bundy's successor. But by then Johnson was already eight months down the track that he had chosen in July of 1965. When he Americanized the war, he neither made consistent use of Bundy nor put one of his own in Bundy's place. For personal advice, distinct from Pentagon and State, LBJ looked nowhere in the White House and relied instead on friends outside whose views were not subjected to the daily grind of staff work. One was a Washington lawyer, very well-connected; another was a Justice of the Supreme Court.[61] They saw the risks he saw and urged him on. Lacking their own staff work they could only echo aims, not map the means either backward or forward.

As for Nixon, the peculiar circumstances of his own career left him in 1969 with two disparate sets of old associates, one dating from the Eisenhower era, the other from his long road back; one mainly from the Fifties, the other from the Sixties; one mainly Washingtonian, the other Californian; one steeped in governing, the other in campaigning. This makes it all too neat, but not by much. A number of these people he brought with him to the White House and accorded senior status: from the older set, Bryce Harlow, Arthur Burns, and Herbert Klein; from the newer set, most notably, Haldeman and Ehrlichman.[62] The new people then pushed the old aside, and Moynihan too.[63] By 1971, for most intents and purposes, the "old" associates in Nixon's House were those campaigners of the Sixties, advertising men or lawyers from the Coast, political indeed but with no previous experience of government at all—and no sense of having missed anything. They were loyal, empathetic, and ignorant. Ignorance and arrogance combined in Watergate. Nixon might well have done better all alone. And had a Haldeman possessed the feel for government of, say, a Harlow, sharing the values of long-time practitioners, Nixon probably would have filled out his term.

Nixon's aides sought only to preserve his interests as they understood them. Knowing nothing of Rooseveltian distinctions—how could they— these men perceived no difference between White House and Executive Office or, indeed, between their President and the Executive branch. They thought it was his to run and theirs to hold in a tight grip on his behalf. The impulse for their evil-doing was of a piece with their approach to presidential duty. They thought the Constitution's "take-care" clause made him a general manager as though ours were a unitary government with powers hierarchical, not shared. This was a thoroughly unsophisticated view, but being who they were they scarcely can be blamed for that. He, being who he was, could scarcely tell them otherwise; his only previous executive experience had been as a mere spectator in Eisenhower's White House. And Democratic Presidents had left behind clouds of misleading rhetoric. Kennedy and his young men had also left behind an early image of interventionist vigor. Johnson, for his part, had left misleading practices and even plans. But worst of all was the rhetoric.

Rooseveltian practice dealt selectively with choices. It emphasized the choices that the Constitution and key statutes pressed upon the President. His task was to consider them, prepare the country for them, articulate them, defend them (or amend them): choices in the conduct of diplomacy, choices in the use of troops abroad or at home, choices of nominees to send the Senate, of economic policies to urge on Congress or the private sector, of legislation to propose or veto, of departmental budgets to endorse or cut—choices of all these and also of what he should say about them, how, to whom, and when. ''Management'' for FDR was found in the finesse of shaping, airing or delaying just such choices, while evading others that he did not have to make.

This expresses what he did when he was most successful, an ideal of what to do, but what he said was rather different. In 1937 his Committee on Administrative Management called for presidential staffs along with departmental reorganization. It couched its proposals in terms he endorsed, terms taken from a thirty-year tradition of executive reform running back to the Progressive era:

> . . . the President is the Chief Executive and administrator within the Federal system and service. . . . canons of efficiency require the establishment of a responsible and effective chief executive as the center of energy, direction, and administrative management; the systematic organization of all activities. . . . the establishment of appropriate managerial and staff agencies. . . .

When Roosevelt sent this to the Hill he decked it out in strong language.[64] Thereafter, the theme was repeated for another thirty years by public and private studies under presidential sponsorship. In 1949 there came the First Hoover Commission, with most of its conclusions blessed by Truman. In 1967 there followed the Heineman Task Force, an unpublicized review for LBJ on which he brooded without action, but which his successor's aides got hold of, liked, and used.[65] Nixon's men thought they were carrying on and tidying up what Democrats did badly but had always meant to do.

In this belief they had support from what they could discern of Johnson's practice, bolstered by imperfect understanding of the Heineman report. LBJ had intermittently turned his enormous energies away from choices he could not escape to other people's choices that he wished they would make differently or better. These were choices mostly in the realm of social policy on implementing actions for the Great Society, choices about ways and means of doing (or reviewing) what his previous stream of statutes had empowered a variety of agencies to do. That stream had so entwined these agencies in one another's business that they frequently did nothing, did it badly, did it double, or endeavored to kick it upstairs.[66] Not only was there more entanglement of programs as compared, say, with the Eisenhower years, there were now more programs to entangle, and more agencies to run them, and more supergrades to man them. A whole new subconstituency, a Great Society officaldom, arose to press on LBJ the operating choices they would not or could not make, a new dimension for his clerkship, and because the Great Society was his, he was a deeply interested, indeed an eager clerk. He was willing enough to shoulder their work, but all too often unable, the war saw to that. In frustration he considered things like departmental realignment, and a stronger Executive Office; meanwhile he let Joseph Califano, Sorensen's successor (shorn of speech-writing), assemble enough junior aides to plug away at operational coordination in the interstices of legislative programming.[67] Califano's work set something of a precedent for Ehrlichman's Domestic Council.

Johnson's interventions, real and fancied, squared with his personal priorities, amounting to an option not an absolute requirement. Nixon's associates apparently missed that nuance. Unlike foreign policy, set by the Constitution, or economic policy, a heritage of the Depression, social policy did not—at least not yet— confront them with a mandate for the President to intervene in operating choices day by day. Not being mandatory, interventions of the sort were optional. He could reach down, or anyway could try, wherever he saw need or reason for his purposes. Most Presidents, emphatically including FDR, had intervened selectively in departmental choices, although rarely on so broad a front as Johnson, which may have helped mislead the Nixon men. "It is all your trouble, not mine," Roosevelt once remarked to cabinet members on a matter he did not want for himself. Nixon was free to do the same. Perhaps his aides did not know that. Or if they did they wanted to make sure that he, and they, were free to do the opposite at will, rather than disclaim responsibility. So they endeavored to create a system, an "Administrative Presidency" in Richard Nathan's phrase,[68] that could guarantee Nixon or his agents mastery at any time of anybody's choices, anywhere on the domestic side of government. They put the whole elaborate center of their system in the White House, attracting vast amounts of second-string activity, while trying at the same time to spare Nixon detail.[69] And all the while they thought that they were doing him a service.

Thirty years before, Smith and others around Roosevelt, men who had coped with growing government since the New Deal, including operational control of the economy in wartime, gave some thought to presidential staff work for the postwar period which then seemed likely to produce a range of novel programs in domestic spheres. Eyeing both the White House and his Bureau, Smith sought to leave the first alone, the President's own, while adding to the second a new staff concerned with substance. The Budget Bureau then as now was dominated by the budget process and its coloration, money. Smith proposed to parallel his present organization with a new one, focused not on money but on policies and programs in the context of national development. As the older entity produced the federal budget, among other things, this new one would do staff work on the nation's economic budget, called for by the pending full employment bill. Here would be a center both for substantive review of programs and for longer-range planning, but unlike the National Resources Planning Board, an agency divorced from action which had fallen by the wayside during the war, this center would be wrapped around an action-forcing process leading straight to the President and on to Congress, a process as direct as budgeting, potentially as sturdy. The two would combine at Smith's desk, one step short of the White House, making him indeed the chief of institutional staff. But both perspectives still would run the gauntlet of the personal, with FDR still separately advised on that. Smith's concept had a challenge in the then Director of War Mobilization and Reconversion, Fred M. Vinson, Roosevelt's adjudicator of disputes among the war-time agencies in economic management. Vinson wanted staff work on the Economic Budget for his own, envisaging a peace-time unit separate from Smith's Bureau, that would help at once to formulate and to coordinate domestic programs.[70] There would then have been two institutional staffs, and two chiefs to boot. Roosevelt might have liked that. But he died, and later to the mutual chagrin of Vinson (who had taken his ambitions with him to the Treasury), and his OWMR successor, and Smith—a trinity of claimants blocking one another—Congress passed a different bill creating a new agency to do a lesser job, the Council of Economic Advisers. OWMR soon after was allowed to lapse. The Treasury did not expand. The Budget Bureau never realized Smith's hopes. Neither has its successor, OMB.

Had Roosevelt lived and chosen one of these alternatives, and gained congressional assent and implemented it, then in due course a Johnson might have found himself less frustrated, a Nixon and his novices might have been more content to take the Presidency as they found it. Roosevelt's pattern might have meant more to them because in its completed form it would have seemed more relevant. Besides, had its revival under Kennedy included a strong programmatic staff, its major features might well have been handed down intact through Johnson to Nixon. The Bundy office, to be sure, required some repairs after Johnson, but in all events it was a special case: Nixon knew exactly what he wished to do with that, and Kissinger did it for him. In the absence of these might-have-beens, however, the suggestion of events since 1960, or for that matter, 1952, is that no continuity of pattern, no stability of doctrine, and precious little lore survives from one Administration to the next about a matter so important to a President as where to put advisers, how to use them, whom to seek.[71] Staffing the Presidency now is a game played catch-as-catch-can, with very few rules.

A President's experience once carried some rules forward. Party differences have played a part in staffing patterns up to now but even that amount of continuity seems transient. The Democrats to date were all professional politicians who admired FDR, whereas Eisenhower was an amateur and so was Nixon's patternmaker, Haldeman. But Roosevelt is long-gone. Professionalism may contribute something further. Ford's White House is notable for having in it more political associates with government experience who knew him when their status matched his own, or nearly so, than any President since Roosevelt. Still, Ford owes nothing to Roosevelt's example. And not since 1945 have we had a President whose previous experience had been at once elective and executive. Amateurism can afflict professional campaigners, as we know from Nixon's case, and many cases tell us now that moving down from Congress to the White House calls for vast amounts of training on the job. Experience, at least the kind one gets these days, is not a stable source of continuity in presidential staffing. Neither is anything else.

No matter how he organized his Office, a President in Roosevelt's circumstances had the continuity of some advisers he could not escape: the congressional leadership, the barons of his party, and those members of his Cabinet—scarcely all but usually some—whose weight in politics assured them of his ear. There thus was some advice he at least had to hear. This was collegial advice as I have used the term, but also interested, concerned, familial advice, for these men shared at least a party tie of more than casual interest to them all, creating for each one of them not only long-term stakes but also lasting loyalties. What makes the instability of presidential staffing seem so stark today is that this context has all but vanished, part of it declining with our party organizations and the rest of it suspended by persistent ticket splitting. While Congress and the President wear different party labels he chooses between loyalists who are less than colleagues—lacking a sufficiency of independent power—and colleagues who in party terms cannot be loyal to him. Moreover Congress, whether viewed as men or customs, has been changing fast since LBJ's majorities, to say nothing of FDR's. Now it is uncertain what a restored party tie might bring by way of powerful and loyal associates for Presidents.

Retrospect can induce romance; it would be easy to see more than actually was there in Roosevelt's dealings with those partisan advisers. Their relations neither put his powers in commission, nor gave us anything approaching party discipline as Englishmen conceive it. James MacGregor Burns, indeed, once savaged FDR for failing to be serious in seeking party government.[72] Let Burns be a reminder of how far we were from that. But something is better than nothing. Of colleagues with family feeling, Ford now has none.

VIII

Our system now encounters two opposed conditions simultaneously. On the one hand, a President is still possessed of constitutional and statutory duties, with associated expectations, far in excess of his own assured capacity to carry through. On the other hand, congressional and public moods since Watergate, piled on electoral politics in recent years, drain all stability and certainty out of the terms on which a President once sought support from others whose authority or influence could reinforce his own. The gap between responsibility and capability grows wider. Besides, in Congress and the press and universities are many voices urging, by the light of Watergate, to make this gap still wider. A President may not be able to do many things alone, on his own say-so, but the few he can contrive alarm a lot of people, nowadays, with reason. Nixon sufficed for that, let alone Johnson.

Still, we shall not soon eliminate the Presidency, or even dent it much, which is to say we shall not soon reduce by much the powers that a man now tries to parlay into outcomes of his choice. Since 1973 we have had an outpouring of proposed new laws to make a bad king weak (all of which are subject to the difficulty that they weaken good kings too). But the relief at Ford's accession showed a lack of disposition to pursue the matter far. The Washington community depends upon its kings to be its clerks and fears to weaken them unduly. Public sentiment has been monarchical throughout most of this century. In 1977, the man who sits where Nixon did will also sit where Johnson championed the civil rights of blacks, where drums rolled after Kennedy, where Eisenhower had an eight-year hero's welcome, and so back to FDR, to Wilson, and the other Roosevelt, looming up behind them Lincoln, Jackson, Washington. As Henry Jones Ford noted long ago, we deal here with the oldest form of human governance, elective kingship.[73] Like it or not, it is solidly grounded.

The difficulty remains: a President with powers as before remains a man whose power is unstable, often insufficient or, indeed, perverse. Military orders to one side, he bargains now for most things in a context so uncertain that results may reflect neither what he chooses nor what anybody advocates but something wholly unforeseen, or stalemate. Avoidance of such consequences may depend on nothing more substantial than his skill combined with luck from case to case. In military choices, to say nothing of diplomacy, his skill combined with luck can be the only thing between us and disaster. Americans quite naturally mistrust so much dependence upon someone else's skill. A President has reason to dislike it too. The obverse of uncertainty is isolation for him, lacking colleagues who not only might contain him but could also lend support. Containment appeals to citizens; Presidents yearn for support. Looking toward the clashes over policy in coming years— homeowners versus oil suppliers, ecologists versus energy producers, bondholders versus streetcleaners, taxpayers versus teachers, workers versus pensioners, suburbs versus cities, everybody versus "welfare," race versus race, and so forth in domestic terms to say nothing of foreign affairs—the men elected to the Presidency in 1976 and 1980, and perhaps still more in 1984 will need all the support they can get. How they are to get it, if at all, becomes a major question for our governmental system. Whether, if they get it, they will do so on a basis that at once helps them and reassures the rest of us is still another question. Both are to be answered in our politics. The answers will come clear, I think, within the next decade. Belatedly we then shall be done with "mid-century."

I see four ways whereby support for Presidents might be enhanced and

stabilized, and relatively soon. These are alternatives, although not mutually exclusive: a constitutional reform, a Wildavskian retreat, a television personality, or a
revival of parties-in-government (which does not mean restoration of old party
organizations). Let me conclude this chapter with a sketch of each.

First, and least likely in my view is constitutional reform. Students of our
government have recently discussed reforms like a congressional dismissal of the
President combined with dissolution of both Houses.[74] Ten years from now this may
have been transmogrified into discussion of their dissolution without his departure,
in short his dismissal of them. If this sounds French, it must be said that De Gaulle's
constitution is the only one at hand to have been framed for the precise eventuality
that modern Presidents might have to govern without party ties to ease the pains of
"separated powers." The President of the Fifth Republic has a Premier, dependent
on him, taking heat and doing chores from day to day; a right of referendum,
moving issues from the legislators to the voters at his option; a legislature which if
organized against him he dissolves at will after a year; emergency power to rule by
decree; and a seven-year term with no limit on re-election. In the absence of majority
support from legislators during that first year, all these, large as they are, might not
suffice to sustain presidential preponderance in France. The case has not yet arisen.
Even so, in the United States such things are bound to seem an antidote for presidential impotence. But I cannot see them moving beyond the discusssion stage. For a
crisis so severe as to induce congressional approval, much less ratification by the
states, seems quite severe enough to yield the President what Clinton Rossiter once
termed our Constitutional Dictatorship, a plenitude of powers in a national
emergency evoking crisis consensus. Nothing less could budge Congress, yet with it
an elected President needs no new powers.

Second is the interesting prospect Aaron Wildavsky offers us, his tongue only a
little in his cheek:

When you bite the hand that feeds you it moves out of range. . . .

The response to ever increasing complexity will be ever increasing simplicity. This is
the rationale behind wholesaling instead of retailing domestic policies . . . revenue
sharing . . . family assistance . . . negative income taxes. . . . "Here is a lot of
trouble," these presidential policies seem to say, "so remember the trauma is all yours
and none of mine."

Future Presidents will be preoccupied with operating strategic levers, not with making
tactical moves. They will see their power stakes . . . in giving away their power. . . .
The Cabinet . . . will undergo a visible revival because the President will trade a little
power for a lot of protection. . . . spread the blame.

The "offensive retreat" will not be the work of a single President. . . . But as Presidents discover . . . sickness in health and ignorance in education they will worry more
about their own welfare.[75]

In Wildavsky's home state, California, "lower expectations" has become the cry of two successive governors, Republican and Democratic. Why not next the President in Washington? Lower expectations far enough, or direct them elsewhere, and the remainder might more readily be balanced by available support. The flexibility that Roosevelt had when expectations rose would be recovered in the process of assisting their decline.

This strikes me as ingenious, likely to be tried, and transient. If it is accomplished in the next decade, I think it will have been undone soon after. The Presidency's clerkship, I surmise, is too entrenched, too institutionalized, with far too many parts of both the public and the private sectors too dependent—and insistent—on routine performance, for incumbents to sustain the role of Roosevelt in reverse. Public expectations if once lowered will be raised again, as Congressmen, officials, journalists, and interest groups extract initiatives and judgments labeled "by the President," in order to have something to respond to or react against. Perhaps I am too much impressed by organizational routines on both sides of the extractive process. At any rate I do not see successive Presidents escaping them, or not for long. Here, however, is an area where changes of detail are now worth watching carefully for signs of clerkly duties being shifted from the President.

Third is a three-way combination of nationalized politics, weighted toward the suburbs, television as a source at once of news and entertainment, and a presidential master of the medium, like FDR with radio. We had a brief precursor under Kennedy, although political conditions were not then as ripe as they are now. The medium is even more pervasive now, and its technology still more advanced. We await the potential master: convincing, engaging, concerned, and alert. I do not know who that may be, but think the next decade quite likely to produce him. The last decade, after all, was not shorn of possibilities: Kennedy's two brothers. The years ahead should bring to prominence at least as many prospects; one of them may very well be nominated and elected President.

If so, he might be able to attract, and hold, and mobilize suburbanites across the country, partisans for *him*, with influence themselves in interest groups of many sorts (including what are now called "public" interest groups) and also in assorted firms or unions. Certain of their chieftains he might then attach as allies, along with the state governors, or other elective officers, whose sources of support he happened to have tapped. From his following he then might fashion not a "party," in the old sense, or a "movement" in the usage of the Sixties, but instead a sort of tribe, those lesser chiefs and all. The problem once he had it would be how to keep it, still worse how to pass it on.

Fourth is strengthened party leadership in Congress as a basis for restoring— better still, enlarging—the collegial relationship downtown. We now have grown accustomed to look back upon the Rayburn-Johnson-Eisenhower era as a time when the congressional leadership was strong. But at that time, in a classic study, David B. Truman characterized it as inherently weak, the leadership of a "truncated" majority which valued leaders the less because they could not press the President in party terms or transmit heat (and information) from him. Lacking access to the White House as a party right, leaders of the House and Senate, jealous bodies both, lacked even a place where they could meet on neutral ground.[76] If strong colleagues are wanted, there is need to do better than that.

For most of this century, congressional reforms have moved in the opposite direction. They have mostly been reforms in a Progressive spirit, accenting responsiveness and openness, not power and assuredly not power at the center. Even such a "neutral" change as increased staff for members and committees—which has transformed Congress since Franklin Roosevelt's time—contributes to dispersion in both Houses and adds layers to the legislative process.

Currently, however, reacting to the Nixon years, both Houses have imposed upon themselves or now discuss reformed procedures that would offer striking opportunities to a cohesive party leadership if only there were one.[77] Of these the most important is assuredly the new congressional budget, now undergoing its first trials. Whether, in the absence of strong leadership beforehand, budget resolutions can themselves induce cohesion, opportunities creating appetites, is at once doubtful and crucial. And the need for cohesion in Congress as a whole, encompassing both Houses at the same time, makes the case still harder. Up to now this has been something rarely seen and never yet sustained for long. In 1948, had Senator Taft been able to impose his program on the House Republicans, I do not doubt their party would have won the next election. What he could not do then might Senate budgeteers be able to do now? If so, we are indeed upon the verge of new-found colleagues for a President. If not, all is as-was, and the reforms become but pegs on which to hang more subcommittee meetings and more staffs. Since Roosevelt's time, Congress has acquired quantities of both. These have not made its members notably more influential at the White House: if anything, the reverse.

At least it can be said that in the budget process Congress has reached for a tool which—if it musters leadership to handle—does create a sort of parity with any President, across the board of governmental programs. In the hands of his partisans this promises familial relations as never before. In the other party's hands it promises coherent conflict. We shall see. Of all details to watch with care in the years just ahead, none will convey more portents for the future than details of organization and procedure, whether strengthening or weakening, in the first few congressional budgets.

Relations between President and Congress are affected not only by reforms on Capitol Hill but also by nominating processes across the country. Nationalization of our politics, long awaited, often heralded, may now be fast approaching. National issues now may well have local impacts less disparate than before, more nearly shared wherever the issues run. Disparate impacts used to keep most congressmen and senators distinct from one another and from presidential candidates, because they faced electorates with differing hopes and fears. Differences grew sharpest at the stage of nomination where electorates were smallest and most specialized. *Convergent* local impacts, therefore, ought in time to induce a convergence of criteria for nominations. This should draw a party's nominees much closer than before and should sustain their fellow-feeling once elected. Even down the length of Pennsylvania Avenue, the sense that the same views on the same issues might have like effects in everybody's primary elections (or conventions) ought to bolster everybody's consciousness of party ties.

Sixteen years ago I argued that the Sixties were too soon for this. Chapters 3 and 5 make the point twice over.[78] The Seventies, I then thought to myself, might find a party's President and legislators warming to each other as they felt more heat in common. The Seventies then seemed a long way off. Now that they are here, I think about the Eighties. At midpoint in this decade much depends on whether ticket splitting will abate enough to put the White House under the same party label as Congress. Much depends as well on what becomes of splinter parties during 1976, on whether we escape a national primary thereafter, and on who then represents congressional districts, also states, in national conventions: followers of candidates or sponsors of congressmen. Or do these become the same? Finally, a lot turns on the retirement rate in coming years among congressional incumbents, not least from current junior ranks, together with the eagerness of Presidents to seek out and support replacements.

Since FDR's unhappy "purge" of 1938, Presidents have shied away from open intervention in House and Senate primaries. Nixon seems to have done otherwise in 1972, but his once instance scarcely makes a trend. Unless successive Presidents grow bolder, the convergence of those nominating processes may now be more delayed than I would once have guessed. Without convergence at the stage of nomination there will be severe constraints on party loyalties at the stage of legislation. Nominations are the root realities in party life. But Presidents have reason to be bolder than before: so little else is real in party life, these days, that intervention now can scarcely hurt them.

At the start of this century, in Theodore Roosevelt's time, scholars of the stamp of Wilson and Ford were clear about the means whereby our government could gain enough authority, under enough restraint, to cope responsibly with industrialism and world power: link the powers of the President to those of the House Speaker. The Speaker then was the embodiment of Congress, or at least of that part subject, like the President, to popular election. This formulation made sense at the time and suitably amended does so still. The first of my four alternatives is probably unreal; the second very likely evanescent; the third, taken alone, is at best unstable; the third and fourth together make a suitable amendment. When we find a President who handles television as well as TR did the press, let us encourage him to try to put his friends in Congress, and encourage them to try to build a leadership he cannot help but hear.

CHAPTER 11

Hazards of Transition

Watching President Jimmy Carter in early 1979 sparked the question, is the Presidency possible? During the winter months I lectured on nine campuses where the question was often raised. I had to answer in the following terms.

There are at least four ways to address that question. Of these the first is physical: The memoranda to be read—300 pages daily I am told in Carter's case, down from 450 his first year—the visitors, the trips, the phone calls, meetings, ceremonies in their ever-flowing streams grind a man down. Carter's photographs now make him look a decade older than the candidate of just three years ago. Yet he, like recent predecessors, is more nearly master of his time than Truman was, more nearly able to deflect those streams at will, scheduling himself to suit his own sense of priorities.[1] Truman, 10 years older to begin with, also aged in-office but he lived and flourished for a generation after. The nation survives still. In this respect the Presidency certainly seems possible: Carter *likes* to read.

A second way to treat the question is moral and emotional. The Presidency's biggest burden for a sensible incumbent is American possession of intercontinental nuclear capability when other nations—someday perhaps terrorists as well—possess it too. Even though there has not been an overt, nuclear confrontation between superpowers for a generation, Presidents continue to be shadowed by responsibility for actions risking the irreparable consequences noted in Chapter 9. Citizens repress and so forget. Presidents apparently cannot. When Carter tied his reputation to peace efforts in the Middle East, he saw the area, reportedly, as corresponding to the Balkans before World War I: the source of instability most likely to lure super-powers into mutual miscalculation. His insistence on SALT II may be comparable. As Jonathan Schell wrote of President Nixon,

> . . . the advent of nuclear weapons has done nothing less than place the President in a radically new relation to the whole of human reality. He along with whoever is responsible in the Soviet Union has become the hinge of human existence. . . . he or his Soviet counterpart can snuff it out as one might blow out a candle. . . .[2]

No code of ethics suitable to private life leaves the decision to incinerate a hemisphere, or even to take actions risking such an outcome, in the hands of a mere human, fallible, imperfect. Such things are for God, not for a man or woman. Yet in our public life no Diety has shown a disposition to assume the burden; humans are left to their own devices; so long as their societies allow for such decisions, some person or other has to take responsibility. Why not the President? That's part of what he's paid for. The burden may be *in*human, but some*body* must bear it. In these terms Carter's Presidency is as much or little possible for him as for his predecessors back to Eisenhower when *mutual* nuclear risks began.

A third way to look at the question of presidential possibility is intellectual—again in human terms—when conventional wisdom fails, the experts disagree and confusion dominates. In many spheres of social and economic policy the Seventies are such a time. They feature disillusionment with governmental grants and regulatory processes along with more of both, a high inflation rate combined with unemployment, a sharply falling dollar without promptly rising exports, investment problems, productivity lags, energy gaps, and so forth, all amidst unceasing argument or puzzlement among economists. Keynesians and monetarists counter each other's claims while lawyers mediate and politicians grope. It is a far cry from "main-line" consensus in the optimistic Sixties.

Probably, however, the late Seventies are less confused, and certainly no more so, than the early Thirties. The Great Depression overthrew old attitudes and introduced a host of incompatible hypotheses all thrust on politicians by assertive experts. It was said of FDR in 1933 that he was ready to try anything; within limits, constitutional and capitalist, he did. His programs reflected the babble around him. There is no evidence that the confusion burdened him unduly and effects on public policy, dubious in substance, were quite helpful psychologically. If he and his countrymen then thought the Presidency possible in this respect, it still must be presumed so.

Confusion then was not confined to economics and administration; it extended also to the country's international role, changing since World War I as we gained, relative to others, in potential power. Relatively speaking we are now on the downward slope, again confused but not necessarily more so. To see the fall of Saigon and become dependent on imported oil in one decade seems no more baffling than to face a second World War while still working up a retrospective rage against the first.

A fourth way of approaching possibilities for Presidents is operational. That means addressing the question in low-level working terms. This seems mundane compared to the three other ways, but it is fitting in the context of this book. Let me proceed to do it.

The question becomes this: can a President keep the Presidency going, turn out the work that keeps government going, and hand both on, reasonably intact, to his successor? This requires coping with the streams of choices that result in troop deployments, foreign aid, press briefings, public appearances, congressional agendas, stances *against* adverse economic trends, calls *for* social goals or sacrifices, and so forth clear around the circle of his five constituencies. Considering the contradictory expectations generated by the President's formal powers, coping includes keeping a degree of credibility in his twin roles as chief of government and chief of state.

Keeping the game going is a relatively humble aim. There is no need to raise the standard very high. Minimal effectiveness suffices. Yet Nixon drained domestic credibility out of his roles. Ford's case is mooted by the terms of his accession and his failure of election. On Carter all the evidence is not yet in. Taken operationally, the question of capacity to cope these days invites a problematical response: "yes . . . maybe."

What is minimally effective? Watergate may shove a Nixon off the chart but to what higher standard should we hold a Carter?

The standard I instinctively invoke—the presidential operation as I first came close to it—is Truman's, nothing high-and-mighty about that. Operationally his first two years were troubled and uncertain amidst postwar reconversion and the onset of cold war. Robert Donovan now gives us in detail the ups and downs of it.[3] Symbolizing all, approval for the President in Gallup polls fell sharply to a first term low of 32 percent. In 1946, the Democratic National Committee urged him *not* to campaign for congressmen lest *he* worsen *their* prospects. Comparatively speaking, the Carter of 1978 saw nothing to match that! But Truman saw nothing in 1946 to match what faced him later, during the Korean War. For his last two years he governed with approval ratings in the range of 32 to 23 percent, the lowest that the Gallup poll records for any President save Nixon in the final months before his resignation.[4]

Yet a generation later Truman is in vogue, remembered now for strength in foreign policy (if anything too much of it), persistence in domestic spheres—ploughing ground for LBJ to harvest—and forthrightness in style; plain-spoken, Midwestern, himself. Denigrated then, fashionable now: on that standard the Presidency surely remains possible.

The Truman standard is too low for Carter's critics. Almost from the outset of his term, and savagely at intervals since his first summer, press commentators and congressional critics have deplored Carter's deficiencies in ways suggestive of a markedly higher standard, apparently compounded out of pieces of performance by the Presidents *since* Truman, as Washingtonians recall them.

To characterize these briefly, one is Johnson's skills with Congress, especially in 1965 (sometimes the press looks back as far as Franklin Roosevelt's Hundred Days of 1933). Another is Dwight Eisenhower's popularity, hence credibility: for eight years his approval rating held high above 50 percent, except once, for one month only, when it dropped to 49 percent. (In much of Carter's second year his rating hovered around 40 percent.) A third is Nixon's strategic sense as manifested by the opening to Peking, the so-called detente with Moscow, and in politics by his plan to back John Connally for 1976.[5] Add, fourth, John Kennedy's performance on TV, which had become by 1963 a masterful affair, of "star" quality, unfailingly of interest, hence always entertaining on an entertainment medium. Finally, fifth, is an implicit Golden Age when White House aides were under tight control, truly anonymous and deferential to their seniors in the great departments. Carter himself contributed to this with early talk of "Cabinet government." But Ford and Nixon do not qualify, nor LBJ, nor Kennedy; few critics can remember farther back, so this is vague.

Carter in his first two years lived up to none of these images and was lambasted in the press for lacking all. As random examples from his first year:

> . . . Carter, anything but a master strategist, is dealing with a Congress that . . . has grown suspicious. . . .[6]
>
> "I have never heard so many suggestions of ineptness about a new Administration" says a Democratic senator's staff member. . . .[7]
>
> The President decides even the petty questions himself. He attends to minute details to an obsessive degree. . . .[8]
>
> There seemed to be no raison d'etre for this Administration . . . little imagination or inspiration in 1977. . . .[9]

And at the end of two years, as *The Wall Street Journal* noted:

> Criticism escalates . . . long time sympathizers grow disillusioned. Fred Dutton . . . "I don't see him getting hold of this" . . . Harry McPherson . . . "He needs to convey a stronger sense there is some fire in his belly" . . . A Democratic pollster ". . . Stability has to come from the top and I'm not sure he can provide it" . . . . Fred Wertheimer "[he falls short] in commanding the attention of the American people" . . .[10]

Both standards need adjustment. The Truman standard, I concede, is low. Governing against the grain of popular support piles up a lot of costs. Militarization of our foreign aid, depredations of McCarthyism, twenty years of isolation from Peking, fifteen years of stalemate on domestic programs, such things are in part by-products of his public standing. Yet the standard raised by Carter's critics seems to me too high, higher than realism counsels or necessity compels.

Too much is expected of a President in Carter's shoes. This is of a piece with very general tendencies throughout the period since FDR. Washingtonians, like less attentive publics, tend to project on the Presidency expectations far exceeding anyone's assured capacity to carry through. Objectively, 1977 had little in common with 1965; still, as Carter started out the LBJ analogy filled many minds, some of them in his own entourage. Whatever were they thinking of? Ignorance is bliss.

II

Carter's aides, with expectations now reduced, defend their man by pointing to specific trends in government that would have baffled even LBJ. Scholars note these too and even have a term for them, "atomization," the coinage of a keen observer from abroad, Anthony King.[11] The term suggests undifferentiated dust, which goes too far, but taken very relatively it is useful shorthand for a number of developments in recent years. It highlights, among other things, four trends that seem to complicate the job of being President and give Carter's defenders sorely needed ammunition.

First, Congress becomes more dispersed, less of an entity, than ever since the early 19th Century. In 1885, a time of relatively strong congressional parties, Woodrow Wilson characterized Congress as a "government by the Chairmen of the Standing Committees . . ."[12] There are far more committees today (including *sub*-committees) and the chairmen, on the average, have decidedly less power. They command few votes. No longer ago than Truman's time the Hill had 180 subcommittees; there are almost twice as many now. As recently as Johnson's time a bargain with a standing committee chairman was a deal; now it often is only a hope. The same can be said of party leaders whose positions have been weakening for decades; however hard they try they often can't deliver votes. Congressmen and Senators revert to what they were much earlier than Wilson: assorted individuals, loosely grouped in state or subject-matter caucuses, staring over their shoulders at the interests (and the media) back home.

The fix on home and fear of it is striking; so are the resultant shifts in sentiment of members on short notice. In 1978, when Californians voted cuts in local property taxation, reacting to a special situation in their state, congressional liberals from almost every state appeared to change their stances as decidedly and rapidly as isolationists after Pearl Harbor. I exaggerate but slightly.

Second, the "Administration" at the other end of Pennsylvania Avenue becomes more fragmented, less coherent than ever (and coherence was never a strong point). The body of senior officials appointed by the President, removable at will, distinct from civil servants and supposedly controlling them, numbers over 700 Cabinet and sub-Cabinet members, assistant secretaries, deputies, special assistants, and the like. But in the three Administrations before Carter's the incumbents of those posts had changed, on average, every second year.[13] There is no indication yet that this has altered very much. If not, these are the shortest-termers in the

Washington community, comparing poorly with equivalents in Congress, press, bureaucracies, interest groups, and law firms alike. No wonder there is incoherence here.

Meanwhile, the tasks those officials are supposed to superintend proliferate. In LBJ's time some 200 novel, mostly complicated grants in aid were authorized by Congress and established deep inside executive departments. Also under LBJ, still more under Nixon, complex regulatory programs in such sectors as health, safety, education, and environment were added to the duties of executive officials. No wonder there is fragmentation.[14]

Third, interest groups proliferate and also tend toward permanence, most notably that current villain of the press, the "single-interest" group. It is as though the single taxers, the free-silverites, the prohibitionists, the suffragettes were working still in Washington with branches dotting the congressional districts, funded by direct mail drives, managed by full-time professionals, attentive all at once to budgets, bills and nominations, schooled as well as anyone in media events, and able to negotiate at both ends of the Avenue.

In actuality we have, instead, the pro and ante groups on equal rights for women, gun control, abortion, SALT, and dozens more. Alongside these are headquarters offices or branches, legal counsel, trade associations representing corporations, unions, universities, churches, hospitals, states, cities, also doctors, scientists, and teachers, among others—the institutions and professions well entrenched in our society—to say nothing of outlets for the altruism of professionals, the "public interest" groups like Common Cause. Foreign governments are represented too, not only by their embassies but also by their lawyers. The time-horizons of all these are long. Many are strong financially. Most plan to stay in business indefinitely. And almost all are staffed as though they could.

Fourth, staffs increase all over town (with counterparts of sorts in the state capitals and the big cities). Four years ago I thought of noting this—but didn't—as an institutional detail for Chapter 10. Now I emphasize it as far more than a detail; quantitative growth is such as to suggest a qualitative change. For example, full-time professionals employed by interest groups in Washington alone are said to number 15,000 now, perhaps 10 times as many as in Truman's years (a shaky estimate).[15] Administration staffs have grown to suit, around the principal officials from the President on down to the most junior assistant secretary. The White House is indicative. Under Carter, creeping up since his first year, professional assistants bearing White House titles number nearly 40 with like numbers, closely linked, in National Security and Domestic Policy staffs: 120-odd compared to under 30 at the Truman peak in the first year of the Korean War. Carter's case is disappointing in a Democrat (see Chapter 10) but possibly inevitable. And Congress has been staffed up almost out of recognition, with its members almost out of sight: professional aides to subcommittees number some 3000 now, up from 400; professionals on personal staffs, 10,000, up from 2000; all in 30 years.[16]

The rise of professional staff is virtually a full-employment program for the professional middle classes. Presumably it is encouraging to graduates of law and business schools, along with newer schools of public policy and management. It also is a source of what Hugh Heclo has called "issue networks," shifting clusters of attentive individuals in government and out, at every level, who seem to dominate what coalition-building, hence what governing, is done.[17] Heclo writes as though elective politicians had almost no role at all; this goes too far: some Senators and Congressmen are very active members of those networks, running their own staffs when the mood strikes them, while a President relates to most networks at least as clerk. But Heclo's point is telling; most coalition-builders, much of the time, are nonelective aides, professionals among professionals, a faceless glob of semipermanent and semisovereign Washingtonians. Moreover many congressmen and staffs are indistinguishable, sharing status in "team" fashion. Elective faces fade into the crowd.

By way of full-time civilian personnel the Federal government has scarcely grown in 30 years (then and now below three million). Adding contract personnel would scarcely double it. But that "glob," that professional crowd, is vastly larger than it was and grows apace.

It can be argued that a President in office is advantaged by this situation. Comparatively, it should leave him standing tall. His is the place legitimated by a national election after nationwide campaigning. He can claim *some* authority in *every* sphere of action at the very time that, relatively speaking, claims of other individuals in government are weakening. What he may do—or not do—helps frame agendas for all others. His face is almost constantly on TV network news. He cannot help but be seen by constituents of every congressman and interest group. The more attention paid to him "back home" the more he counts with them. The more he counts with them the more he matters to the program managers in the departments who depend on congressmen for laws and funds. Standing tall can be its own reward.

And standing so a President is not inhibited these days by pledges to or threats from party barons—for there are none, not in the old sense. As Chapter 10 points out the local leaders and financial backers once so critical in presidential politics are all but gone, a vanishing breed. Their functions are assumed by primaries and media, campaign consultants, mailings, and political-action committees. Changes in nominating processes and in campaigns match all the changes sketched above, with comparable effect on institutions: "atomization."[18]

Thus a Carter could spend two years before March 1976, as "Jimmy who?" the early but unknown campaigner out of "nowhere," (which is what four years as Governor of Georgia evidently meant across the country), then be President-elect eight months later.[19] In 1960, even in 1968, this simply could not have occurred. In 1940 something else occurred: Wendell Willkie did not get nominated on his own; a faction reached for him.[20]

Lacking party baggage, old commitments, or a record, Carter was ostensibly well-placed to make the most of a position sticking up above the professional crowd, untrammeled by competitors up there and free to rally everyone's constituents to him; the citizens against the Washingtonians.

This actually may have been Carter's logic in 1976. He voiced something like it then. So did his aides. So indeed did others. With qualifications as to television style, and not foreseeing "who-ness," this is the logic I, for one, put forward at the close of Chapter 10.

But in his first two years, at least, the logic did not work for Carter. On the contrary, aside from temporary rallying at moments of high hope for Middle Eastern peace, congressional and press reactions to the President along with polls and other signs suggested not that he stood tall but rather that he barely kept from sinking out of sight. Dispersion elsewhere and professional crowding did not add to his comparative advantages—not anyway to his effective use of them—in those years.

This often is ascribed to Carter's operating style and set aside as idiosyncratic, but I think we need go farther. Along with his own starting sense of power and of purpose, and in part shaped by them, Carter's style contributed, no doubt; his speech-writer, James Fallows, vividly portrays the links, suggestive of a President more unpolitical in some respects than Eisenhower.[21] But more systemic things appear to have contributed as well. If so, the weakness in the logic will outlast the Carter Presidency.

For one thing, Carter suffered from the very scale, diversity, complexity of his initial legislative program. He began as a legislative activist in what had been since FDR the Democratic President's tradition. A large share of the measures Carter sought, all of it controversial, much of it redistributive, was within the jurisdiction of the Senate Finance Committee: energy policy, tax reform, welfare reform, health insurance, social security financing. With unexpected vigor the committee chairman, Senator Long, proceeded to stalemate the President on every score. Long had behind him shifting but effective groups of members to defend the status quo or otherwise oppose Carter, and back of them a strong array of regional and economic interests. "Atomization" is a handy tag, but what it means has to be squared with Long's performance (his among others). Traditional party ties are very nearly pulverized but constitutional structure is intact. Separated institutions continue to share powers. The Senate represents strong interests of (and in) the several states; the House has localitis as the Constitution intended; executive initiative is checked; except as interests can be coalesced not much is done domestically, and anyone advantaged by that structure is as free as any President to try his hand at coalition-building through the issue networks. In that Long was experienced, Carter a novice. Besides Long was defending, not proposing.

Another blow to the logic of comparative advantage during Carter's first two years is that what came to be his chief objectives then—partly his own doing, partly history's—required implementation by executives outside the government, in places where the President's authority was weakest, where his constitutional and statutory powers were attenuated or did not apply: decision-makers in the private sector and in foreign governments. At home he called for energy conservation, price and wage stabilization; abroad for SALT from Moscow, peace agreements from Jerusalem and Cairo, to say nothing of Amman, normalization from Peking (and acquiescence in Taipai); these things among others. Each required action on the part of many persons shielded from him by our Bill of Rights, or by their sovereignty. These persons were not only individuals—like automobile drivers—but more centrally the managements of organizations, each with established aims, accustomed routines, internal politics, and limited capacity for change, to say nothing of will. Carter might be "chief executive" but *these* were his executants, at *their* option, not his. Command outran his constitutional authority and statutes too. With prices and wages for example, although facing an inflation rate three times as high as Nixon's during 1971, Carter could not even do what Nixon had done: invoke standby authority for mandatory controls. In 1978 there was no such authority; Congress had let it lapse. To seek restoration—even had Carter wished, which he did not—was to invite anticipatory increases, a cure to worsen the disease. Among his reasons for not wishing was the fear, based on experience, of organizational incapacity combined with foot-dragging.

In addition, Carter evidently suffered from a consequence of being "Jimmy who?" before election: afterwards few hearts throbbed. Nowhere in the country did he seem to stir strong loyalties pro *or* con. A lackluster campaign, a low vote, was followed by a tepid national reaction to his person and his programs. There were at first some titillating questions: what could be the meaning in the White House of a twice-born Georgia Baptist and proclaimed "outsider"? All too many answers were suggested by the Lance affair (to which I will return). For eight months he on one side, Congress, press and interests on the other side, stared at each other, then they cut him up: presumably they noticed that he had not won the citizens. "Jimmy who?" was followed by "who cares?"

A further cause of Carter's inability to exploit his presumed advantages is that he ran afoul of special hazards history reserves for new Administrations. These are transition hazards, associated with newness *in* office, also with newness *to* it. Being in both senses "newer" than its predecessors, the Carter Administration seemed particularly prone to these. But no Administration has escaped them all, or can. And Carter's newness may be symptomatic of the future. Nominating processes and campaigns could continue to evolve along the lines of 1976. That is a sobering thought. Too many transitions like Carter's, too often, might indeed make the Presidency impossible.

Carter's third year found him in a three-fold bind. History now pressed him with a run of hard events. Electioneering was almost upon him, as with Ford, and unlike Kennedy or even Nixon. Yet Carter brought to his third year diminished resources of Washington reputation and of popular prestige; in these respects he was worse off than any other elected President of modern times. His diminution seems to be associated with a set of self-inflicted wounds ascribable to newness. In long perspective this may come to appear too specific; Carter may appear instead the victim of a national reaction after Vietnam and Watergate, a transient phenomenon that happened to encompass him. But the very possibility that Carter may have victimized himself suggests that his successors might do so as well, a troubling prospect.

With that prospect in mind, let me present what I regard as hazardous for them and speculate on means to lessen risks. I start with some assumptions. By no means do transitions offer necessarily the worst risks that a President may face during his term, nor are they sources of the worst mistakes some Presidents have made. But Carter's plight suggests that hazards of transition rise as "atomization" proceeds. The changes in our system seem to make these hazards worse, at once more frequent and more costly for a President. That, at least, is how relationships appear in Carter's time, for reasons I will shortly state. Still, even though the risks grow worse, they seem to be the sort about which something might be done, a hopeful note. When wounds are self-inflicted they are subject to avoidance by self-consciousness. Regardless of outside events and independent of external institutions, risks here are highly influenced by those who run them. They, alas, are just the persons least disposed to see them. Transition hazards turn on that. Yet carefulness could help, awareness might induce it. Hence what follows.

A President's transition can be defined in two ways, narrowly by the time-span between election and inaugural, broadly by the time until he and his principal associates become familiar with the work they have to do, including what to ask of one another and what to expect in response. Transition in the first sense lasts approximately eleven weeks. Transition in the second stretches on until about the time, two years after election, when the "new" Administration has experienced both sessions of a Congress, along with friends and adversaries overseas, and begins to see the shape of the events, hence commitments, that will dominate the presidential term.

The eleven weeks are hazardous because they are so few. They leave but little time to turn a campaign into an Administration, which takes office three weeks *after* Congress does. There has to be a pattern for the presidential staff and initial appointments to suit. There have to be Cabinet and sub-Cabinet appointments, along with understandings on appointments down the line and on procedures to produce them (and to place campaigners). There has to be a legislative program or at least a holding-action with a start upon specifics. There has to be a point of view toward diplomatic and defense initiatives left dangling by the previous Administration. The outgoing regime presents a budget just as it departs; there has to be a point of view on that. There has to be a "memorable" Inaugural Address. Furthermore, importantly, the new look of the President-elect—candidate no longer—has to be impressed upon a temporarily attentive public and an insatiably curious Washington.

These among many other things press in upon campaigners, happy, exhausted, adrenalin flowing, cramped in perspective, needing above all else to adjust their own psychologies from campaigning to governing. The tyranny of time allows them scarcely any break between one and the other; worse, unless they are remarkably self-aware, the work of the eleven weeks can seem deceptively like more campaigning.

We have had four such transitions in modern times—1952, 1960, 1968 and 1976—leaving aside that instantaneous phenomenon, Vice-Presidential succession. Of these four, Kennedy's seems to have been smoothest, most nearly successful in all those respects at once, thus giving him a head-start on Inauguration Day (some of which he soon lost at the Bay of Pigs). Carter's transition almost surely was the roughest, with inordinate time squandered on internecine warfare at staff levels and the least adjustment of erstwhile campaigners to new roles. Kennedy's people leaped into governance, Carter's hung back.

Ironically, Carter had put far more funds and personnel into "transition planning," separate from campaigning, than had any of his predecessors. This proved to be part of his problem: parallel staffs beforehand led to bloodshed after. The inevitable triumph of the tried-and-true campaigners helped dilute the planners' emphasis on governance.

From election to inauguration Carter's people scrambled. Their difficulties may have been compounded by the fact that Ford, the outgoing President, had himself been defeated, unlike Truman, Eisenhower, or Johnson. Access to Ford's budgeting was less than Truman had given to Eisenhower's staff, or Eisenhower to Kennedy's. Carter's aides were kept out of top-level reviews.[22] Few things are more sobering than presidential choices as they manifest themselves in budgetary arguments; for Carter's staff the dosage was delayed. More important may well be the fact that due to legislation passed at Kennedy's urging, Carter had up to $2 million in appropriated funds for preinaugural salaries and expenses. With eager, young campaigners thirsting for Washington, the result was a Carter transition staff six times the size of Kennedy's. Only Carter's fiat held it down to that. Some funds were returned. But the money fueled the arguments that raged in Carter's entourage and almost guaranteed him a big White House staff, filling the Ford slots, with assignments unsettled into January, six to eight weeks behind Kennedy. Carter's time, meanwhile, was spent on Cabinet choices. Kennedy had tossed most of these off and sent his designees to Washington to study their new roles; Carter deliberated, stressing the importance of department heads in his intended scheme of things. The incompatibility of a big staff, prospectively competitive with them, may have escaped him then, or maybe he was hedging bets. While he recruited Cabinet members he remained mostly at home, in Plains, Georgia, remote from his transition staff in Washington and from its quarrels. In Plains there were few excitements except softball games, which he himself played grimly. He thus incurred the wrath of his assigned reporters (whose counterparts in 1960 had enjoyed more pleasures, better stories, and no grimness at Hyannis Port, Palm Beach, Georgetown, and Manhattan). For much of this he was to pay high prices in due course.[23]

By hindsight, Carter would have been much better off to keep his planning effort both informal and anonymous before election and conducted in such terms as not to threaten his campaigners (unless he meant to make them squirm perpetually, which he did not). After election he would have done well to begin by thinking out and organizing his initial White House staff, which then could do or delegate the work of further planning. A temporary staff linked to careerists in the OMB—the source of institutional memory—could have handled such a delegation. Were there to be additional transition staff its focus should have been on the departments, and its future too. A useful rule for Carter would have been: add bodies to *your* Office only as *you* feel need. Before inaugural he and his staff, however constituted, should not have been so far apart as Plains and Washington. He should have kept a closer eye on them. If for symbolic reasons he avoided Washington, so had Nixon eight years earlier, settling with his staff in midtown Manhattan. Carter could have chosen Atlanta. Better still he could have kept on the move, frequently in Washington but not yet of it. At every point, Carter could have drawn upon experienced Washingtonians to inform his personal judgment. This is something no campaigner could do for him and that staff would be unlikely to encourage. He would have had to manage it himself; apparently he saw no need. All these "shoulds" and "coulds" resemble things that JFK did somewhat accidentally with a minimum of planning. His transition, in the narrow sense, was marked by serendipity. Carter's was not.

The eleven-week scramble is the by-product of a reform adopted hastily and cheerfully in 1933 to cure what then seemed a disastrously long time between election and inaugural. Under the provisions of the Constitution at that time, there were four months from FDR's election to his swearing-in on March 4, 1933. On March 3 the old Congress departed, with the new one out of town until December unless *he* should call it into special session. That timing looks marvelous today. In 1933 it looked terrible: in those four months the country's banking system had collapsed. The Twentieth Amendment to the Constitution thereupon insured against the same thing happening again in the same way. Like other constitutional changes this had an unintended side-effect: the contemporary scramble. Eleven weeks proved troublesome enough to Carter. Had Lincoln faced so short a span, with Congress thrust upon him, possibly the Civil War would never have gotten started, or if once begun would have been run from Capitol Hill and bungled still more badly than by him.

Might-have-beens aside, the troubles of transition narrowly defined, the weeks before a January swearing-in, have *not* proved worse, thus far, than those associated with the months of governing thereafter. On the contrary, the greater hazards come then. For these months are a learning time and those who learn are prone to misperceptions of a characteristic kind. Here lie the distinctive hazards of transition. The paradigm is not a Carter case but Kennedy's. Doing well in the eleven weeks did not keep him from doing badly afterwards. Indeed the sense of having mastered those exacting weeks brought on euphoria, itself a source of trouble. This instance has a label, "Bay of Pigs." It is a classic case. To sketch it is to illustrate those hazards.

III

The 1960 election was very close. Kennedy defeated Nixon, then Vice-President, by less than one percent of the popular vote. The retiring President, still immensely liked, campaigned but little for unexplained reasons: health we now are told.[24] Nixon campaigned hard but his incumbency sometimes was an embarrassment in Eisenhower's absence from the hustings.

The campaign featured four TV "debates" in which the candidates were questioned by third parties and made comments on each other's answers. During the fourth debate, Kennedy attacked Eisenhower's relative passivity in face of Fidel Castro's Cuban revolution: Castro's regime had been proclaimed as Communist after achieving power, expropriating and exporting (mostly to Miami) a proportion of its upper and middle classes, allying with the Soviets, and sending revolutionaries south. Without much forethought Kennedy was forceful; Nixon was furious but did not let it show, reacting calmly. He knew but could not say that Eisenhower, months before, had authorized the Central Intelligence Agency to prepare him the option of a counter-revolution whereby Cubans, with our help, could unseat Castro.[25]

Nixon was the angrier because he thought that Kennedy, briefed as a candidate by CIA, knew of this too, which he did not. Only when elected was he told of it, with details spread before him after he took office in January 1961. Then Kennedy discovered something that had grown beyond an option almost to the size of a demand, deadlines attached. In Guatemala, where the Agency some years before had superintended a successful revolution, its operational arm was training a Brigade of some 1400 Cubans recruited from Miami. Training would be completed soon. It then was planned to send them off on their own ships, protected by their own aircraft—equipment covertly supplied, of course, from Washington—for an amphibious landing in southcentral Cuba near the city of Trinidad. This was close to mountains much like those where Castro had himself begun as a guerrilla. The Brigade would seize and hold a beachhead in the name of a new government. Once the beachhead was secured this government would land on Cuban soil, would call for popular revolt and, as the people rose, would seek American recognition; this, once granted, would permit overt supply and other forms of aid if needed. Should the beachhead fail to hold for any reason, the Brigade could fade into the mountains and begin guerrilla action. American support, while covert, would continue. Castro, if not eliminated, would still suffer pain. The plan thus could not altogether fail.

The planners stressed to Kennedy that implementation was urgent. There seemed to be two deadlines. Castro's obsolescent air force could be dealt with before May, but then it would be modernized, with jets from Moscow flown by pilots trained in Prague, more than a match for Brigadeers possessing only aircraft of the sort they might have bought on the world market. Besides, the Guatemalan government was anxious for the Brigade and its trainers to move along. They were a large, attention-attracting, increasingly talky crowd. And where were they to go if not to Cuba? To Miami? (Where they then could talk their heads off about General Eisenhower's cancelled plan.)

Kennedy was cautious. He knew this undertaking was far larger than the CIA had tried before. He knew amphibious landings were no joke. He feared covert support on such a scale would be disclosed. And he refused to countenance overt U.S. involvement. His Inaugural Address had stressed that a new generation, freshly come to power, was at once determined and idealistic. As he began he wanted to appear neither weak nor a warmonger, least of all an unprovoked aggressor.

So, as was characteristic of him, he sought a second opinion on CIA's plan. He sought it from the "pros" in using troops, the Joint Chiefs of Staff. The Chiefs acting alone, without staff for secrecy's sake, reviewed the plan CIA put before them. They responded that they thought it had a "fair chance of success," noting with approval the prospective rising and the fallback to the mountains in case of failure. The Chiefs were not asked whether their response would be the same if they were put in charge, a question that would have brought their own planners into play, exposing Army and Marine Corps reservations. Rather they were asked, merely, to comment on somebody else's operation taken on its face. At least that is the way they understood the question; if more was wanted from them, Kennedy failed to convey it. They also understood that he embodied the new generation. They did not, holdovers all and well into their fifties; he was 43. And they had heard or read him in that fourth debate.

For weeks after this word from JCS, Kennedy continued to discuss refinements of the plan with those involved at CIA. Adding opinions he brought into secret conclave the Secretary of Defense, Robert McNamara, and the Secretary of State, Dean Rusk. McNamara leaned on one of his assistant secretaries, William Bundy, a CIA alumnus who, by chance, had also been a college associate of the CIA's chief planner for this venture, Richard Bissell. Bundy's brother McGeorge was the President's own assistant for national security affairs. Reassured by Bissell, whom they all admired, and impressed by the calm confidence of Allan Dulles, CIA's Director, these men became early advocates.

Not so Rusk, who may well have had doubts but never voiced them plainly, seemed to question his own jurisdiction in the matter, and for reasons of security kept all his people uninformed and out. The Under Secretary sat in for him once and was distressed, but never got back in. Not even their intelligence officials were cued in. If leaks occurred on this, they would not come from State! Rusk, an old government hand, was a believer in compartmentation.

So was Dulles. CIA's operational arm was wholly separate from its estimates arm, the evaluators of intelligence (working with State's officials and with military counterparts). They could easily be walled off, and were, when security seemed to require. This was such a time. The evaluators were not told that operational colleagues had informed the JCS and others of a likely rising against Castro; had they known they would have scoffed: their impression of the prospects inside Cuba differed sharply. But they did not know; they were not asked.

Kennedy did not know that they did not know. Procedures inside CIA were mysteries to him. He would have been appalled. But he did worry about leaks, about the loss of cover for American support, and he had reason: Cubans in Guatemala had long since begun to interest the American press. By the time plans were completed they were pretty well-known in Miami and New York. Still, for Rusk and Dulles, Kennedy's worry vindicated compartmenting Washington.

Thus one of the two buttresses for optimism from the JCS rested on sand, the unsupported hopes of self-interested planners for a Cuban rising. The other buttress was soon kicked away by further planning: the landing site was moved some 70 miles west. Between it and the mountains there now intervened a swamp. Kennedy, Rusk, McNamara, and their aides missed the significance of that. They supported the move to reduce the landing's visible scale, thereby, they hoped, improving chances that it would look wholly Cuban. The Chiefs, not asked explicitly, made no new estimate of chances for success; they did, however, see the revised plans. This left the President assuming they approved.

Facing deadlines that he did not question, confidence from Dulles and the admirable Bissell, apparent optimism from the JCS, its basis unexplored, Kennedy acceded. He set one condition, namely that whatever happened he would not approve the direct use of American armed forces. (In this he probably was influenced by two opponents of the venture he consulted on the side.) Dulles and Bissell agreed, the Chiefs did not object; they simply may not have believed him.

So the Brigade set off in April 1961. There ensued a classic demonstration of Murphy's Law: if anything can go wrong, it will. It did. One strike against Havana's Air Force was mishandled and aroused suspicion of American support; a second strike was cancelled to reduce U.S. embarrassment. Castro's planes appeared over the beachhead, more of them and better flown than planners had foreseen. What matter jets and pilots? These were good enough. One of their first bombs blew up the Brigade's communications ship, which unaccountably contained, as well, much of its ammunition. A second ammunition ship, slow to unload, was also sunk. Castro's police efficiently jailed 100,000 Cubans; there was no hint of a rising. Castro's troops, efficient too, well-armed and mobile (to American surprise), soon reached the beach and moved on the invaders. An air attack was desperately improvised and Kennedy bent his ban on direct involvement just enough to let our naval fighters give air cover to the Brigade's bombers. Alas, the hour was coordinated but not the time zones: fighters flying off our carriers near Cuba left the scene before the bombers, flown from Nicaragua, got there; Castro's people shot the latter down or chased them off.

And never mind what Bissell planned, the CIA instructors in the Guatemalan camp had not taught their trainees to head for mountains, least of all through swamps. (They had been taught instead to count on U.S. forces.) Besides, a swamp was no place for guerrillas in the age of helicopters, of which Castro had his share. So some of the invaders died; a few swam out to sea and were picked up by our patrols; most surrendered. These were jailed and subsequently ransomed by the Kennedys for medicine and other useful things that Castro wanted.

Kennedy looked like a fool, and felt like one. At home approval of him in the Gallup poll actually rose, a rally-round-the-flag effect, which only made him think the worse of popular perceptions. But his professional reputation fell in many quarters and this hurt. Abroad he managed to seem heedlessly aggressive in the eyes of friends, weakly indecisive in the eyes of adversaries. That double vision registered in Senate circles also, to say nothing of officialdom. So diplomatic and congressional advisers told him, carrying coals to Newcastle. He writhed at being thought a clod, and worried about being thought a patsy, especially in Moscow and Havana. By all accounts he was still worrying when, nine months later, he stepped up American support for South Vietnam. Throughout his term he sanctioned further CIA activities, small scale and thus deniable, against Castro.[26]

In this Bay of Pigs affair the new regime's decision-making showed two striking features, ignorance and hopefulness. The ignorance was tinged with innocence, the hopefulness with arrogance.

Consider the ignorance first. The newcomers, except for Rusk and William Bundy, were new not only to the jobs they held, but also to the Executive Branch. They were, moreover, mostly new to one another. Kennedy, indeed, scarcely knew Rusk and McNamara when he appointed them, nor they each other. Even those who knew each other had not done so in their present roles. Kennedy, a Harvard Overseer, had admired McGeorge Bundy, Harvard's premier Dean, a far cry from their new relationship. And so forth. By April 1961 none of these men had taken one another's measure in their new positions well enough to know what they should credit and what they should discount, when. Nor in that sense did they know any of the holdovers, nor the latter them.

The Bundys, reasoning too readily from other roles, thought they knew all about Bissell. The President may have thought so too. Before he came to office he saw Bissell as the one man he knew well enough to trust in the intelligence community.[27] But Bissell had now to play advocate; the other three were cast as skeptics and as judge. He understood his part, they fumbled theirs. In this lies so much innocence!

The innocence is of a piece with JFK's referral to the Chiefs of Staff and with his stress on secrecy: innocently ignorant of consequences in the bureaucratic context. The new men, for the most part, knew no more about the histories of institutions than they knew of one another. The wall inside the CIA was quite unknown to most. The histories of policy were often closed books too.

Ignorance was joined by hopefulness. Dulles and Bissell aside, who knew the arguments surrounding Eisenhower's turn from tolerance for Castro to an interest in creation of an option to unseat him? Who cared? In such cases, unconcern is usual. The very changeover conduces to it. New replaces old, and vigor tiredness; sharp exhilaration drowns out dull experience. The White House shines with fresh paint and the West Wing with fresh faces. Possibilities seem, for the moment, infinite because so many personalities are still unknown, relations still potential. All is heightened by the fact that for a Kennedy or Carter and their aides, arrival at the White House after years of hard campaigning is like reaching an oasis in the desert: faultless air conditioning, matchless switchboard, superb secretaries, visitors by appointment only (press included), cars on call, along with tennis, saunas, helicopters for the President and even, if he wishes (LBJ did), instant Fresca.

Everywhere there is a sense of a page turning, a new chapter in the country's history, a new chance too. And with it, irresistibly, there comes the sense, "they" couldn't, wouldn't, didn't, but "we" will. We just have done the hardest thing there is to do in politics. Governing has got to be a pleasure by comparison: we won, so we can! The psychology is partly that of having climbed one mountain so the next looks easy, partly that of having had a run of luck that surely can't turn now!

The arrogance that goes with this is native to contemporary nominations and campaigns, and to the young who man them. There are some parallels among the brash young men of 1961 and 1969 and 1976, but Kennedy and his aides also were distinctive. Their self-confidence, their "can-do" stance reflected personal accomplishments apart from their campaigning, and reflected also consciousness of being very smart. As a group they were exceptionally able and exceptionally brainy and they knew it, each and all, the President included. Also, in those distant days they relished "Kennedy luck." No wonder that a Rusk, Assistant Secretary of State in Truman's time when old-style southern courtesy held sway on foreign matters, spoke with a muffled voice or not at all in Kennedy group meetings. Reportedly they never ceased to shock him.

Ignorance and hopefulness alike were tempered by the Bay of Pigs experience, a lot of innocence was lost, also a share of arrogance. Nothing is more salutary for the smart than to do something patently absurd, and so they saw it. Being smart they set themselves to learn from it, the President especially, and subsequent events suggest they did, in Laos, Berlin, and the Cuban Missile Crisis. Overlearning was done too, no doubt, and some of it by others, for instance LBJ in the Dominican affair of 1965: 20 thousand troops to squash a local insurrection.

Transition troubles may have silver linings, but not always. The Bay of Pigs was short, sharp, shocking, and soon over, with a lot of obvious lessons scattered in its wake. But new Administrations are not often so well served by their transitional mistakes. Consider Carter's "pig," his nearest thing to Kennedy's in terms of immediate impact on professional reputation: the Lance affair. History will be hard put to find in that much compensation. Dropping Bertram Lance from the Administration could turn out by hindsight to have saved later embarrassment; much depends on what eventually becomes of him. But easier ways to manage that abounded, both before and after July 1977. Peering hard I see no silver lining in what happened then.

IV

In November 1976, shortly after the election, Carter announced as his Budget Director-designate Bert Lance, a friend, backer, and leading Atlanta banker. The appointment was well received in business circles and in Carter's entourage. Lance, a forceful and ebullient man, enormously self-confident, soon made his presence felt. As the new Administration first took hold in 1977 it became apparent that he would be more than his title suggested: he would have easy access to the President on any subject, alongside but not through or under anybody in the White House. For the EPG, the Economic Policy Group, whose other members were ill-matched by temperament or operating style or both, Lance's personality and access soon seemed indispensible to help his colleagues stabilize relations with each other and with Carter.

On the domestic side of government almost everybody came to look toward Lance for access, help, decisiveness, except for the most senior White House aides who saw the President as readily as he did. Hamilton Jordan, the political adviser, Jody Powell, the press secretary, Frank Moore, the congressional liaison, these and others, Georgians all, respected Lance, enjoyed him, and apparently regarded him as one with them but on a different plane, their elder and an independent counselor as well as family friend, the President's and Mrs. Carter's too. His standing as a banker and a liaison for business, overshadowing the Secretary of the Treasury, added to his White House reputation: Georgian among Georgians, he stood out.

In June 1977, Lance faced a personal problem. Before his confirmation by the Senate he had promised the committee that reviewed his nomination to divest himself within the year of stock in the Atlanta bank he formerly had run. This followed the stern logic of Carter's own pronouncements against conflict-of-interest, as well as Senate strictures in recent years. The bank's new management then wrote off certain losses; this caused its stock to fall in price. To sell within the year, before the price recovered, could cost Lance a major portion of his capital and otherwise embarrass him financially. He was so highly leveraged that bankruptcy did not appear impossible. This seemed an exorbitant charge for public service. He inquired of his White House colleagues whether he could not go back to the Senate committee for an extension of time. It was an unusual request. In the years since such provisos had become the norm, the custom was to leave them be lest a reopening unsettle the appointment. But Bert was a special case; his colleagues sympathized; his self-confidence pulled them along. At least four senior White House aides were variously consulted. So was the committee chairman, Senator Ribicoff of Connecticut. Impressed with Lance, and sympathetic too, Ribicoff was cordial. This satisfied the White House and Lance got a green light. How much Carter involved himself at this stage is not clear.[28]

The previous November, when Lance's appointment was announced, his banking practices in Calhoun, Georgia, where he got his start, had been under some scrutiny by the Comptroller of the Currency (the Treasury Department office regulating banks) and also by the Justice Department. But both inquiries had ended shortly after, without any charges against him. Some Carter aides had known this; some of Ribicoff's had learned it later, before confirmation. Apparently it rang few bells in their minds then, and none in June.

So Carter's White House counsel, Robert Lipshutz, wrote to Ribicoff on Lance's behalf, formally requesting an extension. Trouble started. Washington newsmen noticed, among them William Safire, a *New York Times* columnist and former Nixon aide on the alert against a Democratic double standard. That letter "had a clank of falsity," he recalled later, "I knew Lance was hiding something."[29] With Safire in the van, setting the pace—he would win a Pulitzer Prize for his columns—reporters began digging into Lancian finance. Early on they found that Lance had bought his stock with money borrowed from one northern bank and refinanced by another; until the stock was sold his debt remained outstanding. Extension of the time for sale would thus prolong not one but two potential conflicts of interest. Newsmen fanned out from there. Investigative journalists descended on Calhoun, Atlanta, and the Federal agencies, along with banks in New York and Chicago. Adverse allegations followed. To answer these Lance went before the Ribicoff committee three times in July. He was jovial and patient, and he soon got his reward. On July 25, Ribicoff denounced the allegations as a "smear," and was supported by the ranking minority member, Senator Percy.

This should have ended it, in White House calculations, but did not. Committee calculations had produced a self-protective call to the Comptroller of the Currency for an immediate report on Lance's banking practices. The Comptroller was a Carter appointee and his careerists smarted under criticism. Both were defensive, both responded with a will. Their report came August 17. It found no evidence of criminal offenses but was critical on several scores, among them frequent overdrafts in Lance's Calhoun years by him and by the members of his family. They always replaced the money but had used it when they wanted it as though it were their own. This jolted journalists and citizens at large who yearned for overdrafts themselves but couldn't get them. These, Lance later argued, were the usual thing for managements of smaller banks. Maybe so, but saying so cost him the support of most bankers.

Lance gained however, for a time, the President's support. From the moment of the first adverse news stories, Carter had distanced himself to Lance's evident discomfiture. But when the Comptroller cleared Lance of criminality, the President decided to endorse him; firmness, it was thought, could end the matter. "Bert," said Carter on national TV, "I'm proud of you." Behind the affectionate comment lay a remarkable failure of staff work. Reportedly neither Carter nor his closest aides had read the Comptroller's text, relying instead on a summary from Lipshutz.

This happened August 18; to the Washington press it evidently seemed a challenge and was taken so. Republicans in Congress watched with satisfaction, recalling Watergate, and kept score on the newsmen. Journalists recalled it too and kept score on themselves. Investigative efforts were redoubled. Lance's Atlanta bank had owned an airplane and his use of it, along with Carter's during the campaign, became a field for depth reporting. So did Lance's personal finances in the years when he was buying banks, and now that he was selling (or wasn't). So did the fact that Federal agencies had disposed of their inquiries after career officials learned who was to be the new Budget Director. Underlining every implication, the then Acting Comptroller, a careerist, had actually endorsed Lance for the job in an egregious letter to the Ribicoff committee.

By Labor Day the charges had reached such a pitch that Ribicoff was crying *mea culpa*. Those overdrafts rankled. It also appeared possible that Lance had used one bank's deposits with another as, in effect, collateral to finance his own borrowing. He was already in a dual conflict of interest on his Federal job, stockholder and debtor both while helping to make economic policy. Now there would be more investigations just as budget season started. Ribicoff and Percy visited the President to say that Lance must go. A week later Senator Byrd, the Majority Leader, publicly called Lance's resignation "inevitable." Carter's praise was 24 days old.

On September 15, the Ribicoff committee reconvened and Lance appeared before it in his own defense, making a strong showing on live television for three days, with coverage to match the high points of the Senate Watergate hearings five years earlier. Lance took the offensive; it was expertly done—appropriately so with Clark M. Clifford as his counsel—and it may have saved his personal reputation for a time, but could not save his job.[30] Too many Senators seemed unconvinced, so did too many reporters, and anyway official inquiries were cranking up again, manned by careerists eager to show vigor in their agencies. Lance's resignation followed in five days. The President accepted it, with every sign of pain but none of further indecision, and his friend retreated to Atlanta, stopping off in Calhoun for a rousing welcome.

Lance left Washington in late September. His White House colleagues from the President down were evidently sorry to see him go. Indeed they were distressed if not embittered; some seemed disoriented too. Relationships around the Executive

Office were in disarray without him and had now to be refashioned, or at worst endured (the case, it seems, with economic policy relationships). But many former colleagues also were relieved. For nine weeks Lance's troubles had preoccupied them all, fascinated Senators, galvanized the press, and led the nightly news. And these were to have been the weeks a strong Administration put the heat on Senate leadership to match the Speaker's efforts for the energy proposals Carter had presented four months earlier—while summoning the country to "the moral equivalent of war." What Senate leaders could have done with or about determined opposition from the Senate Finance Committee remains something of a mystery, but summer was the time to lay the groundwork.

Instead there came the Lance affair. By the time it was over it had put a period to Carter's honeymoon, played hob with his professional reputation, and cast doubt on the affinity he claimed to have with voters. The doubts grew stronger as successive polls showed they had less and less affinity with him. Between August and September his Gallup poll approval rating fell from 66 to 54 percent; that winter it began to fall again, down to 40 percent by April of his second year. There, with minor variations, it remained for many months. These ratings traced an early pattern more like Truman's or Ford's than like other elective Presidents.[31] Was Jimmy-who-ness functionally equivalent to the Vice-Presidency? Yet at Truman's elbow were the troubles of reconversion, at Ford's the slide into recession. Nothing comparable jostled Carter as his public standing fell.

Carter's prestige followed his reputation down, rather than diverging as in Kennedy's case. The fall of 1977 was a time when Washingtonians were sneering. Does that explain what happened to his standing in the winter?[32] It is hard to resist the suggested causal connection. Washington reactions to the Lance affair could not have been the only influence on general public attitudes: many whites were shocked by the Panama Treaty, many blacks upset by cautiousness toward teenaged unemployment.[33] But outside the ghettos it appears that in the fall of 1977 nothing very awful was occurring, by way of events to trouble private lives. Without such touchstones and not knowing Jimmy, millions may have taken as their own the tone of television commentators who in turn had read the columnists on Lance. Viewers may not get their news from magazines and papers, but TV producers, editors, and anchormen do.

Led by the press corps, Washingtonians of every stripe felt free to turn on Carter then, and often did it with a special relish: "He had been *so* moralistic," one respected reporter told me, ". . . 'I'll never lie to you,' et cetera, and that awful time at Plains, and now it turned out he was just as we surmised: no better than the rest of them, if that." This may be to confuse the Carter idiom with Carter, a problem for the secular observer from the North or West. But that's what Washingtonians so often are and where so many hail from. The handling of the Lance affair played to their every prejudice.

By hindsight it seems obvious that Lance, for his own sake as well as Carter's, should never have sought an extension. Instead, he should have either stood his losses or left office to the deep regret of all. One hears Senators chorusing: "Come back, come back, you useful man and never mind the stock." At worst Lance would have had to be an elder statesman for a time until his stock was sold. Then Carter could have brought him back more reputable than ever (unless of course the press had been aroused by something else).

Hindsight beats foresight. Still, substantial clues to this conclusion were available in June of 1977. Safire aside, a boring summer stretched ahead without convention, or campaign, or war to occupy a national press corps relishing corporate virtue after Watergate, itching to display impartiality, cool to Carter personally, and bursting with would-be Woodwards and Bernsteins.[34] Any Federal inquiry that ended as a matter of discretion might appear a "cover up," a thing still at the front of people's minds. And senatorial judgments often were no better than the staff work that preceded them; Ribicoff's staff had a mixed reputation.

These are quintessentially "insider" clues, matters of Washington lore, far from obvious, it seems, to Carter's Georgians when they gave Lance his green light. That was their Rubicon, comparable to JFK's assent for CIA. If they paused over clues like these and probed them, nothing now suggests it. Memoirs may disclose more than I find. Meanwhile, I presume that they did not. They evidently had done nothing like it in November and they let this second chance pass, doing no more in June. What more was there to do? They *knew* Bert. They also knew his clout and felt his confidence. They waved him on his way. As for Watergate and what that whole experience had meant to those who lived through it in Washington, the Carter men were elsewhere at the time, living through something else, the plans for their extraordinary campaign.[35]

Here again is ignorance in innocence, but ignorance of rather different things. A Kennedy would have known nuances in journalistic attitudes and senatorial staffing. (A Carter might have read more carefully and questioned more precisely JCS opinions.) And here again is hopefulness, accompanied by arrogance of rather different quality, naive not glittery, we-decent-people rather than we-happy-few.

Each new Administration seems to bring its special blend of ignorance and hopefulness, of innocence with arrogance (except for Ford and Truman who had never fought to get there and were far from arrogant as they arrived). Differences begin with the particulars of ignorance. For JFK, the mystery was executive operations. For Johnson it was foreign governments. For Nixon it was evidently eastern journalists and liberal Democrats. For Carter it appears to have been Washington nuances. If so, Carter perhaps had the worst of it. Thanks to "atomization" in the third decade of television, his were the particulars where subtleties change fastest, while mistakes are subject to the swiftest public punishment in reputation or prestige or both. Presumably these same conditions will confront Carter's successor.

The punishment that Carter took after the Lance affair was cumulative. Much of it had been stored up by "piglets" in preceding months attributable to the same cause, ignorance of nuances in interest-group, congressional, and diplomatic dealings, let alone the press: Carter's postelection stay in Plains was very likely Piglet

Number One. Others followed rapidly. Among them was a plan for $50 rebates to all taxpayers, first publicly announced—delighting millions—and then publicly withdrawn. Another was a quite gratuitous assault on water projects treasured in the South and West, financed by Congress, which Carter first declared must stop and then under pressure accepted. There also came a casual yet dramatic burst of talk on human rights just at the crux of Soviet-American arrangements for new SALT talks. This was followed by a bold American initiative in those talks for which Moscow had not been prepared. Immediately after came the Carter plan on energy, complex and multifaceted yet indecisive at its core, presented to the interest groups and Congress—and to Carter's own economists—with scarcely any advance consultation. It was presented, moreover, as the biggest challenge in national life. Then, once the Speaker had rallied the House, energy was treated by the White House as though it were but one of many legislative imperatives. "Priorities" is a word Carter discovered later; the delay was still another "piglet." And these were interspersed with quite extraordinary gaffes in the minutiae of congressional relations. The whole of Washington had watched in wonderment. After Lance, all too many watchers stopped wondering.

Since then, a number of nuances have been learned (some say overlearned). By early 1979 the White House was repeating few of these mistakes. In some respects indeed it had improved upon the staff work of previous regimes, as in "public liaison" under Anne Wexler. But Carter's reputation only slowly (if at all) registered improvements in performance. The slowness in 1979 attests to the severity of punishment in 1977. And his public prestige remained down, indeed fell further, overtaken by accumulated irritants in private lives, most notably inflation.

"Mistake" is a word that bears watching. What went wrong in the Lance affair—and presumably these others—is not that Carter's chosen object was mistaken necessarily, but rather, much more narrowly, that as he chose it he did not make a sufficient effort to identify and weigh even the likely risks that many an experienced Washingtonian could have spelled out for him. All that was required was thought about the press corps and the bureaucrats in an awareness that two inquiries had stopped after election. Had the implications been set forth it is conceivable, at least to me, that Carter would have sanctioned an approach to Ribicoff if Lance still wished. For Carter needed Lance and wanted him; nothing in the record shows he was mistaken about Lance's usefulness since taking office. But had Carter and Lance grasped what they were facing, weighed the risks, and gone ahead, they surely would have gone prepared, which plainly they were not. Lance turned to Clifford in August; he was needed in June, if not sooner.

"Mistake" is thus a reference here to means, not aims. If Carter's aim of keeping Lance was wrong, it was at least shared widely at the start, by Ribicoff's committee among others. The same point can be made, and still more strongly, with regard to the fiasco at the Bay of Pigs. If JFK felt he must have the Brigade out of Guatemala but not griping in Miami, which perhaps became his immediate aim, there was nothing necessarily mistaken about that. Democrats, at any rate, would have agreed in droves, and also, presumably, Eisenhower. But this assumes that Kennedy made reasonably sure his clients would not land in Castro's jails—for that he wanted least, less even than Miami. "Reasonably sure" means something no more esoteric than a swamp. Kennedy, at a minimum, needed to take care that there really were mountains, with room for guerrillas in them, and that they knew how to reach them, wanted to, and could. Instead he sanctioned plans and set restrictions that together led them straight to jail at maximum embarrassment to him.

It can be argued that in both these cases what was lacking could not have been learned in any other way. I think it might. Compared to Kennedy or Carter, Nixon in his first year seems to have had no "pig" and few "piglets," which suggests that there is something to be said for the vicarious experience of a long Vice-Presidency. This aside, Presidents and White House aides learn constantly from their first day, educated by streams of necessitous activities in every sphere. Ignorance of men, roles, institutions, policies—and nuances—will wear away. So much is unavoidable that there scarcely seems need to rush the learning process with discretionary actions of unusual sorts, especially not actions unfamiliar to the old hands too. Both Bissell's invasion plan and Lance's extension of time were in that category. Both were unusual for all concerned, not least but not alone the new Administration. One lesson, possibly, is to postpone the novelties, or anyway to look at them with special care.

Postponement seems to many a false counsel. The error of attempting more than one knows how to do (or think about) is twin to that of not attempting what one could do (or get by with) if one tried. I argue for postponement still. Transitions are not forever, ignorance wears off, hopefulness cools down, and if the novelties are not impelled by sheer necessity (by deadlines that stand up to harder scrutiny than Kennedy gave those alleged in 1961), it should be worth a forfeit of presumptive gains to skirt the losses lurking where one's ignorance and hopefulness combine. But this is an argument each new Administration finds repugnant, almost by definition. Slow starts are not in fashion. From New Year's to Inaugural there come the feature articles on Roosevelt's Hundred Days.

So the alternative is carefulness. Alarm bells ought to ring at sight of the unusual, especially on unfamiliar ground. Alas, they did not ring for Kennedy or Carter. Nobody had set them.

V

In the twenty years since Nixon lost to Kennedy we have had five new Presidents, as against three in the twenty years before. Since 1960 only the then incumbent, Eisenhower, has completed two terms. Kennedy lasted three years and was killed. Johnson lasted five and was almost compelled to retire. Nixon too had five before he was virtually impeached. Ford finished out the term and was defeated for election. Carter now appears intent upon a second term.

Whatever may occur in 1980, five Presidents in 20 years already have brought us as many transitions. Between now and 2000 we cannot constitutionally have fewer than three Presidents and could again have five (or even more). That prospect dims the positive advantages our changing system could in theory give a President. Transition hazards were among the factors that combined to keep Carter from standing tall. His successors face these hazards too. They too in their ways will be ignorant and hopeful. The same can be said of their staffs!

Five transitions instead of three could make the hazards worse. Each changeover spells scramble, discomfiture, reshuffling, adjustment for the issue networkers of Washington. In self-defense the networks should grow thicker, more complex, more interactive, more entrenched, and their relationships should have more nuances with every changeover. Career officialdom should burrow down as far from sight as possible. If we change Administrations at the present rate for long, the subtleties of Washington may soon confound the very Washingtonians who looked askance at Carter.

Since we cannot determine in advance whether a President will live or die, much less win nomination and election to a second term, we cannot guarantee against five or more changes every generation. The problem might be eased by lengthening the presidential term. Six years was Nixon's notion, now proposed by Connally and Carter too, but with the dubious feature of no reelection. This makes the Presidency less accountable while guaranteeing more transitions than the Constitution now requires.

Constitutional reform aside, the Kennedy and Carter cases would suggest that nothing within practicable reach could ease the hazards of transition more than realism about them in the media, more tolerance for taking time, also for taking pratfalls. We need to popularize the idea that a learning process is at once inevitable and legitimate, that ignorance in some significant respects is every new man's fate (hence ours) bound to produce adjustments, disappointments, changes, and reversals both in policy and personnel. If that idea were sanctioned by attentive publics it might spread toward inattentives on the one hand and toward candidates on the other. Someday a President-elect might feel that he could say to newsmen (and himself) ''there *won't* be any 'Hundred Days;' I *can't* know how I really want to organize my White House, ask me again next year; we *don't* yet understand how campaign pledges fit events and trends as yet unknown to us, that's what four years are for''—and so forth.

Paradoxically, a lowering of expectations all around might help a President in Carter's shoes stand taller than he did, the better to be seen and heard and felt because his reputation and prestige were not mortgaged to nuances that he had yet to learn. High expectations helped to pull him down in his first years, the (unacknowledged) learning time. Acknowledge it and possibly another Carter rises in the eyes of Washingtonians and citizens alike.

Realistic expectations could be less productive in a case like Truman's or like LBJ's. For them transition in the narrow sense was indistinguishable from transition in the broad sense. Between the news and swearing-in they may have had two hours, but the Presidency actually began for them the moment FDR and Kennedy died. Then and thereafter what was wanted from them by the press and Washingtonians in general, *and* mass publics, was assurance of effective continuity: the king is dead, long live the king. God forbid that he should be unready to be king, or not know how, or not feel up to it. Johnson's situation was extreme because his predecessor had been killed, the country frightened. Truman's problem in the aftermath of Roosevelt's death was easier; he made it harder for himself, as Chapter 5 records, by being humble. He then went through a phase of shooting from the hip. His professional reputation suffered with attentive publics (even he deplored in later years his abrupt cancellation of Land Lease, an early ''piglet''). Truman's public standing was upheld by the flag until the war's end, then it dropped. Johnson, by contrast, rose in Washington's regard and popular prestige alike. ''Let us continue'' was his watchword and he visibly improved upon the doing. Approbation followed, fueled by relief.

Johnson faced the unprecedented challenge of assuming office and then running for election in the same first year; that year he seemed to do everything right. He displayed skills as President that smacked of faultless expertise, not of learning on the job. He did this partly by deferring issues in the foreign field, not least Vietnam decisions, where he felt least expert; he made his case for doing so by claiming continuity. In the short run this sufficed to keep his show of skillfulness unblemished. Mastery was what the country evidently wanted to observe and what it saw (as long as he kept those decisions at arm's length). In the circumstances realism would have been unpopular, perhaps even unrealistic.

Ford, the third Vice-President to take over in modern times, did have some advance warning, although less than is commonly supposed because he feared to seem a plotter against Nixon.[36] Once in office, Ford faced an extraordinary variant of Johnson's problem. Succeeding a disgraced man, but not himself legitimated by a popular election, Ford needed to assure the continuity of office by his demonstrated *difference* from his predecessor. This called not for mastery—a good thing because Ford did not have Johnson's skills—but rather for unquestionable decency. That he managed to convey for just a month, then blurred it when he pardoned Nixon who had not yet even been indicted.

The pardon seems a matter less of newness than of conscience, sympathy, or party calculation. It may have cost Ford his election three years later. So much for calculation. If and as he thought about Republicans he may have done so more as Minority Leader (which he had been) than as presidential candidate for 1976 (which he had not yet chosen to become). In that sense Ford was certainly new. But sympathy and conscience could have done the deed regardless. Nixon, he reportedly was told, seemed suicidal.[37]

Soon after pardoning Nixon, Ford convened a summit meeting of economists; there he declared war on inflation, unfortunately just as recession was about to show itself. That war, complete with WIN buttons (for "whip inflation now"), became a veritable "pig."[38] Ford's reputation slumped, his prestige was already falling, and the media bore down on him as scornfully as four years afterwards on Carter.[39]

More realism about necessary learning time might well have left Ford's critics doing just as they did. Indeed, realism on that score may not be what was lacking in this instance. Before the pardon Ford was hailed regardless of transition troubles. After the pardon few were in a mood to make excuses.

To counsel realism, therefore, is to offer Presidents no universal remedy for the adverse effects of newness on the job. In the best case I doubt that these could be evaded altogether. Not even LBJ accomplished that. All he did was herd his "pigs" ahead of him, until he turned from what he knew to deal with Ho Chi Minh.

What realism cannot cure might be assuaged by other things. One of them is carefulness from case to case, as indicated above. And after that, presumably, comes a technique not often used by Presidents, confession-and-avoidance. In April 1961, JFK on television took responsibility for everything that had gone wrong. "Defeat is an orphan," he said and claimed parentage. The phrase was memorable, and that went into his professional reputation on the plus side. As for his popular prestige, the gallant gesture evidently pushed it all the higher. Such a thing is too much to expect of LBJ once well into his war, but not of somebody less desperately engaged, as for example Carter. Yet Carter personally was ill-equipped to do it—ill-equipped, at any rate, during his first two years. He lacked the personal style to stir a national audience. And very possibly, after the Lance affair he lacked the audience.

Transition troubles were but one of the systemic difficulties holding Carter down in his first years, denying him presumed advantages of placement where constituents could readily distinguish him from "Washington" and rally to him. The other difficulties, as I note above, combined a lack of constitutional and statutory powers with an insufficient popular response to supplement them. Except in times of widely perceived crisis, like the depths of the Depression or the start of World War II, this combination in some guise has drawn laments from every modern President. Carter's case is not new, but only Ford or Truman offer analogs to "who cares?" in the aftermath of "Jimmy who?" Confession-and-avoidance is a technique open only when relationships of trust have been established, or at least of warm and welcoming response. Carter's relationships were frail. The trouble that accrued to him from newness on the public scene thus reinforced the trouble from his newness in the Presidency. These overlapped. And at their juncture they were rendered worse by his personal style on television.

VI

Television is at once the primary news source for most Americans, the vehicle for national political campaigns, a crucial means to sell consumer goods, and an almost universal source of entertainment. These four may well be put in reverse order of importance. Even so, the President of the United States deals with the general public through this medium, and his presumed effectiveness as a performer on it enters into his professional reputation, especially when he is new. The presumption runs to public impact, hard to judge, but here as much as elsewhere in our politics, or more, appearance counts. The body of this book was written before television came of age as a news source.[40] By light of Carter's first two years some comments are in order.

The Carter television style in his first years gave rise to a standard complaint by supporters, let alone critics: if only he had used TV as JFK did, or as FDR used radio, then millions should have come to "care," at least enough to sway dispersed, home-haunted members of contemporary Congresses (possibly excluding Senator Long). Domestically, this could have given Carter carrots to entice and sticks to beat the private sector. It even could have eased his way abroad, somewhat, enhancing his assurance and bolstering his cautions. Carter's television personality lent credence to the logic of "if only." During those years he answered questions well and often held press conferences, but these were shown mid-mornings or midafternoons and snippets on the network news were cogent but not lively. His written speeches on prime time were soporific, a matter partly of soft tone and curious cadence, partly a reflection of his public personality, toned down, "de-pomped."

Carter is by no means the first President who failed to stir a television audience. Since the commercial medium was launched in Truman's time, all except Kennedy have been mediocre or worse in reading prime-time speeches, save at moments of high drama centered not on their technique but on their powers or the backdrop of events. Ford, Nixon, Johnson, Eisenhower, Truman: rarely did they manage to inspire on TV, oftener than not they bored. This can be written off to various deficiencies in personal style. So can Carter's flatness. It may tell us no more than that John Kennedy's assassination broke the natural order of political succession and delayed the coming of a TV generation. But it may be saying something more. It may suggest that exposition or defense of public policy is harder on TV than on the radio (to say nothing of print) because *spectators* seek and easily can find more interesting forms of entertainment.

It is not clear that style alone keeps Presidents from turning television viewers into lobbyists with Congressmen or interest groups or other institutions. Kennedy, despite his style, could not arouse the countryside for prompt congressional action even on tax reduction, let alone civil rights. LBJ, in contrast, bulled them through with every show of immense popular support, evoked not by his entertainment value but by "let us continue," with Kennedy dead. In Chapter 5, I argued:

> Events determine audience attention for a President. They also make his actions more important than his words. When constituents grow conscious of his relevance to them they are already learning—from events. By then his telling will convey no lesson independent of the things he seems to do within the context of events.
>
> . . . What Roosevelt taught in 1933 was governed only by the future. He had no

presidential past, nor had the Nation a remembered precedent. . . . But for a President in other circumstances talk and action may take meaning from "last time" as well as next, and teaching thus is placed in double jeopardy.[41]

So it was when TV had not yet become the chief news source for most Americans, and when it only had begun to be a captivating source of adult entertainment. So it seems still. But nowadays the medium itself is at the podium, another party to the whole transaction, molding presidential words and even the events to its dimensions as an entertainer and to ours as spectators.

Style aside, this puts a President in triple jeopardy. He needs events behind him, something Johnson had in his first year but Carter lacked. As the years pass he needs a break from what they conjure up. And now he also needs a break from visual associations. How will watchers know whether to laugh or cry? Not from his words alone; what does his body say? What do the recollections of his *person* add: "remember how he looked before. . . .?" If one must be a talking head on TV—and all Presidents are that—previous associations seem to count. Seeing is believing when the head is Walter Cronkite's. LBJ in 1964, although no Kennedy, was reassuringly familiar. In 1977 Carter remained strange. (Now he too grows familiar; if he gains a second term even his cadences may reassure, the more so as his audience recalls him on election night.) Cronkite, of course, has the extra advantage of trust, a thing in relatively short supply for Presidents throughout the Nineteen-Seventies.[42]

Carter began his first term with no gift for reading texts on television, no sharp events to dramatize his multitude of programs, and no record in the minds of viewers save his own astonishing emergence from obscurity. This asset then was dissipated by a set of misadventures culminating in the Lance affair. However ripe the Congress and the issue networks seemed for presidential pressure through constituents, Carter could not turn TV to his account in making them constituents for him.

Can anyone? Spectators may never be convertible to followers if that means *doing* something. Or as suggested by the Selma March of 1965, the "Saturday Night Massacre" of 1974, and other powerful sights, viewers may become doers when the drama of the human scene is matched by something handy to be done just then—like heading South or wiring the White House—and not otherwise. Besides, there is the over-exposure problem, a constant menace for contemporary Presidents. Almost-daily snippets on the nightly news blend into something both continuous and bland. Franklin Roosevelt would have hated it (see Chapter 5); now there may be no way to avoid it.

A feature of the Presidency's clerkship nowadays is giving Cronkite and his fellow anchormen their leads some nights each week. Along with over-exposure comes the menace of under-reaction. It is fed by sights and dramas from around the world each day, a minute or so apiece, bunched between commercials, with the

President (no matter what he says or does) one more of the same, usually less active hence less interesting.

Still, the question remains open. Since the anti-New Deal coalition wore away in Congress, since professional staffs gained their present prominence in Washington, since Heclo's issue networks came to be a—perhaps *the*—dominating feature of the town, we have not had a President whose ease with the news medium matched JFK's, to say no more of FDR with radio or TR, for that matter, with the wire-services. Nor has the ease been bolstered by a long-familiar face evoking feelings of respect or love.

Indeed no recent President, not even Kennedy, has been prepared to use this medium as its habitual practitioners do, emphasizing visuals, action, conflict, turning ease to account in commentary. No President thus far has felt he had the talent both to do that and still appear "presidential."

It will be interesting to see what happens if we get someone who can. Despite its disadvantages, TV undoubtedly has been of use to Presidents. Even the untalented set its agenda by their choices, and when backed by strong events combined with striking visuals they score points. When Prime Minister Begin and President Sadat of Israel and Egypt came from Camp David to the White House in September 1978, and there announced on TV an agreement in principle, their happy praise of Carter who had mediated for a week—warmly human compliments with byplay back and forth—sent his approval in the Gallup poll up temporarily from 42 to 56 percent. It is to be presumed, therefore, that if a President were talented on television, easy with it, innovative in its use, he then should have a better chance than Carter did of minimizing or repairing his transitional mistakes, both in terms of consequences for his Washington reputation and of impact on his popular prestige.

Reputation and prestige are nothing new for Presidents—as Chapters 4 and 5 attest—but television probably has modified the terms of their relationship and use. Personal impressions of the man's own skill and will once dominated Washington opinion, while his general public standing once reflected, in the main, events that shook the private lives of less attentive persons. Twenty years ago I argued that these factors were autonomous and frequently diverged. So they did with Kennedy's Bay of Pigs. By Nixon's time we saw occasions—notably the Saturday Night Massacre (see Chapter 10)—where Washingtonians reacted much like other citizens. Prestige then merged with reputation quite directly. In Carter's first year I believe we saw the opposite: professional opinions shaped the general view, no less directly, in the absence of much pocketbook—or patriotic—change. So I have interpreted the Gallup poll reports on Carter in the winter of 1977−78. When the range of his approval ratings fell from the "mid-fifties" to the bottom of the "forties," it was Washington reactions as transmitted by TV—by newscasts, talk shows, stand-up comics, drawing on and supplemented through print media of course—that evidently guided mass opinion. At least I find no sharp events affecting private lives to offer causal competition.[43]

At the same time that prestige seems likelier than formerly to reflect reputation it may come to matter more *in* reputation. A President's capacity to draw and stir a television audience seems every bit as interesting to current Washingtonians as his ability to wield his formal powers. Their interest is his opportunity. While national party organizations fall away, while congressional party discipline relaxes, while interest groups proliferate and issue networks rise, a President who wishes to compete for leadership in framing policy and shaping coalitions has to make the most he can out of his popular connection. Anticipating home reactions, Washingtonians who sway before a breeze from tax revolt in California are vulnerable to any breeze from home that presidential words and sights can stir. If he is deemed effective on the tube they will anticipate. That is the essence of professional reputation.

At the opposite extreme the question arises whether anyone could govern now as Truman did for two years with the disapproval of three-quarters of his countrymen. Nixon has contributed the precedent of resignation.

These comments on the possible effects and use of television bring us back to the last paragraph of Chapter 10 and to the prospect of a President whose skills embrace at once the forging of strong links to bind the group around him and arousal of responses in a television audience. The person who can do these things appears well placed, compared with Carter, to overcome Jimmy-who-ness, if he suffers something like it, and to ease the usual hazards of transition. He may, however, face a special hazard of his own: his talent for TV may of itself lead him astray, encouraging a special sort of innocence.

VII

The President with television talent will be likely to put his very talent at the center of his hopes when he takes office. If this means striving for a balance with the Washington professionals, seeking advantageous ground to bargain on, then well and good. Anticipated reactions should make them respectful of attractiveness on TV, at least while it is not demonstrably irrelevant (and that takes time to show). But if the President envisages substantial innovations, whether conservative or liberal, then almost everything in modern history cries caution to such hopes unless accompanied by crises with potential for consensus. Even then TV is no cure-all!

Crises of that sort have not been features of our landscape since the Nineteen-Forties. Are the issues of the Eighties likely to produce them? I think of many issues that will almost surely be divisive, not consensual. On the other hand, at least two might contain the seeds of an old-style consensus: sustained fuel shortages and terrorism. Even the possibility distinguishes the years ahead from those behind us and might give a new incumbent reason for his hopes.

Looking toward the Sixties, I wrote twenty years ago that:

> . . . barring deep depression or unlimited war . . . nothing in experience suggests that we shall see either consensus of the sort available to FDR in 1933 and 1942, or popular

demand for constitutional adjustments likely to assist a President. . . . crisis consensus
. . . is probably beyond the reach of the next President. We may have priced ourselves
out of the market for "productive" crises on the pattern Roosevelt knew—productive in
the sense of strengthening his chance for sustained support within the system. Judging
from the Fifties, neither limited war nor limited depression is productive in these terms.
Anything unlimited will probably break the system.[44]

Judging from the Seventies one could say the same for inflation or for a revived cold
war. But independence of the Arabs might yet come to be consensual, if technological advances offer light at the end of the tunnel. (An environmental threat big, close,
and indisputable might someday offer something comparable.) And widespread
terrorism would provoke consensual outrage, I believe, regardless of its source and
never mind what lies at the end of the tunnel. This last is double-edged; the first,
however, appears promising as Carter saw, perhaps prematurely, in 1977 and since.
Carter's efforts, at the least, break ground for a successor if not for himself.

Moreover, my prediction for the Sixties was deficient in at least one respect: it
did not allow for what I might call "in-house" consensus—consensus *without*
crisis. By this I mean a closely woven web of accommodations among interests,
entangling most, which mass publics more nearly acquiesce in than expected. Such
a thing requires on the one hand weaving of the most skilled sort in Washington and
on the other hand sufficient satisfaction about private lives to nurture acquiescence
in the country. The modern prototype is LBJ's consensus on domestic programs
during 1965, the so-called Great Society. Relatively speaking, Washington was
smaller, professionals fewer, the press corps both less numerous and less assured
than now. Johnson had to reach farther for some of the interests he entangled in his
web than a successor may need to do: the town grows; everything is more accessible. The same can be said of influentials. Whoever lives elsewhere is represented
there at increasingly high levels, or summoned there on increasingly short notice.
By the year 2000 modern Washington may be a capital something like traditional
London. Then in-house consensus becomes all the easier. There is a real Establishment of personal relations on the inside. From the outside nothing may be needed
save acceptance. The President who seems adept at helping to secure that is accorded local standing as a *primus inter pares*. Responding to him or reacting against
him spurs accommodation.

Johnson's in-house consensus lasted a bare two years. At that it may have
made a stronger showing longer than its like could do today. For atomization
weakens coalition-building, to say nothing of maintenance, and substitutes but
transient majorities, "coalitions built in sand," as Anthony King puts it. How could
such things sustain consensus without crisis? King seems to imply that they
couldn't.[45] I sometimes think they might. Washingtonians are splintered among
interests, specialties, and home-communities, to be sure. But simultaneously they
all become part of the same Establishment, their own community. May it not come
to have some interests of its own? Already their town is inward-looking; despite its

myriad connections to the country its inhabitants do not confuse themselves with countrymen, or *vice versa*. They share frames of reference, life-styles, media, traditions, customs, even language, lending Washington as strong a regional identity as any part of the United States. To that extent they are not building wholly in the sand when they pursue accommodations with each other.

Still, at least for a time King is probably right. Johnsonian consensus seems less likely in the Eighties than in 1964. For one thing it is harder under "atomized" conditions, King's point. For another thing the private satisfactions yielding acquiescence outside Washington seem incompatible with sharply-felt inflation—to say nothing of spot shortages. Unexpected price rises may well have done as much as draft calls, casualties, and riots to dissolve acceptance of the Great Society. The Eighties promise to be haunted by fears of inflation. Given the poor prospects for in-house consensus we do well to focus on the prospects for productive crises.

Issues that might come to yield consensus in the Eighties almost certainly would call for stricter measures of accomplishment than in the Thirties. Amidst the bank failures of 1933, with a quarter of the work force unemployed, FDR could say "the only thing we have to fear is fear itself," proclaim that Federal action held the key, and reap a psychological reward from almost any sort of act. Six years after Roosevelt spoke, unemployment still was first among the country's social problems to be mastered only in the Second World War. Energy, environment, or terror could not yield productive results on such terms. Their content is too technical, the options too specific. As for future Great Societies, or opposites by way of devolution, tax reduction, the same thing seems to hold. In-house consensus, if and when it comes again, is likely to be woven out of technical materials on quite specific lines.

This counsels special care in a new President's first years; if he is talented on television all the more so. Drawing a consensus from a crisis situation when the technical and the specific dominate the task could not be easy at any time. (Neither could weaving one without a crisis.) How much harder must the task be in a learning time! Specific implementation efforts, technical in scope, necessarily depend on Federal specialists, interacting with bureaucracies at state and local levels and throughout the private sector: oil companies, utilities, police, among others. Here are organizations piled on organizations, each with little-known career-lines, incentives, and routines that shape its capabilities. Alternatively, efforts run through the Defense or State or Treasury Departments, blunt instruments all three, to foreign organizations still less known.

The intricacies of motivating bureaucrats in complex organizations are likelier than not to have escaped the President with talent for TV. In the United States skilled public presentation is identified with advocacy, acting, or reporting; most of our administrators grow up tongue-tied. Moreover in our politics proficiency at legislative, interest-group, and press relations is more visible and more rewarding than administration. Yet balancing the public and administrative feasibilities—the uses of events *and* the capacities of institutions—seems essential for the President who seeks to make the most of any prospects for consensus. The less he may have dealt with organizations in the past, the more he needs to comprehend. The more proficient as a user of events, the less he may conceive he has to learn. In this could lie his special innocence. It heightens both his stakes and ours in hazards of transition for a person with his talent.

VIII

Is the Presidency possible? Even in the humble sense of keeping the game going, handing on the office reasonably intact? Well into the television age, threatened by inflation, badgered by spot shortages, tied to an increasingly complex technology with little room for unskilled blacks, and tied as well into a world economy with little patience for low productivity, the answer turns in large part on events and organizations beyond presidential control or subject in uncertain ways to presidential influence. Revival of the cold war, if that comes, or a new form of nuclear vulnerability adds more uncertainties. These are compounded by revival of an old American tradition, the mistrustful public mood, reacting against social optimism in the Sixties together with Vietnam and Watergate. That mood may now accommodate and carry on alongside a renewal of exaggerated expectations for *some* President's performance, if not Carter's than the next man's. One needs my Truman standard to encourage hope. This combination keeps an answer problematical.

It seems the more so because politics is so unhinged from parties, while the crowd of Washingtonians so frequently escapes political direction by the leadership at *either* end of Pennsylvania Avenue. We currently have neither an "Imperial Presidency" as popularly understood nor have we congressional government in Wilson's terms, rule by the chairmen of committees.[46] Rather we have some of each and much of neither as we drift with the crowd. The amalgam is hard to describe, harder to understand, hardest for the so-called Chief Executive to manage.

Looking well ahead, however, if events and resources allow, it may be that we now approach an *ad hoc* transformation of our working political system, which without disturbing formal structure might afford us two main elements collaborating in constructive tension.

Carter's campaign against "Washington" in 1976 may not have been the oddity most Washingtonians then thought it. Roughly put, that town's professional crowd seems now to be emerging as our functional equivalent for almost everything in Paris save the President of the Republic and for almost everything in London save the senior Cabinet Ministers. Those political chief executives are supposed to rise above parochial interests, if and as they can, pursuing integrative goals, embodying the whole, and taking the ultimate rap. As such they are supposed to balance off the permanent establishment, indeed to guide it, giving an accountable, elective, human cast to governance. Our nearest counterpart for them remains the President of the United States, and closely grouped around him perhaps half a dozen senior aides, perhaps as many department heads (if he is lucky), together with a handful of congressional leaders (if he is wise) who have their own interests in integration and in him. Most of the rest, the lower-level aides, administrators, civil servants, legislators and their staffs, along with private-sector staffs are part of, dominated by, responsive to, or smothered in the crowd. To balance it and guide it he and his little band would have to show both skill and will in their own work, building reputation, and capacity on television (also off) to attract other people's clients and constituents. Otherwise that crowd might smother him. For its part it contains connections, skills, and energies, within each issue network and among them, indispensible to comprehend the substance of our problems and to bridge the separations of our institutions. These things the President needs as much as Washingtonians need him to be their clerk. And if, besides, enough of them decide they have to heed his guidance or at least treat with him on it, then perhaps the stage is set for constructive tension.

This could not be a tension between anything so simple as two unitary actors labeled "Congress" and "President" or "Interests" and "Executive," even though procedures, legislative or administrative, would confer advantages and frame particular actions. Functionally a closer counterpart might be relations between London's two sets of careerists, MP's and civil servants, who observe some tacit treaties which allow them to collaborate in governing yet argue all the while.[47]

Britain's career systems are but distantly analogous. Lacking set career-lines, most issue-oriented Washingtonians have yet to work out treaties even with each other. They scarcely have a consciousness of group identity. Within the complex structure of our formal system they divide now on exceedingly fine lines of interest, market, section, service, subsidy, also to some extent of race, religion, sex. Yet their relationships elaborately crisscross these lines; acquaintance follows, and recruitment; do's-and-don'ts accumulate; possibly, with time, these just might turn a crowd into some sort of working entity possessing better defined membership and roles.

Alone of major modern governments, the United States has had no stiffening element in its political system, no politicized army, no preponderant party, no communist cadres, no French bureaucracy. Our nearest counterparts were old style national parties, mushy by comparison and now, as organizations, virtually defunct. But now by inadvertence if not accident, tenuously, almost imperceptibly, there may be coming at what C. Wright Mills called "middle levels of power," a curious, vigorous substitute, the issue networkers, professional men and women settling down in Washington: the lawyers, engineers, economists, the former military officers, the MBA's or MPP's, or MPH's or MD's, appointive, elective, nonprofit, or private, in short the crowd. It is not elitist by Paris standards, nor coherent by the standards of say, Cairo, nor disciplined in even Belgrade's terms. But it becomes more meritocratic, more continuous, more self-absorbed, perhaps more of an entity, than many of its members seem to think. What may it be in twenty years? Perhaps as incoherent as our other institutions, indeed adding, just as now, to incoherence in the rest of them, but possibly a stiffener. If so we need a lively Presidency alongside, with an independent popular connection. If not we need the Presidency still more, and Gaullist constitutions could be much in fashion.

Nowadays we also lack determinate *political* career-lines. Where those are to come from seems a still less settled question. But conceivably it too might be resolved by evolution of the professional crowd. Might an elective specialty emerge, with Congress as its clubhouse? Do Senators Culver, Hart, and Moynihan, or Congressman Cheney, Ford's former chief of staff, imply a trend?[48]

These are mere speculations but they do suggest that "atomization" may foreshadow reconstruction, not collapse. Two big things in Washington that, relatively speaking, were but small things twenty years ago are television news and the professional crowd. Between them they account for much of the dispersion since then in other things like party organization. They might yet become pillars of a reconstruction yielding more effectiveness than we have seen of late in White House contributions to governmental outcomes. This is, of course, a long shot and would take substantial time.

Meanwhile, those with responsibility for operations day by day should be encouraged to do what they can, the rest of us should be encouraged to do likewise, and transitions offer opportunities for doing. Here official carefulness combined with public realism, bolstered by occasional confession-and-avoidance, actually might help in concrete cases to improve the prospects for a President's effectiveness. Such things may be marginal but that is how in the United States thus far, the Civil War aside, we deal with our problems of governance. Maybe what we need instead is thoroughgoing constitutional reform. This often is suggested. But while waiting for it (a long wait in my view), we and our Presidents-elect could try to cope a little better than before with their assumption of the office and their learning-time in office. Recognizing that it has to be a time of special hazards is a first step.

Notes

Chapter 2

[1]Robert J. Donovan, *Eisenhower: The Inside Story,* New York: Harper, 1956, p. 151.

[2]These and later references to the dismissal of General MacArthur and the background of that action are based on the following sources: "The Military Situation in the Far East," *Hearings,* U.S. Senate Committee on Armed Services and Committee on Foreign Relations, 82d Cong., 1st sess., Washington: 1951, parts 1−5 (referred to hereafter as *MacArthur Hearings*); Memoirs by Harry S. Truman, Vol. 2, *Years of Trial and Hope,* Garden City, Doubleday, 1956, copr. 1956 Time Inc., chaps. 23−28.

There has been some supplementation of these sources by interviews with former President Truman in December 1955, and in February 1958, and by personal notes made at the time. For general background I would refer the reader to Walter Millis, Harvey C. Mansfield, and Harold Stein, *Arms and the State,* New York: Twentieth Century Fund, 1958, chap. 7.

[3]As reported in the *New York Times,* March 8, 1951 and reproduced in the *MacArthur Hearings,* part 5, pp. 3540−3541.

[4](See also, note 31, Chapter 10.) These and succeeding references to the steel seizure and related events are based on the case study by Grant McConnell, *The President Seizes the Steel Mills,* Inter-University Case Program, University, Ala.; University of Alabama Press, 1960, supplemented extensively by personal notes made at the time and by interviews with former President Truman in December 1955.

For an illuminating documentation of public and legal developments before and after seizure, the reader is referred to Alan F. Westin, *The Anatomy of a Constitutional Law Case,* New York: Macmillan, 1958. See also Truman *Memoirs,* Vol 2, chap. 29.

[5]These and succeeding references to the Little Rock affair are based on the following sources: news reports and texts of documents appearing in *Southern School News* and the *New York Times;* former Congressman Brooks Hays's personal account *A Southern Moderate*

Speaks, Chapel Hill: University of North Carolina Press, 1959; the personal account by the former Superintendent of Schools, Virgil T. Blossom, *It Has Happened Here,* New York: Harper, 1959, especially pp. 120 ff.; Corinne Silverman's case study, *The Little Rock Story,* Inter-University Case Program, no. 41, University, Ala.: University of Alabama Press, 1958. These sources were supplemented by interviews in February and April 1958 with three members of the White House staff.

[6]Truman *Memoirs,* Vol. 2, p. 442.

[7]Harry S. Ashmore, *An Epitaph for Dixie,* New York: Norton, 1958, p. 41.

[8]In the period before this action by the District Court, Sawyer's delay was based, in part, on the advice of Commerce legal staff after consultation with Justice attorneys preparing the government's case. The Justice lawyers feared that action on wages would complicate their argument before the court. The lawyers in the White House were unimpressed by this concern; it is doubtful that the Acting Attorney General shared it, either. But Sawyer was the official in charge of the mills, and these were the attorneys in charge of the case. Their preference buttressed his inclination, and the responsibility was his.

[9]The emergency-disputes provisions of the Taft-Hartley Act, which Truman so far had refused to invoke in this case, require as their first step appointment of a fact-finding board. Only after its report, if he deems its findings justify such action, is the President authorized to have the Attorney General seek an injunction from the courts forbidding a work stoppage for 80 days. Hence the first step, fact-finding, neither stops a strike in progress nor automatically commits a President to the use of an injunction.

[10]Truman *Memoirs,* Vol. 2, p. 448.

[11]As indicated especially in MacArthur's message to the Veterans of Foreign Wars, which was "withdrawn" on presidential order of August 26, 1950. By then, an advance text had already been released to the press and was carried in full in *U.S. News and World Report,* September 1, 1950, Vol. 29, no. 9, pp, 32–34. The text is reproduced in the *MacArthur Hearings,* part 5, p. 3477.

[12]Transcript of presidential press conference, July 17, 1957, in *Public Papers of the Presidents: Dwight D. Eisenhower,* 1957, Washington: The National Archives, 1958, p. 546.

[13]Henry A. Kissinger, *Nuclear Weapons and Foreign Policy,* New York: Harper, for the Council on Foreign Relations, 1957, pp. 50–51.

Notes

Chapter 3

[1]The reader will want to keep in mind the distinction between two senses in which the word *power* is employed. When I have used the word (or its plural) to refer to formal constitutional, statutory, or customary authority, it is either qualified by the adjective "formal" or placed in quotation marks as "power(s)." Where I have used it in the sense of effective influence upon the conduct of others, it appears without quotation marks (and always in the singular). Where clarity and convenience permit, *authority* is substituted for "power" in the first sense and *influence* for power in the second sense.

[2]See, for example, his press conference of July 22, 1959, as reported in the *New York Times* for July 23, 1959.

[3]See Douglass Cater, *The Fourth Branch of Government*, Boston: Houghton-Mifflin, 1959.

[4]With the exception of the Vice-Presidency, of course.

[5]See David B. Truman's illuminating study of party relationships in the 81st Congress, *The Congressional Party*, New York: Wiley, 1959, especially chaps. 4, 6, and 8.

[6]As Secretary of the Interior in 1939, Harold Ickes refused to approve the sale of helium to Germany despite the insistence of the State Department and the urging of President Roosevelt. Without the Secretary's approval, such sales were forbidden by statute. See *The Secret Diaries of Harold L. Ickes,* New York: Simon and Schuster, 1954, Vol. 2, especially pp. 391–393, 396–399. See also Michael J. Reagan, "The Helium Controversy," in the forthcoming case book on civil-military relations prepared for the Twentieth Century Fund under the editorial direction of Harold Stein.

In this instance the statutory authority ran to the Secretary as a matter of *his* discretion. A President is unlikely to fire Cabinet officers for the conscientious exercise of such authority. If the President did so, their successors might well be embarrassed both publicly and at the

Capitol were they to reverse decisions previously taken. As for a President's authority to set aside discretionary determinations of this sort, it rests, if it exists at all, on shaky legal ground not likely to be trod save in the gravest of situations.

[7]Truman's *Memoirs* indicate that having tried and failed to make Stevenson an avowed candidate in the spring of 1952, the President decided to support the candidacy of Vice President Barkley. But Barkley withdrew early in the convention for lack of key northern support. Though Truman is silent on the matter, Barkley's active candidacy nearly was revived during the balloting, but the forces then aligning to revive it were led by opponents of Truman's Fair Deal, principally Southerners. As a practical matter, the President could not have lent his weight to *their* endeavors and could back no one but Stevenson to counter them. The latter's strength could not be shifted, then, to Harriman or Kefauver. Instead the other Notherners had to be withdrawn. Truman helped withdraw them. But he had no other option. See Memoirs by Harry S. Truman, Vol. 2, *Years of Trial and Hope,* Garden City; Double-day, 1956, copr. 1956 Time Inc., pp. 495–496.

[8]The reference is to Stassen's public statement of July 23, 1956, calling for Nixon's replacement on the Republican ticket by Governor Herter of Massachusetts, the later Secretary of State. Stassen's statement was issued after a conference with the President. Eisenhower's public statements on the vice-presidential nomination, both before and after Stassen's call, permit of alternative inferences: either that the President would have preferred another candidate, provided this could be arranged without a showing of White House dictation, or that he wanted Nixon on condition that the latter could show popular appeal. In the event, neither result was achieved. Eisenhower's own remarks lent strength to rapid party moves which smothered Stassen's effort. Nixon's nomination thus was guaranteed too quickly to appear the consequences of popular demand. For the public record on this matter see reported statements by Eisenhower, Nixon, Stassen, Herter, and Leonard Hall (the National Republican Chairman) in the *New York Times* for March, 1, 8, 15, 16; April 27; July 15, 16, 25–31; August 3, 4, 17, 23, 1956. See also the account from private sources by Earl Mazo in *Richard Nixon: A Personal and Political Portrait,* New York: Harper, 1959, pp. 158–187.

[9]Stenographic transcript of presidential press conference, October 19, 1950, on file in the Truman Library at Independence, Missouri.

[10]Jonathan Daniels, *Frontier on the Potomac,* New York: Macmillan, 1946, pp. 31–32.

[11]Transcript of presidential press conference, June 18, 1958, in *Public Papers of the Presidents: Dwight D. Eisenhower, 1958*, Washington: The National Archives, 1959, p. 479. In the summer of 1958, a congressional investigation into the affairs of a New England textile manufacturer, Bernard Goldfine, revealed that Sherman Adams had accepted various gifts and favors from him (the most notoriety attached to a vicuña coat). Adams also had made inquiries about the status of a Federal Communications Commission proceeding in which Goldfine was involved. In September 1958, Adams was allowed to resign. The episode was highly publicized and much discussed in that year's congressional campaigns.

[12]As reported in Marriner S. Eccles, *Beckoning Frontiers,* New York: Knopf, 1951, p. 336.

[13]In drawing together these observations on the Marshall Plan, I have relied on the record of personal participation by Joseph M. Jones, *The Fifteen Weeks,* New York: Viking, 1955, especially pp. 89–256; on the recent study by Harry Bayard Price, *The Marshall Plan and Its Meaning,* Ithaca: Cornell University Press, 1955, especially pp. 1–86; on the Truman

Memoirs, Vol. 2, chaps. 7−9; on Arthur H. Vandenberg, Jr., editor, *The Private Papers of Senator Vandenberg,* Boston: Houghton Mifflin, 1952, especially pp. 373 ff.; and on notes of my own made at the time. This is an instance of policy development not covered, to my knowledge, by any of the university programs engaged in the production of case studies.

[14]Secretary Marshall's speech, formally suggesting what became known as the Marshall Plan, was made at Harvard on June 5, 1947. On June 20 the President vetoed the Taft-Hartley Act; his veto was overridden three days later. On June 16 he vetoed the first of two tax reduction bills (HR 1) passed at the first session of the 80th Congress; the second of these (HR 3950), a replacement for the other, he also disapproved on July 18. In both instances his veto was narrowly sustained.

[15]*Private Papers of Senator Vandenberg,* pp. 378−379 and 446.

[16]The initial reluctance of Secretary of the Treasury, John Snyder, to support large-scale spending overseas became a matter of public knowledge on June 25, 1947. At a press conference on that day he interpreted Marshall's Harvard speech as a call on Europeans to help themselves, by themselves. At another press conference the same day, Marshall for his own part had indicated that the U.S. would consider helping programs on which Europeans agreed. The next day Truman held a press conference and was asked the inevitable question. He replied, "General Marshall and I are in complete agreement." When pressed further, Truman remarked sharply, "The Secretary of the Treasury and the Secretary of State and the President are in complete agreement." Thus the President cut Snyder off, but had programing gathered less momentum overseas, no doubt he would have been heard from again as time passed and opportunity offered.

The foregoing quotations are from the stenographic transcript of the presidential press conference June 26, 1947, on file in the Truman Library at Independence, Missouri.

[17]A remark made in December 1955, three years after he left office, but not unrepresentative of views he expressed, on occasion, while he was President.

[18]This might also be taken as testimony to the political timidity of officials in the State Department and the Budget Bureau where that fear seems to have been strongest. However, conversations at the time with White House aides incline me to believe that there, too, interjection of the price issue was thought a gamble and a risk. For further comment see my "Congress and the Fair Deal: A Legislative Balance Sheet," *Public Policy,* Cambridge: Harvard University Press, 1954, Vol. 5, pp. 362−364.

Notes

Chapter 4

[1]Carl J. Friedrich, "Public Policy and the Nature of Administrative Responsibility," *Public Policy,* Vol. 1, Cambridge: Harvard University Press, 1940, pp. 3–24.

[2]Quotation from stenographic transcript of presidential press conference, July 12, 1951, on file in the Truman Library at Independence, Missouri.

[3]For this account I am indebted to the technician in question.

[4]Unfortunately at the time this was written, the debacle of budget presentation and related development in 1957 had not been made the subject of an intensive case study published or in preparation by the usual university sources. Such a study is now planned by the Inter-University Case Program. Until its release, however, this is an instance in which I have had to break my general rule that the readers of this book should be able to lay hands readily upon another and more detailed treatment of its illustrative material.

In the absence of other treatments, these and succeeding observations rest, primarily, on interviews with a number of officials in the White House, the Executive Office agencies, and three of the executive departments. Various congressional assistants and committee staff members were interviewed, as well, along with several members of the Washington press corps. I am indebted to them all for my understanding as reflected in the text. These interviews were conducted in December 1956, in April, June, and October 1957, and in January, March, and April 1958. The *Congressional Record* and the *New York Times*, of course, provided an essential framework.

[5]From the transcript of the President's remarks November 7, 1956, in *Public Papers of the Presidents: Dwight D. Eisenhower, 1956,* Washington: The National Archives, 1958, p. 1090.

[6]*New York Times,* January 17, 1957. For the full text of the comments quoted in this

news account see "The Budget for 1958," *Hearings*, U.S. House of Representatives, Committee on Appropriations, 85th Cong., 1st sess., Washington: 1957, pp. 5, 7, 14.

[7] Transcript of presidential press conference, January 23, 1957, in *Public Papers of the Presidents, 1957*, pp. 73–74.

[8] Paul H. Douglas, "A New Isolationism: Ripple or Tide?" *New York Times Magazine*, August 18, 1957, p. 10.

[9] *New York Times*, March 7, 1957.

[10] House Resolution 190, 85th Cong., 1st sess.

[11] Letter from the President to the Speaker of the House of Representatives, April 18, 1957, in *Public Papers of the Presidents, 1957*, p. 301.

[12] Transcript of presidential press conference, March 27, 1957, *ibid.*, p. 223.

[13] William S. White in the *New York Times*, March 28, 1957.

[14] On April 2 the President addressed the Washington Conference for the Advertising Council. On April 3, he spoke at the Fifth Annual Republican Women's National Conference. See texts in *Public Papers of the Presidents, 1957*, pp. 233–237, and pp. 256–259.

[15] Transcript of presidential press conference, May 15, 1957, *ibid.*, pp. 353, 355–356.

[16] Transcript of presidential press conference, May 22, 1957, *ibid.*, pp. 399–400.

[17] James Reston in the *New York Times*, May 23, 1957.

[18] Specifically, 203 Democrats and 39 Republicans voted against the increase; 140 Republicans and 11 Democrats voted for it. This vote was taken May 29, 1957.

[19] Letter from the President, June 25, 1957, to Representative Freylingheusen (R., N.J.) and comments of the latter as reported in the *New York Times*, June 26, 1957.

[20] For current reactions see the *Congressional Record*, 85th Cong., 1st sess., July 19, 1957, Vol. 103, pp. 12121–12122 and pp. 12136–12138. For retrospective comment see the *Congressional Record*, 85th Cong., 2nd sess., April 17, 1958, Vol. 104, pp. 6666–6667.

[21] The parliamentary sequence was as follows: In the Committee of the Whole, a so-called "Powell-type" amendment, barring grants to states with segregated schools, was offered by a New York Republican and was adopted 136–105 (teller vote). A Wisconsin Republican then offered an amendment to strike grants-in-aid. Immediately, another amendment was offered by one of the bill's Republican supporters. This would have stricken the previously adopted anti-segregation proviso and at the same time made all grants-in-aid subject to the Administration's formula of "need." During the debate that followed, two of the Democratic members of the House Labor and Education Committee urged all proponents of the bill to support this last amendment. At that point, the Democratic Chairman of the House Rules Committee, Smith of Virginia, offered a motion to strike out everything but the enacting clause, which meant no bill at all. This motion was adopted 153–126 (teller vote). The House then confirmed that action by a roll-call vote of 208–203, with 111 Republicans and 97 Democrats supporting, 77 Republicans and 126 Democrats opposing.

[22] Transcript of presidential press conference, July 31, 1957, in *Public Papers of the Presidents, 1957*, p. 576.

[23] Transcript of presidential press conference, July 3, 1957, *ibid.*, p. 521. The sentence order has been changed slightly for the sake of clarity. The provisions in question comprised Title III of the bill (HR 6127).

[24] As quoted in the *New York Times*, January 10, 1958, Eisenhower's address had been delivered January 9.

[25]William S. White in the *New York Times,* January 19, 1958.

[26]*Ibid.*

[27]Text of the President's State of the Union Message, January 9, 1958, in the *Public Papers of the Presidents, 1958,* pp. 2–15.

[28]Transcript of presidential press conference, January 15, 1958, in the *New York Times,* January 16, 1958. See also The Transcript in *Public Papers of the Presidents, 1958,* p. 92, where one phrase does not appear.

[29]Address by President Eisenhower to Republican rally in Chicago, January 20, 1958, as reported in the *New York Times,* January 21, 1958.

[30]Perhaps the classic instance was Eisenhower's stand in 1959 on the Development Loan Fund, which had been the central feature of his foreign aid program two years before. In 1957 the President had urged long-term financing for the Fund by borrowings from Treasury in lieu of annual appropriations. This recommendation was then rejected by Congress on economy grounds, and the Fund was established with appropriated funds. In 1959, however, the Senate Foreign Relations Committee prepared to shift the Fund's financing; this was considered indispensable by most committee members if the Fund were to achieve its purposes, and for various reasons 1959 seemed a propitious year to make the change. When the committee bill reached the floor, however, the Republican leadership speaking for Eisenhower opposed the change on economy grounds. The President now urged financing through appropriations. The Senate ultimately acted as he recommended. The comments of the Foreign Relations Committee Chairman, Fulbright of Arkansas, make instructive reading. See *Congressional Record,* 86th Congress, 1st sess., July 1, 1959, Vol. 105, no. 110, pp. 11316 ff., and July 2, 1959, Vol. 105, no. 111, pp. 11426 ff.

[31]See my "Presidency and Legislation: The Growth of Central Clearance," *American Political Science Review,* Vol. 48, no. 3, (September 1954), p. 656.

Notes

Chapter 5

[1]See Pendleton Herring, *Presidential Leadership,* New York: Rinehart, 1940, especially pp. 52–72.

[2]For detailed discussion see Paul Hammond's study ''Super-Carriers and B-36 Bombers: Appropriations, Strategy, and Politics,'' in the forthcoming case book on civil-military relations prepared for the Twentieth Century Fund under the editorial direction of Harold Stein.

[3]The Army's line on that occasion was set by General Ridgway, then Chief of Staff. For details see his *Soldier: The Memoirs of Matthew B. Ridgway,* New York: Harper, 1956, pp. 286ff., and Glenn Snyder's case study on the origins of the ''New Look'' in the forthcoming case book on civil-military relations prepared for the Columbia University Institute of War and Peace Studies under the editorial direction of W.T.R. Fox.

[4]Early in January 1958 Lieutenant General James Gavin, then chief of Army missile research, requested retirement, effective March 31, 1958, avowedly in order to fight the Army's case from the outside, a procedure scorned by Navy leaders when Truman occupied the White House.

[5]Just before his death in 1956, Anthony Leviero of the *New York Times,* one of the ablest Pentagon reporters, told me that in his judgment no Chief of Staff could have resisted service pressure from below for public ''revolt'' against the ''New Look'' in 1954, had anyone of lesser military reputation then been President. It must be added, though, that General Ridgway might have tried to smother a revolt in any case. For Ridgway was that relative rarity among the Chiefs of recent years, a ''professional'' in the sense of Samuel Huntington's ideal-type.

[6]Louis Harris, ''How Voters Feel About Ike's Health,'' *Collier's,* July 20, 1956, Vol. 138, p. 17ff.

[7]As reported in the *New York Times,* April 14, 1945.

[8]For further comment which seems sound to me, see Elmo Roper, *You and Your Leaders,* New York: Morrow, 1957, pp. 139–144.

[9]These and all following "approval" and "disapproval" figures are taken from the records of the Gallup Poll through the courtesy of Dr. George Gallup, director of the American Institute of Public Opinion, Princeton, N.J. Great care must be taken in using these data. I have suggested their leading limitations in the text. But there is very little else available which attempts to measure what I call "prestige." And Gallup's figures have one great advantage: they have been compiled by the same source, in much the same way, for over 20 years. For present purposes they have a second great advantage: they are very widely read in Washington. Despite disclaimers, they are widely taken to approximate reality.

[10]For whatever it is worth, Truman's previous "low" had been 32 percent, recorded in the two months of October and November 1946, hard upon that year's beef shortage and mid-term elections. His next lowest approval figure, 36 percent, was recorded in April 1948, the month of final action on the Marshall Plan, two months after his civil rights message to Congress and the unrelated bolt of Henry Wallace from the Democratic Party. Between these two low points of 1946 and 1948, the Gallup figures would suggest that Truman's "borrowing" of prestige during 1947 (as described in Chapter 3) boosted his own to a marked degree. Gallup's "approval" questions for the months of February, March, June, July, and October 1947 elicited a favorable response in the following proportions: 48, 60, 57, 54, and 55 percent. The March "high" coincided with announcement of the Truman Doctrine shortly after a display of presidential firmness on a coal strike. As indicators of a *relatively* lasting *upward* shift of range, these figures illustrate the obverse of examples cited in my text. Truman, of course, looked far less partisan and far less like a candidate in 1947 than in 1948. Approval tumbled at the start of the latter year. It rose again, after his surprise election, to 69 per cent in January 1949. In all these instances, the indicated months are the months when surveys were made.

[11]For whatever it is worth, Eisenhower's first term "low" was 57 percent, recorded in November 1954. This coincided with the mid-term elections and a critical stage of the first Quemoy-Matsu crisis. It is the only recorded instance in his first five years where approval dropped below 60 percent. Indeed, two months later, in January 1955, the figure was 69 per-cent. His 1958 "low" of 49 percent in April coincided with what turned out to be the bottom of the 1958 recession. His 1958 "high" of 58 percent in August followed close upon the unopposed landing of troops in Lebanon and the easing of tension in the Middle East. These conjunctions are in terms of dates when surveys were made, not necessarily of the release dates for results.

[12]Through 1959, up to the time of writing, Eisenhower's record of approval in these polls has been 58 percent in February, 59 percent in March, 60 percent in April, 61 percent in May, and 62 percent in June.

[13]Lest any reader be misled, let me note that I would not pose these questions in this fashion if I thought the *second* term, as such, a dominant factor shaping the dimensions of those particular losses of prestige. I do not. Had the events of 1957–1958 or those of 1950–1951 occurred four years earlier, I know no reason to suppose the results for prestige would have been very different.

Gallup's data do suggest, however, that *some* down-trend in "approval" and *some* lessening of variations upward *may* be characteristic in second terms. Other things aside, a "boredom" factor may have played a part in Truman's case and Eisenhower's. There is, of course, no guarding against boredom unless, as in the case of F.D.R., one gets involved in a new play like his "War Presidency."

[14]It is suggestive, though of course not proof of anything, that "approval" of Eisenhower in the Gallup Poll was at a low for 1958 in April when opinion leaders were the loudest in their criticism of his "inactivity" or "indecision" on antirecession measures, and reached its high, that year, in August after he had intervened dramatically in Lebanon, an "active" and "decisive" move by which, as matters stood, no one was being hurt.

[15]These appearances are Gallup's again. "Approval" of Eisenhower, as measured by the Gallup Poll, reached a first term "high" of 79 percent in August 1955, compared with two secondary highs of 75 percent in September 1953 and in December 1955. Excluding the three highs, approval in these polls during his first three years averaged approximately 67 percent. As has been noted previously, his all-time "low," up to the time of writing, was 49 percent in April 1958. During the twelve months of 1957 his average had been approximately 65 percent. Averages, of course, will have the least significance of any figures of this sort. I note them here only to give a crude frame of reference for the high and low results.

[16]See note 11, chap. 3.

[17]For what it may be worth, a Gallup Poll taken in May 1951 showed approval of Truman only one percentage point above his all-time low of 23 percent. That low was reached just six months later, amidst charges of corruption and a stalemate in Korean truce talks.

[18]From the summer of 1945 to late autumn 1946, Truman's approval, as measured by the Gallup Poll, dropped continuously and precipitously from 87 to 32 percent. Early in his third year it rose as high as 60 percent, and after temporary stabilization in the "fifties," dropped to 36 percent early in 1948; it climbed steeply, again, late in the year. In Eisenhower's case, the comparable figures show a mild down-trend, broken by many upward variations from an early high of 75 percent to a low of 57 percent in late autumn 1954. An upward trend appears immediately after, with approval at 69 percent in January 1955, and at 79 percent in August, amidst the "Geneva spirit." Thereafter, there was temporary stabilization in the middle of the seventies, followed by a mild slump to a "low" of 67 percent in 1956, with a sharp move up again by the end of the year to 79 percent in January 1957.

[19]In most of Roosevelt's years and most of Truman's, C.E. Hooper's rating service reigned supreme in radio. Hooper ratings were expressed as proportions of "actual" to "potential" audience among radio users in homes, based on a sampling of "radio-homes" with telephones in 36 cities. A multiplier of approximately 1.3 was used to convert sets into listeners. Not every presidential address received a Hooper rating in those years, but virtually all major addresses were rated through April 1948. The termination of these ratings could be due, I assume, to someone's loss of interest at the networks or in the White House. From 1935 to 1939 most addresses were also rated by another service, the Cooperative Association of Broadcasters (CAB), then maintained jointly by the networks.

Television began to be a presidential medium in Truman's second term. As its use spread, three different commercial rating services developed, each determining its ratings in a different and noncomparable way (and each, of course, excluding radio). Trendex ratings are based on a sampling of "television homes" with telephones in fifteen major urban areas across the country. Results are compiled on all viewing hours, but coverage is limited to one week out of four. Nielsen and ARB ratings are drawn from a national sample of all "television homes'' (the data are obtained in different ways), but results are regularly compiled only on commercial programs in the case of Nielsen.

The data-gathering techniques of these three television services are such as to render their results, when and as available, noncomparable across service lines or with the older Hooper ratings. Moreover, in earlier years it was customary to pre-empt *all* networks for live coverage of major presidential addresses; this is no longer current practice with respect to either medium. In consequence, only the older radio ratings provide an internally consistent measure of presidential audiences for comparable addresses when network listeners were left no option but to listen or turn off their sets. To the extent that I have relied upon such data for the purpose of relative comparisons, only Hooper ratings have been used.

[20]These and other radio and television ratings cited in this chapter were furnished through the courtesy of Jay Eliasberg and Rose Marie O'Reilly of the Columbia Broadcasting System. CBS compilations of Hooper and CAB ratings on presidential addresses are acknowledged with particular gratitude.

[21]The dates, days, times, subjects, and ratings of these eight evening addresses are as follows:

Date	Day	Eastern Time	Subject	Rating
10/30/45	Tues.	10 P.M.	Wage and price policy	43.8
1/3/46	Thurs.	Same	Program for the year ahead	49.4
5/24/46	Fri.	11 P.M.	Railroad strike	34.4
6/29/46	Sat.	10 P.M.	Veto of price control bill	31.8
10/14/46	Mon.	Same	Lifting of controls on meat	57.6
6/20/47	Fri.	Same	Taft-Hartley veto	30.7
10/24/47	Fri.	Same	Special session of Congress	34.3
3/17/48	Wed.	10:30 P.M.	Foreign policy and defense	31.0

[22]For a brief indication of the steps leading toward beef decontrol, see Memoirs by Harry S. Truman, Vol. I, *Year of Decisions,* Garden City: Doubleday, 1955, copr. 1955 Time Inc., pp. 488–491. For a quick review of the economic and political setting see Eric Goldman, *The Crucial Decade,* New York: Knopf, 1956, chap. 3.

[23]The dates, days, times, subjects, and ratings of these six Roosevelt addresses are as follows:

Date	Day	Eastern Time	Subject	Rating
5/27/41	Tues.	10:30 P.M.	Unlimited emergency	69.8
9/11/41	Thurs.	10 P.M.	"Shoot first" naval policy	67.0
12/ 9/41	Tues.	Same	Report on Pearl Harbor	79.0
2/23/42	Mon.	Same	Report on the war	78.1
4/28/42	Tues.	Same	Economic policy	61.8
10/12/42	Mon.	Same	Report on the war	58.9

[24]Unfortunately, no one of the television services has compiled ratings on all the Eisenhower "fireside chats" in 1957 and 1958, the two years checked for purposes of this study. Or, more precisely, if any of the services *has* rated them all, my inquiries have not produced its findings. (The White House may know more than I have found.) Moreover, in his second term, Eisenhower ceased pre-empting all the networks for his evening addresses; on some occasions he was carried "live" by two, on most by one. This is a tribute, I would gather, to television economics and to White House fear of viewers' anger at no choice. In consequence, at this time, I have been unable to assemble Eisenhower ratings in a reasonably complete, consistent series, on the order of those readily obtainable from radio ratings of Roosevelt and of Truman in the 1940's.

[25]For details on the staging which preceded presentation of the legislative program for 1954, see my "Presidency and Legislation: Planning the President's Program," *American Political Science Review,* Vol. 49, no. 4 (December 1955), especially pp. 980–996.

[26]The reference is to Eisenhower's "fireside chat" of January 4, 1954, when he discussed his legislative program in general terms on the eve of his State of the Union address to Congress. His Trendex rating on that occasion was 73.1 percent, compared with equivalent ratings of 50.7 percent for his fireside chat of June 3, 1953, and of 52.5 percent for that of April 5, 1954. All three addresses were carried live by all networks.

[27]Franklin D. Roosevelt to Ray Stannard Baker, March 20, 1935. This letter is included in the Roosevelt Library collection at Hyde Park, New York.

[28]These attributions of intent to Truman, as well as comments on advice received by him, are drawn from notes made at the time. But they can be inferred from his own words. See especially: his message to Congress of July 19, 1950, outlining his post-Korean legislative proposals; his subsequent letters of August 1 and 18, 1950, concerning the addition of price controls; and his press conference of June 29, 1950, in which, among other things, he accepted a reporter's characterization of Korea as a "police action." See also the press conference of July 27, 1950, in which he distinguished the then situation from "all-out mobilization."

[29]Woodrow Wilson, *Constitutional Government in the United States,* New York: Columbia University Press, 1908, p. 81.

[30]For revealing comment see Robert Sherwood, *Roosevelt and Hopkins,* New York: Harper, 1948, pp. 428–438.

Notes

Chapter 6

[1]Transcript of presidential press conference, January 23, 1957 in *Public Papers of the Presidents: Dwight D. Eisenhower, 1957,* Washington: The National Archives, 1958, p. 73.

[2]This and subsequent references to Cabinet discussions on the January 1957 budget are drawn from interviews with two participants and with five responsible officials or consultants who were briefed by participants immediately after. The persons contributing these recollections at first or second hand were members, respectively, of the White House staff, the Bureau of the Budget, the Council of Economic Advisers, and three Cabinet departments, including Treasury. These interviews were conducted in February and March 1957, and in February 1958. I found no substantial differences in the accounts from these various sources. Even a year later, the incidents described were remembered vividly by those consulted; it is easy to see why.

[3]Report of Secretary Humphrey's press conference, *New York Times,* January 17, 1957. For the full text of the Secretary's statement see "The Budget for 1958," *Hearings,* U.S. House of Representatives, Committee on Appropriations, 85th Cong., 1st sess., Washington: 1957, pp. 1−3.

[4]Budget Message in *Public Papers of the Presidents: 1957,* pp. 40ff.

[5]For details see Warner Schilling's forthcoming case study, "Fiscal 1950," now in preparation for the Columbia University Institute of War and Peace Studies, under the editorial direction of William T. R. Fox. For highlights see my "Presidency and Legislation: Planning the President's Program," *American Political Science Review,* Vol. 49, no. 4 (December 1955); especially pp. 1005 ff.

[6]*Addresses of the President of the United States and the Director of the Bureau of the Budget at the Eleventh Regular Meeting of the Business Organization of the Government,* Washington: Government Printing Office, 1926, p. 8.

[7]Transcript of presidential press conference, March 3, 1957 in *Public Papers of the Presidents, 1957,* p. 222.

[8]Harold Stassen, then Special Assistant to the President for Disarmament, a post he would retain for one more year, was a regular attender at Eisenhower's Cabinet meetings. From his specialized and institutionally insecure position Stassen tended to be free with his advice on matters of domestic policy, where almost always he appeared well-briefed, articulate, and "liberal." Add these "sins" to his well-known differences with Dulles and to his ill-fated "dump Nixon" move in 1956, and it is not surprising that in the words of one very close observer:

> Nothing probably shook the President's confidence so much, or did more to confirm Humphrey's faith in his own opinion, than hearing Stassen argue that the budget as it stood was both good economics and good politics. . . . As a matter of fact, his exposition was first-rate, forceful and clear, which probably made things worse. . . . Certainly nothing could have made the budget's other friends more cautious in their good words for it . . . they were embarrassed, naturally; they had to keep their standing in the club, which was hard enough in that atmosphere without being classed with Stassen, so to speak.

One of my informants goes so far as to assert that this single factor holds the key to the whole episode of presidential sanction for the Humphrey press conference.

[9]The limitations native to such meetings are discussed at length in Richard F. Fenno, Jr., *The President's Cabinet,* Cambridge: Harvard University Press, 1959. See especially chaps. 3 and 4.

[10]The reference is to House Resolution 190, mentioned in Chapter 4, *supra* p. 136.

Although there were obvious risks in disciplining Humphrey, I have found no indication that these weighed heavily with Eisenhower, personally, when he made his public response to the former's press remarks. However, one cannot be certain from outside.

[11]In addition to the incidents described in this chapter, indications of a President's dependence on himself will be found in each of the three cases of "command" presented earlier. For other instances not treated in this book, the reader is referred to the various case studies cited in these notes.

[12](See also, note 44, Chapter 10.) In preparing this account of Korean developments during the fall of 1950 I have relied, in part, on notes of my own made at this time, on interviews with former President Truman, and on interviews with five former officials then at key staff levels in the State and Defense Departments, and the White House. These interviews were conducted in August and December 1954, in June and December 1955, and in January 1956, in February 1958, and in May 1959. Except where otherwise noted, quotations in this account of Korean developments during the fall of 1950 are taken from Memoirs by Harry S. Truman, Vol. 2, *Years of Trial and Hope,* Garden City: Doubleday, 1956, copr. 1956 Time Inc., chaps. 22–24. Except where otherwise noted, dates and similar specific references have been drawn from three sources: from testimony and appendices in "The Military Situation in the Far East," *Hearings,* U.S. Senate Foreign Relations and Armed Services Committee, 82d Cong., 1st sess., Washington: 1951, parts 1–5 (referred to hereafter as the *MacArthur Hearings*); from the *Department of State Bulletin,* Vol. 23, nos. 576–597, July 17–December 11, 1950; and from the United Nations General Assembly, *Official Records,* Fifth Session, First Committee, 346th–353rd meetings, September 30–October 4, 1950. All dates are given as of Washington, not Korea.

For a more detailed account of these developments which puts them in the context of the war's whole course from its inception ot the start of truce negotiations in July 1951, the reader is referred to Martin Lichterman's penetrating case study "To the Yalu and Back," prepared for the Twentieth Century Fund under Harold Stein's editorial direction and now in press. A less detailed treatment which differs somewhat in interpretation both from Lichterman's and from my own is found in Walter Millis's section of *Arms and the State,* New York: Twentieth Century Fund, 1958, chap. 7.

[13]For a chronological account of the decision to intervene in Korea (which was really a succession of decisions taken between June 26 and June 30, 1950), see Beverly Smith, "The White House Story: Why We Went to War in Korea," *Saturday Evening Post,* Vol. 224, no. 19 (November 10, 1951), pp. 22ff. A very useful comment on the notions in the minds of those who counseled intervention—notions which also were to affect the choices of September and October, 1950—will be found in Alexander L. George's "American Policy-Making and the North Korean Aggression," *World Politics,* Vol. 7, no. 2 (January 1955), pp. 209–232.

[14]Truman *Memoirs,* Vol. 2, p. 341.

[15]Truman spoke in San Francisco October 17, 1950. The preceding May he had traveled by train in leisurely fashion, to and from a dedication of Grand Coulee Dam, a tour reflecting his apparent hope to raise the strength and change the mix of Democrats in Congress at the mid-term elections. (In effect, this was a hope to match the precedent of 1934 with roughly the results of 1958.) The hope was not realized, of course, though Democratic losses in both Houses were less, proportionately and absolutely, than in the three preceding off-year elections.

[16]Truman *Memoirs,* Vol. 2, p. 359.

[17]*Ibid.,* p. 360.

[18]At the time, United Kingdom, Australian and Philippine ground forces were serving under MacArthur; Turkish and Thai contingents were en route; a Canadian contingent was in formation. Next to the Americans, the Commonwealth—and in the Commonwealth, the UK—gave the principal outside assistance to the South Koreans; hence the emphasis on British views in this account. The ratio of Commonwealth to U.S. participation is suggested by the fact that (as of October) *one* Commonwealth and *seven* American divisions were engaged. I surmise that in November another Commonwealth division would have more than doubled British influence with Washington, but Atlee chose to strip his garrisons no further.

[19]Transcript of presidential press conference, September 21, 1950, on file in the Truman Library at Independence. It should be noted that as early as September 1, the President virtually had pledged some sort of UN action—without specifying UN *means*–by stating in a fireside address to the country that "Under the direction and guidance of the UN, we, with others, will do our part to help them [the Koreans] enjoy . . . free, independent, and united [government] . . . ." This theme, "the UN will decide," also had been sounded before Inchon in some public statements by other American officials, especially by Acheson and by Phillip Jessup, State's Ambassador-at-Large. For occasions and texts see *Department of State Bulletin,* Vol. 23, nos. 583, 584, and 585, September 4, 11, and 18, 1950.

[20]The resolution was proposed to the Political (First) Committee on September 30 by Australia, Brazil, Cuba, the Netherlands, Norway, Pakistan, the Philippines, and the United Kingdom; a sponsorship designed to emphasize its international character. But drafting and negotiation of this sponsorship were largely in the hands of the State Department and the U.S. delegation.

[21]The text of the October 7 resolution on which I have relied is found in the *MacArthur Hearings,* Part 3, pp. 2436–2437. Alternatively, see *Department of State Bulletin.* Vol. 23, no. 590, October 23, 1950.

[22]The abstainers were Egypt, India, Lebanon, Saudi Arabia, Syria, Yemen, and Yugoslavia. The negative votes were cast by the Soviet Union (3), Poland, and Czechoslovakia.

[23]On September 24 the Indian Ambassador at Peking reported having had disturbing conversations with a Chinese military source. See K. M. Panikkar, *In Two Chinas: Memoirs of a Diplomat,* London: Allen and Unwin, 1955, p. 108. On September 30, the Chinese Foreign Minister, in a speech to a committee of the People's Political Consultative Conference, said, according to news reports, that Peking "could not supinely tolerate the crossing of the parallel," and "could not stand aside." Far more specific threats had been made far more formally about Formosa for months past, yet in that quarter Peking had remained supine. To allied foreign offices this apparently seemed more of the same in a minor key. Ninety miles of open water and an American fleet separated Formosa from mainland China; no such barrier divided China from North Korea. The difference does not seem to have made much impression upon allied diplomats in September 1950.

[24]Truman *Memoirs,* Vol. 2, p. 362. See also, Panikkar, *Memoirs,* pp. 109–110.

[25]Leland Goodrich, *Korea: A Study of U.S. Policy in the United Nations,* New York: Council on Foreign Relations, 1956, p. 136.

[26]Marshall had succeeded Louis Johnson as Defense Secretary on September 21, in time to share, in form at least, in post-Inchon decisions.

[27]Truman *Memoirs,* Vol. 2, p. 362.

[28]*Ibid.,* p. 373.

[29]See *ibid.,* pp. 373–380 for texts of MacArthur cables November 4, 6, and 7 and for account of following action in Washington.

[30]*Ibid.,* p. 380.

[31]*Ibid.,* pp. 378–379.

[32]S.L.A. Marshall, *The River and the Gauntlet,* New York: Morrow, 1953, p. 1.

[33]For further detail see the Lichterman study cited in note 12.

[34]On November 28, coincidentally, John Hersey was at the White House and attended Truman's usual morning staff meeting in preparation for his memorable "Profile" published serially by *The New Yorker* the following spring. Hersey's account of Truman's announcement to his staff that the Chinese had intervened full-force sheds considerable light on the motivations and responses of this President. See John Hersey, "Mr. President, II—Ten O'Clock Meeting," *The New Yorker,* April 14, 1951, pp. 38ff. In general, it can be said that Hersey's series is the most enlightening single source as yet available on Truman as President and on the daily tasks of being President in our time. It is superb reporting.

Notes

Chapter 7

[1]The reference is to the *Report of the President's Committee on Administrative Management,* Washington: Government Printing Office, 1937. For background see the second volume of reminiscences by the Committee's chairman, Louis Brownlow, *A Passion for Anonymity,* Chicago: University of Chicago Press, 1958, chaps. 28, 30, 31, and 33.

[2]These so-called "staff" facilities around the President are actually an odd assortment of personal and institutional staffs and of interagency committees. Their development has never been traced satisfactorily, nor their operations analyzed in depth, by any single source. Indeed, some of these facilities have yet to be discussed in any depth by any source. There is now underway a study of the institutionalized Presidency by Rowland Egger. When published, his work should do a great deal to further understanding of the Presidency as an institution.

[3]Clinton Rossiter, *The American Presidency,* New York: Harcourt Brace, 1956, p. 104.

[4]Exposure to detail can be carried too far, of course. Herbert Hoover is perhaps the classic instance of a man who went too far. For example, Hoover personally read and approved every letter sent by the Budget Bureau to executive agencies "clearing" their individual replies to congressional inquiries on legislation. In suggesting that a President be his own staff director, I would not urge that he routinely do the work of the whole staff. One admires Hoover's industry but not his judgment of what to take upon himself and what to leave to others.

[5]Arthur M. Schlesinger, Jr., *The Age of Roosevelt,* Vol. 2, *The Coming of the New Deal,* Boston: Houghton Mifflin, 1959, pp. 522–523.

This and later quotations are drawn from Schlesinger's characterization of Roosevelt in his earlier years. It often is assumed that in his last years, during the Second World War, Roosevelt was a "changed man"; that in his handling of military strategy and foreign policy, then his prime concerns, he became virtually the creature of his Chiefs of Staff. What his biographers will make of this, I do not know. But it is clear that they will deal with contradictory evidence. For a suggestive reading which discounts the "change" see William Emerson, "Franklin Roosevelt as Commander in Chief in World War II," *Military Affairs,* Vol. 22, no. 4 (Winter, 1958–1959), pp. 181 ff. See also Harvey Mansfield with Harold Stein. *Arms and the State,* New York: Twentieth Century Fund, 1959. Part one, chap. 3.

For a detailed case study of Roosevelt in action toward the end, see Paul Hammond's "Directives for the Occupation of Germany: The Washington Controversy," prepared for the Twentieth Century Fund under the editorial direction of Harold Stein and now in press. This shows Roosevelt a tired man indeed, whose foot slipped now and then, as at Quebec, but by no means a "changed" one. It also shows what I suspect may be the key to understanding F.D.R.'s War Presidency: that his personal perspective often coincided with the judgments of his military advisers, *but not for their reasons.* His personal, political judgment *may* have failed to keep pace with events, as Emerson suggests, although the evidence is inconclusive. But this is not to say that he failed to consult—and to inform—himself as politician, in much the same way he always had. And judging from what I have learned about his final conversations just before his death, it may be that he was fast catching up with events or was abreast of them; if so he was ahead of most of his advisers. At least it can be said that he was in the process of evaluating Soviet-American relations and that no one can claim certain knowledge of the way his mind was moving on the problems his successor shortly faced. The man whose mind remained unfathomed by associates was scarcely a changed man.

[6]Schlesinger, *Roosevelt,* Vol. 2, p. 528.

[7]*Ibid.,* p. 528.

[8]The classic instances of miscalculation on Roosevelt's part would seem to be his initial presentation of Supreme Court reform in 1937 and his careless choice of objects and of tactics for his party "purge," so-called, in 1938. See James M. Burns, *Roosevelt: The Lion and the Fox,* New York: Harcourt Brace, 1956, especially pp. 291 ff. and pp. 358 ff.

Many writers regard as a third such instance the "unconditional surrender" formula of 1943. I wonder. From a President's perspective that formula in that year may have been, among other things, a way to keep doors open rather than a way to slam them shut, at a time when the "balance of administrative power," in Arthur Schlesinger's phrase, remained indeterminate at home and abroad. Winston Churchill's comments are worth noting in this connection; see his *The Hinge of Fate,* Boston: Houghton Mifflin, 1950, pp. 685–691.

[9]These general observations on the workings of the Eisenhower "staff system" are drawn from periodic interviews with staff officials in the White House and with certain others whose work kept them in close contact with the White House. Fifteen individuals were interviewed at least once; three in the White House and four outside were interviewed three times or more, at intervals, constituting a rough sort of "panel." These interviews were conducted in January and June 1954, in April, June, and December 1955, in June 1956, in April and October 1957, in January, February, March, and April 1958, and in April 1959.

[10]This comment, made in personal conversation, dates from January 1958, three years before the close of Eisenhower's term.

[11]See Robert J. Donovan, *Eisenhower: The Inside Story,* New York: Harper, 1956, chaps. 2, 4, 6, 10, 23, 25.

[12]*Ibid.,* p. 357.

[13]For a summary of Eisenhower's political involvement as a potential candidate from

1947 on see Marquis Childs, *Eisenhower: Captive Hero,* New York: Harcourt Brace, 1958, chaps. 6–7.

[14]*Ibid.,* p. 117.

[15]Transcript of presidential press conference, May 31, 1955, as reported in the *New York Times,* June 1, 1955.

[16]The quotations are from Robert Donovan's account of Eisenhower's conference with twelve close associates in January 1956, on the question of a second term. See Donovan, *Eisenhower,* pp. 394–395.

[17]*Ibid.,* p. 402.

[18]See Memoirs by Harry S. Truman, Vol. I, *Year of Decisions,* Garden City: Doubleday, 1955, copr. 1955 Time Inc., for example, pp. 328–329.

[19]I am indebted to former President Truman for permitting me to read his photostatic copy of the portion of the Harold Smith diary that covers the first fifteen months of Mr. Truman's Presidency. Smith, who had been Budget Director since 1939 resigned in July 1946.

[20]Transcript of Presidential press conference for the American Society of Newspaper Editors, April 17, 1952, on file in the Truman Library at Independence, Missouri.

[21]Jack Redding, *Inside the Democratic Party,* Indianapolis and New York: Bobbs-Merrill, 1958, p. 133. Reprinted by permission of the Bobbs-Merrill Company, Inc.

[22]For further discussion see my "Congress and the Fair Deal: A Legislative Balance Sheet," *Public Policy,* Vol. 5, Cambridge: Harvard University Press, 1954, especially pp. 374–378.

Notes

Chapter 8

[1] Arthur M. Schlesinger, Jr., *The Age of Roosevelt,* Vol. 2, *The Coming of the New Deal,* Boston: Houghton Mifflin, 1959, p. 529.

[2] See Chapter 7, p. 226.

[3] Edward S. Corwin, *The President: Office and Powers,* 4th ed., New York: New York University Press, 1957, p. 312.

[4] Woodrow Wilson, *Constitutional Government in the United States,* New York: Columbia University Press, 1908, pp. 79–80.

Notes

Chapter 9

[1]What follows first appeared in the French edition of this book published in 1968. It represents an adaptation and enlargement of testimony before the Senate Subcommittee on National Security Staffing and Operations, March 25, 1963 (see "Administration of National Security," *Hearings,* U. S. Senate Committee on Operations, 88th Congress, 1st Sess., Washington: 1963, Part I, pp. 74–84), together with enlargement of an article, "Kennedy in the Presidency," *Political Science Quarterly,* Vol. LXXIX, No. 3, September 1964.

[2]The Bay of Pigs in southern Cuba was the site of an unsuccessful invasion attempted by CIA-trained exiles from the Castro regime. For details see Chapter 11.

Notes

Chapter 10

¹The discussion is in Woodrow Wilson, *Congressional Government,* New York: Meridian Books, 1956, "Preface to Fifteenth Edition."

²Henry Jones Ford, *The Rise and Growth of American Politics,* New York: Macmillan, 1898, chap. xxii, a remarkable exposition which may have done much to educate Woodrow Wilson.

³I use the term "Watergate" to refer in the first instance to the break-in and attempted bugging in June 1972, of the Democratic National Committee headquarters in the Watergate complex in Washington, D.C. In addition I use the term to refer to what former Attorney General John Mitchell once characterized as "do-it-yourself . . . White House horrors," associated with the so-called "Plumbers' Unit" in the White House, with the offices of Charles Colson, and John Dean, White House Counsel, and with the Security Office of The Committee to Re-elect the President (CREEP). The ramifications are almost endless. For an introductory tour see Carl Bernstein and Bob Woodward, *All the President's Men,* New York: Simon and Schuster, 1974.

⁴For a summary of this sequence see Theodore H. White, *Breach of Faith; The Fall of Richard Nixon,* New York: Atheneum, 1975, especially chap. 10.

⁵For a summary of the MacArthur case see pp. 79–81.

⁶See pp. 172–173.

⁷See White, *Breach of Faith,* pp. 13–29.

⁸Doris H. Kearns, *Lyndon B. Johnson and the American Dream,* New York: Harper, 1975, chap. 12.

⁹For contrasting versions of the sequence of events see Townsend Hoopes, "The Fight for the President's Mind, and the Men Who Won It," *Atlantic Monthly,* Vol. 224 (October 1969), pp. 97–114, and Lyndon B. Johnson, *The Vantage Point,* New York: Holt, Rinehart and Winston, 1971, especially pp. 380–437. See also Kearns, *Johnson,* chap. 12.

[10]See pp. 167–168.

[11]"Transcripts of Eight Recorded Presidential Conversations," p. 183 (March 22, 1973), *Hearings,* Committee on the Judiciary, House of Representatives, 93rd Congress, 2nd Session (May-June 1974), Serial No. 34.

[12]See, for example, Peter W. Sperlich, "Bargaining and Overload: An Essay on *Presidential Power*" in Aaron Wildavsky, ed., *The Presidency,* Boston: Little and Brown, 1969, pp. 168–192.

[13]The references are to H. R. Haldeman, Assistant to the President and Chief of Staff, campaign aide in 1960, 1962, and 1968, and former Los Angeles advertising executive; John Ehrlichman, Assistant to the President for Domestic Affairs, campaign aide in 1960 and 1968, and former Seattle lawyer; Egil Krogh, an Ehrlichman assistant and former Seattle associate who was detailed from the Domestic Council staff to head the special investigative unit in the White House which became known as the "Plumbers"; Daniel Ellsberg, former Defense Department official and RAND consultant who leaked a Defense Department historical study (the Pentagon papers) to *The New York Times* and was subsequently prosecuted unsuccessfully. With Ehrlichman's approval, Krogh's unit illegally rifled the files of Ellsberg's Los Angeles psychiatrist, seeking material with which to discredit him publicly.

[14]For Nixon's practice, see the forthcoming study by Stephen Hess of the Brookings Institution on the uses of Cabinet and staff by modern Presidents. For further details, see William Safire, *Before the Fall,* New York: Doubleday, 1975, especially pp. 112–117.

[15]"In [Nixon's] first four years as President, he held only thirty-one press conferences. By contrast, Kennedy held sixty-four in slightly less than three years; Johnson held 126 in slightly more than five years; Eisenhower had 193 in eight years; Truman had 322 in almost eight years, and Roosevelt had 998 in just over twelve years." David Wise, *The Politics of Lying,* New York: Random House, 1973, p. 246. See also Elmer E. Cornwell, *Presidential Leadership of Public Opinion,* Bloomington, Indiana: University of Indiana Press, 1965.

[16]Nixon's first Secretary of the Interior, Walter Hickel, was forced out of office in November 1970 apparently because of disagreement over the Cambodian incursion that Hickel had voiced publicly in May. His aides reported then, as part of his complaint, that he had been able to see Nixon only twice in fifteen months. See *The New York Times,* May 7, 1970, pp. 1, 18.

[17]See Hess, note 14, chapters on Johnson and Nixon. For background on Johnson developments in program formulation and in legislative liaison see respectively Joseph A. Califano, Jr., *A Presidential Nation,* New York: W. W. Norton, 1975, especially pp. 19–25, 37–52; and Lawrence F. O'Brien, *No Final Victories,* Garden City, New York: Doubleday, 1974, especially pp. 181–197 which deal also with liaison under Kennedy.

[18]In the 86th Congress, the Democrats had majorities of 281 to 152 in the House and 65 to 35 in the Senate, Eisenhower vetoed or pocket-vetoed 20 bills during the first session; Congress succeeded only once in five attempts to override. (For a comment on the "new Eisenhower" of 1959 see pp. 82–84). By comparison, Ford, after his third month, faced the 94th Congress with the House Democratic by 289 to 145 and the Senate by 61 to 38. In his first fourteen months of office Ford vetoed or pocket-vetoed 39 bills. As of October 15, 1975, Congress had failed in eight attempts to override, succeeding in seven others.

[19]See pp. 115–122.

[20]Chalmers Roberts, "The Day We Didn't Go to War," *The Reporter,* Vol. 11, no. 4 (September 14, 1954). *The Pentagon Papers: The Defense Department History of United*

States Decisionmaking on Vietnam, 4 vols., The Senator Gravel edition, Boston: Beacon Press, 1971, Vol. 1, especially pp. 88—107, 443—487.

21See Richard E. Neustadt and Graham T. Allison, "Afterword" in Robert F. Kennedy, *Thirteen Days,* New York: Norton, 1971, pp. 118—150.

22See Arthur M. Schlesinger, Jr., *The Imperial Presidency,* Boston: Houghton Mifflin, 1973, pp. 189—190.

23"Nobody" means civilians outside the Defense and State Departments and the White House. I presume that there was consultation with military advisers, field commanders, and the government at Saigon, perhaps also with Pnom Penh. For available details see *The New York Times,* June 14, 1970, pp. 1, 18; see also David R. Maxey, "How Nixon Decided to Invade Cambodia," *Look,* Vol. 34, no. 16 (August 11, 1970), pp. 22—25.

24See Schlesinger, *Imperial Presidency,* pp. 127—176.

25See War Powers Resolution, 87 Stat. 555, enacted in November 1973 over Nixon's veto.

26See Congressional Budget and Impoundment Control Act, 88 Stat. 297, enacted July 12, 1974.

27See Federal Election Campaign Act Amendments of 1974, 88 Stat. 1263, enacted October 15, 1974. As this is written, most of the provisions are under legal challenge and the case is being argued in the Supreme Court.

28For suggestive commentary see David S. Broder, *The Party's Over: The Failure of Politics in America,* New York: Harper & Row, 1972.

29*US* v. *Nixon* 418 US 683. The Court's opinion prescribed only that in a criminal case before a court a concrete need for evidence took precedence over a generalized assertion of executive privilege unrelated to defense or diplomacy. The opinion was respectful of that privilege, as such, grounding it indeed in the Constitution and suggesting it might well be absolute for national security affairs.

30To give a rough idea of the dimensions of these various shifts in scale of Federal undertakings, the following "before" and "after" indications are offered: From 1932 to 1937, direct Federal relief and work relief rose from zero to $2.527 billion, while in the same period public works expenditures went from $499 million to $1.102 billion. From 1949 to 1953, Federally guaranteed home mortgages grew from $465 million to $2.498 billion. From 1956 to 1959, Federal aid for highways jumped from $783 million to $2.709 billion. During the Sixties, Federal aid to education and manpower training grew from $2.533 billion in 1965 to reach $6.135 billion by 1967, while Federal health aid soared from $1.73 billion in 1965 to $11.696 billion in 1969. (All figures are outlays taken from *The Budget of the United States,* various fiscal years, Washington, D.C., U.S. Government Printing Office.)

As one index of the governmental impact of increased Federal efforts in the Sixties, the number of Federal categorical grants to state and local governments rose from 160 in 1962 to 379 in 1967, 109 of which had been added in 1965 alone; see Advisory Commission on Intergovernmental Relations, *Fiscal Balance in the American Federal System,* Washington, D.C., 1967, Vol. 1, pp. 140—144.

31See Chapter 2. Truman's then Secretary of Commerce, Charles Sawyer, who figures in my account of the steel seizure, complained in his memoirs that I had failed to consult him and had distorted his role. I plead guilty to the first. While doing research in Independence, I had asked Mr. Truman to arrange for me to see Sawyer. Mr. Truman chose not to do it or it slipped his mind. I decided not to press. So I did not see Sawyer and for that I have always been sorry. Had I done so, however, I am confident that I would not have altered my account in any substantial way. With due respect I prefer mine to his and trust my sources as decidedly more accurate than his memory as reported in his book. The difference, of course, may be in large part a matter of perspective. I was reporting his behavior as it looked from the White House; he reports it as it looked to him. See Charles S. Sawyer, *Concerns of a Conservative Democrat,* Carbondale, Illinois: Southern Illinois University Press, 1968, especially pp. 274–277, 379–381.

Another problematical work in this regard is Maeva Marcus, *Truman and the Steel Seizure Case: The Limits of Presidential Power,* New York: Columbia University Press, 1977. While she does not support Secretary Sawyer's account, neither does she support mine with respect to the character of partial wage and price increases aborted by the Supreme Court's stay order of May 3. In a long footnote (ch. 5, note 13, pp. 289–290) she speculates on the matter. Oddly, in later notes she cites key pieces of evidence on which I relied, apparently without understanding their significance. See ch. 6, note 92, pp. 306–307; ch. 7, note 49, p. 316, also note 70, p. 320. On page 147 she quotes the President's injunction to negotiators on the morning of May 3, concerning changes in wages and working conditions that would be put into effect if no agreement were reached. These were precisely the increases of which I wrote. She seems unaware of that. I think I might have helped Ms. Marcus connect this up, but I was on leave when she sought an interview.

[32]See p. 279.

[33]See Jonathan Schell, "Reflections on the Nixon Years," *The New Yorker* Vol. 51, Nos. 15–20 (June 2, 9, 16, 23, and 30 and July 7, 1975).

[34]For sympathetic commentary and significant illustrations, see Kearns, *Johnson,* especially chaps. 8 and 11, and William Safire, *Before the Fall,* especially pp. 97–106, 341–365, 599–627, and 688–693.

[35]George Reedy, *The Twilight of the Presidency,* New York: New American Library, 1970, p. xiv.

[36]William H. Herndon and Jesse W. Weik, *Herndon's Life of Lincoln,* New York: Albert and Charles Boni, 1930, p. 304.

[37]See p. 250.

[38]See James David Barber, *The Presidential Character: Predicting Performance in the White House,* Englewood Cliffs, New Jersey: Prentice-Hall, 1972, especially chaps. 2–5, 10–13.

[39]*Ibid.,* p. 12.

[40]See p. 252.

[41]On the specifics of Johnson's decision in the summer of 1965, *The Pentagon Papers* indicates that his military advisers then were estimating needed American combat forces in Vietnam at between 200,000 and 400,000 men; most thought that the final total would crowd the upper end of that range. At the time, Johnson actually committed 44 battalions or about 175,000 men (estimates of the effective size of this commitment varied from 175,000 to 219,000). The plan on which he operated specified only that an additional 24 battalions would be used in the second phase of the plan. This was not presented to him as an upper limit. But the plan did presume an end to the American involvement in hostilities by January 1, 1968—two and a half years ahead. Initially—July 28, 1965—Johnson publically presented his decision only as one of sending 50,000 men above previous deployments of 75,000 announced by McNamara in June; hence his *public* commitment of troops was only 125,000. See in note 20 *The Pentagon Papers,* Vol. 3, pp. 462–485.

[42]See Kearns, *Johnson,* chap. 9; see also Rowland Evans and Robert Novak, *Lyndon B.*

Johnson: The Exercise of Power, New York: The New American Library, 1966, pp. 530–556; Barber, *Presidential Character,* pp. 32–42; and O'Brien, *No Final Victories,* pp. 189–193.

[43]Kearns (*Johnson,* chap. 9) quotes Johnson as saying retrospectively:

> I knew from the start. . . . If I left the woman I really loved—the Great Society—in order to fight that bitch of a war . . . then I would lose everything at home. All my programs. All my hopes. . . . dreams. . . .
>
> Oh, I could see it coming all right, history provided too many cases where the sound of the bugle put an immediate end to the hopes and dreams of the best reformers: the Spanish-American War . . . World War I . . . World War II. . . . Once the war began then all those conservatives in Congress would use it as a weapon against the Great Society. . . . And the Generals. . . . I didn't like anything about it, but I think the situation in South Vietnam bothered me most. They never seemed able to get themselves together.

This squares with what several members of Johnson's staff told me in 1965 and 1966 that he was saying to them at the time. Of course as he saw many different things he said them selectively to those who wanted to hear each.

[44]See pp. 123–146. Subsequent research by other scholars with access to more sources casts doubt upon one facet of my account, namely the degree of worry and the kind of consultation at the top of the State and Defense Departments in the last ten days before MacArthur's November offensive. There may have been less worry than my sources led me to think and also less meaningful consultation. If so, the behavior of Dean Acheson, Omar Bradley, and George Marshall, to say nothing of then Assistant Secretary of State Dean Rusk, seems to me still *less* defensible, and Truman still more imposed upon, than I thought when I wrote. For a summary of later scholarship and an overview of the period see Alexander L. George and Richard Smoke, *Deterrence in American Foreign Policy,* New York, Columbia University Press, 1974, chap. 7.

[45]There are as yet no definitive short histories of the Watergate affair. For an overview readers would do well to start with Safire, *Before the Fall,* which has the merit of approaching Nixon sympathetically. White, *Breach of Faith,* summarizes from start to finish in a relatively straightforward way marred by the author's sense of personal betrayal. Nothing substitutes for the grueling but superbly organized *Statement of Information,* especially Books I–VIII, Hearings, Committee on the Judiciary, House of Representatives, 93rd Congress, 2nd Session, May-June 1974.

[46]See Nixon's private assurance to the South Vietnamese in letters to President Thieu on November 14, 1972, and January 5, 1973, just before the signing of the Paris peace accords. The Nixon letter of January 5, 1973, became public at the time of South Vietnam's collapse two years later, while President Ford lamented inability to intervene. See *The New York Times,* May 1, 1975, p. 16, for text of the letters.

[47]For further discussion on this point, intended for students, not Presidents, see Graham T. Allison, *The Massachusetts Medical School Case,* Kennedy School Case Program, Harvard University, case number C14–75–001, 1975. For a briefer version see Allison, "Implementation Analysis: 'The Missing Chapter' in Conventional Analysis. A Teaching Exercise," *Benefit-Cost and Policy Analysis: 1974,* Chicago: Aldine Publishing Company, 1975, pp. 369–391.

[48]Ernest R. May, *"Lessons" of the Past: The Use and Misuse of History in American Foreign Policy,* New York: Oxford University Press, 1973, chap. 5, "Analysis: Bombing for Peace." See also the reports issued by the United States Strategic Bombing Survey, especially *The Effects of Strategic Bombing on Japan's War Economy,* Washington, D.C.: Overall Economic Effects Division, 1946; *Overall Report* (European War), Washington, D.C.: U.S. Strategic Bombing Survey, 1945; and *Japanese Air Power,* Washington, D.C.: U.S. Strategic Bombing Survey, 1946.

It is worth noting that Nixon's Christmas bombing of December 1972 was of a different nature than those ordered by Johnson; the Christmas bombing had limited objectives, did not strike at the heart of the North Vietnamese war effort, and was not intended to persuade them to withdraw from the South.

[49]See my testimony before the Senate Subcommittee on National Security and International Operations, June 29, 1965 (see "Conduct of National Security Policy," *Hearings,* U.S. Senate Committee on Operations, 89th Congress, 1st Session, Washington, D.C.: 1965, Part 3, pp. 119–149). See also in Note 20 *The Pentagon Papers,* Vol. 2, pp. 717–728, Vol. 3, pp. 43–44, and Vol. 4, pp. 615–619.

[50]I came to this conclusion not long after publishing the book while trying to advise then Senator John F. Kennedy on problems he would face in staffing the White House should he win the 1960 race. In 1963 I sought to make amends by publishing an article which dealt extensively with Roosevelt's staffing pattern and briefly with Kennedy's experience thus far in adapting it. The piece was written in September 1963. See "Approaches to Staffing the Presidency: Notes on FDR and JFK," *American Political Science Review,* Vol. LVII, no. 4 (December 1963), pp. 855–864.

[51]All numbers are author's estimates drawn from the *Congressional Directory* and the *Government Organization Manual,* with some adjustments for uniformity, supplemented by interviews.

[52]See Hugh Heclo, "OMB and the Presidency—the Problems of 'Neutral Competence,' " *The Public Interest,* no. 38 (Winter 1975), pp. 80–98.

[53]Harold D. Smith was the first Director of the Budget after Budget Bureau status was raised under the recommendation of the President's Committee on Administrative Management. Smith was appointed in 1939 and took over a staff of 40 which he built in two years time to more than 400, giving the place its modern character and indeed making it more central to the Presidency than ever before or since. The war rather lessened Bureau status, although not Smith's own, but his relationship with Roosevelt was not matched under Truman and after the war Smith departed. Bureau history in Truman's years belongs to Smith's successor, James E. Webb.

[54]Harry L. Hopkins, a native Iowan and professional welfare administrator, began his association with Roosevelt when Hopkins served as deputy administrator and then administrator of the relief program established by Roosevelt in New York in 1931. When Roosevelt moved into the White House in 1933, he brought Hopkins along to head the Federal Emergency Relief Administration, an agency similar to the one run by Hopkins in New York. Hopkins went on to serve as chief of the Civil Works Administration and the Works Progress Administration. In 1938 he was appointed Secretary of Commerce, a post he held until 1940. During the war, Hopkins undertook diplomatic missions for Roosevelt, making frequent trips to Britain and the Soviet Union. He died in 1945. See Robert E. Sherwood, *Roosevelt and Hopkins: An Intimate History,* New York: Harper, 1946.

[55]This characterization is adapted from my 1963 article, "Approaches to Staffing the Presidency," pp. 856–857.

[56]Theodore Sorensen was Special Counsel to the President under Kennedy, having come with him from the Senate. Samuel Rosenman had been Counsel to the Governor with FDR in Albany and joined him at the White House in 1941, remaining there through Truman's first year. See Theodore C. Sorensen, *Decision-Making in the White House: the Olive Branch or the Arrows*, New York: Columbia University Press, 1963, and Samuel I. Rosenman, *Working with Roosevelt*, New York: Harper, 1952.

[57]McGeorge Bundy, who served Kennedy and then Johnson as Special Assistant to the President for National Security Affairs, came to the post in 1961 from the deanship of Harvard's Faculty of Arts and Sciences, and left at the start of 1966 to assume the presidency of the Ford Foundation. Bundy was the first holder of that White House title to have a strong substantive role. His predecessors under Eisenhower had served rather as committee secretaries than as staff advisers. Bundy thus is properly regarded as the founder of the staff unit which later under Nixon was enlarged by Henry Kissinger. While a professor of government at Harvard, Kissinger became Nelson Rockefeller's foreign policy adviser. In 1969, Kissinger took over the Bundy office as Assistant to the President for National Security Affairs. Nixon subsequently made him Secretary of State, after which he held both jobs at once until late 1975 when Ford separated the two again, promoting Kissinger's former deputy to the White House assistantship.

[58]Clark M. Clifford, who succeeded Rosenman in 1946 as Special Counsel to the President, came to Truman out of naval service highly recommended by close, mutual friends. Before the war, Clifford had been a successful young attorney in St. Louis. Clifford left his White House post in early 1950 and resumed law practice, this time in Washington, which he interrupted for consulting services to Eisenhower, Kennedy, and Johnson. Clifford was Secretary of Defense in LBJ's last year.

[59]With background in Massachusetts politics and brief previous experience on Capitol Hill, Lawrence O'Brien became chief of Kennedy's legislative liaison staff in 1961 and stayed on under Johnson until 1967 when LBJ appointed him Postmaster General. He continued to aid Johnson on legislative matters through 1968. O'Brien later served as Chairman of the Democratic National Committee and as Commissioner of the National Basketball Association. See O'Brien, *No Final Victories*.

[60]Walter W. Jenkins had been a principal assistant to Johnson in the Senate and the Vice-Presidency and came to the White House as a sort of coordinator for staff operations, really a jack-of-all-trades. His service was exemplary; it broke his health; he left in October 1964.

[61]The one was Clark Clifford, the other Abe Fortas.

[62]Arthur F. Burns, a professor of economics at Columbia, chaired the Council of Economic Advisors from 1953 to 1956 and during that period became a close personal advisor to Nixon. Burns joined the Nixon White House in 1969 as Counselor to the President and later took over as Chairman of the Federal Reserve Board. Bryce N. Harlow, a former staff chief of the House Armed Services Committee under both Republican and Democratic chairmen, served on Eisenhower's legislative liaison staff from 1953 to 1961. Nixon brought him back from January 1969 to December 1970. After the Watergate scandal broke, Harlow returned again for a brief period as Counselor to the President, part of Nixon's attempt to shore up his staff without Haldeman and company. Herbert G. Klein, a longtime Nixon friend and editor

of the *San Diego Union*, handled press relations during Nixon's 1952, 1956 and 1960 campaigns for national office. In 1969 he joined the White House staff as Director of Communications, a new post, honorific but not very potent, not to be confused with the press secretaryship.

[63]For a summary and characterization of the process whereby Nixon's White House was consolidated under Haldeman and Ehrlichman (and Kissinger), see Safire, *Before the Fall,* pp. 10, 278–293, and 463–473. Daniel P. Moynihan, a Harvard professor of government with experience in the Kennedy and Johnson administrations, came to the Nixon White House in 1969 to direct staff work on urban affairs. The Family Assistance Plan of 1969 was a chief result. Ehrlichman succeeded him and Moynihan returned to Harvard in 1971. He has since served as Ambassador to India and to the United Nations.

[64]See President's Committee on Administrative Management, *Report with Special Studies,* Washington, D.C.: U.S. Government Printing Office, 1937, pp. 2–3. Roosevelt's recommendations went to Congress on January 12, 1937. His message is printed with the Committee's Report.

[65]See Commission on Organization of the Executive Branch of Government, "General Management of the Executive Branch," Washington, D.C.: Government Printing Office, February 1949.

President Johnson's second and principal task force on questions of government structure was charged in 1967 to review the organization of the entire Executive Branch. Its members included Ben W. Heineman (chairman), Frederick M. Bohen (executive secretary), McGeorge Bundy, William Capron, Hale Champion, Kermit Gordon, Herbert Kaufman, Richard Lee, Bayliss Manning, Robert McNamara, and Charles Schultze. The existence of this task force was never publicized and its report never published. President Johnson did not make the report available to his successor, but task force members, I am told, shared their findings with members of Nixon's counterpart, the so-called Ash Council which generated the Reorganization Plans of 1970–1971.

[66]For detailed illustrations and suggestive analyses see Martha Derthick, *Uncontrollable Spending for Social Services Grants,* Washington, D.C.: The Brookings Institution, 1975, and Bernard J. Frieden and Marshall Kaplan, *The Politics of Neglect: Urban Aid From Model Cities to Revenue Sharing,* Cambridge, Mass.: The MIT Press, 1975. See also James L. Sundquist and David W. Davis, *Making Federalism Work,* Washington, D.C.: The Brookings Institution, 1969.

[67]Joseph Califano came from the Defense Department to the White House in 1965 to replace Bill Moyers in what once had been Sorensen's work on development of legislative programs. Califano remained at the White House until 1969. His book on the Presidency is cited in note 15.

[68]The reference is to Richard P. Nathan, *The Plot That Failed: Nixon and the Administrative Presidency,* New York: Wiley, 1975, especially chaps. 3 and 4. This is a thoughtful review and assessment of staff development under Nixon by a close observer and sometime participant. Nathan finds a strong policy motivation for the systemization to which I refer. Others ascribe it to a far less substantive orientation, mainly control for control's sake.

[69]For illustrations of "second-string activity," see Derthick, *Uncontrollable Spending,* pp. 43–70.

[70]Fred M. Vinson, former congressman and circuit judge as well as wartime economic stabilizer, served as Truman's Secretary of the Treasury and then as Chief Justice of the

Supreme Court. When Vinson went to the Treasury, he became an advocate of locating the policy staff work there. He was succeeded at OWMR by John R. Steelman who championed that location for both policy development and program coordination. Smith too had had ideas about program coordination. For this he planned to draw upon his Bureau's then Division of Administrative Management in combination with the Bureau's field offices, eyes-and-ears facilities, of which there were then four; he hoped for more. Observations on Smith's plans and views are drawn from contemporary notes and a review of Budget Bureau files in 1949.

[71]This troubles some other observers less than it does me. See Stephen Hess, note 14. See also Thomas E. Cronin, *The State of the Presidency*, Boston: Little Brown, 1975, chap. 5.

[72]See James MacGregor Burns, *Roosevelt: The Lion and the Fox*, New York: Harcourt Brace, and Company, 1956, "Epilogue."

[73]Henry Jones Ford, *Rise and Growth of American Politics*, p. 293.

[74]See for example James L. Sundquist, "Reflections on Watergate: Lessons for Public Administration," *Public Administration Review*, Vol. 34, no. 5 (September-October 1974), pp. 453-461.

[75]See Aaron Wildavsky, "The Past and Future Presidency," *The Public Interest*, no. 41 (Fall 1975), pp. 56-76; quotations from pp. 71-73.

[76]David B. Truman, *The Congressional Party*, New York: Wiley, 1959, especially chap. 8.

[77]For a number of proposals see Walter F. Mondale, *The Accountability of Power: Toward A Responsible Presidency*, forthcoming. See also Califano, *A Presidential Nation*, Schlesinger, *The Imperial Presidency*, chap. 11, and Theodore C. Sorensen, *Watchman in the Night: Presidential Accountability After Watergate*, Cambridge, Mass.: The MIT Press, 1975, Part III.

[78]See pp. 101-102 and 255-259.

Notes

Chapter 11

[1]The great change came with Eisenhower's heart attack. See Chapter 10.

[2]Jonathan Schell, "The Time of Illusion: VI—Credibility," *The New Yorker*, July 7, 1975, p. 61.

[3]Robert Donovan, *Conflict & Crisis, The Presidency of Harry S. Truman, 1945–1948*, New York: Norton, 1977, esp. pp. 15–305.

[4]For detail on Truman polls see Chapter 5, note 10. Nixon polls first slipped below 30 percent in October 1973 (the "Saturday Night Massacre") and again in February 1974 after which they fluctuated between 26 and 24 percent. Gallup polls are used because they are the only such "approval" measures reaching back in an unbroken line, with roughly the same questions and interview technique, for 40 years. See Chapter 5, note 9.

[5]Henry Kissinger no doubt can claim a share in the strategic thinking internationally, but Connally seems to have been Nixon's very own conception. Judging by appearances, early in Nixon's second term he looked ahead three years to using every resource that the White House then commanded (presumably including surplus campaign funds from 1972) for the sake of gaining Connally the Republican nomination in 1976. Not in this century has any other President laid plans of such importance for political realignment with as much deliberation or so far ahead. See Harry S. Dent, *The Prodigal South Returns to Power*, New York: Wiley, 1976, esp. pp. 269–280.

[6]Richard H. Rovere, "Letter from Washington," *The New Yorker*, October 11, 1977. The reference to Lance is explained later in this chapter.

[7]Charles Mohr, *The New York Times*, October 23, 1977, p. 1, col. 4.

[8]Curtis Wilkie, *The Boston Sunday Globe*, January 1, 1978, p. A4.

[9]Ibid.

[10]*The Wall Street Journal*, "Washington Wire," February 23, 1979. For a more elabo-

rate midterm appraisal see a six-part series by James Deakin in the *St. Louis Post-Dispatch*, November 12, 1978, *et seq.*

[11]See Anthony King, *The New American Political System*, Washington: American Enterprise Institute, 1978, esp. pp. 388–395. For elaboration of the following characterizations see especially essays by Hugh Heclo (Chapter 3), Samuel C. Patterson (Chapter 4), Jeane Kirkpatrick (Chapter 7), and Richard Brody (Chapter 8). See also the essay by Fred I. Greenstein on the Presidency.

[12]See Woodrow Wilson, *Congressional Government*, Boston: Houghton Miflin, 1885, p. 102.

[13]See Hugh Heclo, "Issue Networks and the Executive Establishment," in Anthony King, *System*. See also Heclo, *A Government of Strangers*, Washington: Brookings Institution, 1978, esp. pp. 84–109.

[14]For further comment see Chapter 10, esp. note 30. See also Heclo, *Strangers*.

[15]For various estimates see *Newsweek*, November 16, 1978, p. 48 ff; *Time*, August 7, 1978, p. 15 ff; see also, *The New York Times*, November 14, 1978, pp. 1, B 14.

[16]See Samuel C. Patterson, "The Semi-Sovereign Congress," in Anthony King, *System*, pp. 163–166. For comprehensive data through 1974 see Harrison W. Fox and Susan W. Hammond, "The Growth of Congressional Staffs" in Harvey C. Mansfield, Sr. (ed.), *Congress Against the President*, New York: Praeger, 1975.

[17]See Hugh Heclo in Anthony King, *System*, esp. pp. 98–108. Regarding the eleven-week prelude to assumption of office, while this is short in American terms it is astonishingly long in, say, British, where a few hours suffice. But Britain has two career systems, appointive *and* elective. The new Cabinet has been there all along across the aisle.

[18]See Austin Ranney, Jeane Kirkpatrick, and Richard Brody in Anthony King, *System*. See also James David Barber, (ed.), *Race for the Presidency*, New York: Prentice Hall, 1978. For campaign-media interactions see also the forthcoming book by Christopher Arterton, tentatively titled "Media Politics: The News Strategies of Presidential Campaigns."

[19]For an insightful account of the Carter campaign from first to last see Jules Witcover, *Marathon*, New York: Viking, 1977.

[20]On the Republican side in 1940, a group of old-style barons from the party's Eastern, internationalist wing coalesced around a previously unknown businessman, Wendell Willkie, and pushed him through the party's national convention. But differences are as striking as similarities: There were barons to get together and the convention was the place to push, still the arena for *negotiating* nominations rather than for registering what primaries-and-media have done: with an almost obligatory decision on the first ballot.

[21]See James Fallows, "The Passionless President," *Atlantic Monthly*, May, 1979, pp. 33–48. As Fallows explains, President Carter failed to grasp, in his first Congress, the need for strategy, hence priorities, with respect to a multiplicity of preelection pledges shaped in the image of the traditional Democratic coalition. This may be because he had no strong sense of where *he* wished to go, as a matter of substance. So Fallows suggests, without recognizing how common it has been for Presidents to acquire their specific substantive commitments after they take office, well after, shaped by events (see Chapter 9).

Fallows also indicates that Carter failed to reach out beyond half a dozen senior aides, almost all Georgian, to arouse and keep the loyalties of his second and third echelon assistants. Had he reached he could have had them for the asking; evidently he did not. The evidence runs beyond Fallows. Far less than Ford or even Nixon, remote though he was, did

Carter build himself a "team." So every interview suggests, in what may be the saddest aspect of his early years. Yet nothing stood against it save his operating style, a striking commentary on his managerial skills as President.

[22]Truman, who made the first arrangements, let Eisenhower's designee sit in on all meetings at the then Budget Bureau, including Director's Review. Kennedy reappointed Eisenhower's Deputy Director, which came to the same thing. Ford's OMB Director denied Carter's people comparable access, apparently without any awareness of the older precedents. So much for the "institutional memory" of the only organization in the President's entourage supposed to possess one.

[23]These comments are drawn from first-hand observations in 1952 and 1960, from interviews with Budget Bureau staff, incoming White House aides, and transition consultants in 1968, and from telephone interviews (for the most part) with comparable sources in 1976. I was hospitalized that year in late November, thus unable to observe or interview in person except for three days, November 12–14. My observations were facilitated differently at different times by various positions. In 1952 I was on Truman's staff. In 1960 I served as Special Consultant to Kennedy on White House organization and related transition matters. In 1968 I consulted with the transition task force chaired by Frank Lindsey that the Institute of Politics at Harvard sponsored for the benefit of Nixon's staff. In 1976 I consulted before the election with Carter's transition planners, continuing somewhat by telephone thereafter.

[24]According to Nixon, Mrs. Eisenhower begged him to keep her husband out of it as far as possible, but not to reveal her concern. Nixon says he did so to the President's chagrin, since Eisenhower wanted to campaign extensively. Had he done so Nixon probably would have been elected. See Richard M. Nixon, *Memoirs,* New York: Grossett and Dunlap, 1978, pp. 221–222.

[25]For this and subsequent detail about the Bay of Pigs affair I rely on Arthur M. Schlesinger Jr.'s accounts in *A Thousand Days,* Boston: Houghton Miflin, 1965, pp. 206–297, and in *Robert Kennedy and His Times,* Boston: Houghton Miflin, 1978, pp. 443–449. For the latter Schlesinger had access to Robert Kennedy's still-closed file on the "Cuba Study Group," a post-mortem in which he participated at his brother's request. The summary of that post-mortem has been released by the National Security Council under the Freedom of Information Act: see General Maxwell Taylor, "Narrative of the Anti-Castro Cuban Operation ZAPATA," June 13, 1961. I have also reviewed the account in Theodore Sorensen's *Kennedy,* New York: Harper, 1965. In addition, I have considered my own notes of conversations at the time with senior members of the White House staff. (I then was serving as a consultant to the President on organizational problems.) Missing from this data is a crucial commentary on the Cuban affair, which I read then: a brave and thoughtful lesson-learning memorandum, written as the beachhead was collapsing, addressed to the President by his new Special Assistant for National Security Affairs, McGeorge Bundy. This presumably will be available at the Kennedy Library in Boston after declassification in the normal course. As I recall, it was a candid, probing critique, not outdone by commentaries since.

[26]Schlesinger, *Robert Kennedy*; see especially pp. 474–496. Schlesinger argues that neither President Kennedy nor his brother Robert, then Attorney General, had sanctioned or knew anything about assassination attempts against Castro. Robert Kennedy, however, presumably with JFK's approval in a general way, helped launch a low-level harassment operation that CIA apparently continued long after he lost contact with it. (The Miami Cubans of Watergate fame were engaged in that.) And that both Kennedys were strongly, personally

antipathetic to the Castro regime may have been taken by CIA officials as a general, if indirect and inexplicit authorization for many strange endeavors cooked up by odd characters in their employ.

[27]So Kennedy told me in November 1960, when I pressed on him a scheme to match the Allen Dulles reappointment with a personal assistant of his own. He wondered why; I urged that he check my outsider's view with an insider he could trust; he must know one. Assenting, he said he did: "Dick Bissell." For Kennedy it was a real misfortune that his trusted insider already had the duty to develop Eisenhower's option against Castro.

[28]This and subsequent characterizations of Bert Lance and his affair rest on press coverage in the *New York Times, Washington Post,* and *National Journal,* from July to October 1977 supplemented by contemporaneous interviews with four OMB and White House aides. During the period I served intermittently as an OMB consultant on White House reorganization. This provides some first-hand feeling for relations and assumptions, but not in depth to match those of April, 1961. My consulting assignments were not comparable. Moreover no definitive accounts by others have been published yet to match those on the Bay of Pigs. What I offer here are personal impressions checked as closely as I can.

[29]*Newsweek,* April 23, 1979, p. 88.

[30]Clark M. Clifford, a Washington attorney of extraordinary judgment and high standing with the press, had been a close advisor to Truman, Kennedy, and Johnson. See note 58, Chapter 10. By 1977 Clifford had become a sort of symbol of Washington savvy.

[31]In 13 postwar months, Truman's approval rating in the Gallup poll fell from 82 to 32 percent, followed by unstable recoveries (and slumps) with a first term high of 60 percent after Greek-Turkish aid in early 1947. Ford, in just five months, slid from 71 to 38 percent; then he too had unstable recoveries with a high of 51 percent in the summer of 1975, then a drop back to the "thirties." Carter, beginning at 70 percent approval, dropped in 13 months to 40 percent and hovered there until September 1978 when success at the Camp David summit was followed by a rating of 56 percent; the next winter he had slid again into the "forties" tending down. As for the other elected Presidents since these polls began, Eisenhower, Kennedy, Johnson, and Nixon, none dropped below 60 percent approval in his first two years except Nixon, and he only to 55 percent.

[32]It is suggestive that Gallup approval ratings *rose* five points, with disapproval falling commensurately, for one two-week period immediately after Lance's televised testimony and publicized departure. He may have gained credit for his stance, and the President for letting him go relatively gracefully. But this was a blip in the pattern; Carter lost those five points immediately after and did not regain them. Is this because direct public perceptions were corrected as the word came in from columnists and commentators? That seems likely.

[33]For a near-term assessment of public attitudes within a month of Lance's resignation see Adam Clymer, *The New York Times,* November 2, 1977, p. 1, col. 5. Clymer reports the findings of a *Times*—CBS survey in mid-October.

[34]The reference is to the *Washington Post* reporters on assignments from the metropolitan desk who first broke the Watergate story, became national figures, wrote best-sellers, collected royalties in seven figures, and became the heroes of a smash hit in the movies, "All the President's Men."

[35]During 1974, his last year as Governor of Georgia, Carter worked with the Democratic National Committee on congressional campaigns, moving around the country, making acquaintances. His senior White House aides-to-be were, for the most part, already involved and working in Atlanta. See Witcover, *Marathon.*

[36]See, among others, Ron Nessen, *It Sure Looks Different from the Inside,* Chicago: Playboy Press, 1978, pp. 29–39.

[37]There are disputed allegations that the then White House Chief of Staff, Alexander Haig, who orchestrated Nixon's resignation made himself a mental note to get the man a pardon later, which he then did by representing Nixon's physical and psychological plight to Ford. There are also very different allegations that Ford's primary motive was political, to get the divisive Nixon issue behind the Republican Party in 1974, rather than in 1975 or 1976 after Nixon's court trial and what everyone foresaw, his probable conviction of conspiring to obstruct justice.

[38]For some detail and sympathetic treatment of accompanying transition difficulties see the forthcoming book by Roger Porter, tentatively titled "Presidential Policy Making: The EPB Experience." See also Nessen, *Inside.*

[39]Ford's approval ratings in the Gallup poll fell from 71 percent in August to 50 percent in September, 55 percent in October, 38 percent in January. The decline began with his pardon of Nixon and resumed with the onset of recession. How much the WIN affair contributed in light of the pardon to that 50 percent is anybody's guess. Contemporary observation in the Washington community suggests that his professional reputation suffered rather more from WIN than from the pardon. That may be reflected in Ford's *later* public standing.

[40]In his intriguing book on television news, centered on NBC, outdated now in several technical and reportorial respects but still of use conceptually, Edward Jay Epstein suggests the fall of 1963 as a time of maturation for the medium in terms of news. That was when two of the three network news shows were extended from radio's traditional 15 minutes to the present half-hour. See his *News from Nowhere,* New York: Random House, 1973, esp. Chapter 3. Moreover, only weeks later, the television networks gave almost constant coverage through four days to President Kennedy's assassination and its aftermath, his funeral, including live the murder of his assassin. Many observers think that this conferred on TV a whole new status as a news source and extraordinary credibility in the public mind; apparently it also gave news a substantial boost in the minds of TV executives.

[41]See Chapter 5.

[42]For a detailed instance of resultant problems see my *Swine Flu Affair, Decision-Making on a Slippery Disease,* with Harvey V. Fineberg, Washington: GPO, 1978, Stock No. 017-000-00210-4; esp. pp. 26–30 and 63–71. The President concerned was Ford not Carter, a distinction without a difference in terms of those problems.

[43]Something of the same sort seems to have occurred with Ford. In the fall of 1975, long after popular reaction to his pardon and to subsequent recession—and then loss of Saigon—had shown up in his poll ratings, these sagged again, from the high "forties" to the low where they remained for months. This followed an outburst of derision in the columns and by anchormen (and comics), making much of moments when Ford physically had stumbled in the sight of mini-cams, the dread invention of the age.

[44]See Chapter 8.

[45]See King, *System,* esp. pp. 388–394.

[46]Arthur M. Schlesinger, Jr. coined the term "Imperial Presidency" as the title for a book on the historical expansion of claimed prerogatives since Truman's time in national security affairs, including use of troops abroad. Placed in historical context as this was, and reminiscent of the arguments over "imperialism" 80 years ago, the usage seems to me unexceptionable. Schlesinger himself enlarged the meaning of the term at the book's end

when he included chapters on Nixon's conduct in domestic spheres; after the book's publication the term became synonymous with anything or everything its users disliked in Nixon's Presidency, also Johnson's, and on back to FDR, but especially with presidential initiatives apart from Congress in the years since World War II; also with presidential style in Nixon's years and Johnson's; also with memories, often exaggerated, of respectfulness shown Presidents before Nixon's fall. The upshot is a usage I regard as so exaggerated in its implications for command, its underplaying of persuasion, hence bargaining, as to be very misleading. That Presidents could command within the narrow range of Schlesinger's original usage— and can today at least as well as FDR before Pearl Harbor—seems unquestionable and still a matter of concern and importance in its own right (see Chapter 9). See Arthur M. Schlesinger, Jr. *The Imperial Presidency,* Boston: Houghton Mifflin, 1975.

[47]For elaboration of the "tacit treaty" notion see my "White House and Whitehall," in Anthony King, (ed.), *The British Prime Minister,* London: Macmillan, 1969.

[48]Senator John Culver of Iowa started as a Senate staffer. Gary Hart of Colorado started on the staff of the Interior Secretary. Daniel Patrick Moynihan of New York worked in four administrations before seeking elective office. Richard Cheney of Wyoming worked his way up the White House ladder. This foursome is suggestive but no more than that.

Index